A Political Romance

Also by Susan K. Foley

WOMEN IN FRANCE SINCE 1789: the Meanings of Difference

under the name Susan K. Grogan
FLORA TRISTAN: Life Stories
FRENCH SOCIALISM AND SEXUAL DIFFERENCE: Women and
the New Society, 1803–44

Also by Charles Sowerwine

FRANCE SINCE 1870: Culture, Society and the Making of the Republic
SISTERS OR CITIZENS? Women and Socialism in France Since 1876
MADELEINE PELLETIER: Une Féministe dans L'Arène politique
(*with Claude Maignien*)

A Political Romance

Léon Gambetta, Léonie Léon and the Making of the French Republic, 1872–82

Susan K. Foley

and

Charles Sowerwine

First published 2012 by
PALGRAVE MACMILLAN

Palgrave Macmillan in the UK is an imprint of Macmillan Publishers Limited, registered in England, company number 785998, of Houndmills, Basingstoke, Hampshire RG21 6XS.

Palgrave Macmillan in the US is a division of St Martin's Press LLC, 175 Fifth Avenue, New York, NY 10010.

Palgrave Macmillan is the global academic imprint of the above companies and has companies and representatives throughout the world.

Palgrave® and Macmillan® are registered trademarks in the United States, the United Kingdom, Europe and other countries.

ISBN 978–0–230–20686–1

This book is printed on paper suitable for recycling and made from fully managed and sustained forest sources. Logging, pulping and manufacturing processes are expected to conform to the environmental regulations of the country of origin.

A catalogue record for this book is available from the British Library.

A catalog record for this book is available from the Library of Congress.

10   9   8   7   6   5   4   3   2   1
21   20   19   18   17   16   15   14   13   12

Printed and Bound in the United States of America
by Edwards Brothers Malloy, Inc.

For
Niamh
Orvis
Ned
Mabel
and others still to come

Contents

List of Illustrations

List of Maps

Preface

Generations of French schoolchildren remember Léon Gambetta for one exploit: in 1870, he escaped the Prussian siege of Paris in a hot-air balloon, landed near Tours, and raised a fresh army 100,000 strong. Some also remember him for the pivotal role he then played in obtaining passage of a republican constitution, and in bringing the vast majority to accept the Republic as the framework within which to pursue their vision for France. Many works treat Gambetta's role in political history. This book takes another approach, focusing on the romance between Gambetta and Léonie Léon, the partnership which lay behind his political accomplishments.

Léonie Léon was Gambetta's lover and confidante throughout his campaign for the Republic, from 1872 until his untimely death in 1882. Their romance was based not only on the passion each felt for the other, but also on the passion each felt for politics and for the Republic. Indeed, the Republic was almost a third party in their relationship. Early in their liaison, Léon wrote to Gambetta: 'I want you to devote yourself completely to this Republic, your goddess, whose supremacy in your heart I accept'; her goal, she went on, would be 'to equal her in your affections'. [1] Theirs was not only a passionate affair but also a political relationship between two people who were committed to the Republic; it was a political romance.

This romance has been neglected, but it is significant in French history. Gambetta and, through this romance, Léon, played a key role in what Sanford Elwitt called the 'making' of the French Republic.[2] Gambetta does not now enjoy the reputation of a founding father, like George Washington or Simon Bolivar. Yet it was Gambetta who effected the compromises which ensured passage of the Constitution of 1875, providing a framework within which the Republic grew and put down deep roots, and it was Gambetta who articulated a vision of the Republic and brought the vast majority of the French to accept the Republic as the framework within which to work for their vision of France.

Before 1875, every major change in that vision had been realized through a change of regime; no regime had lasted more than twenty years. Since 1875, France has never ceased to be a Republic, with the exception of the Vichy Regime, brought to power with German victory in 1940 and driven from power with German defeat in 1944. To be sure,

Gambetta did not found the Third Republic single-handedly. Indeed, the very question of whether individuals really make history or simply ride its shifting tides is hotly debated. But individuals are still required and Gambetta was the individual whose acts made the Republic, however much one may argue that the society and the polity were already moving that way.[3]

This book studies Gambetta and Léon's romantic and political partnership, using their extensive correspondence. They wrote nearly every day during the ten years of their liaison. Gambetta confided in his 'Minerva' and she provided knowledgeable and forthright counsel. Their correspondence brings to light a dialogue which enabled Gambetta to nurture his spirit, clarify his thoughts, and decide his actions. It discloses to us a partnership strongly marked by the gender structures of their society and thus allows us to probe the impact of those structures upon individuals. It also offers a vantage point for situating this couple in Parisian life and culture of the 1870s, opening a window onto the leisure pursuits and the intellectual and artistic issues which interested the educated bourgeoisie.

Both Gambetta and Léon wrote beautiful love letters, distinguished by soaring, passionate prose. The letters reveal Léonie Léon, the otherwise unknown figure who was Gambetta's intimate partner in love and politics, and they document her key role in Gambetta's life and political thinking. The letters reveal Léon Gambetta, the man behind the politician, and they offer a much deeper, warmer figure than do the standard biographies. We learn of his hesitations, uncertainties, and insecurities, as well as of his profound commitment to the Republic. We discover a principled man, who compromised in seeking to realize his project, to build the Republic, but who never lost sight of his goal. And the letters reveal how his participation in a deeply loving relationship with Léon – the only truly intimate relationship among his many friendships – enabled him to navigate the often choppy political seas.

Some of Gambetta's letters to Léon were published in a 1938 collection of his correspondence, but most of his and all of her letters – 1076 in all – remain unpublished and largely ignored. Professor Françoise Gaspard brought this unpublished correspondence to our attention. Having been a Deputy during President Mitterrand's first term (1981–8), she was involved in the state's purchase, in 1984, of a set of Gambetta's letters to Léon. The collection of which that set forms a part is now held in the Bibliothèque de l'Assemblée Nationale. While other writers have made some use of these letters to illuminate Gambetta's career, this book makes the letters its inspiration and the romance its keystone.

We hope that the letters and their authors may engage others as they have engaged us.

Many people helped us in the writing of this book. We are particularly grateful to Professor Françoise Gaspard, to whom we owe our encounter with the letters. We thank M. Fabrice Costa, Director of the Bibliothèque de l'Assemblée Nationale, who graciously gave us permission to copy and use the letters. We give special thanks to Mme Catherine Déalberto, his assistant, who went beyond the call of duty, supporting our endeavour in every way, explaining the intricacies of the collection, and finding new materials for us. Her support made this project possible. We also thank Mme Dominique Parcollet, Archivist at Sciences Po, for her help with the Archives of Émile Pillias.

Many friends and colleagues have given generous assistance and we thank them sincerely. M. Thierry Dumanoir, curator of les Jardies, the couple's country home, threw open the house and facilitated our research. His wife, Mme Nicole Zucca, a fellow researcher into Léon's life and writings, generously supported and encouraged our project, enabling us to visit Léon's apartment and its balcony overlooking the gardens she tended with Gambetta. We remain in their debt.

David Garrioch, Catherine Kovesi, Charlotte Macdonald, Véronique Magnol-Malhache, Jean-Yves Mollier, Val Noone, Kerry Murphy, Sabina Ratner, Sîan Reynolds, and Jean-Claude Yon shared their professional expertise with us, and their help has enriched the book. Our friends in the Melbourne Life Writing Group read drafts and made many valuable suggestions. Dr Barbara Burge assisted us on medical questions. Alice Garner, Julie Kalman and James Cannon gave substantial help in the research for this book. Chandra Jayasuriya prepared the maps. We acknowledge a grant from the Australian Research Council, which made possible such wonderful research support.

Christine Ranft's editorial work was thorough, careful and conscientious. We are very grateful to her. We were continually heartened by the patient support of our editors at Palgrave Macmillan, Michael Strang and Ruth Ireland, even when the project stalled. May this book justify their patience.

Susan K. Foley
Charles Sowerwine
Melbourne, October 2011

Key

Residences of Léon Gambetta and of Léonie Léon

1 5, rue Bréa: Léon family's first Parisian residence

2 7, rue Bonaparte: Léonie and Émilie Léon's Parisian apartment for receiving male visitors

3 12, ave Montaigne: Gambetta's Paris residence until 1876

4 14, rue Soufflot: Léon family's residence from 1879

5 53, rue de la Chaussée-d'Antin: Gambetta's apartment 1876–8, adjoining office of *La République française*

6 57, rue Saint-Didier: Gambetta's residence 1881–2

7 2, ave Perrichont; Léon's home after Gambetta's death

8 Hôtel du Ministre des Affaires étrangères (quai d'Orsay): Ministry of Foreign Affairs, Gambetta's residence during his ministry Nov. 1881–Jan. 1882

9 Palais Bourbon/Hôtel de Lassay: Gambetta's residence during his tenure as President of the Chamber 1879–81

Places of interest to Léon and Gambetta

10 Collège Sainte-Barbe

11 Institut de France (seat of Académie française and other academies)

12 Arsenal Museum

13 Cluny Museum (now Museum of the Middle Ages)

14 Grands Magasins du Louvre (Louvre Department Store)

15 Palais Royal

16 Panthéon

17 Church of Saint Augustine

18 Maison Dorée (restaurant)

Theatres Léon and Gambetta frequented

19 Comédie-française (Théâtre français)

20 Opéra (Palais Garnier)

21 Opéra-Comique

22 Théâtre du Gymnase

23 Théâtre-Lyrique (later Théâtre-Lyrique de la Gaïté)

24 Théâtre du Palais-Royal

25 Théâtre des Variétés

26 Théâtre du Vaudeville

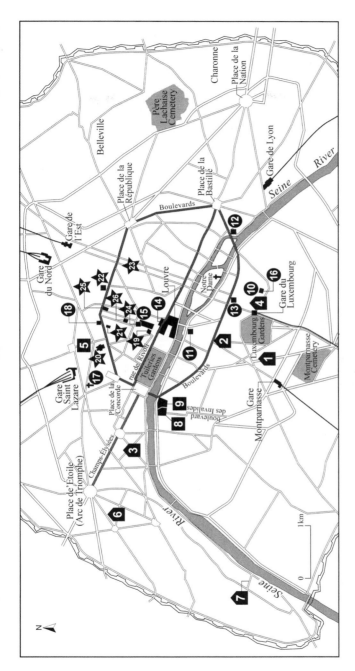

Map 1 Paris *c.*1880: sites mentioned in the text

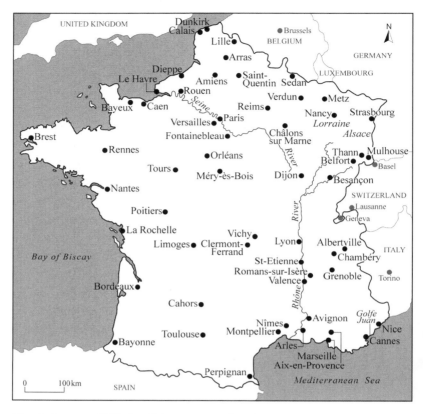

Map 2   France *c*.1880: Localities mentioned in the text

Dear Beloved Darling,

I too have rummaged through, explored, my box [of letters]! What admirable pages! What steadfast sentiment, what delicate and searching wisdom! What good sense in these letters, wingèd like butterflies! And what certainty of insight, what good grace in enduring ill fortune, what accuracy in foreseeing on the horizon the glimmers of the dawn which must bring victory. I have re-read them all, and filed them all: I am a lot richer than you, you have reached nearly a thousand. I don't want to accept this inferiority; look at the bottom of your jealous caskets, I must have somewhere a collection I mislaid. Not that I can count on numbers to bear the comparison without too much disadvantage. Oh! No, I don't have such pretensions this evening; I am delighted and I place my pride in having inspired you and not in having equalled you. I say that with the sincerity of the artist and the passion of the lover. You don't recognize your own talent, you underestimate yourself; when you like, we will re-read together this amorous Iliad, not to increase your love but to recompense your spirit.

Moving on, I found that adorable photo that you've been asking about for so long, but I'm keeping it because it's truly worthy of its subject.

I've finally decided to move house definitively, my last packing is done, Saturday and Sunday, François will give himself to this agreeable task, and Monday I'll be installed.

It's on my mind that I nearly confessed to you that I'm busy Saturday, however if you want to come I will promise you not to be more than two hours with the doctor; otherwise come Monday or Tuesday, I will be all yours.

If la Chine *[Léon's son, Alphonse] permits you to come tomorrow (for we must think of everything), I will be at the rue Montaigne until 7 o'clock.*

You will see in the paper the disgusting scandal that took place at Versailles: I was at the Budget Commission. Finances are useful from many points of view.

I embrace you with the same passion that I read you,

I belong to you

Léon

Introduction: 'What admirable pages!'

Léonie Léon and Léon Gambetta – we will refer to them by their family names, Léon and Gambetta – exchanged letters almost every day. They could neither marry nor live together, given Gambetta's political aspirations and Léon's past as a courtesan. As a result, their letters addressed not only the couple's love and desire and the political issues with which they were constantly concerned, but also their daily lives: their reading, their rambles in the countryside, their trips to the theatre and the Salon, and the Parisian life in which they were so deeply immersed. The diversity of the letters makes them particularly valuable to the historian.

A sizable collection of letters from both sides of this correspondence has survived, something that is quite rare. The collection is, to be sure, incomplete: of some five to six thousand letters,[2] 1165 remain (495 by Léon, 670 by Gambetta).[3] The collection is also uneven. There are very few letters by Léon for 1880 and 1882 and none at all for 1874 and 1875, at least among those that are dated. And the dating of some of Gambetta's and many of Léon's letters is uncertain: the envelopes originally used to order her letters have disappeared and internal evidence in the letters shows that some are out of sequence as they are currently organized.

While Gambetta's letters are preserved in their original form, Léon's survive only in typed transcripts. Those transcripts, however, were purchased along with the original letters in 1938, and experts authenticated both the originals and the transcripts. Indeed, the purchase was initiated by the then President of the Chamber of Deputies, Édouard Herriot, himself a distinguished historian (and later a member of the Académie française). The originals and the transcripts remained together for two years, until the originals were stolen during the war.[4] It is certain that the transcripts are generally accurate, therefore, although

3

there are a few uncertain readings of Léon's difficult handwriting. Their perfect fit with Gambetta's letters confirms that they are a 'pair' to his letters.

These letters are, above all, love letters, rich, touching and often profound in their sentiments. They deal with the whole range of the couple's preoccupations, personal and political, over a decade that proved crucial for France. They allow us to catch significant glimpses of the interchange between the lovers, illuminating what drew them together and kept their relationship alive. Moreover, in revealing the epistolary dynamics of an intimate liaison, the letters tell us much about the emotional economy of 1870s bourgeois society and its cultural practices.

Unlike some personal letters, such as those circulated within the family of an absent correspondent,[5] the letters between Léon and Gambetta were entirely private. This does not mean that they offer a more 'accurate' account of the events they discuss, though they may offer a different account from one presented for public consumption. Rather, they offer an account shaped by the logic of the letter-writing relationship. That logic centres on the bond between the correspondents, the current state of their relationship, and their hopes for its future. That is particularly the case with love letters. In writing a study focused on Gambetta and Léon's love letters, we aim to explore the dynamics of their relationship, as it was lived in its many dimensions. Their relationship is at the heart of this study, just as it was at the heart of their letters.

Love letters may no longer be part of the common experience of lovers, but they have a very long history. Those between Abelard and Heloïse, written in the twelfth century, remain among the foremost examples of the genre.[6] The love letter is not a static form, however, but a culturally specific one. It assumed a heightened erotic and emotional form with the rise of 'romantic love,' which gradually brought together sexuality, love and (eventually) marriage during the course of the nineteenth century.[7] Specialized letter-writing manuals like *The Lovers' Handbook*, with their guidelines for conveying ardour and agony, helped to construct what it meant to be 'in love', and showed how to present oneself as someone 'in love' in the letter.[8] The letters of Léon and Gambetta are remarkable examples of the nineteenth-century love letter.

These letters are also remarkable for their elegant prose and their diverse subject matter. Both correspondents excelled in the epistolary skills valued in nineteenth-century French culture, skills instilled in bourgeois children during their formative years and throughout their education. Léon and Gambetta wrote their letters within the conventions that governed letter writing in their day; knowing those conventions enabled them to express their meaning deliberately on paper and to interpret what the other wrote in reply.[9] These letters are thus a particular example of a familiar practice, replicating in their own individual voices the conventions found in other love letters of their day.[10] To re-enter the world of the nineteenth-century writer of love letters requires a deliberate effort to engage with the practices of the time, with the florid prose and hyperbole, which were then required but which may seem impossibly inflated today.

Simply by being written, the love letter expresses desire, and the material object speaks of love even before it is opened. The familiar handwriting on the envelope heralds the presence of the beloved, a presence often reiterated, in the nineteenth century, by the lover's monogram: the letters 'LG' superimposed on each other, in Gambetta's case, or the intertwined letters 'LL' in Léon's case.[11] The lover who puts pen to paper is seeking to affirm her or his love for the recipient, and the recipient reads the letter searching for that message. Whatever the topic of discussion, the lovers' exchange is shaped by the state of their relationship; the exchange is designed to woo, to delight, to reassure, to seek reassurance, to express hurt, forgiveness, or any other of the thousands of emotions that lovers undergo. Even the discussions of politics in these letters were part of an exchange of passion; politics provided another vehicle for the expression of attachment, devotion and need. The lovers were in fact aware of the epistolary treasure they were creating: 'what admirable pages!' Gambetta exclaimed in a letter to Léon, discussing the richness of their own correspondence.[12]

If these letters reveal the dynamics of the relationship between Gambetta and Léon, they also provide a point of entry into their world. This was a world in which the sons of shopkeepers, like Gambetta, newly enfranchised and increasingly educated, were coming into their own as a political constituency. It was a world, moreover, where urban renewal was transforming the city and new wealth was enriching urban life, making leisure and pleasure central to bourgeois lifestyles. It was a world where courtesans like Léon were familiar figures, though they occupied a severely restricted place in society.

Above all, the bourgeois world of the 1870s was deeply marked by gender norms that shaped the divergent life chances and expectations of both men and women. If Gambetta and Léon shared a deep passion for politics and for the Republic, if they discussed politics constantly, it was nevertheless the case that women were excluded from participation in electoral politics in the Republic. They could not vote or hold office.

Legal impediments that defined women as dependants, not as autonomous individuals, made it difficult to conceive of them in the political realm. Politics was emphatically coded 'male' in the public imagination and women's direct participation in the affairs of government was, for most people (both men and women), literally unthinkable. Arguments for women's suffrage, raised periodically throughout the century by small groups of feminists, were readily dismissed.[13]

Bourgeois women exerted considerable social power, but they were confined to the fringes of political life and to circumscribed 'feminine' roles. As a courtesan, lacking both social respectability and personal wealth, Léon could not host a political salon or finance Gambetta's political campaigns, as other women did. She could, however, be Gambetta's confidante and counsellor. The letters reveal the aura of significance with which they invested this role. The gendered structure of political life is thrown into relief by these letters, as they detail the couple's differing involvement in politics and the meanings which they ascribed to that difference.

This book breaks new ground in examining Léon and Gambetta's relationship and their world primarily through the lens of their decade-long correspondence. We are not, to be sure, the first historians to use the letters. Both Jacques Chastenet and J. P. T. Bury were granted access to Gambetta's correspondence when it was still in private hands. They used it, as well as Léon's letters, to inform their studies of Gambetta's political career and the foundation of the Third Republic.[14] Recent biographies of Gambetta, and a number of political histories of the era, have also made some use of the letters.[15] But none has focused on the couple or on their correspondence. Instead, these studies used the letters as evidence about Gambetta's political and public action. Indeed, they devoted almost no attention to Gambetta's emotional life with Léonie Léon, to Léon herself, to the couple in their time, and to the correspondence as an epistolary object worthy of consideration in its own right.

The one scholar to have made Léonie Léon a serious subject of study wrote the only existing biography of her in 1935, before the correspondence resurfaced. Émile Pillias conducted extensive historical research and uncovered many important documents, some of which have since disappeared. He interviewed a number of surviving friends of Gambetta, especially Jeanne Scheurer-Kestner (Mme Marcellin Pellet), who made available to him her lengthy correspondence with Léon after Gambetta's death. But he never managed to locate the letters between Gambetta and Léon.[16]

To date, only Camille Servan-Schreiber, in her *Maîtrise*, has undertaken a study of these letters.[17] We have profited from her work and extended its focus considerably in this book. We have supplemented the letters with a wide variety of other sources to further illuminate the account the correspondence provides. Such sources have also enabled us to trace the couple's lives before their relationship began and to examine Léon's later life, as well as the ways both were remembered after their deaths.

The book is in three parts. Part I begins by outlining the couple's lives before their relationship began, and then provides a chronological narrative of the evolution of their political and personal lives from 1872 to 1879. The narrative then pauses to explore three themes in Part II: the couple's leisure pursuits, their intellectual and cultural interests, and the intersecting dynamics of religion and anticlericalism in their lives. Part III resumes the chronological narrative, taking the account from 1879 to 1882 (when Gambetta died), and thence to Léon's death in 1906. It then briefly traces the process of memorialization that saw Gambetta's apotheosis in 1920 and the subsequent decline of his reputation. An epilogue outlines the history of the couple's letters after their deaths.

Part I
Years of Hope, 1872–1877

My dear adored soul,

You are divine, and I am the happiest of mortals, a mortal whom a goddess has honoured with her favours. I owe everything to you, I attribute everything to you, and I won't allow you to lose for one second your awareness of the moral good that I draw from your superiority in every order. However much you underestimate yourself, humiliate yourself, I will always remind you of your true role and your true power.

I am conscious of being, I am so aware of being an altogether different man since that unforgettable day of 27 April. I attribute to that day part of the grateful admiration that makes your tenderness sweeter and more profound for me in the indissoluble love that has bound our lives together.

I am enormously tired, I cough from time to time despite the sunshine and the delicious potion of mother Legay. I sigh only for your return and I await you Friday morning so that we can go roaming together and take delight in my happiness.

I kiss you as I love you.

[Léon Gambetta]

1

'The unforgettable day of 27 April'

On 14 November 1868, Léon Gambetta, then a young lawyer, made a sensational speech for the defence at the Baudin trial, a political trial in which republican journalists were prosecuted by Napoleon III's Second Empire. Gambetta's speech was a dramatic attack on the regime. It brought him instant renown and he won a seat in the legislature the following year. Watching his performance in the audience that day, Léonie Léon was captivated. She set out to attract his attention, but it was to take four years for Gambetta to respond to her advances. The relationship they began in 1872 ended only with Gambetta's sudden death a decade later.

Reading their story with hindsight, through the medium of the love letters they left behind, we might imagine a fairy tale in which Léonie Léon fell in love with Gambetta at first sight, attracted by his charm and his powerful oratory. But it is likely that her advances were more calculated than that. His charisma and bright prospects made him an ideal catch for a courtesan seeking a new protector: her previous protector had been dismissed to the provinces in 1867 after losing favour with the imperial regime. Léon's behaviour following the Baudin trial was not that of a bedazzled maiden with stars in her eyes, but that of a determined woman with nothing to lose, least of all her reputation. Deploying the 'cheek' of the courtesan, Léon sought every possible way to meet Gambetta.[2] She accosted him as he left meetings, but he paid her no attention. She wrote him fan letters, but he did not reply. She seated herself in his compartment on the train as he returned to Paris from meetings of the National Assembly at Versailles, but he ignored her. She even followed him across the border to Spain and knocked on his door, only to be turned away by his aunt.[3]

Such active pursuit of a man was inconceivable for a 'respectable' woman and marked Léon as a woman of ill repute, a courtesan. A courtesan was a high-class prostitute. Unlike a 'common prostitute', she did not solicit on the streets or work in a brothel, nor was she paid for each transaction. A courtesan usually had regular clients who repaid her services with generous gifts that enabled leading courtesans to become extremely wealthy. Strict social codes excluded such women from society, and especially from contact with 'respectable' women.[4]

A Belgian police officer who tailed Léon and Gambetta in 1873 described her as follows: '1.6 metres [5 feet 2 inches] tall, oval face, pale complexion, fine and pointed nose, chestnut brown hair, aged 27 to 28 years. Lively and exuberant bearing.'[5] She apparently looked younger than her 35 years. The description is borne out by the one surviving photograph (Figure 1.1). It shows an unremarkable face, not one whose great beauty might have attracted attention. She is dressed fashionably in the style of the 1870s, but her outfit is quite restrained compared to some that she is later reported wearing. It is certainly not brash or sexually alluring. The high-necked dress – perhaps taffeta, perhaps silk – is trimmed very simply, with braid defining the bodice and sleeves. Léon's long, dark hair curls down below her shoulders, pulled back off her face and held in place by a small hat whose ribbons tie under her chin. She sits straight-backed in half-profile, her hands folded in her lap, her head turned towards the viewer. Her gaze meets ours and she gives the hint of a smile, but this is the face of a serious woman.

A portrait based on this photo, produced shortly after Léon's death at the age of 68, is better known. It romanticizes a young Léon, softening her features and transforming her into a beauty who might have attracted a great statesman (Figure 1.2). This image was produced by Jean Coraboeuf, a portraitist known for his patriotism as well as for his images of 'the eternal feminine.' It implicitly supported the narrative of a great romance, countering rumours of Léon's nefarious influence on Gambetta.[6]

If the photograph is a fair representation, it supports the view that Gambetta was captivated not by Léon's stunning beauty, but by her wit and intelligence. Léon lacked the public profile that might have attracted to her bed the fabulously wealthy or the aristocratic. As she observed Gambetta at the Baudin trial in 1868, however, he must have seemed exactly what she was looking for in a protector. He was an emerging public identity but, given his background and limited resources – he was the son of a shopkeeper – she faced no competition for his affection from the *grandes horizontales*, the famous courtesans. Competition came

Figure 1.1 Léonie Léon: sole known photograph, 1872 (Archives Sciences Po, Fonds Pillias)

in the form of the little-known actress, Marie Meersmans, who also heard him at the Baudin trial and who snared him immediately.[7]

The fact that Léon set her sights on Gambetta suggests that she already had a preference for political men. Her former lover (the only one we know by name apart from Gambetta, and perhaps her only other protector) was

Figure 1.2   Léonie Léon: pencil drawing by Jean-Alexandre Coraboeuf, 1907, after the 1872 photo (given to Les Jardies by P-B Gheusi, 3 January 1935; © Centre des monuments nationaux / Philippe Berthé)

Louis-Alphonse Hyrvoix, Inspector-General of the Police of the Imperial Residences for Emperor Napoleon III. Hyrvoix was not a political figure in his own right, but his duties kept him constantly in the Emperor's company. He was an observer at the heart of the political action; a source, perhaps, of interesting news and confidences. Gambetta's later reference to 'returning' Léon to her place in the Legislative Body suggests that she frequented parliamentary debates before she met him.[8] That, in turn, would help to explain why she was in the audience to hear Gambetta's scintillating speech in the political trial of November 1868.

Léon Gambetta had yet to achieve political success or fame in 1868. With a background in the republican student movement and then as a junior associate of the established republican lawyer Jules de Jouy, Gambetta was close to the republican leadership but not yet part of it. His friend, the republican photographer Étienne Carjat, snapped his image several times in the 1860s. These pictures show an attractive man, with regular features framed by the collar-length hair and full beard that had become associated with republicanism. Portrayed in half-profile, as he usually was, the glass eye that had resulted from a childhood accident could not be seen, and he was yet to develop the large paunch of indulgent middle age (Figure 1.3). The rumpled suit attested to Gambetta's limited means and modest origins, but his bearing suggested his self-confidence and his aspirations.[9]

Léon was still pursuing Gambetta when, on 19 July 1870, France fell into Bismarck's trap and declared war on Prussia. The war went badly and, on 2 September 1870, Napoleon III surrendered his army to the Prussians at Sedan. The Second Empire lost all legitimacy. Gambetta was one of the recognized republican figures who stepped in to direct the popular uprising that followed. He became Minister of the Interior in the new 'Government of National Defence'.

As the French armies surrendered and Prussian forces put Paris under siege, Gambetta took a balloon flight to Tours in an attempt to rally the country for further efforts against the enemy. Not only did he manage to land successfully behind enemy lines, but he also managed to raise a new army of 100,000 men. Unavailing in the end, this attempt nevertheless made Gambetta a national hero. His fame spread beyond France, too. From far-flung New Zealand, Jane Maria Atkinson quizzed her friend, Margaret Taylor, then visiting Germany: 'Who is Gambetta? It is not a French name and new to me.' In Britain in 1872, *Vanity Fair* featured him in its series of portraits of famous statesmen.[10]

Prussia defeated France and elections were held for a new National Assembly. Gambetta was elected in ten seats, but in an extremely popular patriotic gesture, he chose to represent a district in occupied Alsace. On 1 March, the Assembly ratified the treaty that took Alsace and Lorraine from France and made them part of the new German Empire. Gambetta and twenty-seven others resigned from the Assembly in protest.

Figure 1.3 Léon Gambetta: the young Republican, *c.*1868 (Bibliothèque Historique de la Ville de Paris; Roger-Viollet)

The new French government was led by the veteran politician Adolphe Thiers, who had first been President of the Council of Ministers (Prime Minister) for King Louis-Philippe in 1836. The people of Paris, enraged by the treaty and by the conservative government's policies, rebelled on 18 March 1871 and Thiers' government fled to Versailles. Paris militants organized the Paris Commune, which governed the city for two months.

Gambetta, however, was not in Paris. Having resigned from the National Assembly, he travelled south to visit his family in Cahors, a small city 100 kilometres north of Toulouse. He then went on to San Sebastian, on the Spanish coast, remaining there, in the company of his then mistress, Marie Meersmans, while Thiers led the repression of the Paris Commune. Like a number of republican figures, Gambetta quietly distanced himself from both this suicidal uprising and the government that crushed it mercilessly.

In June 1871, by-elections were held for a number of vacant seats in the Assembly. Gambetta re-entered the political fray and was elected by the firmly republican, working-class district of Belleville, on the northern outskirts of Paris. A scintillating orator and quick-witted debater, he soon emerged as the parliamentary leader of the republicans against the monarchists and Bonapartists. His position was reinforced when he got financial backing to found a major daily newspaper, of which he was the guiding force until his death. *La République française* first appeared on Tuesday, 7 November 1871.[11]

Only in April 1872 did Gambetta finally take notice of Léonie Léon's relentless efforts to meet him. Having had an associate check that her overtures were not a monarchist trap, he agreed to meet her after the Saturday session of the Assembly on 27 April. They returned together by carriage to Léon's Paris apartment, where their affair began. They subsequently celebrated this date as their anniversary. As Gambetta later wrote to Léon, 'I am conscious of being, I am . . . aware of being an altogether different man since that unforgettable day of 27 April.'[12]

Fallen woman, rising star

Léon and Gambetta were both thirty-four when their relationship began. She was born on 6 November 1838; he was born seven months earlier, on 2 April. It was not unusual for a man to be unmarried at that age: he needed time to establish himself in business or a career and have the solid financial prospects that would attract a woman's family. Lacking the inherited wealth of the comfortable bourgeoisie, surviving on the parliamentary salary intended only as a supplementary income, Gambetta was still not a good marriage proposition in 1872. But an affair conducted with discretion posed no threat to his professional or social advancement. A woman of thirty-four, however, was well past marriageable age. Had Léonie Léon come from a solid bourgeois family, she would have been presented with a husband as she approached the age of twenty. But Léon's background had made such a scenario impossible.

Léon's star had fallen long before she encountered Gambetta in 1868. Léon's paternal grandmother, Adélaïde Goupille, was born on the island of Guadeloupe, in what was then the French Caribbean, the child of a slave mother and the Frenchman who owned her. This lineage counted against Léon in such a racialist age. She was later described as 'Creole', although neither Coraboeuf's portrait of Léon, nor the police report describing her in 1873, captured her mixed ancestry.[13]

Adélaïde Goupille was deserted by her first husband. She obtained a divorce, legalized by the French Revolution, and married Jacob Léon, a Jew. Their son Émile, who was to be Léonie's father, was born in Guadeloupe in 1795. At the age of fourteen, Émile Léon enlisted as a cabin boy in the French navy. At fifteen, when the English captured Guadeloupe from the French, he committed himself to France, choosing exile rather than take an oath of loyalty to George III.[14]

In 1812, Émile Léon's mother moved to France and settled in Caen. The following year, he left the navy and began a new career in the army, which may have looked more promising given England's dominance of the seas. He then began a slow thirty-three year progression to the rank of Colonel.[15]

During this time, France went through a succession of different regimes and Émile Léon adjusted his loyalties accordingly. He had signed up at the age of fourteen and had no alternative career to pursue when the Napoleonic Wars ceased. To re-enlist, as he did, was not unusual. Émile Pillias describes Léonie Léon as the 'daughter of an Orleanist'. But personal loyalty to the duc d'Orléans (eldest son of King Louis-Philippe), whom he served as aide-de-camp in the 1830s, did not necessarily represent a political stance. After Napoleon's defeat, Léon served the Bourbon kings for fifteen years, the Orleans king for eighteen years, and the Emperor Napoleon III for twelve more years. While he was finally promoted Colonel in 1846 under the Orleanist regime, he was named Commandant of the Dunkirk Garrison in 1848 under the Second Republic, and received the Legion of Honour in 1853 from the Second Empire. Léon's loyalties lay with the ruler of the day; nothing suggests a strong political affiliation.[16]

Émile Léon met his future wife, Marie Sauzy, while based in Perpignan. Their first daughter, Marie-Émilie, was born there in November 1829. Their second daughter, Marie-Léonie, known simply as Léonie, was born in Paris nine years later. Serving officers required permission to marry and the woman they married required a dowry, a relic of noble dominance of the officer corps. Sauzy probably lacked a dowry, because Léon acknowledged paternity of his daughters but the couple did not marry until 11 April 1840. Émile Léon legitimated his two daughters at that time.[17]

The Léon family lived a peripatetic life in a series of garrison towns until 1848, when Colonel Léon assumed command of the military base at Dunkirk. Léon was ten when her father took up this important post, so she grew up as the daughter of a man of standing in the local community. She was educated at the convent school run by the Daughters of the Sacred Hearts of Jesus and Mary, who were known as the Louvencourt Sisters after their founder. They had opened a school at Dunkirk in 1847.[18]

Like most Catholic schools, this school sought to produce 'good Christians, possessed of a solid and enlightened piety'. To this effect, the Louvencourt sisters established two confraternities in their schools, one devoted to the Virgin Mary for the older girls, another to the Holy Angels for the younger ones. Léon duly became a 'child of Mary' in her adolescence, indicating that she exhibited the requisite piety and good conduct to be admitted. Children of Mary were expected to imitate the virtues of the Virgin, amongst which purity of heart and modesty ranked highly.[19]

The academic quality of girls' schools varied widely in this period. Léon later complained of the 'stupid convent where [she] learned nothing about life'; she regretted not having attended the famous school of the Legion of Honour near Paris, established by Napoleon I for daughters of members of the Legion, but her father did not receive that honour until she was fifteen, about the age when her schooling would have ended. By the standards of the day, however, the Louvencourt sisters provided a reasonable education for girls. They had a particular interest in the education of the 'ruling classes'. Their rule encouraged them to 'inspire in their students the desire to learn' and the textbooks they themselves produced – for classes in French language, history, and mythology – suggest serious scholarship. Léon's letters reveal a well-read young woman with a broad general knowledge of history, literature and music. Such an education was seen as fitting bourgeois girls for marriage, and it is safe to assume that Léon's parents hoped for a suitable marriage for her once they had amassed a small dowry.[20]

The illness and sudden death of Colonel Léon destroyed such hopes. Diagnosed insane in September 1860, he refused to eat and died a month later in the asylum at Charenton, near Paris, the institution made famous by the Marquis de Sade. Mme Léon and her daughters were left in poverty, with a meagre inheritance (2909 francs, 727 of which went to each daughter) and a pension of 1175 francs per year, after the Colonel's fifty years and nine months of military service.[21] A minimum income of 5000 francs per year was necessary to live in a bourgeois fashion, with one servant, but without a life in high society.[22] In the 1870s, school directors usually earned 6000 francs a year, while secondary teachers of the lowest rank earned between 1500 and 2000 francs a year. An income below this was incompatible even with a petit-bourgeois lifestyle.[23] And indeed, the police later reported that rent on the apartment to which the family moved after the Colonel's death was more than Mme Léon's pension.[24]

With their father's death, Léonie Léon and her sister lost not only their home in Dunkirk, but also the respectable social position that they had enjoyed there. They were adults, aged 21 and 30. Their miniscule inheritance would be quickly spent. They faced poverty on their mother's pension and penury on her death, when her pension would cease. Marriage was now out of the question. The daughters lacked dowries and they now suffered from the stigma of their father's mental illness, as well as from doubtful ancestry and illegitimacy: their birth certificates would always betray that they were born outside wedlock.[25]

The sisters' options for supporting themselves were few, and all were unattractive. Moreover, the suddenness of their father's decline gave them little time to adjust their expectations and devise a strategy for survival. They could, perhaps, have found positions as governesses, the conventional solution for gentlewomen fallen on hard times. This would have meant living meekly and in poverty. Becoming seamstresses or domestic servants would have been even more humiliating, and promised even less financial security.

Whether they became courtesans by choice or default, however, is impossible to say. Most courtesans came from modest origins; women from wealthy families did not face such a choice. Women with a degree of education who had not been able to assume an honest profession – like Léonie Léon – formed an identifiable category amongst the ranks of the courtesans.[26] This life promised a level of bourgeois comfort, but the courtesan was nevertheless a glorified prostitute.

A young woman with Léon's Catholic background and education would not have chosen this life lightly. Indeed, the 'choice' may have been thrust upon her as a result of succumbing to 'temptation', or even to duress. But once she had succumbed, there was no way back. To join the ranks of courtesans or demimondaines (women on the edge of society) was to become a 'fallen woman'. As Léon was to discover, that fall was beyond redemption.

How Léon came into the arms of her 'protector', Louis-Alphonse Hyrvoix, is unknown. Hyrvoix was, by all accounts, charming and kind: his letters to his sons, who had lost their mother very young, are a delight to read.[27] His later conduct towards Léon shows that he was also honourable. But how did the penniless daughter of an obscure army officer meet the man responsible for the Emperor's personal security, a figure of some importance in Empire society? The few records of Léon's life before she met Gambetta give no clue. We are left with conjecture and circumstantial evidence.

The family moved to Paris in 1860 upon the Colonel's death. This move spared them the shame of a public downfall in the town where they were known. Taking an apartment near the Montparnasse cemetery (where the Colonel was buried), perhaps offered some personal consolation.[28] But it is unlikely that they could have met the costs of a Paris apartment without additional financial support. This was especially true once they moved to an apartment at 7, rue Bonaparte, about 1861. This was a much wealthier neighbourhood; it was located in the heart of the sixth arrondissement of Paris, near the river Seine. Their apartment was between the expensive first and second floors, on the 'mezzanine' floor, where smaller and cheaper apartments could be found (Figure 1.4).[29]

It is possible that Léon had met Hyrvoix in Dunkirk, when he accompanied the Emperor on his customary visits to army garrisons, and re-established contact with him once she arrived in Paris. The rue Bonaparte was only a ten-minute walk across the Seine from the Tuileries Palace – the Emperor's residence, destroyed in the fires of 1871 – where Hyrvoix worked. It is not inconceivable that Hyrvoix paid for the apartment on the rue Bonaparte, where his mistress could live within easy walking distance but not so close as to risk indiscretion. However, the date at which Léon's relationship with Hyrvoix began is unknown: all we know is that they had entered a liaison by 1864.[30] That leaves up to four years during which Léon had no obvious means of support.

It is equally possible, therefore, and perhaps more likely, that Léon and her sister established themselves as courtesans soon after arriving in the capital. The proximity of the apartment on the rue Bonaparte to the centre of government made it ideal, not just for the mistress of

Figure 1.4   7, rue Bonaparte, Paris, 2010: Léon's apartment was on the *entresol*, behind the small windows above the ground floor (photo by the authors)

Hyrvoix, but for courtesans who sought their clients amongst public officials, the men whom the police later observed frequenting this address.[31] It is likely, too, that Léon's work as a courtesan brought her to Hyrvoix's attention. His job was not limited to ensuring the Emperor's security; he also recruited and investigated the young women who took the Emperor's fancy (Napoleon III was an infamous philanderer).[32] Reputedly, too, Hyrvoix ensured the silence of any of the Emperor's conquests who contemplated speaking out about her experience.[33] Perhaps Hyrvoix took advantage of his position to make some conquests himself: Léon was only one of several women with whom he apparently had liaisons during his years in the Emperor's personal service.[34]

From their liaison came a son, Alphonse Léon, born on 5 February 1865 in Bordeaux. There is no doubt about the child's paternity. Two months later, Hyrvoix made a will leaving 30,000 francs to the child: a generous gesture that would have been unthinkable unless Alphonse was undoubtedly his son, since he had no legal obligations to either mother or child. Hyrvoix' legitimate son was in no doubt, either, about Alphonse's paternity. This gesture suggests that Léon's relationship with Hyrvoix was an exclusive one. However, neither Hyrvoix nor Léon was listed on Alphonse's birth certificate: Léon maintained throughout her life the fiction that he was her nephew. In his will, Hyrvoix named Mme Léon senior as Alphonse's guardian, which indicates that he cooperated in this fiction.[35]

In 1867, Hyrvoix was dismissed. According to one account, the Empress was furious when she overheard Hyrvoix telling the Emperor that, just as Parisians in the 1780s had blamed Marie-Antoinette – 'the Austrian woman' – for their woes, in the 1860s they were blaming 'the Spanish woman', the Empress.[36] In fact, Hyrvoix's dismissal was part of a broader battle between court factions. He had made a number of reports to the Emperor about the Empress' extravagances and his reports infuriated Eugénie's faction. Napoleon III placated them by consigning Hyrvoix to a bureaucratic job in the provinces.[37]

Léon could hardly have accompanied Hyrvoix as his mistress to a small provincial town, even had she wished to, but his departure left her in difficult circumstances. Whether he provided financial support for Léon and their son, who was now three years old, we do not know. Police reports from 1874 assert that Léon had a concession for a Bureau de Tabac (a state-licensed tobacco shop) in the provincial town of Arras, which she sub-let.[38] These concessions had been allocated since Napoleon I's time to widows and orphans of soldiers, to ensure them a modest income. Perhaps Hyrvoix arranged one for Léon. But such an income – a few hundred francs per year – was insufficient to live even a modest life in Paris. It was nowhere near what Léon spent, living in a wealthy neighbourhood, wearing stylish clothes from expensive shops, and travelling everywhere by cab. According to the police, Léonie and Émilie Léon frequently received 'rich visitors and deputies' in the apartment on the rue Bonaparte.[39] If we cannot be sure about Léon's lifestyle before her relationship with Hyrvoix, we can be sure that she lived by high-class prostitution after his departure. Her 'fall' was then complete.

Gambetta's star, on the other hand, had risen slowly but surely throughout these years. Like Léon, Gambetta grew up on the fringes of the bourgeoisie, belonging to the aspirational rather than the established middle class. A bright and ambitious boy, his fate was more securely in his own hands than was Léon's. His father, an Italian from Genoa, ran a successful grocery store in Cahors and married the daughter of the local pharmacist. Thus Gambetta bore an Italian name, but his mother was a quintessential product of provincial France and his upbringing was entirely French. He attended the local Catholic school until his father placed him in the state secondary school in Cahors. The curriculum, with its emphasis on rhetoric, history, Latin, Greek, French, and the classics, shaped his adult thinking, imbuing him with a love of classical culture and a talent for public speaking.[40]

Gambetta obtained the baccalaureate of letters in 1856: one of only 2071 young men in France to pass that year. The 'bac' not only opened professional careers like law, but also opened the door to bourgeois status. Gambetta was thus prepared to represent what he would later call the 'new social stratum' – wage and salary earners, peasants, artisans, even shopkeepers – demanding greater representation in the polity. He also took his first step towards becoming 'the great patriot,' as he would later be known: because his father was Italian, he had to make a declaration of nationality to become French. Although he always loved Italy, he made a conscious decision in 1859 to take French citizenship at a time when dual citizenship was unknown.[41]

Instead of staying in Cahors to take over the grocery, Gambetta (aided by his mother and aunt) prevailed on his father to allow him to study law in Paris. His exuberant nature made him many friends among students and young professionals. Alphonse Daudet later remembered his sociability, his ready gestures of intimacy (*le geste tutoyeur*), walking arm in arm with his friends.[42] Many remained his devoted friends for life. Eugène Spuller later declared that he had 'given himself completely' to Gambetta, who 'knew from the very first day that I would remain faithful forever.'[43]

From these years, he also acquired a reputation as a 'bar-room orator' (*orateur d'estaminet*) and one who frequented dancers and actresses. This reputation was later fostered by his political enemies. It is not at all certain that it is merited. Claims at the time about the dissolute life of young republicans often reflected the disdain of bourgeois commentators who found popular sociability crude and uncultivated.[44] For people without spacious and well-heated apartments, however, cafés were attractive places to meet with friends. Moreover, since political gatherings were prohibited or severely curtailed, cafés were also one of the few alternative sites for political discussion, hence their close surveillance by the police.[45] Gambetta admitted to his father that he hadn't 'always worked with the regularity of the clock' and had even given in to 'dangerous impulses and crazy behaviour'. But he studied seriously when necessary and was admitted to the bar in 1860.[46]

By this time, Gambetta was known as a fervent republican. His legal work and a few newspaper articles brought him to the attention of republican leaders. In mid-1862, having been a member of a republican defence team for men accused of belonging to a secret society, he was invited to join the law practice of Adolphe Crémieux, former leader of the Second Republic of 1848.[47] Many republicans had high expectations for Gambetta by 1868. His speech at the Baudin trial would confirm their hopes and enable him to emerge onto the wider political stage.

At the trial, opposition journalists were accused of 'disturbing public order and exciting hatred and scorn of the government'.[48] They had opened a subscription to build a monument to Jean-Baptiste Baudin, a republican politician killed in 1851 as Louis-Napoleon Bonaparte crushed the Republic proclaimed in 1848. The subscription campaign and the resulting trial recalled the Empire's origins in a coup d'état.

This promised to be the biggest confrontation to date between the regime and the emerging generation of republicans. All Paris, indeed all France, was agog. Previous trials of the regime's opponents had already turned into political events, since other channels of political expression were closed. *Le Figaro* reported crowds of people trying to get seats, keen to witness the clash. Many republicans attended the trial; Edmond Adam returned to Paris just to be there. A formal system for allocating tickets to spectators separated the classes: as one court reporter noted, those in lace and perfume were seated at the front, while those in workers' clothes, reeking of garlic sausage, crowded together at the back. People of influence could even petition the presiding judge for places.[49]

Léon, the former mistress of an important Empire official, whose current clients included Deputies to the *Corps législatif* (Legislative Body), would have had no trouble getting a ticket and probably had a front-row seat.[50] Léon's interest in the trial no doubt reflected her interest in politics, but may also have been heightened by an emerging sense that the regime was floundering while the republicans were gaining strength.

Léon thus witnessed the sensational courtroom drama on 14 November 1868, when Gambetta made the defence plea for Charles Delescluze, the first of the accused journalists. His stunning condemnation of the Empire brought him instant renown. The prosecutor, by detailing the 'crimes' of Delescluze since 1848 and thus bringing those events into consideration, inadvertently handed Gambetta a powerful weapon. Gambetta reinterpreted those events, putting the Empire itself on trial. Revealing for the first time the powerful oratory that was to be his trademark, he lambasted the regime that had outlawed the motto of the Republic and of Delescluze's newspaper, 'liberty, equality, fraternity':

> Yes! On 2 December [1851], around a pretender, assembled men unknown in France before that day, men who had neither talent, nor honour, nor rank, nor position, men who, in every era, are the accomplices of violent seizures of power, men of whom one can repeat what Sallust said of the throng that surrounded Catiline, what Caesar himself said in sketching the portrait of [Catiline's] accomplices . . . 'A handful of men ruined by debt and crime,' as Corneille translated it.

He continued, claiming 2 December – the date of Louis-Napoléon's coup d'état – as a republican anniversary:

> This anniversary that you don't want, we proclaim it, we take it for our own; we will celebrate it always, incessantly; each year, it will be the anniversary of our dead until the day when the country, back in control, commands a great national expiation in the name of liberty, of equality, of fraternity.

The audience burst into frenzied applause. Gambetta's client received a harsh sentence but Gambetta became an overnight sensation.[51]

Republicans were ecstatic. Juliette Adam recalled:

> I thought my father would go mad as a result of Gambetta's speech. He wanted to go and 'kiss the boots of the orator.' We were all saying: 'We have a leader.' . . . In the Latin Quarter, the Café Procope [a republican stronghold] boiled over with excitement.[52]

The regime got its verdict, but in the process its prestige and legitimacy suffered a serious blow. Gambetta was a national hero; an emerging leader whose oratory drew republicans together. He offered hope that republicans might summon the unity and strength to contest, and to replace, Napoleon III's imperial regime. For Léonie Léon, seated in the audience watching this powerful and exciting man, this was to prove a life-changing moment.

My Dear and only beloved,

What powerful magic do you work on me? Your letter sparkling with wit and with love spread fire through my whole being! If I delay until next Tuesday or Friday the joy of being close to you again in that heady atmosphere of voluptuous pleasure, don't think, I beg you, that this is due to fear of you or of me. Whatever happens, I will never retract the unreserved, entire gift I made to you of my whole being, and when my head rests on your heart it is with unlimited confidence, knowing perfectly well that it is the heart of an honest man in the fullest sense of the word; the noblest of all hearts, the only one worthy of being adored. You are and every day you will be increasingly the pure source from which I draw life, happiness and all the ideas that I have yet to acquire. I don't want to conceive a thought that hasn't been inspired by you. I want to be so completely immersed in you that I am no longer aware of my own existence!

Events don't always work out according to my desires and my days are far from being spun from pink silk and gold. I will be free on Tuesday from six o'clock and all day Friday. I say Friday deliberately so as not to deprive you of the political soirée on Saturday. Tell me which day do you prefer? Don't feel obliged to say the first out of politeness. I believe firmly in your present tenderness. As for that of the future, la Rochefoucault [sic] says: 'We can no more vouch for the duration of our feelings than for that of our life'.

I spent three hours in Paris on Wednesday, I saw my doctor and put to him the question that occupied us last Saturday. Is the heart an organ or a muscle? He replied that we were both partly right and that we had to unite our opinions to be completely correct, the heart is a muscular organ.

I think you are too hard on the almost necessary irritability of the little hero of the bourgeoisie [Adolphe Thiers]. His outbursts of stubbornness are as many victories over these remnants of the aristocracy who have inherited only their names from their gentlemen fathers; they make the country realize the weakness of a party which no longer has any foundation in France, and will eventually discourage these faded stars bearing coats of arms, and their satellites too. As for the Bonapartists, that's a different matter, they have soaring hopes.

Reply speedily, dear adored one, my imagination has resumed its flight towards the unexplored heights to which your ideal love transports me, and there I remain in ecstasy, contemplating day and night the vast and radiant horizon that this fusion of our hearts, our souls, our intelligences, in a pure, noble, elevated goal, enables me to glimpse, and I love you!

Yours

Léonie

2

'I want you to devote yourself to the Republic'

On 27 April 1872, the man on whom Léonie Léon had set her sights finally consented to meet her. As Gambetta later recalled, 'we met, were smitten by each other, gave ourselves to each other'.[2] After four years of assiduous effort to achieve her goal, Léon was surely seeking a long-term relationship; Gambetta, already in a relationship with Marie Meersmans, may have anticipated only a casual affair. But the liaison between Gambetta and Léon gradually evolved into a serious commitment, and then into a shared family life that included Léon's son and even her dogs.

From the beginning, this relationship was both lived in the flesh and embellished through the letter. Gambetta wrote passionately four days after their first encounter: 'When will I see you again? . . . I am on tenterhooks. Let me see your beautiful eyes or I will go out of my mind and be no use to anybody.' Léon replied to this or an equally seductive letter: 'What powerful magic do you work on me? Your letter sparkling with wit and with love spread fire through my whole being!'[3]

From the beginning, too, this mutual passion had a strong political dimension. Léon's first letter not only spoke of love, but also resumed a political discussion that had begun face-to-face. These initial letters set the tone for the couple's correspondence across the decade that followed. Their letters – simultaneously tokens of love, snapshots of daily life, and documents of political strategy – fostered a liaison that was at once an intimate relationship and a political partnership.

A liaison unfolds

Despite fervent protestations of love, the relationship between Gambetta and Léon did not run smoothly at first. Léon was often unavailable when Gambetta wanted to see her. In June 1872, an aggrieved Gambetta was insisting that she must 'make [herself] free', she must 'finally arrange [her] return' to Paris. But Léon kept repeating: 'It isn't possible for me to spend tomorrow Monday at your knees . . . I hope to be able to give you Tuesday evening and all day Wednesday, or another day if you prefer.' She 'had to return to the fold', she explained.[4]

Léon lived at Bourg-la-Reine, nine kilometres (five miles) south of Paris, with her mother, her son Alphonse, and her sister Émilie.[5] Her visits to Paris had to accommodate her domestic situation. They had to be coordinated with her sister's use of the apartment they shared on the rue Bonaparte at which, the police later reported, they both entertained clients. As Léon wrote to Gambetta one Tuesday: 'since you hadn't yet expressed the desire to see me this week, [my sister] has chosen Wednesday and Thursday. I will only be able to come Friday and I will expect you from 2pm.'[6]

Léon also had to negotiate her absences with her mother, and her new relationship was a subject of conflict between them. Gambetta noted that he had 'awakened unpleasantly the curiosity and the indiscretion of your entourage'. Léon prohibited Gambetta from visiting her at Bourg-la-Reine, adding: 'I have already endured two quite sharp attacks. This morning I lied with an aplomb that I didn't believe I was capable of, I hope I have thereby gained a few hours of peace.' We can infer that Gambetta's visit stirred up a hornet's nest in the family. Did Mme Léon not wish to be confronted with the reality of her daughter's source of income? Or did she regard Gambetta as a dangerous extremist?[7]

If their relationship was to flourish, both Léon and Gambetta needed to extricate themselves from their past lives. Perhaps they judged it prudent to see how this new liaison developed, however, before burning their bridges. Gambetta continued his affair with the Belgian-born demimondaine, Marie Meersmans. She had caught Gambetta's attention following the Baudin trial by posing as a plaintiff seeking legal advice, and their affair lasted at least until September 1872. He sent her a number of ardent love letters, although only one of those that survives was written after he met Léon.[8]

Gambetta would have realized from Léon's conduct that she was a courtesan, not a 'respectable' woman. Respectable women did not pursue men. Nor did they smoke cigarettes. And Léon apparently revealed something of her past during the first weeks of their relationship. Writing to his 'Magdalena' (a reference to the biblical Mary Magdalene, traditionally represented as a prostitute), Gambetta urged her, 'tell me everything': 'nothing can alter or cool my adoration. I fear nothing except being kept in the dark. Speak, speak, my sweet mistress; I want to take you again [*te reprendre*], by going back over your life to your most bitter memories.'[9]

Léon soon referred to herself as Gambetta's 'morganatic wife', claiming a unique status for her relationship with him. She nevertheless continued seeing clients until at least 1874. Only substantial financial support from Gambetta, including support for her family, would have enabled her to dispense with them. The letters do not raise the delicate issue of finances – discussing money was taboo for a courtesan, reducing her to a 'common prostitute' – and this makes it difficult to establish the point at which Léon became exclusively Gambetta's mistress. But Gambetta, still a struggling politician without a private income, could not yet support Léon.[10]

Whether Léon knew of the existence of Marie Meersmans is impossible to say, but she probably suspected that Gambetta had other romantic interests. She wanted to establish an exclusive relationship with him: did she envisage marriage, or simply having a sole protector and discarding other clients? 'I've been reflecting since this morning', she wrote, 'that it is an unspeakable naivety for a woman with some experience of life to try to convince the man she loves, not only of the immensity of the feelings he inspires, but also of the impossibility of tolerating any rival.' She acknowledged that 'coquettish ploys' would more readily keep Gambetta's love aflame than declarations of her 'endless fidelity', but she insisted that she was not interested in playing that game.[11] This was a 'coquettish ploy' itself, however, given that Léon was in no position to promise 'endless fidelity'.

Léon responded indignantly to Gambetta's initial assumption that theirs was simply a sexual relationship in which he could assume her availability: this was an assertion of her status as courtesan and aspiring mistress, rather than 'common prostitute'. 'I will not see you until your spirit has regained ascendancy over your senses', she wrote in an early letter. 'I don't want to be desired but loved.' Gambetta swiftly acknowledged his misdemeanours: 'I fear that I tire you, and that you are afraid of me. I swear however that I will never again have to reproach myself with the slightest violence. I am impatient to swear an oath at your knees.' He was deeply apologetic again a week later: 'I can't think about what happened without trembling, I ask myself how I could have lost my reason . . . I swear to you that an impure design never entered my soul. I am sorry and furious . . . How right you were to recall me to duty and to decency'.[12]

Perhaps Gambetta had approached Léon crudely; perhaps he had even attempted to force himself on her. Having apologized to Léon,

Gambetta noted: 'I believe that in the future we must better organize the use of our time; I must know in advance when you will arrive in Paris, when you are obliged to leave, and the period between should be allocated in minute detail for the greater well-being of your avid worshipper.'[13] Gambetta was still intent on making the best use of the time available, suggesting that he still thought of Léon as a courtesan. Léon wanted to put the relationship on a less crude footing. Remarkably, however, Gambetta accepted Léon's reproaches rather than abandoning her for easier pickings.

Gambetta clearly found something particularly attractive in Léon. His persistence supports the view that bourgeois men, who from the mid-nineteenth century increasingly kept mistresses, were searching for emotional satisfaction, not just for sexual gratification. Men desired 'some semblance of seduction, of feeling, even of attachment', as Alain Corbin argues.[14] Perhaps Léon's demands reflected an awareness of that male desire. But perhaps they indicated a parallel desire for fantasy on Léon's part; a belief that what she was offering – and what Gambetta offered in return – was not a commercial exchange of sexual favours for money, but a romance and a meeting of minds.

An epistolary affair

If Léon feared rivals like Marie Meersmans, she had several trump cards to play against them, not least her talent as a correspondent. She may have complained about her 'stupid education', but her letters are intelligent, well informed and witty, reflecting a broad-ranging knowledge of literature and culture. Gambetta's letters are equally well written and interesting. Clearly, the letters themselves provided delight and were an incentive to pursue the physical relationship.[15]

In the early years, Léon and Gambetta met only once or twice a week, but they quickly established the practice of exchanging daily letters. At midnight on 1 June 1872, barely six weeks after their first meeting, Gambetta wrote to Léon, 'I will prove to you prosaically the perfect exactitude of my devotion. Every evening, putting the newspaper to bed, I slip into the outgoing mail the letter which is destined for you and which leaves by the morning's mail.' Léon treasured Gambetta's letters as he did hers. In August 1872 he re-read Léon's letters, which he then 'organized and put in a pretty little pink box, in the most private recesses of [his] desk'. A year later, Léon 're-read nearly a hundred of [his] dear and ravishing letters, in which the spirit and the heart do battle for poetry and finesse'.[16]

Since neither Gambetta nor Léon could offer an exclusive relationship, passionate letters were vital to convey the importance they
attached to this relationship and their hopes for its future. Each of the
lovers deployed the carefully crafted letter in order to attach the other
more closely.[17] Léon's reaffirmation of her sexual union with Gambetta,
in her first surviving letter, served that purpose: 'Whatever happens
I will never retract the unreserved, complete gift I made to you of my
entire person, and when my head rests on your heart it is with unlimited confidence, knowing fully that it is the heart of an honest man
in the fullest sense of the word; the noblest of all hearts, the only one
worthy of being adored.' Gambetta, likewise, pressed his 'dear idol' for
another rendezvous. He begged his 'dear Madonna': reserve 'at least one
day a week for your despairing and starving Léon'.[18]

Such epistolary excesses signalled devotion and desire. So, too, did
Léon's 'coquettish ploys' that tantalized Gambetta by hinting at sexual
pleasure: 'The more I understand you, the more certain I become that
you need to be loved, spoiled, adored, idolized incessantly', she wrote.
Promising Gambetta 'relaxation' and 'an affection without bounds', she
continued: 'If you really feel the desire to see me again and think that
an hour or two spent with me might distract you, do you some good,
I don't believe it's necessary to feel as strong as Hercules to come as far
as [my apartment on] the rue Bonaparte.'[19]

Expressions of doubt and despair surfaced periodically in their letters,
calling for reaffirmation of the other's devotion. Léon was 'filled with
terror' by one of Gambetta's letters. Gambetta feared that Léon was
'indifferent' because her letter was 'cold, lifeless'. Worse, he feared that
she was 'putting him to the test', even 'playing with him'. Indeed she
was: 'You are certainly more experienced in military strategy than in
that of love', she wrote, when he accepted her suggestion that he delay
replying to her letter. He was supposed to have rejected such an idea out
of hand. Gambetta protested his love: 'How can I speak to you, write to
you, consult you on the thoughts that occupy me or besiege me when
I have this horrible anguish: does she truly love me?' He closed, asking
rhetorically: 'What can I do? I love you madly and I'm always afraid of
losing you. I throw myself at your feet and beg you to let me remain
there.'[20]

The couple's letters repeatedly expressed their frustration at failing
to find words to convey the passion they felt. They turned to the letters of others in search of inspiration. Letter writing was a valued social
accomplishment at the time, and collections of correspondence were
popular reading.[21] Léon and Gambetta compared their own epistolary

efforts to those of such literary celebrities as Prosper Mérimée, Honoré de Balzac and Pierre Lanfrey; they studied letters by noted stylists such as Madame de Maintenon and Madame du Deffand (the correspondent of Horace Walpole). Léon declared Gambetta's 'epistolary poetry' far superior to 'Lanfrey's dry pose' and 'Mérimée's pretentiousness'. Gambetta even surpassed Balzac, her 'ex-divinity'. Balzac failed to convey 'the extremely varied and infinite nuances' of love: 'he sprinkles his amorous accounts with theories that reveal a profound ignorance of the delicious emotions that fill my memory at this moment'.[22]

Each letter was an emotional weather vane signalling its writer's desire: each was scrutinized for any sign of cooling affections. Léon wrote anxiously in October 1873: 'Your letter this morning was really disappointing, not that it was cold; our language is not rich enough to furnish expressions suited to all states of mind . . . but the soul is somehow absent . . . you must have been preoccupied, distracted while writing it.' Gambetta responded that 'paper doesn't suffice for me any longer; no matter how I fill it with my ardour, it's in vain', and he reaffirmed explicitly his desire for her: 'only your real presence can slake my thirst'. Léon replied with relief: 'This time your dear mind was indeed fully focused on me because each line, each word of your incomparable letter makes my heart beat faster, I am bedazzled with happiness and I am at your feet in ecstasy for the rest of my life!'[23]

The letters of late 1873 were increasingly emphatic in their expression of love, overflowing with hyperbole as nineteenth-century love letters typically did. 'You are the most inexhaustible, the most marvellous, the most exquisite *artiste* that nature ever formed in her finest hours of prodigality and magnificence', Gambetta wrote in November 1873, 'I am dazzled and exhausted.' Léonie Léon replied the same day: 'My Léon, my life, my idol, didn't this marvellous evening surpass all the others, and can I complain about sufferings that are compensated for by such raptures? My worship for you, that I thought infinite, has grown again since yesterday.'[24]

Their love letters were, in part, a linguistic game, exploring the possibilities provided by language to express love and desire. Sometimes (but rarely) brevity struck the right chord, as when Gambetta wrote:

I adore you.
I will always adore you. I have adored you from all eternity.
Do you remember?
Your
Léon.[25]

Léon's reply excelled in its extravagance:

> This supreme hour will be eternally present in my thoughts! This pale ray of the setting sun will envelop my whole life with its gentle light! We have contemplated the infinite face to face, we have felt and understood it. You have initiated this soul born of your breath to such divine mysteries, and what adoration does it not owe you in exchange for the ineffable delights with which you fill it? Such a letter, I throw myself at your feet bathed in love and gratitude, [I leave] to tomorrow the affairs of this world.[26]

Letters like these certainly suggest the sexual ardour of the union between Gambetta and Léon. They led the historian Jacques Chastenet to suggest that Léon was 'remarkably expert in [sexual] caresses', responsible for introducing Gambetta to a 'marvellous carnal kingdom' hitherto unknown to him.[27] Chastenet neglects the role of hyperbole in achieving the love letter's primary goal, that of reaffirming and validating all aspects of a relationship.

There is no doubt, however, that sex played a major role in their relationship. As well as the inflated, sometimes orgasmic language of the letters in general, there is one explicit letter extant which confirms that this is a valid reading of the letters. Léon destroyed some letters, allowing us to infer that there were other similar letters. She may have saved this letter because of its political content and its testimony to Gambetta's faith in her judgement. It is probably she who deleted some key words, but it is still surprising that she did not cut whole lines, as she occasionally did in other letters.

In this letter, Gambetta apologized for having failed to write his daily letter: 'My remorse was calmed by reading that delicious letter in which you retrace the divine ecstasies with which you intoxicated me in that incomparable Friday of tenderness and of [*deleted*].' He went on to apologize further about their encounter: 'I was furious that I allowed myself to come too quickly, . . . I even came from the momentary [*deleted*] which you gained from my eagerness, I will make up for it and impose on you a tender revenge.'[28]

Sexual pleasure – which they were apparently able to discuss explicitly – was certainly important. But, as with other courtesans, it came as part of a 'package', which included wit, conversation, and intelligent discussion – and, in Léon's case at least, enticing letters, which confirmed not only the pleasure but also the emotional validity of their sexual intimacy.[29] For Gambetta and Léon, the 'package' included, most importantly, an interest in politics. Léon's appeal to Gambetta – and Gambetta's appeal to her – lay precisely in the combination of all these attractions in a single individual.

'I want you to devote yourself completely to the Republic'

From the start, Léon metaphorically aligned herself with Gambetta's 'goddess', the Republic, 'whose supremacy in your heart I accept . . . because it also offers me a goal to aim for, that of equalling her in your affections one day through my love and abnegation.'[30] To ally herself with the Republic was to enhance her desirability for Gambetta and she deployed her feminine strategy with skill.

Léon was nevertheless profoundly engaged with politics and this was part of Gambetta's attraction for her. She chided Gambetta in one early letter, 'Why didn't you mention politics, knowing the immense attraction exercised on my spirit by this fascinating preoccupation, this element in which I would like to have lived exclusively? Wasn't it that noble passion that drew my thoughts to your personality, my admiration to your actions, my gaze to your person and my heart to your great and innumerable perfections?' Léon adored the public figure, the powerful and commanding orator, not merely the lover who visited her in secret. In this respect she resembled other women who lived their lives in the embrace of political men, and for whom the excitement of politics was inextricable from the erotic appeal of the individual politician.[31]

Conforming to gender expectations, Léon explicitly positioned herself as passive spectator to Gambetta's political activity, writing in the spring of 1873: 'I am passionate about your politics, and it's a joy for me to follow you wherever it requires your exclusive attention.' She wrote '*your* politics', even though she was actively involved in Gambetta's political decision-making. She presented – and Gambetta accepted – her role as strictly feminine, a support role played behind the scenes. Despite her declaration that politics was 'the domain in which [she] would like to have lived exclusively', she never envisaged female suffrage or acknowledged the admittedly rare feminist declarations of her time.[32]

Gambetta's political life centred on the National Assembly, where he was the republicans' most powerful speaker. Léonie Léon was frequently in the audience, like many other women. The National Assembly may have been an exclusively male political forum, but women were highly visible in the galleries as witnesses to the male political process. Their luminous dresses contrasted with the sea of black suits below, space and colour eloquently expressing the separation along sex lines that characterized politics at that time. Camille Pelletan, a radical young journalist and republican, wrote disparagingly of the National Assembly in 1873:

> The entire balcony, during the major sessions, is multi-coloured thanks to the women's outfits, in which all the shades of the rainbow sparkle, and which are surmounted by shrubberies full of corolla and liana, wheat fields speckled with poppies, hanging gardens inspired by those of Semiramis, bird of paradise feathers, and cornucopias overflowing with grapes and fruit, that women wear on their heads as pretexts for hats.[33]

The Assembly sat in the theatre built for the marriage of King Louis XVI and Marie-Antoinette, and Pelletan's description reflected his criticism of the decorative excess and moral corruption of the monarchy. He viewed women's presence in the public galleries of what had now become the Republic's debating chamber as a threat to male virtue in the new political order as well.

In fact, many women had strong political loyalties, and all the political leaders had female supporters who applauded, encouraged and affirmed them.[34] Commentators might dismiss women's attendance as a matter of fashion rather than conviction, but women like Léon espoused political causes passionately, and observing the debates was vital to their informed engagement with politics.[35] As Léon would note in 1876: 'It is quite difficult to assess fully from a distance the value of a parliamentary day as important as yesterday; the expressions, even the intonations are sometimes rays of light that are not available to the reader.'[36] Only attendance gave the 'feel' of the political contest and brought it to life. For devotees like Léon, it was also a form of vicarious participation.

Gambetta loved to have Léon in the audience at the National Assembly. He sent her tickets regularly and expressed disappointment if she failed to come. Léon was 'enthusiastic' about attending, eager to witness the 'drama of Versailles'. Sometimes fate intervened to delay her: 'I had relied too much on my watch which was fast,' she explained on one occasion, 'and I burned a large handful of hair with the curling iron . . . the consternation produced by this scorching was one of the causes of my lateness.'[37]

Just getting to Versailles from Bourg-la-Reine was not easy. Léon had to travel to Paris by train, cross Paris by coach, and then take a second train to Versailles. At times she excused herself: 'I won't go to Paris tomorrow Tuesday unless you've sent me a ticket for the Chamber and you are going to speak, otherwise I won't come till Thursday.' But this was not due to a lack of political interest. She continued in the same letter, celebrating recent republican by-election wins: 'I am triumphant about the elections; what matter if these frightful reactionaries have seduced a few waverers in order to give themselves an absurd majority; France is yours at heart, if not yet in fact!'[38]

Léon's pleasure in attending parliamentary sessions was clearly entangled with her love for Gambetta. She wrote early in their relationship:

> I fully understand your political obsession, so I am deeply touched that you thought to obtain a ticket for me at such a moment. If you have one I will gladly take advantage of it. But the Chamber no longer holds an irresistible attraction for me except when I can enjoy your wonderful eloquence and study the effect it produces on everybody's physiognomy.[39]

The 'irresistible attraction' of politics was obviously not new, but it had been transformed by her passionate love for Gambetta. Moreover, his 'wonderful eloquence' – attested to by many others – enraptured her, stirring the emotions of a lover. The prospect of hearing him speak in the Assembly made her heart 'tremble in anticipation, thinking of all the noble and delightful emotions that await it!'[40]

The seductive power of Gambetta's voice was even more powerful in those special moments when he declaimed a speech in private, just for her. Describing to Gambetta 'the delightful emotions that your vibrant voice causes in me', she added on one occasion: 'Never has it sounded so harmonious to me as during our last meeting. I said to you: Speak, speak again, and I listened, my soul plunged in an indescribable intoxication. This single memory, this single joy will suffice for the happiness of my entire life!'[41]

Léon's political role alongside Gambetta was not confined to applauding his oratory. She was his confidante, commenting on his speeches, debating policy with him, and offering advice.[42] Léon lived vicariously the drama of the early 1870s as republicans, with Gambetta in the vanguard, tried to wrest government of the nominal Republic from a monarchist majority bent on a restoration. Léon gave renewed energy to Gambetta, whose battles with colleagues in the faction-ridden republican movement were often as difficult as those with his monarchist opponents.

The survival of the Republic, still at best uncertain in 1872, was uppermost in the couple's political considerations. They worried about the likely actions of the head of government, Adolphe Thiers. An advocate of constitutional monarchy, Thiers had been influential in installing King Louis-Philippe on the throne following the 1830 Revolution. He resurrected his political career in the 1860s, accepting the Empire so long as it, in turn, committed itself to what he called 'the necessary freedoms'.

After the Republic was proclaimed in 1870, Thiers opposed republican efforts to continue the war. This put him at odds with Gambetta, who led those efforts, most famously by his daring balloon flight to raise a fresh army. Peace proved more appealing to the French electorate than a hopeless if heroic struggle. In the elections of February 1871, the republicans were associated with the effort to continue a widely detested war; monarchists stood for an end to the war and won a huge majority. Thiers became provisional 'Head of the Executive Power' – not President – pending 'a decision on the institutions of France'.

Thus the Republic so recently proclaimed came to be governed by monarchists. With peace, however, they lost their trump card, and Thiers soon came to support a Republic, but one with constitutional arrangements to entrench the power of elites against what he had famously called the 'vile multitude'. Gambetta stood not only for a Republic, but for a thoroughgoing democracy. The 1869 Belleville Manifesto, on which he was elected to the Legislative Assembly, called for 'the most profound application of universal suffrage [in fact only for men]; . . . freedom of press, of assembly, of association, separation of Church and state; compulsory, free and secular primary education; secondary education free by competitive examination.' This programme seemed so extreme that its supporters were labelled 'radical' republicans. The name stuck. Gambetta's wartime exploits only added to his reputation as a radical.[43]

The contest between Thiers and Gambetta from 1872 was thus a contest to fight off any attempt at restoration and then to define the Republic. Convinced that Thiers remained a monarchist at heart, many republicans feared that he would support a restoration if the opportunity arose. This was the first political issue that Léon discussed with Gambetta.[44] Gambetta's strategy, worked out with Léon over the years, was to attract moderates, even to the point of accepting an undemocratic Senate, but to maintain his republican following.

Day to day tactics were more difficult than this broad strategy. Gambetta wavered between confidence in his ability to work with or outwit Thiers, and fury at the political intrigues of the 'little master'. July 1872 saw him sure that he had the upper hand and could bend

Thiers to his will. In a lengthy exploration of the issues, he advised Léon not to be 'too quickly alarmed' by Thiers' seesawing politics. Thiers had 'burned his bridges with the right', who would 'never forgive him'. 'Despite appearances', he continued, 'despite the unfortunate retractions he comes out with, we have the President in our hands and we know how to extract from him the services that he can still provide before signing up to honest and true Democracy.'[45]

Always independent, Léon disagreed: 'I don't believe the right are as vindictive and particular as you describe them. On the contrary, I am certain that they would receive M. Thiers with open arms, and like the father of the prodigal son, would heartily forgive his excursion to the left provided he set himself again to the task of reconstructing some throne or other.' Having disagreed, however, she resumed a pose of deference and admiration. She 'await[ed] the hour of combat without concern; hoping that the master [Thiers] has finally understood that you alone can offer him real support'.[46]

Léon's cautious political instincts were evident in her letters and she constantly urged moderation, which became Gambetta's strategy. Any outburst of radicalism on Gambetta's part, she insisted, would play into the hands of his political enemies and alienate Thiers, whereas he could disarm them all by a display of cool reserve. After watching Gambetta's performance in the Assembly one day, Léon was full of encouragement:

> I contemplated you with rapture, with your proud, gracious and calm poses. Oh! persevere I beg you in that moderation which astonishes and exasperates your enemies; they are even saying that you are playing a comedy of moderation to dupe the undecided conservatives; but it enthralls and fills with enthusiasm all those who don't know you and who wonder about this monstrous calumny that had deceived them.[47]

By-election results throughout 1872 boosted the republicans' confidence. 'What I am reading about the elections thrills me, dear child of destiny', wrote Léon. She added an erotic twist to Gambetta's political triumphs: '[Destiny] too is in love with you and satisfies all your desires willingly. Who could resist your irresistible smile?' But Léon also expressed concern about the election trends. Suspicious of those who would push for a more radical Republic, she added: 'I fear this socialist tide which after having been held in check for so long will come swirling around your feet roaring and frothing. Get ready to master this torrent, to say to it: "you will go no further".'[48]

Léon here alluded to divisions amongst the republicans that had a long history. Republicanism in France had its origins in revolutionary politics, in the popular uprisings of 1792 and 1848. The proclamation of the Third Republic in 1870 in the wake of the Emperor's defeat placed it in the same tradition, and the Paris Commune of 1871 highlighted its radical potential. But Gambetta was at pains to transform the image of republicanism, to sever its links with violence and highlight the virtues of 'honest and true Democracy'.

His challenge was to shape a moderate republicanism that would appeal to a broad electorate, thus forestalling a monarchist restoration. In order to do so, he had to contain the 'intransigents' or 'Extreme Left' (Léon's 'socialist tide'). They were considered 'extreme' at a time when even democracy, as Gambetta's Belleville Programme proposed, was a radical idea, and functioning republics almost unknown. They looked back to the short-lived Second Republic of 1848 and sought social reforms to promote equality (hence Léon's 'socialist' slur). For them, changes to the political system were not enough.

Thus the 'radical' Gambetta – who was in fact moderating his views – was outflanked by this 'Extreme Left', whose increasing appeal to his electors was to cause him many problems. But while those 'Extreme Left' republicans regarded him as too conservative, others still regarded him as a radical. These diverse impressions hindered his attempt to form a united republican party in the 1870s, and made many wary of his quest for power.[49]

'Marked on the forehead by destiny'

If the Republic was to come to power via the ballot box, embedding a republican culture in the electorate was critical to success. Gambetta's numerous speaking tours, like his newspaper, were designed to create such a culture. With parliament in recess in September 1872, and with an eye to further by-elections in October, Gambetta toured Eastern France. Léon associated herself vicariously with this mission, reaffirming the feminine self-abnegation that sometimes framed her contributions to their political discussions. 'Since this sad separation is necessary', she wrote, 'I'm anxious to know that you have left. You must be nostalgic for applause, just as I am to enjoy and, in my solitude, to take delight in the triumphs that await you.'[50]

Since their relationship was still not an exclusive one, separation put their mutual devotion to the test. Léon's anxiety about Gambetta's fidelity rose when she received a letter written on the notepaper of 'a Madame or Mademoiselle Denoir'. She feared the 'legions of young and seductive women quite prepared to lay siege to [Gambetta's] heart' and, signing off as 'Penelope', begged him not to allow himself 'to be charmed by any Calypso'.[51]

Her anxiety would have been greater still had she seen the note Gambetta wrote to Marie Meersmans shortly after his departure: 'My dear little darling [*mignonne*], It's been three long days since I left you!' He closed this letter asking her to be patient and to 'count on the fidelity of your loving Loulou'. Clearly, he had not yet terminated his affair with Meersmans, despite the many adoring letters he wrote to Léon. She, for her part, was still trapped in the life of a courtesan. She nevertheless reminded Gambetta of why she deserved his attention: her only merit, she claimed, was 'that of adoring you with all the ardour of a soul of which you are the first and will be the only love!' She simultaneously disavowed the significance of other sexual relationships in her life and implicitly appealed for a commitment on Gambetta's part.[52]

Political triumphs were quick to come for Gambetta and Léon was quick to praise them. Thousands of workers turned out to hear him in the manufacturing towns around Lyon. He then moved into the Savoy region, where a speech was scheduled for Chambéry on 22 September – anniversary of the declaration of the first Republic in 1792. Léon had clearly been apprised of the contents of this speech and was full of anticipation: 'Does my destiny not lie in strewing flowers on the sometimes arid path that leads to your triumph? But if the wonderful harangue of the 22nd that I am nevertheless awaiting with feverish impatience is the last step on this thorny route, my delightful mission will have been very short!'[53]

When the Prefect banned the scheduled public meeting at Chambéry, Gambetta repeated his speech in a series of 'private' gatherings.[54] Rather than muzzling Gambetta, the Prefect had enhanced his prestige and popularity. Léon was enraptured:

> From all I've read about your entry into Chambéry I can only compare it to that of Alexander the Great into Babylon; like that prince, like Caesar, like all the great men marked on the forehead by destiny to personify in themselves an entire epoch, you have that prestige which fascinates and what's more that persuasive eloquence which, in instilling confidence, gives birth to devotion. Will my most ingenious, most passionate, most infinite devotion suffice, on its own, to fill the void left in your heart after the warm and exuberant tenderness of the people of Savoy?[55]

As Léon reasserted her love, she kept herself in the political frame beside Gambetta as the courageous woman waiting for her man.

The most significant speech of Gambetta's campaign was to come on 26 September at Grenoble, where six thousand people turned out to welcome him. He repeated his praise for the Republic and democracy, and criticized the current regime, which severely restricted freedom of speech and assembly and maintained a state of emergency in a number of departments. Gambetta criticized the bourgeoisie's reluctance to accept that the monarchy was finished, making one of his most controversial declarations:

> Haven't we seen appear across the country . . . a new personnel of electoral politics, a new personnel of universal suffrage? Haven't we seen the workers of town and countryside, this world of labour to whom the future belongs, make its entry into political affairs? . . . Yes, I sense, I feel, I announce, the arrival and the presence in politics of a new social stratum . . . which is far, indeed, from being inferior to its predecessors.[56]

By the 'new social stratum' and the 'world of labour', Gambetta meant all those who depended on wages and salary, including peasants, artisans, and even shopkeepers like his father. But this speech outraged his political opponents: by appealing to the 'world of labour' for support, he was engaging in class warfare. They attacked him furiously in the months that followed.

Back in Paris, Gambetta set out to achieve a dissolution of the Assembly followed by general elections, which he was convinced would eliminate many of the monarchists in the Assembly. Their election in 1871, he believed, reflected the fraught conditions at the end of the war, when parts of the country were still occupied by Prussian troops. On 14 December, he gave a two-hour speech in the Assembly in support of dissolution, but the vote was 483 to 196 against him. Gambetta tried to reassure Léon, taking refuge in his masculine capabilities in words that betray his insecurity: 'On the subject of politics, you must calm down, put your mind at ease. The situation . . . is a little confused, but I am used to navigating in the fog and I can assure you that we have left behind the dangerous channels, we are on the high seas, we are saved.' He insisted: 'universal suffrage will soon seal our destinies and those of our young Republic'.[57]

Léon remained sceptical about Gambetta's analysis, although she smothered her disagreement in 'sentiments of adoration, gratitude and infinite love'. 'I have read and meditated a lot on your letter and I do not completely share your opinion on the situation at the present moment', she wrote. She offered her own incisive interpretation instead: the monarchists realized that a Republic was inevitable, so they planned 'to deceive the country by establishing . . . a constitutional monarchy under the title of a Republic. They hope, thanks to the mutilation of universal suffrage and the creation of an Orleanist second Chamber, to one day hand the presidency of this monarcho-republic to the duc d'Aumale.'[58] She was right, although Gambetta later turned the Senate into a bastion of republicanism.

Thiers had committed himself officially to the Republic in 1872 but, under increasing pressure from the monarchists, his ministry now embarked on a series of anti-democratic and anti-republican measures. Léon was furious when the monarchists established an enquiry into the actions of the Government of National Defence of 1870, specifically targeting Gambetta. She was incredulous when Gambetta and his followers supported a motion of confidence in the commission conducting it. In one of her longest letters to Gambetta, Léon poured out her feelings in a rush of angry and ungrammatical prose:

> You make me feel all the passions in succession. Yesterday for the first time I felt hatred and vengeance to such a degree that I understood Judith and Charlotte Corday.[59] Are you aware of all the harm you have done by supporting Broglie's motion, giving this despicable commission complete leisure, complete ease to spin for you a web in which, like an imprudent fly, you allow yourself to be enveloped and which leads you, hands and feet tied, towards a verdict by the ministers and you accept this decision. . . .

She was equally furious about those targeting Gambetta, and about Thiers in particular:

> As for M. Thiers, at the very moment that you have just done him a service, sacrificing your convictions in order to enable his affairs to triumph, he authorizes such a scandal and allows a frenzied assembly to sow throughout France suspicion, distrust, uncertainty about your loyalty[,] on the eve of the prorogation[,] without giving you time for a complete justification.[60]

Unlike the letters in which she deferred to Gambetta's better judgement, or subordinated herself to his political mission, Léon here took the initiative, intent on defending Gambetta's reputation. She identified so strongly with him and his mission that her response could hardly have been more intense had she been targeted herself.

Thiers' hold on power by mid-1873 was fragile. The monarchists undermined him despite his anti-republican concessions; the republicans were increasingly loath to support him against the monarchists. As Léon observed: 'when he needs your strength to shore up his shaky power, [he] becomes republican only to become a monarchist again the day that his ambition makes him dream once again of the votes of the Right'. 'This time he is at your mercy', she continued, in authoritative rather than self-effacing mode, 'and you must make him pay a high price for the support he requests to preserve his authority.'[61]

By-elections in April and May of 1873 brought matters to a head. The by-election in Paris was critical, and Thiers proposed his aristocratic friend, the comte de Rémusat, as the candidate. The fact that Rémusat had never claimed to be a republican, and sat in the cabinet repressing democracy, made it impossible for Gambetta to support his candidature. But what was the alternative? Léon came up with a Machiavellian plan:

> As for the candidature of M. de Rémusat, wouldn't it be more prudent to put up against the minister someone completely insignificant? If he succumbs in the battle, you could obtain credit in the eyes of the government for having abandoned the terrain to it whilst preserving appearances with regard to your party. If on the other hand your candidate triumphed, your triumph would be even more crushing for the government in that you had only opposed to it a nonentity, which would prove in a striking fashion the strength, the docility of your party and the conviction that your directives inspire![62]

Gambetta did not take this advice but threw his weight behind the largely unknown Désiré Barodet, recent victim of a purge of radical mayors and favoured by the most radical sectors of the republican movement. In an election that was, at heart, a referendum on Thiers' politics, the turnout was a record and the outcome decisive: Barodet was elected by more than 40,000 votes. Worse was to come for Thiers, when four by-elections on 11 May saw three radical republicans elected.[63]

If these results seemed like victory, their disastrous implications were soon evident. Léon noted presciently on 13 May 1873: 'only the growing fury of the reactionaries is to be feared'. She had already observed that 'Mac-Mahonism will be the [refuge] of all the disappointed parties';

she was referring to Marshal Patrice de MacMahon, duc de Magenta, the prominent monarchist waiting in the wings. The monarchists, convinced that the Republic was destined to be dominated by the Extreme Left, now manoeuvered to remove Thiers from office. Eleven days after Léon warned of the Right's 'fury', the Assembly elected Marshal MacMahon as President. An avowed supporter of a Bourbon restoration now headed the Third Republic.[64]

Gambetta versus the 'Old Colonel'

The cabinet appointed by Marshal MacMahon, led by the duc de Broglie, declared all-out war on republicanism. Forty-three departments remained under martial law and their military governors had carte blanche to preserve 'Moral Order', a term which came to designate Broglie's reactionary regime. A wave of purges saw republicans removed from administrative posts. Many republican newspapers were banned. Prosecution of former Communards continued apace, and a counter-attack was launched on republican anticlericalism. The struggle for the Republic seemed back where it had started.

Gambetta devoted himself to keeping up the spirits of rank and file republicans. On 24 June, he gave his customary address at the annual celebration of the birth of General Hoche, a hero of the Revolutionary Wars of the 1790s. Whilst urging calm and obedience to the law, Gambetta rallied his republican audience for the battle at hand: 'Continue to demonstrate by comparisons, by facts, the considerable advantages of republican democracy over all the dynastic and monarchical regimes . . . We are fighting for France!'[65]

Léon thought this speech 'magnificent' and anointed Gambetta as the man of destiny. He showed, she declared, that republicanism was a 'system of politics so consistent with modern philosophy and natural law that it will impose itself on France whatever obstacles these pygmies put before it'. But Broglie asserted privately that it would be 'unpardonable' not to attempt a restoration of the monarchy, and the republicans spent the parliamentary recess, from July to November, preparing for such an attempt. Gambetta helped devise the strategy of reviving local republican committees across the country, and organizing local mayors and officials to take action.[66]

In this busy period of Gambetta's political life, Léon was anxious to keep him mindful of her presence as his political partner. Her loving letter of 1 August served that purpose, putting words into Gambetta's mouth (or thoughts into his mind) as she analysed his latest letter.

'I have re-read your adorable letter a hundred times, to convince myself that politics . . . no longer suffice[s] to fill your life, and that there are hours when your great soul . . . awaits and desires the effusions of mine; and the more this conviction seeps into my heart, the more madly happy and loving I become!'[67]

Gambetta and Léon took a brief holiday in Belgium and Holland in September. This marked a new step in their liaison; it was probably their first time together for more than a few hours. Then, on 22 September, Gambetta began a tour of the South West as part of the republicans' endeavour to shore up support. With her usual tendency to exaggerate his role, Léon transformed his strategic tour into a mission of salvation: 'In showing the promised land to faltering souls, your marvellous eloquence will restore to them the hope and the strength needed to overcome the last remaining obstacles to the triumph of justice and liberty.' This echoed her grand, but less messianic, assessment on an earlier occasion. France was in a stupor, she had suggested then, drugged by the monarchists' poppies: 'Like the sleeping beauty, [France] awaits the prince charming whose words will recall her to life.'[68]

But Léon's political pessimism still reasserted itself on occasion. Two days after sending Gambetta off as pre-emptive victor on 22 September, she wrote: 'I feel very black about politics today. I envisage the present situation extending beyond all expectation, getting worse by the day, and the need to resort to extreme, and always dreadful, measures to save the Republic.' Despite Gambetta's reassurances, Léon remained dubious about the nation's ability to recognize the merits of his politics. 'I put much less store on French patriotism than you do', she wrote. 'It bubbles and sparkles like champagne foam, surges quickly and rises high, but when it comes to the test very little remains in the depths of the heart!'[69]

'I no longer say "I", I feel "we"'

Léon's despondency in late 1873 had a personal dimension: she faced a major family crisis. 'It is stormy in my family', she wrote, as she looked to Gambetta to 'console [her] for so much sadness'. Again, she wrote, 'Don't count on me this week, it's quite impossible. This crisis can't last long and will be ended by one means or another in the next few days.' But she reassured Gambetta: 'Don't preoccupy yourself with my family sorrows dear friend, I find enough strength in your love to endure them alone.'[70]

In October 1873, Léon's 'melancholy' took a clearer form. She linked it to 'the memories of that month of October which carried off my father with the last [autumn] leaves'. But the immediate cause of the crisis lay in the present. Léon's sister Émilie was showing increasing signs of mental instability, having sunk into a deep depression. 'Compared to my sister, Jeremiah was a playful fellow', Léon wrote, and the atmosphere at home was 'sepulchral'. To make matters worse, the crisis made it increasingly difficult for Léon to visit Gambetta, and she was hardly disposed to do so anyway: 'Don't regret not having seen me today', she wrote in early October, 'I would have been very sad company.' They might meet Saturday if she had 'recovered [her] serenity', she suggested. 'Otherwise I will postpone my visit till the following week, because I can't seek the summits of joy when one of my family believes she is dying, nor display to you so often the spectacle of my sorrow!' There was no improvement in November. 'Things are bad at home', she noted cryptically to explain 'the melancholy that overwhelms me despite myself'.[71]

The letters the couple exchanged during this difficult period carried the burden of sustaining their relationship, because other means of doing so were weakened by separation. That they made this epistolary effort illustrates their mutual investment in that relationship. The letters affirmed a sharing of lives, not merely of beds, and often exhibited a poetic licence that attempted to cut through the sadness: 'We are on the summit, in perfect harmony, in an incessant interchange of tenderness and ardour that nothing from here on can weaken or diminish', Gambetta proclaimed in November 1873. 'I no longer say "I", I feel "we".' 'After such raptures one can only remember and be silent for no human word is infinite enough to describe them!' Léon replied.[72]

The techniques of the love letter, its affinity for metaphor and allegory, also enabled Gambetta to stress the importance of his political relationship with Léon throughout this difficult period. Immersed since his youth in the culture of antiquity, he conjured up an array of images from the ancient past as models for Léon. Like the 'nymphs' and 'hamadryads' (tree sprites) who vivified nature in pagan mythology, Léon brought him inner strength.[73]

Gambetta lovingly referred to Léon as his Egeria, the muse who, in legend, had inspired the wise rule of the second king of Rome and was commonly invoked in the 1870s to describe a female confidante. Not content with that familiar allusion to describe their unique partnership, Gambetta imagined 'enter[ing] the apocalyptic life of the old Gallic legends' alongside Léon, he as Vercingetorix, hero of the ancient Gauls, Léon as Veleda, priestess of the Bructeri tribe who also resisted Roman rule. Heroic struggles of the distant past became metaphors for the present. Léon threw herself into her role alongside him: 'Your Veleda is at your feet in ecstasy forever, longing for your fragrant breath and drawing life from your fiery gaze.'[74]

Veleda and Vercingetorix, as well as Egeria, were well known thanks to the weight of classical studies in the secondary school curriculum. Their stories had become embedded in French literature, art, and music, and their images adorned the public gardens and museums of the capital.[75] Since the roles assigned to these figures in cultural memory were consistent with the gender divide of the 1870s, Gambetta could readily imagine Léon's political role alongside him through such imagery.

Epistolary fantasies may have provided a distraction from Léon's personal troubles. But the family crisis came to a head on 12 December, when Émilie Léon was committed to a Paris asylum suffering from persecution mania and hearing voices. Léon sought consolation in Gambetta's arms: 'my suffering self ceases to exist during these hours of ecstasy'.[76] But this family trauma grieved Léon deeply. Perhaps she worried that she would follow in the footsteps of her mentally unstable father and sister. She feared that her 'curious, investigative mind' was being destroyed. 'Everything that might have been piquant, out of the ordinary, original in me is paralysed by the despondency that is overtaking me.' These were significant admissions from a woman whose role consisted in making witty and intelligent conversation, and bringing pleasure to the life of her protector, as Léon well knew. She feared the effect of her melancholy on her relationship with Gambetta: 'I understand the attraction, the charm that an eternally smiling woman offers and I reproach myself with the crime of being unhappy and sad and enveloping you in my dark clouds in return for the ray of happiness with which you enlighten them.'[77]

Gambetta's response was, once again, that of a devoted and loving man, not that of someone in a purely commercial arrangement with a courtesan. A week after Émilie's committal, he affirmed that, 'far from finding your company sad and melancholy, I am pleased to discover you . . . serious, lofty, cheerful, without affectation or embarrassment. That's the way I wanted you and dreamed of you, a true woman.' Her reaction to this tragedy was proof, Gambetta declared, that 'I could not have chosen better and that she whom my heart has elected is the courageous and necessary companion of my ever-changing life.' Gambetta affirmed his commitment to Léon and offered her the highest possible compliment: 'You are associated in my soul with the shared and equal tenderness that I have vowed to my wife and to my country.'[78]

At the end of December 1873, just two weeks after Émilie Léon's committal to the asylum, Gambetta left Paris to visit his family and then join Juliette and Edmond Adam for a few days' vacation at their sumptuous villa near Cannes, on the French Riviera. This prominent republican couple had taken Gambetta under their wing and fostered his career through Juliette's salon. Their sponsorship remained essential. Gambetta emphasized his 'horror' at the forthcoming separation, but Léon was nevertheless jealous: 'Such spring-like weather! It gives me vague ideas of running away, me, riveted to my heavy chains of duty and suffering; it seems to relieve you of them, you who are free to go to Nice to enjoy this sun in all its splendour.'[79]

Writing from the villa a few days later, Gambetta described to Léon an 'incomparable evening with ball and supper'. He enthused about a risqué and anticlerical musical comedy that Mme Adam had written for her guests to perform. 'We had a wonderful time, we supped under Venetian lanterns, overlooking the magnificent panorama of the Golfe Juan.'[80]

Gambetta's holiday without Léon threw her problematic social status into bald relief. Despite the couple's passionate declarations, Léon remained Gambetta's lover, not his wife. She could not join Gambetta at political events, nor at social occasions like this visit with the Adams. Although Juliette Adam had taken a lover after leaving her first husband and then lived with her would-be second husband for several years before her first husband's death, she could not receive the unmarried Léon, still living illegitimately.[81]

Gambetta wrote apologetically: 'In the midst of all these celebrations, I felt alone, I pretended you were participating, I went to bed very pensive, wondering when the day would finally come that you would be the queen of these interludes. That is indeed the least you deserve for all the suffering that destiny has imposed on you thus far. I won't really have deserved your love and done my duty until that is so.'[82] 'Wondering when the day would finally come' perhaps suggests marriage, which did not come on the agenda explicitly for several years. It was certainly Gambetta's way of placating Léon, and perhaps soothing his own guilty conscience. It reaffirmed her special status in his life, despite the fact that she remained a mistress in the shadows.

My adorable master,

What inexhaustible treasures of tenderness are contained in these few lines, dictated and written by that voice of your heart whose softest murmurs are so eloquent!

I really love knowing that you have been carried away by this political whirlwind, in which your ardent spirit finds such intense and unremitting emotion that it eventually finds some charm in resting beside me.

What are the champions of this stillborn monarchy still hoping for? To push the Republicans to the limit with their arbitrary laws and administrative measures? To have grounds to repress a few incidents of disorder and thus buy the undecided votes of fearful people? But in a few days this old struggle of kings against the people will be over; thanks to you, to your energetic foresight, to your persuasive eloquence[,] France will have escaped this final attempt to enslave it; intelligence will reign forever over accident of birth and patriotism will gradually replace personal interest. I don't know when I'll be able to escape this increasingly mind-destroying milieu. As our only distraction, our old men of the academy bombard us with literature but not a word of politics, I am nostalgic for it.

I send you my entire life in a kiss.
Till tomorrow,
Léonie

3

'Thank you for being my strength, my hope'

Marshal MacMahon's assumption of power brought to a head the monarchist challenge to the Republic. This political challenge was intertwined with personal challenges for Gambetta and Léon. The couple had declared their love, but whether a relationship between a courtesan and her protector could evolve into something more enduring was far from certain. It would break the social codes that excluded courtesans from polite society and, given Léon's earlier links to the Empire, pose political dangers as well. Increasingly, too, family problems disrupted Léon's relationship with Gambetta. The political collaboration between the couple enlivened, and was enlivened by, the intimate ties that bound them. But both their political and personal aspirations advanced uncertainly, and their rising and falling hopes on both counts were reflected in their letters.

'Long live the Republic'

The compromises necessary to secure the Republic began to take shape in the latter months of 1873 and came to fruition in 1875. Throughout the summer of 1873, the monarchists had struggled to achieve a restoration. But there were two contenders for the throne, representing divergent views of monarchy. The Bourbon Prince, Henri, clung to the principles of hereditary monarchy that had seen his grandfather, King Charles X, overthrown in the Revolution of 1830. The Orleanist pretender, Philippe d'Orléans, accepted constitutionalism like his grandfather, King Louis-Philippe, whom Thiers had helped put on the throne in place of Charles X. The two princes now disagreed over who should take precedence. Rumours that deals were being done raised monarchist hopes and made Léon anxious. But a series of by-election results in late 1873 were encouraging. 'We're winning everywhere, and with strong majorities', Gambetta noted.[2]

Prospects looked even brighter when negotiations between Bourbons and Orleanists collapsed on 27 October. Léon anticipated Gambetta's imminent victory: 'In a few days, this old struggle of kings against the people will be over; France will have escaped this final attempt to enslave it, thanks to you, to your energetic foresight, to your persuasive eloquence; intelligence will dominate forever over accident of birth and patriotism will gradually substitute for personal interest.' She speculated optimistically that divisions among the monarchists might bring down both MacMahon and Broglie, but still she feared that the Right would somehow steal victory: 'Long live the Republic, yes, but will it be the real one?'[3]

This letter offers clues to Léon's views on fundamental issues and helps explain how she had managed the transition from being the mistress of a Bonapartist official to being Gambetta's lover. The letter points to key elements in Léon's republicanism which are common to both Bonapartism and republicanism, values derived from the French Revolution, from which both traced their origins. Both favoured 'careers open to talent' and rejected birth as the marker of rights, as Léon did in her October letter. Both were associated with patriotism, which Léon also invoked here.

Patriotism had inspired support for Napoleon I at the turn of the nineteenth century. It underpinned support for Napoleon III in the 1850s, as the dream of recapturing French greatness regained momentum. But from the 1860s, the republicans gradually chipped away at the Empire's cultural legitimacy as heir to the Revolutionary tradition.[4] Their claims were boosted by the Second Empire's definitive collapse in 1870. The Republic was increasingly seen as the only vehicle for French regeneration; the only guarantor of national pride and of the 'career open to talent'; the only vehicle, too, for seeking international prestige by participating in the race for colonies.

Many French people were making the transition to republicanism in these years, therefore, as the republicans' growing electoral strength illustrated. Like those voters, Léon became convinced that the future was republican, and Gambetta personified the Republic for her. Indeed, the grandeur and authority with which he represented the Republic had seized her imagination when she first encountered him in 1868. She again articulated her devotion to both Gambetta and the Republic in October 1873: 'You possess a political science against which none have the strength to struggle . . . Your will alone will have installed the Republic in France, and your genius will endow this form of government, so feared, so slandered, with all its brilliance and all its greatness!'[5]

As parliament resumed for the winter session in November 1873, Gambetta wrote to Léon: 'The struggle, the battle begins tomorrow.

Ah! Thank you for being my strength, my support, my hope to this moment. You know, I have never loved so much as on the eve of battle.'[6] He was to play a key role in that battle, leading the republican forces in the Assembly. He possessed the most precious attribute of the politician of his day: a powerful speaking voice. Moreover, his talent for the memorable turn of phrase and the quick-witted reply was invaluable given that the rules governing debate placed few limits on speaking time or on interjections.[7] Gambetta's performances were flamboyant, dramatic, and energetic. Camille Pelletan described him mounting the tribune to attack the Bonapartists:

> Head high, brows imperious, the breast full of passion and superb fire, overflowing with indignation; and with a lofty and absolute gesture, his voice resounding like a fanfare, rending like thunder, he launched on the heads of the Bonapartists the word 'wretches!', whose echo resonated [around the Assembly].[8]

Another observer likened his style to a dance or a symphonic performance, with its swelling rhythms and powerful chords.[9] It was not only Léonie Léon, therefore, who was moved by his performances. They could sway the votes of the assembled deputies too.

There was still no constitution in 1873, so the length of Marshal MacMahon's tenure as Head of State had not been defined. Léon hoped for a quick republican victory: 'Perhaps the Marshal will resign if they don't give him [a term of] ten years and if you manage to form a majority that only gives him five years, you will be the master.'[10] But that was unrealistic in an Assembly dominated by conservatives. MacMahon did not resign when a compromise period of seven years was voted on 20 November.

Gambetta's political duties kept him away from Paris at the beginning of 1874. His southern vacation with Juliette and Edmond Adam extended into a working holiday. He visited Italy to assess the political situation there and then tried to reorganize the quarrelling republicans in the Alpes-Maritimes region. Gambetta sought Léon's forgiveness for such a long absence but scolded her gently for focusing on her misfortunes: he clearly underestimated the impact of her sister's traumatic mental breakdown, which had occurred only three weeks previously. Gambetta was at pains, however, to stress the permanence of the knot that bound them:

> You forget what you can no longer reject or contest, *the alliance is eternal* . . . remember that I have neither joy, nor strength, nor family

more important than you and that you must never again lose sight of the fact that in speaking to me, in writing to me, you are addressing the most loving of men, but also your husband who begs you gently to forgive him this little sermon.[11]

For Gambetta to describe himself as Léon's husband was a significant mark of commitment, but it did not describe the reality of their lives.

Courtesan and protector?

In late January 1874, the police began surveillance of Léonie Léon, staking out her apartment at 7, rue Bonaparte. This was not the first time that she had been the subject of official interest. When Gambetta and Léon had visited Belgium and Holland in September 1873, the police had co-operated across national borders to watch their movements. The Belgian police shadowed them until they boarded their train; French police were waiting in Paris to follow them home. The Belgians had reported: 'this woman claims that her family name is Laguerre and that she is the daughter of a colonel', but the French police quickly identified her as 'none other than Mlle LÉON Léonie'.[12]

This phrasing suggests that they were familiar with her, as they would have been with a courtesan. Surveillance of 'common prostitutes' intensified from the mid-nineteenth century, as the vice squad (*police des moeurs*) endeavoured to remove women from the streets into registered brothels. But secret surveillance of prominent people had also been practised for some time, as Louis Andrieux (who became Prefect of Police in 1879) explained in his memoirs. 'Everyone that counts in Paris for her beauty, her elegance, her wit, her birth, her dress, the entire social elite (*tout Paris*) in fact, has a file.' Just as undercover agents of the Prefect of Police kept dossiers on political figures and social leaders, they also kept dossiers on courtesans and those who associated with them. Dossiers were colour-coded: those concerning political figures were blue; those on 'morality' (*moeurs*) were white. Léon probably had a white dossier from the time she began working as a courtesan, certainly from the time of her liaison with Hyrvoix.[13]

Léon came to police attention in 1873 because she was travelling with Gambetta. In 1874, the police focused their attention directly on her. Perhaps they hoped to find material that could be used to undermine her increasingly popular and powerful lover. The police reports cast little light on Gambetta's political activities, which may explain why the surveillance was short-lived. But they reveal a great deal about the relationship between Gambetta and Léon in early 1874.

As they began their surveillance of Léon, the police agents noted the difficulty of the assignment: in a narrow street with no shop-fronts or other places of concealment, in an apartment block managed by a concierge, discreet observation was near impossible. They therefore gained much of their information by cultivating the neighbours and the concierge. They established that Léon's mother never came there, though her sister Émilie often did. There were no servants, which the police thought unusual in this neighbourhood. The rent, the concierge told them, was 800 francs per year: less than the 1200 francs the police had noted in their 1873 report, but still more than Mme Léon could have afforded to set up her daughters in Paris.[14]

While Gambetta described himself as Léon's husband, and Léon described herself as Gambetta's 'morganatic wife', police reports in January and February 1874 claim that Léon was still living as a courtesan and that Gambetta was her lover, though not yet her exclusive protector. A surveillance report for 22 January described their evening together. Gambetta had arranged this meeting two days earlier: 'It is not by letter that I want to pour out my feelings. I need to see you, to consult you as well, to regain by your side strength, courage and pleasure. I expect you Thursday without fail, I won't go to Versailles that day . . . You can thus choose your time and come and surprise me at my place whenever you wish.'[15]

At 5 pm that Thursday (22 January), Léon emerged from her apartment looking, the police noted, 'flashy [*une toilette tapageuse*]', 'like a streetwalker'. The police agent tailing her was apparently an experienced observer of courtesans, given his description of her outfit: 'she was wearing jade earrings, a straw hat with blue feathers, a velvet beret, a short astrakhan cape, fur-trimmed kid boots, and a flounced skirt with a blue overskirt trimmed with astrakhan'. Her outfit, as well as her lifestyle, showed how far she had departed from her youthful ideals as a Child of Mary, whose virtues included being 'simple and modest in their dress' and 'avoid[ing] attaching any value to the hollow trappings of fashion'. But unlike the Child of Mary or the modest *bourgeoise*, the courtesan needed to attract attention and hint at excitement through her self-presentation.[16]

After purchasing some white braces and cufflinks, Léon arrived at Gambetta's apartment on the rue de Montaigne at 6.15 pm. The couple emerged together an hour later, without Léon's purchases, and got into the waiting cab. They stopped to window shop at a shoe store just behind the Opera, then continued a short distance along the Boulevard des Italiens to the Maison Dorée, the most expensive and most fashionable restaurant in Paris. The Maison Dorée was famous for its cuisine, its magnificent cellar, and the celebrities who frequented it, but also for its private 'salons'. These had curtained 'alcoves' where diners could entertain each other intimately between courses. The word 'alcove' – originally a curtained recess in a bedroom – came in this period to mean a space for illicit sex. The Maison Dorée had two entrances, one for the public restaurant, the other for these more intimate rooms. At 8 pm that evening, Léon and Gambetta took the second entrance.[17]

They re-emerged at midnight and strolled down to the Seine, despite the winter weather. At the Palais Royal, they took a cab. Léon dropped Gambetta at his apartment and was driven to hers, arriving at 1 am. The next day, Gambetta wrote to say how much he missed her. 'I feel empty and I know well by the thought, by the constant memories which come back to my heart that it is you, you alone who are lacking to me.' That same day, however, the police observing Léon's apartment noted that 'several well-dressed Gentlemen visited during the day'.[18]

Despite having been informed that Léon would be absent from Paris for several days, the police continued to watch her apartment fruitlessly. Surveillance resumed successfully in mid-February 1874, and the couple's meetings followed the same pattern as in January. On 18 February, Léon spent three-quarters of an hour with Gambetta before the waiting cab dropped Gambetta at the offices of his newspaper, *La République française*, and then took Léon home. The following day Léon was with Gambetta from 5 pm until almost 7 pm, and two days later, on Saturday, she stayed at his apartment from 6 pm until 7.20 pm.[19]

These meetings resembled the pattern of many liaisons between courtesans and their lovers. They were typically brief, and they typically took place in the early evening. Indeed, 'five to seven' came to mean the time of day a man devoted to his mistress, before he went off to his social engagements. Sometimes Gambetta and Léon went out together for the evening, but they did not spend the night together. It was to be a mark of their growing attachment that such fleeting meetings became a source of frustration, especially to Gambetta, inadequate for the type of relationship they sought to create, one in which there would be time together for emotional and intellectual as well as sexual intimacy in person and not just by letter.

The reports claim that Léon was still seeing other clients in February 1874, almost two years into her relationship with Gambetta: 'The demoiselle Léon, Léonie, receives rich men and deputies into her home.

Her conduct is dubious . . . Émilie, her elder sister, aged 47, behaves in a similar fashion.' The reports also suggest the possibility that Léon had another regular client on the Boulevard des Invalides (a very wealthy neighbourhood on the left bank). She visited an apartment there several times during the period of surveillance: after a brief visit on Wednesday 18 February, she spent an hour there the following day, before spending two hours with Gambetta in the evening. She returned to that apartment on Sunday 22 February. It seems indisputable that, at this time, Léon was sexually involved with men in addition to Gambetta.[20]

As well as providing an insight into the nature of the couple's relationship in early 1874, the reports also provoke questions about sexual health and pregnancy. The fact that Léon had fallen pregnant during an earlier liaison surely made her attentive to the possibility that she could do so again. One historian claims that, in an unsigned 'deathbed confession' attributed to Léon which only he saw, she confessed to having had an abortion, performed by Gambetta's friend and physician, Dr Lannelongue, at an unspecified date.[21] The correspondence is unsurprisingly silent on such delicate matters, but courtesans normally employed an array of condoms, sponges, and douches to safeguard themselves from disease and pregnancy.[22] Perhaps Léon's visit to Karoza's pharmacy, on her way to see Gambetta on 22 January 1874, reflected her attention to such matters. Karoza's pharmacy was on the rue des Petits Champs, just outside the Palais-Royal: it was a well-known location for purchasing contraceptive products.[23]

The police reports detail the variety of Léon's daily activities, not just her rendezvous with Gambetta. They note her shopping expeditions, her visits to the public baths near her apartment, and her meetings with unidentified female friends or family. But the surveillance uncovered nothing that was surprising or useful to Gambetta's political opponents. The fact that he had a mistress was scarcely news, even if Léon had other clients as well.

The surveillance does, however, cast the couple's correspondence, and hence their relationship, in a new light. The rapture expressed in many of their letters suggests a fairy-tale romance and a growing commitment. Indeed, as Gambetta set out in March 1874 on a brief campaign trip to Bordeaux, he predicted a rosy future for himself and Léon: 'The horizon is becoming brighter, we can see dawn breaking; a little longer to wait and we will witness the beautiful sunrise of our shared and happy life.'[24]

Léon's letters from around this time also began to envisage life together with Gambetta: 'You too have experienced this emptiness, this wrenching of the soul which I always experience after leaving you. Nothing is harder to bear than the days following these intimate days when we have so sweetly led the same life.' She went on to write of a more total union: 'It's only since yesterday, my Léon, that your confidence in me was complete enough to abandon to me not only the tender and loving soul of our first days, but also the other incarnation of that soul, the great and sublime genius given by God to France to save it, to transform it.'[25] But despite the expressions of devotion that filled their letters, their lifestyle at the beginning of 1874 did not yet reflect such exclusive devotion. Their passionate letters sought to compensate for the financial and personal impediments that kept them apart.

'This vile Assembly'

Gambetta's search for comfort with Léon intensified in parallel with the political struggle. Marshal MacMahon's continued appointment of reactionary ministries with a brief to attack republicanism set the agenda for the battles of 1874. The ministry installed in May 1873, headed by the duc de Broglie, fell on 16 May 1874 over his proposed second Chamber. To be composed of Cardinals, Marshals and Admirals, it was widely likened to the Assembly of Notables of the Old Regime.[26]

The next step in the conservative push came via the 'Commission of Thirty', charged with drawing up a Constitution. It launched an attack on universal male suffrage, which had been established in France by the Revolution of 1848, but which conservatives had long sought to replace with a property suffrage. Both Gambetta and Léon regarded universal male suffrage as fundamental to the Republic. They held that merit, rather than birth, should determine political rights, at least for men. Léon had deplored the Commission's challenge to the suffrage in 1873 as 'sacrilegious'. Faced with a new attempt to restrict the suffrage in 1874, Gambetta leapt into action. He condemned the move as an 'act of spoliation' which removed long-established political rights. But he also attacked the political incompetence of the move: 'You are completely lacking in political sense if you undertake a task as enormous as disenfranchising 2,500,00 to 3,000,000 voters, without having an exact estimate of either the process or the consequences it could bring.' The Bill was withdrawn for revision.[27]

Gambetta constantly sought Léon's comforting presence as solace for the demands of politics: 'I won't go to Versailles today', he wrote in May. 'I am too tired, I didn't close my eyes at all last night and I need to recover. Nothing in the world can restore my strength like your divine presence so I will wait for you at my place . . . I will dream of your arrival and when you cross the threshold I will devour you with kisses.'[28]

Heading off the Bonapartists occupied Gambetta in mid-1874. Their by-election victory in May alarmed both the republicans and the monarchists. Gambetta went on the offensive in a series of powerful speeches, sparring with the Bonapartist leader, Eugène Rouher, in a vicious debate in the Assembly. He accused the Bonapartists of having 'brought France to her ruin' in the war with Prussia. This infuriated the Bonapartists, and mobs assaulted him at the railway station on 10 and 11 June 1874. Gambetta allayed Léon's concerns: 'I beg you not to worry at all about your friend, he is wonderfully well. The Bonapartists have revealed their sentiments too soon; they have appeared to be formidable before they really are; France has woken up in time.'[29]

The efforts of what Gambetta labelled the 'vile' Assembly to draw up a constitution posed the next challenge. The monarchists who dominated the Assembly wanted to avoid a general election, which they would almost certainly have lost. Until now, many republicans, including Gambetta, had contested the Assembly's right to create a constitution: it had come into being as a provisional government at a moment of crisis when the Empire fell, and by-elections suggested that its majority did not represent the views of the country. Republicans wanted elections instead. But Gambetta was prepared to reconsider if an acceptable constitutional model could be agreed.

The major issue of contention was bicameralism. All but the most conservative republicans regarded a second chamber as an anti-democratic measure, as had Gambetta in the Belleville Programme.[30] Accepting a second chamber – favoured by conservatives as a check on democracy – was a gamble. But, for Gambetta, cajoling moderate, constitutional monarchists (Orleanists for the most part) into accepting the Republic was the most fundamental task. If that required accepting a Senate, the challenge was then to guarantee the primacy of the lower house, and institute an electoral process for the Senate that did not enshrine the old elites. Gambetta would have to accept more compromises than he wished, but in the long run his gamble paid off.

Gambetta worked hard to win republican support for a compromise that accepted a Senate in exchange for ratification of the Republic. 'Half-hopeful' on July 7 that this manoeuvre would pay off, he was 'nearly there' on July 16: 'next week we'll have the Republic'. Victory remained just out of reach for several more days, with the ministry in disarray and the wind 'full in the republican sails'. But the summer vacation began to distract the deputies from reaching a decision, to Gambetta's disgust: 'Today was even worse than yesterday', he wrote to Léon. 'The adjournment and the holidays carried the day over reason, good sense and the interests of the country. I am more discouraged than annoyed at such petty tactics against the rights of France.'[31]

Municipal elections in November 1874 confirmed that the Republic was increasingly the choice of the electorate. 'We have a first glimpse of the vote in large, small and medium-sized towns', Gambetta wrote to Léon following the provincial poll on 22 November. 'It's dazzling. I don't know how the Regime [*Pouvoir*] is going to get out of this one, but it will have a tough dialogue to sustain. The whole of France is rising up and protesting.' A week later, when Paris went to the polls, Gambetta was even more jubilant: 'The elections in Paris are a triumph. It is the most resounding defeat we have ever inflicted on the reactionary troops. We are victorious in 70 of 80 [electoral] colleges, with decisive majorities. Paris is ours; Paris acclaims us.'[32]

But this political message was inserted at mid-point within a poignant statement of love and interdependence that attributed the victory to Léon, as the ellipsis below indicates:

> How would I possibly not love you to madness; are you not my good star, my protective genius [*démon*], indeed my providence? See what magic influence you wield; under your aegis everything succeeds for me, all difficulties dissolve. . . . But this triumph would be only vain pomp if your soul did not belong to me completely, if my heart did not possess you undivided and untroubled; it's to you that I attribute everything, it's for you, you alone, that I carry on with my task and I identify you so strongly with the image of the Fatherland that I love you with the same love and that I embrace you both.[33]

Conventional notions of gender allowed Gambetta to imagine Léon as the inner force through which he triumphed, his 'possession' of her fuelling, and even modelling, his conquest of the nation and its capital. His letter affirmed in striking terms the intertwining of the personal and the political in the lovers' relationship.

'Outside this ring, no love'

In mid-1874, Léonie Léon announced with pride: 'Another beautiful compensation in which I hardly dare believe: it seems that *la Chine* has won the *prix d'honneur* of Sainte-Barbe, awarded yesterday at a ceremony to which all the parents were invited!'[34] *La Chine* was their code name for Léon's son, Alphonse; Sainte-Barbe was the school he attended. This was the first of a growing number of references to the child in the couple's surviving letters. They may have been courtesan and lover, but the fact that Gambetta and Léon had begun to share details of their personal lives on a regular basis was a sign that they were growing deeply attached.

La Chine was a curious term, most readily meaning 'China': perhaps it referred to Alphonse's delicate health. But at that time it was also slang meaning both 'second-hand goods' and 'hard work'. Léon guarded the secret of her son's birth desperately. Perhaps the name referred to her supposed status as his aunt, making him her 'second-hand' child; perhaps it referred to the demands that having a child, particularly a delicate and sickly one, placed on her.[35] Even more curiously, William, the legitimate son of Alphonse's father, Hyrvoix, was nicknamed 'Chino', a name sufficiently similar to raise the possibility that this term of affection had a private meaning for Léon.[36]

Entering domesticity was not smooth sailing for Gambetta. He was sometimes peeved at sharing Léon's time with her son, who had turned nine in February 1874. Choosing familiar political metaphors, he complained of having to 'resign' himself to 'the despotism of this young and insatiable dominator', who sometimes put his 'incontestable veto' on their plans. Gambetta nevertheless made conciliatory gestures to Léon's sentiments, as when he referred to 'our dear little *Chine* – may God keep him well'.[37]

The summer of 1874 was also complicated by ongoing 'difficulties' at home that affected Léon's health but to which she referred only briefly in her letters. These 'difficulties' may have related to the deteriorating health of Émilie Léon (who died in the asylum the following year), or to her relationship with her mother, which was becoming increasingly antagonistic. Léon visited Paris less often, and Gambetta feared that she was withdrawing from him. He appealed for her presence to help him endure 'the ever-increasing problems of [his] political life'. 'I have suffered terribly from this undeserved and involuntary fast', he wrote. 'I really ask your pardon for the problems that politics causes, but I am confident that your political passions will absolve me.' By August their relationship had recovered and Gambetta daydreamed about 'taking you away from here, far away . . . I will try to give you a foretaste of the tokens of affection with which I want to smother you.'[38]

Around this time, Gambetta had two copies made of a ring held in the Cluny Museum, which Saint Louis (King Louis IX, 1214–70) had given to his wife Marguerite. The rings were inscribed with the words, 'outside this ring, no love'. Pillias suggests that the exchange of rings was a compensation for Gambetta's unwillingness to marry Léon. But perhaps it compensated for his inability to do so. While Gambetta must have contributed to Léon's support – that would have been part of their arrangement – it was still unlikely that he could afford to keep her as his exclusive mistress.[39] The parliamentary salary of 9000 francs was intended as a supplement to personal wealth, not a complete income. Gambetta earned an additional 12,000 francs annually as the effective director of *La République française*, and may have received share dividends as well. His total income in 1874, therefore, was probably a little more than 21,000 francs. It was still two years before he would exchange his own apartment on the mezzanine – a sign of financial constraint – for a more substantial apartment, and that move was almost a financial disaster.[40]

To be sure, Gambetta's income was well above the minimum required to live in a modest bourgeois fashion, estimated to be between 5000 and 7000 francs.[41] But it did not go very far in Parisian high society. As an aspiring politician, Gambetta had to dress well, travel, attend Salons, entertain, and be seen in the right places, all of which was extremely expensive. If Gambetta lived well, that was largely due to the generosity of his supporters, who plied him with gifts, 'loans', dinners, holidays, and use of their boxes at the opera and the theatre. He could scarcely ask them for an allowance to maintain Léon.

Moreover, making Léon his exclusive mistress would have required more than paying the rent on the apartment on the rue Bonaparte, as well as on his own. With Émilie committed to the asylum and her mother's pension far from adequate, Léon's financial responsibility for her family increased. There was rent to pay for the house at Bourg-la-Reine and Alphonse's school expenses to meet. And as the police description of Léon indicated, she liked expensive clothes and shopped in the best neighbourhoods. To maintain her in the style she favoured would not have come cheaply.

It is tempting to speculate that, once Léon wore Gambetta's ring, she stopped entertaining other men. Exchanging rings certainly signified commitment by both parties, even though that commitment was not formalized by marriage; it was another affirmation of the value they each placed on this relationship. But the ring was not necessarily a sign that she had become his exclusive mistress. Nor was it necessarily a portent of marriage. Rather, like the passionate and devoted letters the couple exchanged, it was a marker of firm attachment between a man and his lover.

'What a great game politics is when one is winning!'

Having failed to restore the monarchy and faced with alarming election results at the end of 1874, the weakened conservatives played for time, hoping to keep open the possibility of restoration. On 21 January 1875 they put a motion to the Assembly to establish 'temporary powers' for the government of the nation, leaving the question of the permanent form of government – monarchy or Republic – in abeyance. Many Orleanists, however, were beginning to think of compromising to ensure a conservative-dominated Republic rather than holding out for an increasingly unlikely restoration. The motion was rejected. A week later, the Assembly also rejected a statement declaring France a Republic, but it did so more narrowly than in the past.

Finally, on 29 January 1875, a compromise motion negotiated an awkward path between the opposing interests, declaring France a Republic, but with a bicameral National Assembly and a Head of State eligible for re-election. The motion read: 'The President of the Republic will be elected by an absolute majority of votes of the Senate and the Chamber of Deputies united in a National Assembly. He will be appointed for seven years; he is eligible for re-election.' After hours of lobbying in the corridors, the motion was put at 6.45 pm. The Assembly voted for a Republic, but by the narrowest of margins: 353 votes to 352. The republicans were happy to see a definitive end to monarchy and an entrenched system for electing the President that would give due weight to their growing numbers in the Chamber. The Right was happy to have a second chamber and the prospect of MacMahon's continued tenure as a President with substantial executive powers. Further votes on 1 and 2 February established the basic outline of the constitution.[42]

Gambetta was initially optimistic about the constitutional arrangements. When the Assembly voted for the Senate to be elected by universal male suffrage, he shared his excitement with Léon. He could hardly have hoped for more: 'Wonderful day! and decisive, contrary to my first expectations. The Senate will be democratic, elected by direct universal suffrage. We carried the motion with a majority of 12. The disarray at Versailles is extreme, we must push on to the end amid the alarm of the right and the impatience of our friends.' He hoped to complete the 'victory' the following day, believing that 'the Marshal is very close to his political Sedan'.[43]

The following day, however, the Right reorganized to curtail the republicans' gains dramatically. A new motion proposed that a quarter of the Senate be chosen for life by the Assembly, with the remainder elected by an indirect process that favoured rural voters. Gambetta was flatly opposed to this amendment. But his conservative republican colleagues (who had engineered this compromise with the Centre-Right, the Orleanists) persuaded him, and he in turn persuaded most of his supporters. The Extreme Left of the republican movement could not swallow such a departure from democratic principles, but they abstained rather than opposing the measure. When this motion passed, the Republic was finally established on 25 February 1875.[44]

This outcome was nevertheless a political disappointment for Gambetta. It added its weight to the personal tragedy that had struck Léon a few days earlier. Her sister, Émilie, died on 15 February after fifteen months in the asylum. Gambetta's letter of condolence was a model of tender commiseration. 'I felt the blow that has hit you as you yourself did, I didn't know this generous sister, but it seemed to me that I had lost one of my own, so much have I identified myself with you and so much have I come to consider you the new center of my life.'[45] His letter confirmed that, despite the time Émilie had spent in Paris in previous years, Léonie Léon had never introduced her to Gambetta. Their relationship, unlike a marriage, did not extend to next of kin.

Gambetta soon worried that grief over her sister's death was leading Léon into what today would be called depression. 'For your grief, so deep and so touching, I will have all the care it deserves', he wrote, but he worried that she was tearing herself apart. 'I beseech you not to go down that road.' A week later he wrote, 'I consent not to demand your coming to me, but I beg you not to let yourself go, not to abandon yourself . . . All this [political effort] deserves a breath of love and of warm consolation. Only you can give it to me.'[46] Just as he had underestimated the emotional impact on Léon of her sister's committal in 1873, he now seemed surprised that recovering from the loss of an only sibling took more than two weeks. He was certainly feeling sorry for himself, and 'consenting' not to 'demand' Léon's visit underlined the unequal power balance in their relationship. This was the language of a man who paid for his comforts and expected to receive them. But Gambetta may also have been trying to drag Léon out of the abyss of depression. He continued to offer her his love and support when it would have been less troublesome to find a new mistress.

Republican optimism was dampened by the costs of political compromise, and the dissatisfaction of the Extreme Left caused Gambetta increasing problems. Indeed, a republican veteran of 1848 later complained that the new constitution meant 'the stifling of the big towns by the small, of the small by the villages, of the villages by the hamlets. It was the defeat of day by night.' Gambetta's own electorate was chafing at the slow pace of reform and the concessions made to conservatives. In April 1875, he admitted to anxiety as he faced his constituents to explain why he had accepted the most controversial provisions of the constitution, especially the creation of a Senate. 'I'm going to sail into stormy seas [*franchir un grand Cap*] and I won't be free of my emotion until I am on dry land . . . Léonie, *ora pro nobis* [pray for us],' he pleaded. But he succeeded in persuading his constituents that the priority given to rural communes in the Senate electoral process was a democratic measure, rather than an attack on the democratic rights of urban voters like themselves. He charmed this audience, too, addressing their concerns and soothing their ruffled feathers. As Léon put it on another occasion, he 'seduced' his listeners, 'carrying them with [him] rather than convincing them'. Discontented to begin with, they ended up applauding him.[47]

Against these discontents, Gambetta worked hard to maintain republican patience and discipline. 'The situation is still very tense; not to say perilous', he wrote to Léon in May. 'What the President wants is an explosion, a rupture with the left, and I don't want the fault to be on our side for anything in the world. As always, I preach moderation and prudence, but I need to restore my reserves at the feet of my queen.' Gambetta again expressed his need for Léon. 'For the first time in my life[,] discouragement is overtaking me, and it's a very ugly, very unattractive companion.' He even contemplated giving up politics and returning to the law. 'It's in moments like these that I need your fortifying words, your caresses. Where are you, my consoler? And I have to wait until Friday.' His frustration reached a new peak in July, when the conservatives forced through a higher education bill favouring the Catholic Church. Exhausted and suffering from neuralgia, Gambetta wrote miserably to Léon: 'Yet another detestable day. We were furiously defeated by this clerical majority. France is monk-ridden for a long time to come . . . it makes me mad with anger . . . I need to see you, to hear you, to adore you.'[48]

Under the new constitution, Life Senators were to be appointed by the existing National Assembly, after which elections would be held for the remaining Senators. Only then would the Chamber of Deputies be elected. The process began in December 1875. Each of the political factions was desperate to entrench its interests by winning the powerful Life Senator positions. Gambetta adopted the surprising but shrewd strategy of aligning with the Legitimists, the thoroughly unrepentant monarchists for whom only a Bourbon King was a legitimate ruler, in order to thwart the more numerous constitutional monarchists, the Orleanists. The strategy paid enormous dividends, but this only became clear after the event.

The negotiations were slow and tedious and the results were far from certain. Gambetta's separation from Léon added to his woes. The gaps between her visits to Paris seemed endless. If he had considered 'demanding' Léon's presence in March, now he pleaded for her affection, aching for her presence as confidante and lover, as well as for her political advice and reassurance. 'The few instants of rest, of moral and physical refreshment that I find in our fleeting encounters are becoming more and more necessary to me. You must not space them out too much, and I find that [waiting till] this Monday makes a lot of time still to come.' Without Léon's letters for this period it is impossible to explain her absence, although Gambetta suggests that she was bed-ridden with a severe cold. His appeals continued: 'It seems that I am exiled from light and happiness. It is a century since I embraced my sweetheart . . . I call you, I await you, I love you, I embrace you.' He continued the following day: 'I thirst to see you, to gain additional courage and resolution beside you . . . I beg you to take pity on the unhappy one who adores you.'[49]

The Right pulled out all the stops in the Senate contest, mobilizing the Church hierarchy in its cause: 'all the red, black and purple robes, some say even the pope', according to Gambetta. But on December 16 he wrote, relieved and happy, to Léon: 'Despite the scandalous indiscipline of our troops we have triumphed thanks to the disarray, the incompetence of our adversaries . . . ten of ours have been named senators.' In all, republicans from the various factions had fifty-seven Life Senators, compared with only fifteen Legitimists and three Orleanists. His arch-rival, the duc de Broglie, was not among them. This was the sweetest victory for Gambetta, who shared a malicious satisfaction with Léon: 'I have finally been able to enjoy the lasting stupefaction of one de Broglie. Never has a hoarse turkey squawked so pathetically; people were doubled up with laughter.'[50]

The last day of 1875 was a landmark on the path to a fully-fledged Republic: 'At last the final step has been taken, the dissolution has been declared, France is delivered . . . Despite the fatigue of this long and interminable day, I have never felt more full of energy, more joyful, more alive. An enormous weight has been lifted off my chest.' It had been a year of seesawing possibilities and emotions but, as Gambetta observed, 'What a great game politics is when one is winning!'[51]

'Thanks to your precious talisman, I felt my strength redouble'

Successful in the battle to appoint Life Senators, Gambetta now threw himself into campaigning for elections for the remainder of the Senate, due at the end of January 1876. After again trying to unite the divided republicans in Nice and Marseille, he headed to Aix-en-Provence and Arles to drum up electoral support. As a gesture to his absent lover, Gambetta paid tribute to Léon's inspiration: 'Who would have told me four years ago, before I knew you, that I would become a missionary of peace? I never undertake such work without invoking your name.' His trip confirmed that republican prospects, and his own reputation, were strong: 'The dissidents are done for, the reactionaries are buried', he declared, 'we will have wonderful elections, even in the Senate, and the numerous [punitive] measures of the moral order [Broglie's regime] won't be a minor factor in enlarging and extending the victory in the countryside.'[52]

But he had 'had enough of widowhood'. The couple enjoyed a brief reunion in Paris on 22 January, as Gambetta noted after their evening together: 'Leaving you is cruel; being away is terrible, but returning, finding you again, feeling you more beautiful, more perfumed, more adorable than ever! What joy, what inexpressible pleasure [*volupté*]! . . . I have never felt so in love and so greedy for you.' 'Politics can wait', he reaffirmed. 'It it less important than you.'[53]

Under the circumstances, politics could not wait, but at least Gambetta's crucial role in the republican campaign in Paris did not take him away from Léon. The electoral system for the Senate required each political group to compile a list of candidates in each seat. Gambetta's first battle was to ensure that the list of republican candidates for Paris was dominated by moderates, not by conservative or Extreme Left republicans.[54] Léon entered the spirit of the campaign by letter. 'Why not Colonel Denfert[-Rochereau] at number five [on the ballot]?' she asked.[55] In a gesture of love, Gambetta acclaimed her as the hidden source of his victory. 'Your delightful letter this morning perfumed my whole day', he wrote. 'Thanks to this precious talisman I felt my strength redouble, and today I fought and won a beautiful battle. I believe that my list [of candidates] is holding despite the reactionaries on the right and the madmen on the left.'[56]

When Gambetta's favoured candidate and friend, Charles de Freycinet, topped the Senate poll in Paris, Léon was as jubilant as Gambetta. Her letter was an emotional tribute of triumph and adoration: 'I took an indescribable pleasure in reading and re-reading this very happy telegram . . . But I had reached such a pitch of anxiety, that I nevertheless spent a frightful night . . . I really needed Freycynet's [*sic*] victory, your victory my beautiful adored one, to recall me to life.' The republicans won all five Senate seats in Paris, but with 149 Senators to the conservatives' 151, they narrowly failed to win a majority nationally. Gambetta was still reasonably happy, however, since a majority of Senators were at least nominally in favour of preserving the Republic.[57]

Gambetta was off again almost immediately, this time campaigning for the legislative elections that would choose a Chamber of Deputies. The legislative elections, based on universal male suffrage, were to be conducted on a single-member constituency system (*scrutin d'arrondissement*). The first round of these elections was set for 20 February. In seats where no candidate won an absolute majority in this vote, the two leading contenders would run off in a second round of voting, set for 5 March 1876.

A whirlwind trip in early February took Gambetta the length and breadth of the country, to Lille, Avignon and Bordeaux. He was a candidate in all these constituencies himself: seeking election in multiple seats was common at the time, success demonstrating one's nation-wide popularity. During a brief return to Paris on 14 February to campaign for Belleville, which he already represented in the Assembly, he wrote to Léon at 2 am: 'I am exhausted, shattered. Having arrived this morning, I had two enormous meetings this evening . . . I greatly need to see you, to rest on your breast. I have lots of things to tell you.' He left again on 16 February for Marseille and Avignon, where republican prospects were weak. He was greeted with enthusiasm in the towns around Avignon, though Avignon itself remained fiercely Legitimist and was the only seat he stood for and failed to win in this campaign. Even Marseille – 'a real battleground', as he described it to Juliette Adam – welcomed him exultantly.[58]

Gambetta was elected in Paris, Lille, Marseille, and Bordeaux. He chose again to represent the Paris seat of Belleville, leaving the second-runners to take the remaining three seats. Indeed, the republicans won a tremendous victory in the first round of the elections, picking up 300 of the 435 seats outright. Best of all, Louis-Joseph Buffet – formerly President MacMahon's Minister of the Interior and Vice-President of his Council of Ministers, the 'Black Viper' to Gambetta and Léon – was defeated in all the four seats in which he stood. He resigned on 23 February.[59]

Yet another campaign trip was necessary before the second round of the elections on 5 March. Such prolonged absences evoked Gambetta's constant affirmations of love and loyalty in his letters to Léon, whose anxieties about other women surfaced periodically during his absences. 'I don't think that earth has ever seen, since the time of Origen, a man as abstinent and continent as your Léon', Gambetta had declared in October 1874. A year later, he insisted again: 'away from [you] I have eyes and ears only for the Electors'.[60] In early 1876, he again offered epistolary reassurance to the ever-anxious Léon, reiterating his desire to be home, secure in her company. 'The fleeting encounters we have had for two months have only made me more passionate, more loving, more happy to possess you so well and so little', he wrote from Marseille in February. A fortnight later, her reiterated: 'I will be in Paris at 8 am tomorrow . . . Finally I will be able to seek pardon for my absences, for my epistolary neglect, bring you my wreaths and adore you till my thirst, which is extreme, is quenched.'[61]

The second round of the legislative elections clinched a memorable republican victory, the 340 republican deputies almost doubling the tally of 155 conservatives. 'I am broken, but satisfied', Gambetta wrote on election night: 'The Assembly will be extremely new. We can barely count in our ranks 25 former parliamentarians who have already addressed the chamber. . . . It will be a tough job to order and discipline all these people.' Gambetta's prediction was to prove correct, as the factional divisions within the republican cohort hardened in the late 1870s.[62]

In the heat of victory, Léon congratulated Gambetta on his great triumph, inserting herself again into the political narrative. She could not claim to have campaigned alongside him, but she could make a virtue of her role as lover and soul-mate and seek both his gratitude and his adoration: 'Is your sweetheart a silly proud fool to flatter herself that, thanks to her ardent passion, these three years haven't seemed too long to you?'[63] But the euphoria of March 1876 nevertheless proved fleeting. The victorious republicans still faced the task of 'republicanizing' France, against the wishes of a hostile President and their own fragmenting solidarity. And Léon and Gambetta were far from resolving the personal barriers to a life together.

My dear beloved,[1]

You alone were the object of this three-minute meditation that so strongly shocked your despotism, accustomed as it is to having its least fantasies anticipated. I can say that without boasting, because doesn't my entire joy, and my dearest occupation, lie in dreaming of your desires so that I can satisfy them before they have been clearly conceived? I hesitated to tell you the object of these reflections, which saddened me as they crossed my mind, because you didn't seem in the mood to tolerate any observation, whether just or unjust. Remember that this doesn't have the slightest thing to do with me; it is solely about you, about the passion I feel for your glory, and the consistency of your personality, whether as a political or private man. I will always be frank with you although as brief as possible when I am afraid of displeasing you. Won't the splendour of this upstart's mansion somehow undermine the model of dignified simplicity which suited so well the lofty politics of the statesman devoted exclusively to the triumph of a great cause, consecrated unreservedly to the regeneration of France? Luxury[,] to provide an incentive for the arts and trades that pursue it[,] is only a requirement for the one who holds the reigns of power.

You, my beloved, are and will always be my divinity, my cult, and my life. Yours,

Léonie

Till Tuesday if you like or if not whenever you choose. 30 April 76.

4
'I am smiling at your triumph, at our love'

The large republican majority in the first Chamber of Deputies was a two-edged sword. In theory, it promised the possibility of legislating a republican agenda. But with strength of numbers came ideological and political differences. Gambetta's political skills and magic oratory continued to prove vital to the republicans' electoral triumphs. Eventually even President MacMahon could not ignore their victories and had to appoint a republican ministry. But Gambetta's prominence in securing this outcome was also a two-edged sword. It raised his public prestige but created jealousies and resentments amongst his colleagues, who became increasingly critical of his politics of compromise.

The contradictions and frustrations in the personal relationship between Gambetta and Léon also became increasingly apparent. Gambetta wanted more private time with Léon; Léon regretted that she could never entirely share his public life. Gambetta was drawn increasingly into the social whirl of high society, leaving Léon to regret her 'awkward position' in his life. Léon's bouts of melancholy created tension between them and cast a pall over both their lives. The couple had yet to find a basis for their relationship that matched their needs and desires as well as the realities of Gambetta's political position.

'I am battling satisfied egos'

As the new parliament – now bicameral – assembled at Versailles on 8 March 1876, Léon and Gambetta turned their minds to the inevitable power struggle between the republican-dominated Chamber of Deputies and the conservative-controlled Senate. Their epistolary exchange continued to intertwine political debate and expressions of love, the latter serving to enhance or sweeten political differences. Léon's immediate anxiety – that the Orleanist duc d'Audiffret-Pasquier would be elected president of the Senate – produced a dramatic appeal to Gambetta's charismatic power as lover and as politician:

> You bear within yourself the resurrection and the life, and as Renan explains in his life of Jesus, you work miracles simply by your will, your contact and your gaze! But it's not enough to sweep me away enraptured into the infinite spheres that no other woman has reached before me; you must also work the final wonders necessary for the success of your politics, and for that you must fight as hard as possible against the election of Audiffret, I see new dangers in that by the hour.[2]

Léon's letter moved smoothly and almost imperceptibly from amorous ecstasy to political substance. Her reference to Gambetta's friend, the Biblical scholar Ernest Renan, highlighted the broad scope of the ideas that the couple debated. But this reference was a device to praise her lover, to exaggerate his powers and encourage him to do as she wished. In the process, she demonstrated just how closely she observed the political processes that were unfolding.

Gambetta was less worried about Audiffret-Pasquier, who was duly elected President of the Senate, than about the new cabinet. Under the 1875 Constitution, the right to choose a 'Council of Ministers' and appoint its 'President' (the equivalent position today carries the title 'Prime Minister') lay solely in the hands of the Head of State, who now took the title 'President of the Republic'. President MacMahon chose conservative republican Jules Dufaure to head the ministry, ignoring Gambetta's electoral support. 'Had the Constitution of France been as well established as our own', *The Times* commented from London, 'it would have been the duty of the Marshal to call upon M. Gambetta to form a cabinet.'[3]

Despite being the leader of the largest group in the Chamber, however, Gambetta was excluded from the new ministry. Indeed, the President refused to appoint any republicans to the Ministries of Foreign Affairs and of War, assigning the portfolios to conservatives. Gambetta was furious. MacMahon's action went against the spirit, if not the letter, of the constitution. The cabinet was 'stupid and malevolent', he raged, appealing to Léon to replenish his reserves of calm and moderation.[4]

If President MacMahon's intransigence barred the way to a republican government, division among the republicans limited their ability to challenge him. As Gambetta had predicted, the surge in the number of republican deputies created problems of consensus and discipline. They held a wide range of views, which would eventually produce several political parties.

The so-called Left-Centre, the conservative republicans from whose ranks President MacMahon selected his Ministers, were wary of the radicalism of their colleagues and voted on occasion with the Orleanist 'Centre Right'. They remained suspicious of Gambetta, remembering his Belleville Programme of 1869 and his sometimes heavy-handed measures during the Government of National Defence of 1870. If the Left-Centre worried about Gambetta's radical aspirations, he was not radical enough for the Extreme Left, who regarded social reform as integral to the Republic. Like many other republicans, Gambetta regarded them as unrealistic, dismissing them as 'the prehistoric old-beards of 1848'.[5]

Gambetta's Republican Union shared the republican middle ground with Jules Ferry's Republican Left: a division mainly reflecting the play of personalities. But Gambetta's group was by far the largest of the republican factions. It had emerged in a period when compromises with the conservatives were essential to the creation of the Republic: had Gambetta not been able to charm and persuade wavering constitutional monarchists, a restoration may well have occurred in the early 1870s. But by 1876, Gambetta's pursuit of the 'happy medium' was scorned by the Extreme Left, while conservative republicans jealously derided his ambition.

Despite Gambetta's enormous charisma, then, he also alienated people by his forcefulness. His efforts to unite the republican groupings in these years were interpreted as a grab for power rather than as an important political strategy. The Extreme Left, in particular, determined to preserve their independence, and their growing numbers in the Chamber in the late 1870s made them the greatest impediment to Gambetta's hopes for political advancement.[6]

Conflict intensified from April 1876, when Gambetta became President of the powerful Budget Commission of the Chamber of Deputies. This Commission examined budget proposals and vetted spending, giving it oversight of all ministries. Gambetta took this role very seriously, studying systems of finance and taxation. He was committed to ensuring tax relief for consumers (there was no income tax), but his vigilance was seen as further proof of his determination to control others. Léon, however, found it further grounds for praise: 'How your budgetary enthusiasm enraptures me!' she wrote in May, 'I am getting into the subject'. But she also reminded him that she was there when he needed 'relaxation' or 'diversion'.[7]

Gambetta had fended off the 'madmen' of the Extreme Left in drawing up the Senate election lists in January 1876. He was at odds with them again in June over their proposals to reduce the length of military service. More damaging still for Gambetta was conflict over an amnesty for former Communards, those involved in the Paris Commune of 1871, who were regarded as dangerous criminals in conservative circles. Gambetta was not unsympathetic to an amnesty. He had proposed such a measure himself in 1871, and had been highly critical of Thiers' punitive policies in 1872.[8] But now he was facing an impossible task. To shore up the republican majority he needed to keep the Left-Centre and the Centre-Right (the Orleanists) on side, which made it impossible for him to support a total amnesty. But nothing short of a total amnesty was acceptable to the Extreme Left.

During the 1876 election campaign, the Extreme Left had attacked Gambetta's failure to support total amnesty. He himself had spoken of awaiting the 'opportunity' to push such measures and his critics began to denounce his 'opportunism'. Gambetta finally chose to take the word on in a positive sense, using it to defend his policies in a major speech of October that year. Thus was born a new party label: the once Radical Gambetta was now an 'Opportunist', a word which came to cover what became the party of government under the Republic.[9]

The issue of amnesty showed the couple's political partnership at work. It also exposed the different perspectives of the deputy attuned to the political intricacies of factional interplay and delicate negotiation, and the confidante operating outside that world and fundamentally wary of 'the socialist tide'. Léon opted for directness rather than sweet-talk in this instance, criticizing Gambetta's indecisive editorial on amnesty in March 1876: 'All the parties are right to find it unsatisfactory . . . that you don't have a fixed view on this important matter, so I think it would have been preferable to have kept your irresolution to yourself.' Her only suggestion, however, was that Gambetta put a positive spin on his uncertainty, advising the public 'to have absolute confidence in the decision of the Chambers, both of which desire to conciliate the most extensive indulgence possible with respect for the law and the maintenance of order'. This was a formula for a partial and selective amnesty at best. In the end, Gambetta could not reconcile his conflicting loyalties: he abstained from voting when the Chamber rejected the measure decisively in May. His relations with the Extreme Left suffered a severe blow.[10]

As early as six weeks after the republicans' electoral triumph, then, Gambetta wrote to Léon discouraged, looking for solace: 'I am battling satisfied egos, and the sources of aid on which I could count withdrew under one pretext or another. I am clearly nearing a crisis. I feel ill will mobilizing around me, people are a bit tired of me . . . and they want me to pay a high price for the additional power and influence that recent events have brought to my position.'[11]

Gambetta provided further ammunition for his enemies in May when, having taken poor financial advice, he moved his newspaper and his own apartment into a grand building, formerly the residence of a Minister of the Empire, on the prestigious rue de la Chaussée-d'Antin. Léon strongly opposed the move. She condemned 'the rather garish luxury of these premises' and pointed out the likely political damage: 'Won't the magnificence of this upstart's mansion somehow undermine the model of dignified simplicity which suited so well the lofty politics of the statesman devoted exclusively to the triumph of a great cause, consecrated unreservedly to the regeneration of France?' Having been so outspoken, she feared that she had exceeded the bounds of their relationship, and was relieved by his reply: 'I am now reassured about the fear of having incurred your wrath, which led me to spend yesterday . . . a bad day!'[12]

Léon was rightly concerned for Gambetta's reputation in this exchange: his enemies soon circulated rumours about his 'palatial' apartment and its 'silver bath', though it was in a state of disrepair and the 'silver bath' was pewter. But Léon was also defending her own political project: to support the Gambetta of her dreams, the acclaimed republican statesman and hero. Gambetta insisted that he had things under control and would 'give no purchase to malicious gossip', but the issue dogged him for months and was a source of tension with Léon. It contributed to a moment of exasperation in mid-May when, to Léon's astonishment, Gambetta briefly toyed with retirement: 'You have moments of wonderful naivety, my dear great man', she wrote, 'and my smile of incredulity returns when I think that yesterday, between two kisses of a woman who has abandoned everything in order to adore you exclusively, you imagined being able to live simply as a spectator, you who are the centre [of] all internal and external politics, you who are the object of all feminine desire [*convoitise*] and to whom each hour of life brings a triumph, a satisfaction, a hope!' Léon neatly wove her own concerns about other women, and a hint of jealousy at Gambetta's fame and public prominence, into her response.[13]

In June 1876, the conservative-dominated Senate chose the anti-republican ally of President MacMahon, Louis-Joseph Buffet, to fill a vacancy for a Life Senator, adding to Gambetta's political woes. Buffet 'has slipped into the Senate and for the long term', he noted ruefully.

He hoped that 'After such a shock people will feel the need to close ranks, to rally to the flag, to focus and to obey.' But even on such a democratic measure as the election (rather than appointment) of mayors, Gambetta was soundly defeated by votes from fellow republicans.[14]

'My life is intolerable'

The couple's letters during 1876 were filled, as always, with declarations of love and dreams of future happiness together. The political conflicts that bedevilled Gambetta between March and May were offset by the solace he found with Léon. 'Have I ever loved you with as much passion as yesterday? Has any mortal ever felt such sublime emotions?' he asked his 'beautiful adorable and adored' one in April. 'I am proud enough to believe they have not.' Léon, too, acclaimed their love. 'This phase that we are going through would not be so bad if lots of hours like those of yesterday were slipped in. Such an infinite dream of contemplation, an instant of intellectual life, removed from all these mundane affairs that suppress the imagination, hinder the soaring spirit, and paralyse the movements of the heart!'[15]

As Léon's reference to the 'phase' they were going through suggested, there was often a gap between the emotional world the couple created in their letters and the one in which they lived. The flexibility of the letter allowed it to respond to many moods: to crown triumphs or offer solace; to express bliss or despair; to spar playfully with words and ideas. But it also offered an escape from frustrating and unhappy realities. It allowed the couple to enter an imaginary world where love was boundless, and where sorrows and frustrations disappeared. They could re-visit that world whenever they wished by re-reading the love letters they kept and treasured.[16]

The gap between epistolary intimacy and the reality of the couple's separate lives was revealed starkly in Léon's moments of jealousy, which recurred periodically throughout the relationship. Jealousy gave expression to Léon's pain and resentment at her exclusion from the world that Gambetta occupied, the world of salons, dinners and soirées where he was usually the star attraction and often, she feared, the subject of female interest. She was often suspicious of women with close political links to Gambetta. Léon's strong anti-Russian views, for instance, partly reflected her hostility to Russian Princess Lise Troubetzkoï, a wealthy and powerful figure, whose salon drew the Parisian social elite.[17] Like Juliette Adam's salon, this was a world where Gambetta was feted by a woman, but which Léon could not enter. In mid-1876, as Europe debated Russia's expansionist moves in the East, Troubetzkoï (along with Juliette Adam) attempted to persuade Gambetta to favour a French alliance with Russia. But Léon declared, 'I continue to discount Russia, as sharing at no point a common interest with us.'[18]

Gambetta, too, opposed a Russian alliance, as he explained to Juliette Adam. And he realized that Troubetzkoï was a Bonapartist sympathizer. But Léon's hostility to Russia often took a personal form. She nicknamed Troubetzkoï 'the marmoset' – perhaps a reference to her diminutive stature – and made many unflattering allusions to her. She cast doubt on Troubetzkoï's political credentials, perhaps hoping to send a message to Gambetta: 'The tokens of affection that the Marmoset sends you from the top of her palm tree are running around in my head; at heart, that is quite significant and very consoling, if she is truly well-informed about the thinking of foreign courts!'[19]

Léon even referred explicitly to Troubetzkoï's seductive strategies, fearing Gambetta's susceptibility to this engaging woman: 'The marmoset has had the talent to make your chords vibrate twice over', she wrote in May 1876, 'by flying your colours and by lifting a corner of the veil that floats on the diplomatic horizon!' Gambetta objected, and Léon noted that 'this wretched marmoset' was always behind their quarrels. But she took a malicious pleasure as the European powers curtailed Russia's territorial ambitions. Léon wrote in October: 'Let's hope for peace and the obliteration of the cossacks.' 'We will triumph over the cossacks', she repeated in November, 'and on the day that the marmoset tribe bites the dust we will have a celebration!' She was thinking of domestic as well as foreign affairs.[20]

Léon's hostility to Troubetzkoï indicated dissatisfaction with her restricted role in Gambetta's life. By 1876, Gambetta, too, was looking for a change, seeking to end the pattern of brief visits that still typified their relationship. He wrote on 11 March: 'I must offer my apologies for the unceremonious way I fell asleep [last night], if I could only have kept you beside me I would have been completely cured. I am longing for the day when I will obtain this supreme favour. You won't always have the courage to refuse me.' Having Léon stay the night with him would be 'a certain means' to enhance their love, he continued, 'and I am far from giving up on it'. It would also signify a more exclusive engagement between them, compatible with the position of a dedicated mistress who reserved her time for a single man.[21]

Gambetta felt freer to bring Léon home once he moved from his mezzanine on the rue Montaigne to his controversial new apartment on the rue de la Chaussée-d'Antin. It was considerably more spacious, and he could entertain her there. He wrote on 20 May: 'I'll free myself around nine. I'll go first to the rue Bonaparte, unless you prefer that I send the carriage to fetch you; you'll come to join me at the Quai d'Orsay. We'll take a nice walk and then we'll come back to dine and spend the evening in my new apartment.'[22] Gambetta now had a carriage at his disposal, and someone to cook his meals, an indication of his increasing wealth as President of the Budget Commission, though he was not yet free of financial worry.

Léon's personal and family problems nevertheless remained a source of tension and anguish. Rather than solving such problems, Émilie's death may even have exacerbated them. Léon's correspondence increasingly tells of her conflict with her mother, a tale alluded to only cryptically in earlier years. Since Léon and Gambetta now shared more about their personal lives, the stresses and strains of those lives affected their relationship too.

Léon's mother, Marie Sauzy, had had a difficult life. Orphaned at six, an unmarried mother at nineteen, she had finally married Émile Léon at the age of thirty. Widowed at forty-nine, she was forced to rely on her daughters' incomes as courtesans for her survival. Her lack of personal independence frustrated her. Léon later reported the substance of her mother's complaints: 'that I consign her to the countryside where she is dying of boredom etc.'[23] The women's complex family lives and sexual histories, laden with guilt and blame, had shaped a very unhappy relationship.

Ironically, Léon's complaint about her own domestic situation resembled that of her mother. Each felt constrained by the other. Without Émilie to share the burden of care, Léon felt imprisoned at home: she was an 'unfortunate captive' dreaming of freedom. According to Léon, her mother was increasingly demanding and irascible, resentful of her daughter's absences in Paris, and given to 'unimaginable' moods. Only periodic visits from friends of the family relieved Léon from her 'duty' to care for her and keep her company. Léon insisted to Gambetta that she was 'suffering cruelly, intolerably', adding: 'these are not simple adverbs intended to cover a lot of paper!' 'It doesn't take a great effort of imagination to understand that my life is intolerable and that it takes only one new vexation to make the chalice of bitterness, from which I drink each day, overflow.'[24]

The needs of eleven-year-old Alphonse played their part in the difficulties between mother and daughter. In October 1875, Alphonse had entered the eighth grade at the Collège Sainte-Barbe des Champs, the rural annex and junior school of the famous Parisian Collège Sainte-Barbe. In May 1876, as Gambetta was moving to the rue de la

Chausée-d'Antin, Léon and her family left Bourg-la-Reine for Fontenay-aux-Roses, another leafy suburb of the capital, where the school was located. If Mme Léon was 'dying of boredom' by October 1876, Léon herself was restive almost immediately they arrived there: 'This constant rain is increasing my absolute disenchantment with the countryside. A beautiful view is not an inexhaustible pleasure, and I have sufficiently enjoyed all the effects of the light which, depending on the weather and the hour, change the appearance of the vast horizon that I am discovering!' But the family remained at Fontenay-aux-Roses until Alphonse entered the senior school in Paris in October 1879.[25]

Alphonse was also a source of tension between Gambetta and Léon. Only on her deathbed did Léon finally admit that she was Alphonse's mother, not his aunt. The letters do not reveal if she told Gambetta, although her confession at the beginning of their liaison and her constant care for *Chine* suggest that she had. Léon was devoted to her sickly son, mollycoddling him and giving precedence to his needs and demands. Gambetta had hoped that, once Alphonse settled into his new school with new friends, his mother would become less anxious and more readily spend time away from him. But Alphonse – along with his ill-humoured grandmother – continued to dictate the pattern of Léon's visits to Paris. Gambetta was forced to hope that Alphonse would smile propitiously on their plans.[26]

As well as humouring Alphonse, Gambetta also had to accommodate Léon's animals. She was deeply attached to her two little dogs, and often took them to Paris with her. Gambetta took a liking to them – or feigned affection to please Léon – and they gradually became part of the family. 'Bring Fidès', Gambetta had written in March 1875 when arranging Léon's next visit. 'I'll discipline her instead of *la Chine*; I love to see her playing under your skirt.' Now, Gambetta wrote cheerfully about dining with a second dog, Flèje, whom he was minding: 'We are on the best of terms, becoming ever more intimate. I'm as smitten as you.'[27]

But Gambetta did not appreciate the depth of Léon's attachment to her animals. She was deeply grieved when Fidès produced two stillborn pups in June 1876. Five days later, Gambetta carelessly announced the death of Flèje: 'P.S. Bad news, Flèje has given up his soul to the common mother of all beings.' Léon was horrified: 'The sad post-scriptum removed any regret about having delayed my visit until tomorrow! One day's mourning is not too much for this poor, pretty little animal that I raised with such care!'[28]

Gambetta's apology for this faux-pas reflected his grievance at ceding priority in Léon's life to Alphonse and the dogs: 'I understand what proprieties the death of this little wisp of a dog imposed on me, and I am hardly worthy to dry the tears that this sudden and terrible catastrophe must have caused you. But I resign myself with difficulty to taking into account the caprices of the *Chinois* and now I must respect the whole of zoology that intervenes to sadden you.'[29] Nevertheless, the fact that Léon openly expected Gambetta to take her personal life into account was a sign that their relationship had reached a more trusting level than a mistress might have expected. Equally, the fact that Gambetta accommodated Léon's wishes and needs, even whilst complaining, showed the strength of his devotion to her.

'My heart is suffering'

The unhappiness that punctuated Léon's letters in 1876 was not new. The correspondence had, for some time, referred to Léon's 'black thoughts' and a 'sadness' she could not shake off. But her symptoms extended beyond dark moods, suggesting that there was a physical basis for Léon's ill health. In addition to an array of coughs, colds, eye infections and toothaches, from which Gambetta also suffered, Léon began to complain in 1876 of headaches, which worried her because she had never had them before.[30] She also suffered from severe neuralgia, which sometimes left her face swollen and tender: 'I have never felt such sharp, such persistent physical pain as the neuralgia which is easing just this minute at five o'clock, all night long I have walked about my bedroom unable to close my eyes and not knowing where to rest my splitting head!'[31]

Léon's loose combination of physical and 'moral' symptoms was consistent with the contemporary understanding of 'melancholy'. It resembles in some respects what is now called 'depression', which was only gradually defined in the late nineteenth century.[32] Léon and Gambetta sought treatment for her melancholy on a number of occasions. Gambetta repeatedly encouraged her to consult Dr François Siredey, his own doctor, and she did so several times. Gambetta had written in March 1876: 'This very evening I saw Dr Sirdey [*sic*], who immediately enquired about the health of my dear lady. I told him that you had obeyed only half his directives and that consequently you were only half well. He strongly recommended hydrotherapy, saying that he would take responsibility for your prompt recovery if you would obey him for a few weeks.'[33]

Whatever treatment Léon had already received from Siredey, however, had not ended her physical or emotional suffering. The search for successful treatment would continue, and Gambetta would continue to urge Léon to take Dr Siredey's hydrotherapy treatment. He wrote on 30 June 1877: 'I put on my love only one condition, I should say one prayer, that is that you take care of yourself, sacrifice everything to this supreme interest; I want you to take a decisive resolution, I will have no rest unless I see you keeping to a regimen [*vouée à un régime*]; believe me hydrotherapy can give each of us what we need, strength to you, equilibrium to me.'[34]

Even if Léon's suffering had a physical component, it also reflected the difficulties of her life. She was torn between her family duties, her love and responsibility for Alphonse, and her love for Gambetta; his career was surging forward while she was hamstrung by domestic burdens, anxiety and social norms. Léon seemed overcome by this conjuncture. She poured out her despair a little incoherently, exaggerating her vulnerability in an appeal for Gambetta's sympathy: 'The future which is fading away, or sometimes tinged with colour during hours of happiness; at such moments the sombre and menacing thought returns incessantly: alone, and so fragile, caught between an old person and a child! And the terrible solution seems to me the only possible way to overcome so many misfortunes!' This was less a threat of self-destruction, however, than a plea for reaffirmation of Gambetta's love.[35]

Gambetta was quick to respond to Léon's appeal, emphasizing his own suffering and his need for her: 'You came and brought me joy and happiness, you left and I fell back into silence and moral lassitude. When you leave, the day flees, and I am left tired, disgusted by the vileness of politics . . . I spend my time reworking that old tapestry of Penelope known as parliamentary politics, which is falling apart everywhere. As soon as I have sewn up the right, it tears on the left, in the middle.'[36]

But the letters of July 1876, which tell the story mainly from Léon's side, suggest that Gambetta was irritated by Léon's melancholy, and that he complained about her silences. She wrote on 9 July: 'Given your personal preoccupations and my awkward position in your life, it is impossible that I will ever be fully expansive and I find it prudent and more dignified to remain silent when discouragement reaches its greatest heights!' She tried to placate her 'beautiful love', however, by couching her complaint very affectionately, and accompanying it with a flower she had found in a 'delightful gorge' that morning.[37]

Discussion of Léon's moods continued for several days. She argued that there was fault on both sides: 'You are quite unjust to accuse me of keeping silent when you send me off to the drawing room for an hour and you spend three [hours] in the carriage. I believe I suppressed my sorrows completely in order to distract you, and spoke for as long as you wanted to listen to me.' But she clearly wanted to pacify Gambetta and avoid his displeasure, as a mistress would: 'Glum or gay I adore you above all, my beloved, and I cover you with kisses as infinite as my love!' She even quipped the following day, 'In fact everything is improving, even me; and I am ready to prove it to you by an inexhaustible loquacity!'[38]

An uncustomary silence on Léon's part surely disturbed the pattern of a relationship that was heavily invested in words – in poetic declarations of love, and exchanges of ideas about numerous topics. Léon's emotional withdrawal from Gambetta apparently threw him into a gloomy mood as well, making him unable to bounce back from the political stresses that beset him: he even suggested once again that he might give up politics altogether. Léon was incredulous: 'You would make me laugh if I were still capable of doing so, with your disdain for the outside world, you who live, act, speak, write and breathe only for the world and its present and future opinion! This isn't an accusation, far from it, but a simple statement of the facts, a correction of the minutes.' The following day Léon invited Gambetta to compare their respective physical and 'moral' conditions: he could be certain of 'glory' in the future, she reminded him. 'That is the supreme compensation; an inexhaustible source of intoxication!' Again, she seemed resentful that public recognition was not available to her, but there is no sign that she reflected on the gender divide that underpinned this gap in their expectations.[39]

Alphonse was too ill to go to school, adding to the stresses of July. Gambetta was sceptical about the boy's condition. 'Whatever you think', Léon wrote, 'the poor baby wasn't able to enjoy the splendid festival on Sunday: the brass band competition, of which we heard only occasional echoes; the fireworks and illuminations, of which we saw only the remnants carried on the storm.' The doctors diagnosed 'a sort of yellow fever'; medical conferences were called; Léon stayed by the child's bedside, anxious and worried. She wrote miserably: 'So many complications, sorrows and worries. When will we be together again, dear? Our lives and our health are being worn down while we wait for a happiness that recedes as we advance to grasp it.' Yet by 30 July Alphonse was back at school, well enough to enjoy the gift of a watch that Gambetta had sent. Both doctors and mother had apparently misjudged the severity of his condition.[40]

Léon's letters throughout July attempted to negotiate her varied concerns as absent lover and political confidante, harassed daughter and worried mother. She still managed to comment on the political situation, enquiring about proposed legislation and the foreign policy issues that interested Gambetta. But the underlying source of tension between Léon and Gambetta was the fact that her role as his mistress was difficult to reconcile with her family duties and her battle with 'melancholy'. She reminded Gambetta that her 'awkward position in [his] life' prevented complete freedom of expression. She represented herself as the mistress, distracting and amusing her lover regardless of her own feelings. Indeed, she was even more explicit: 'You didn't need to insist, you had already given me to understand that this kind of relationship didn't allow for sorrow, and that when I didn't feel strong enough to overcome mine, I should stay at home.'[41]

Léon feared that she had no future to look forward to with Gambetta in 'this kind of relationship'. Worn down by her own personal problems, she worried that Gambetta's political career would absorb him completely and take him away from her: 'time is passing by, the world is engrossing you, life is flying by; what happiness lost!' In November she would reiterate that anxiety: 'I bitterly regret not having managed to chase away my black butterflies so as better to dispel yours: Life is passing by, youth is disappearing, why not seize the happiness of the present, get drunk on dreams?'[42]

Léon's ongoing bouts of melancholy and her fruitless search for effective treatment demonstrate that her existential angst could not easily be dispelled. But her anxiety could be eased by a more secure relationship with Gambetta. Léon had pointed out early in 1876, as the conflict with her mother intensified: 'It's not plans I lack but the conquest of my freedom which is hard work, not only material freedom but security complete enough to leave me full moral liberty.'[43] She needed, she suggested, a degree of financial support that would ensure her personal independence.

Fragments of evidence indicate that Gambetta was providing that support by mid-1876. When Léon and her family moved to Fontenay-aux-Roses in May that year, they rented the property at Bourg-la-Reine to tenants and employed a chambermaid, so they were clearly doing better financially than a decade previously.[44] Either Léon earned enough to make them more comfortable, or Gambetta assisted them. The latter seems more likely by this time. If she had not become his exclusive mistress when the couple exchanged rings in 1874, she may well have been so now.

Alternatively, that moment may have come a few months later, in August 1876, when Gambetta finally became financially secure. The purchase of the 'upstart's mansion' on the rue de la Chaussée-d'Antin, against which Léon had argued vehemently in April, had been a near-disaster, and on 29 June Gambetta informed Léon that he was 'headed sweetly for ruin'. Léon could not resist saying I told you so: 'Have my warnings against the acquisition of that hotel proved justified enough?' She was, she added, 'deeply sorry to have been right!' However, Edmond Adam and other republican notables came to the rescue. They repaid the loan and reorganized the finances of the *République Française*, which soon assured Gambetta a solid income for the first time in his life.[45]

That income was quite adequate for Gambetta to support a mistress and keep her for his own. As they planned a trip to Germany together for the beginning of September, both reaffirmed their love. 'Life and happiness are you!' wrote Léon. Gambetta anticipated the pleasures of their 'odyssey': 'Long live love and politics, that's the inscription that I will have written on your coat of arms, because you revise both of them for me.'[46]

'I really believe I have won'

The appointment to head the ministry of another conservative republican, Jules Simon, was frustrating for many. Gambetta's Republican Union was still the largest bloc in the Chamber, but Simon was a long-standing opponent of Gambetta and unwilling to advance his agenda. If Gambetta could rely on his close parliamentary allies for political support, he continued to turn passionately to Léon in search of personal reassurance and consolation as the struggle for supremacy unfolded. Each parliamentary battle was fought under her protective gaze; each victory was attributed to her inspiration. Their partnership continued to reflect the gender divide that distinguished Gambetta's male role as active political combatant from Léon's female role as observer. It was an emotional union; one giving expression to their love and mutual need.

Faced with MacMahon's new ministry, Gambetta and Léon discussed the possibility that the President would resort to military force, if necessary, to stave off republicanism. When Léon noted that securing a republican Minister for War would prevent the army being turned against the Republic (a strategy he also supported), Gambetta was enraptured, transposing Léon's reasoned argument into mystical terms: her inspiration was 'more infallible than the most astute instincts of the ancient sorceresses', he declared, continuing: 'I will do as you say. It is always in you that I place my happiness, my joy, my true ambition without renouncing the other [i.e. political] form.'[47]

Similarly, when the Chamber overwhelmingly approved his Budget revisions, which reduced the allocation for priests and ministers of religion, Gambetta turned his success into a declaration of love. 'I took on the Minister of Finance in hand-to-hand combat and we won the finest parliamentary success of the session . . . It is in your eyes, on your lips that I found the grace and honey, found the secret to seduce the souls that were irresolute or ill-humoured the day before.'[48]

Gambetta's choice of a military metaphor reflected the hyper-masculine atmosphere that dominated parliamentary proceedings. Debate in the Chamber was constantly likened to doing battle, fighting a duel, struggling to the death.[49] But Gambetta also paid tribute to Léon for handing him a different sort of weaponry, the power of 'seduction'. To persuade was perceived as feminine, to defeat as masculine, but Gambetta was happy to use both to achieve his ends.

The Chamber's vote on the Budget unleashed a fierce contest for budgetary control with the conservative-dominated Senate. 'The battle is joined', Gambetta advised Léon on 21 December. Indignant that the Senate wanted to reduce 'the Chamber of Deputies, the Chamber of universal suffrage, the Chamber of taxpayers' into a modest advisory body, he planned a motion of no confidence and sought her presence at the debate as an inspiration and a good omen. 'This encounter will probably take place next Tuesday. I want to have you there at Versailles on that day, and to do battle in your presence. That will make me stronger and more confident, and if I succumb at least I will have the consolation of finding you right there next to me.' Despite her inspiration and support, however, he suffered a resounding defeat: the Chamber preferred compromise to another cabinet crisis and new elections.[50]

Gambetta bounced back in January 1877 with a resounding political victory. He was re-elected President of the Budget Commission with an overwhelming majority over Simon's candidate, the eminent banker Henri Germain (founder of the Crédit Lyonnais bank). Moreover, nineteen of his Republican Union colleagues were elected while Simon's Centre Left group had only four members. The Chamber was once again flexing its muscle. An exultant Gambetta attributed his success to Léon: 'He has not really experienced the true exhilaration of political triumph who has not savoured it in love . . . What superiority of strength, of courage, of power do I draw from you as from an inexhaustible store of moral riches . . . The invincible confidence you give me makes everything easy and everything propitious.' He continued to shower Léon with declarations of affection: 'You are the eternal springtime of my love', he declared. 'I will die without being satisfied and I will have loved you all my life with an insatiable tenderness.'[51]

Léon could actually do little to assist Gambetta in his parliamentary battles. But the same adrenalin that inspired his powerful parliamentary speeches also inspired his paeans to his lover. We can only imagine Léon's enraptured responses, since all but two of her letters from 1877 have disappeared. Gambetta's confidence and optimism were at their height. His letters reflect the symbiosis between his relationship with Léon and his career, raising the question of how that relationship might fare in the event of a decline in Gambetta's political fortunes.

In the Chamber, Gambetta continued to challenge Jules Simon and through him President MacMahon. Matters came to a head in May. When Simon several times failed to prevent the Chamber from passing motions that displeased MacMahon, the President forced Simon's resignation. The President thus claimed the right to overrule the will of the Chamber of Deputies, an act widely regarded as 'tantamount to a coup d'état'.[52] The date – 16 May 1877 – would be celebrated in republican history as the moment that heralded the Republic's final triumph over monarchy.

That evening, republican deputies drew up a resolution to demand, once again, a ministry that would 'govern in accordance with . . . republican principles'. When the motion was put to the Chamber the following day, after a powerful speech by Gambetta, it passed overwhelmingly. Gambetta wrote to Léon that evening: 'I have entered battle and I really believe I have won, as you will see in the newspaper. The question is clearly posed for the country now, either a republican government or dissolution. It's evidently dissolution.' The date of this parliamentary encounter was propitious, given that the couple celebrated any dates containing '7' as their anniversary. 'It was the 17th', he noted. 'It was a certain triumph!'[53]

But it was not yet victory. President MacMahon again summoned the duc de Broglie to head a conservative ministry. He prorogued parliament for a month and began a purge of officials, foreshadowing new elections. Gambetta set off campaigning, while Léon played her role as confidante: 'You will read in tomorrow's paper the speech whose main points you saw sketched out', Gambetta wrote to her. 'I believe I followed them faithfully and successfully. I am quite pleased with myself and await your judgement with confidence, but not without impatience.'[54]

When parliament reassembled on 16 June, the President called on the Senate to dissolve the Chamber, but the Chamber was determined to vote no confidence in the ministry first. The debate was furious and Gambetta's oratorical skills were deployed to devastating effect. In a marathon sitting which degenerated at times almost to physical violence, before a gallery packed to overflowing, Gambetta gave one of his most powerful speeches in a debate with Interior Minister Fourtou. Fourtou portrayed the battle between monarchists and republicans in 1877 as a struggle between the 'France of [17]89' and the 'France of [17]93'. In other words, he portrayed his monarchists as high-minded revolutionaries and the republicans as Jacobins, those linked with the Terror of 1793.

Gambetta took the podium, expressing ironic amazement that the die-hard monarchist duc de Broglie had 'suddenly been smitten by republican institutions' derived from the Revolution. Flaying the various dynastic parties and their ambitions, raising the spectre of 'the government of the priests', Gambetta defended universal male suffrage against 'the partisans of ducal supremacy and the oligarchy of a few nobles . . . who don't wish to adapt to democracy, and a congregation [the Jesuits] who want to enslave France'. After trading discursive blows with his opponents for more than two hours, amidst hundreds of interjections and insults, Gambetta collapsed in a pool of perspiration to the deafening cheers of his supporters and the howls of outrage of his enemies. The debate continued for two days, after which time the republicans' vote of no confidence in the government was carried by 363 to 158. On 22 June, the Senate accepted dissolution, making new elections necessary.[55]

Watching the debate in the gallery, the writer Jules Claretie recorded: 'Gambetta was superb, admirable, astonishing. He is going grey, getting fat. But what power there is in this young man. He displayed magnificent bearing, withering responses, historic turns of phrase. This morning's *Officiel* [Hansard] does not capture the lofty, contemptuous irony of the harangue. The ministers on their benches must be frothing with rage.'[56]

Léon was, as always, Gambetta's greatest fan. Having witnessed this contest, she wrote the following day: 'Ah! indeed, my divine love, I understand your exhaustion only too well, and beseech you to preserve yourself for other hours that will sound in the future, when present events are already in the past. I savoured the speech, which I heard much better than I expected to; each of your words is in my heart and continues to ring in my ears with the intonation you gave it.'[57]

'Submit or resign'

Looking forward to the elections, Gambetta discussed his political strategy with Léon, presenting lines of argument and responding to her objections. 'Yesterday evening proved to me for the thousandth time the value of your lofty reason in directing my ideas and actions. I dearly love encountering the objections of your mind in order to jostle with, test, control my own.' Other republican women wrote encouragingly to Gambetta, too, aware of the significance of the political moment. But as they understood, men acted politically on behalf of women: the republican victory would represent, as Gambetta put it to Céline Scheurer-Kestner, 'the triumph of your ideas and of your friends.'[58]

The monarchists looked for any opportunity to destroy Gambetta. Having already tried to incriminate him for his role in the Government of National Defence of 1870, they now seized on a speech he made at Lille in August 1877, prosecuting him and his newspaper for insulting the President. 'When the only authority before which all bow down has spoken', he had said, 'when these millions of Frenchmen, peasants, workers, bourgeois, electors of the free land of France, have made their choice . . . no one, whatever rung of the political or administrative ladder he occupies, can resist. When France has made its sovereign voice heard, believe me, Gentlemen, it will be necessary to submit or resign.' MacMahon's name was not mentioned, but Gambetta's meaning was clear.[59]

Léon was extremely worried about the looming trial, set for 11 September. Gambetta urged her to 'calm down and present impassive scorn to these puerilities', as he did: 'It's wrong to think that this will be a second Baudin trial, it is quite useless to take these political runts so seriously.' He made a date with Léon to go over his 'plan of defence and attack'. 'Hold your indignation in check', he wrote, 'we both need to be cool-headed.'[60]

Gambetta's conviction by the court created a sensation. He himself was undaunted, however, determined to pursue his legal options to the limit. 'I have happily resumed my first career as prosecutor and I plan to make these idiots take a fine trip through the brambles of legal procedure', he wrote cheerfully to Léon. 'They haven't caught me; I strongly doubt that they'll ever catch me . . . so don't take these vile acts for tragedy; one must laugh and make fun of these fools.' This may have been bravado to assuage Léon's concerns, but Gambetta used the legal process to play for time, and his expectation that the republicans would win the elections was reasonable. Indeed, in December the new government would drop the charges against him.[61]

If the prosecution was an irritation to Gambetta, the sudden death of Adolphe Thiers on 3 September 1877 was a major blow to his hopes for advancement, and Gambetta feared 'the consequences of this terrible event'. Thiers had become the benign elder statesman of republicanism, and he may even have reached an agreement with Gambetta that, following a republican victory in the forthcoming elections, Thiers would replace MacMahon as President and would appoint Gambetta to head the ministry. The Right warned of disaster should the republicans – minus Thiers – gain power. But Gambetta countered by publishing a manifesto that Thiers had drafted before his death. 'It is a real masterpiece of good sense, clarity, patriotism, eloquent reason, and serene impartiality', Gambetta wrote to Léon. 'France will hear this voice from beyond the grave, and 14 October [election day] will be in memory of M. Thiers, the finest triumph of his name and his spirit.'[62]

Election day demonstrated the intensity of the battle, with a high voter turnout and a decisive vote: only fifteen seats needed to go to a second round. That evening, as the election results came in, Léon sent a blissful note to Gambetta: 'I am smiling at your resurgence, at your triumph, at our love!' France had heard the republican call and, despite all the machinations of Interior Minister Fourtou, had given them a majority – slightly reduced – of 119.[63]

Despite yet another victory for the republicans, however, President MacMahon remained resolutely opposed to appointing a republican ministry. Gambetta correctly predicted that the President would try for 'some sort of parliamentary patch-up from before 16 May'. That 'patch-up' came when MacMahon again appointed the duc de Broglie as Prime Minister. Even when elections for the General Councils on 4 November saw Broglie lose his own seat, and the republicans gain 113, MacMahon did not accept his resignation.[64]

The republicans drew up their battle plan ahead of the opening of parliament on 7 November 1877. Gambetta was in high spirits, predicting publication of the 'death notices' of the cabinet within weeks. 'On Monday or Tuesday we'll begin to sweep away this rubbish', he wrote. 'I have a ticket for Monday and another for Tuesday, and so on, tomorrow evening I'll arrange things with you for this first one.' Arrangements firmed up two days later: 'the decisive act won't be played until Wednesday or Thursday. So I am keeping to my plan, Tuesday you'll come to dine and sleep in Paris, Wednesday we'll go to Versailles together and come back the same way.'[65]

On 15 November, Gambetta's unsparing denunciation of the Broglie ministry ended three days of fierce debate, and the republicans ended the first skirmish of the new parliament in triumph.[66] But at this moment of glory, Gambetta was dismayed that Léon nowhere to be seen. That evening he wrote expressing his anxiety about her, but also appealing for her consolation:

> I fear that you are ill. I waited in vain for you at the Chamber today, I had written to you yesterday evening, your place was reserved and kept for you; alas! It remained empty throughout the session. My heart was heavy as I mounted the tribune, I needed to have you there, before my eyes; I summoned up your image and it's to you that I addressed my reply to the born enemy of my politics. I think you will be happy with your Léon, judging by the enthusiasm of the assembly, the rout of the right, the crushing of the ministry.[67]

What kept Léon away on this crucial day? A domestic crisis? An insuperable attack of melancholy or anxiety? Her letters for this period have disappeared, taking the answers with them.

The ministry may have been 'crushed' but President MacMahon only accepted its resignation several days later, when even the Senate failed to support Broglie. The next ministry he named, composed of obscure figures who were the butt of republican amusement, lasted only one encounter with the Chamber, resigning on 24 November. As the President hunted around for another candidate to his liking, the republicans turned the financial screws, refusing to vote taxes unless a republican ministry was appointed. Rumours of a coup d'état spread, and Gambetta saw the political climax approaching.[68]

Whatever had troubled Léon ten days previously had clearly been resolved, and Gambetta's confidence was restored: 'I have lots of things to tell you, and lots of advice to seek . . . we are really coming to the end, to submit or resign . . . we have the high ground, and I am more than ever sure of final success if the troops continue to march well and the adversaries continue to wage the campaign.' The situation remained unclear for a fortnight: 'we are marching blind, uncertain of tomorrow, discovering hieroglyphics whose meaning changes daily. We have had three ministries today and will go to sleep tonight hopeful of having a fourth at dawn that will last at least until midday.'[69]

President MacMahon's final attempt to defy the majority was to nominate the hardliner Anselme Batbie. He urged the proclamation of martial law when the Senate resisted his appointment. This was too much even for MacMahon, who was a stickler for the legalities, if not the spirit, of the Constitution. Instead, he decided to nominate a republican, but having declared in May that he would 'rather be overthrown than remain under the orders of [M.] Gambetta', on 13 December he again appointed the conservative Jules Dufaure to head a ministry. This time, however, he gave Dufaure free reign to choose his own cabinet. France finally had a republican ministry. But given Dufaure's desire to placate MacMahon, Gambetta, the leader of the largest republican group in the Chamber, was not among them.[70]

There are no letters between Gambetta and Léon discussing this outcome, despite the fact that this was the moment for which Gambetta, along with his lover, had fought so hard since 1870. He put on a good face to *The Times*: 'How should I be dissatisfied when I see so grievous a crisis so happily ended?'[71] But perhaps in private he expressed views that seemed best kept hidden. His struggle to maintain his influence in the Republican regime that was now beginning was soon underway.

Part II
A Bourgeois Couple in the Third Republic

Adored sweetheart,

You are an incomparable wonder, and I am more and more fanatical about you. I am completely enamoured, and almost feverish from that delightful and intoxicating evening. I would like to have had you for this beautiful day today, but without you nothing invites me to go out, I have stayed reading in my library and in my bedroom, still completely pervaded by your perfume.

It is quite agreed that on Tuesday we will go and visit our beautiful rocks at Fontainebleau, to recall our sweet and tender impressions of the fairy pond and the little amphitheatre of old druidic oaks.

I am really expecting you to come on Monday evening and dine with me so that you will be all adorned on Tuesday morning. Let's take advantage of the fine days, dearest, and since you don't want to go too far, let's at least take a trip around Paris.

I await you, I kiss you as I love you, without stopping.

Your Léon

P.S. The war continues, and I am still hoping!

5
'We'll go and laugh at the Palais-Royal'

Both Gambetta and Léon had come to the capital in their youth in pursuit of personal advancement. Paris was the city of opportunity, unrivalled by any provincial centre. Thanks to the massive programme of urban renewal commissioned by Emperor Napoleon III in 1852 and overseen by the Prefect, Baron Georges-Eugène Haussmann, Paris had gradually been transformed into an impressive imperial capital. By 1870, it offered all the amenities that modern technology could provide. Gone were most of the narrow, dark lanes and ramshackle buildings of the medieval city. Gone, too, were the leather works and slaughterhouses that assailed the senses. Paris became the modern city familiar to today's tourists, with its grand boulevards and sidewalks, its low-rise apartment blocks, its department stores, and its array of parks and gardens.[2] It was the centre of intellectual and cultural life, the home of the leading institutions of education, the law and government. For a courtesan like Léon, or an aspiring lawyer like Gambetta, there was no better place to be.

As a Parisian couple, Gambetta and Léon participated enthusiastically in the capital's bourgeois lifestyle. Their correspondence provides many glimpses into their activities in the rejuvenated city. Léon could not join Gambetta on official occasions, when the rules of respectability held sway. But the city offered anonymity to an illicit couple. Gambetta and Léon took advantage of the social freedom it afforded, sharing many of the leisure and cultural activities of the respectable bourgeoisie.

The pleasures of consumption

Nineteenth-century Paris was increasingly promoted as the leisure capital of the world in the numerous new guides that, unlike their predecessors, focused on pleasure rather than on architecture and history. The explosion of wealth that financed major public works also facilitated a culture of consumption. Both luxury shopping and restaurants had long histories, but they expanded rapidly in the newly reconstructed city, whose broad avenues and footpaths, bordered by shops, restaurants and cafés, offered endless opportunities for indulgence and endless spectacle to passers-by.[3]

Léon and Gambetta enjoyed window-shopping in the fashionable districts, a pastime enhanced with the development of sheet glass and street lighting from the 1860s. They dined in up-market Saint-Germain-des-Près, later the haunt of Sartre and Beauvoir, and joined the throngs promenading on the new footpaths.[4] Shaded by trees during the day, lit by gas lamps at night, and often protected by arcades, the footpaths made strolling in the city a novel pleasure. An English guidebook noted: 'In Paris everything is so broad, that the pedestrian can move with perfect freedom.'[5] The lovers took advantage of that freedom to wander at leisure. They might meet on the Quai d'Orsay to take 'a nice walk' before dinner, or take a 'charming promenade across the centre of our great Paris'.[6]

The couple described their walks around the city in various ways: promenading, strolling, roaming, wandering. 'If it is late we will stay in Paris and stroll [*flâner*] wherever fantasy takes us', Gambetta wrote, 'to the Louvre or the Arsenal [Museums].'[7] The act of 'strolling' (*flânerie*) – walking with no particular destination or objective in mind, observing others and the sights at hand – was a novel feature of the modern city.[8] *Flânerie* originated in the eighteenth century with the first tree-lined boulevards, but the *flâneur* became a central character of modern life thanks to the writings of mid-nineteenth-century poet, Charles Baudelaire.[9] He had envisaged a male *flâneur*, assuming that only men had the right to be on the streets alone and to subject others to their gaze.[10]

Léon, however, was used to wandering unaccompanied, as the police observations showed. And she enjoyed walking around the city with Gambetta. They ran the risk of encountering a friend or acquaintance in the city's streets and gardens. But a man was free to mix with both respectable society and the demimonde, even if a woman could not cross that line. Any acquaintance from polite society whom they met would certainly not have greeted Léon, though she or he may have been curious to see this mysterious mistress about whom Gambetta was so secretive.

When Léon went out alone in the city, it was often to go shopping. Her letters to Gambetta are strewn with references to visits to seamstresses and milliners, as she endeavoured to co-ordinate those appointments with the couple's time together. 'Not at three o'clock exactly, I have the dressmaker', she replied to Gambetta on one occasion, 'at four o'clock instead and then I will be yours alone.' She adjourned their rendezvous again a few weeks later: 'There are dresses in preparation, an appointment with the *artiste* [the seamstress], and given her customary slowness I don't want to put it off. I'd like to meet you when I leave her, not before three but certainly before four!'[11]

Like many bourgeois women, Léon had her outfits made by a seamstress – Mme Tridon – and rarely bought ready-made clothing. While seamstresses often worked for clothing manufacturers by this period, the development from the 1850s of small sewing machines for use in the home also supported seamstresses working on their own account. Hand-finishing remained the norm for quality products. Each new outfit required multiple visits to the dressmaker.[12]

Advance preparation was imperative, therefore, if a garment was needed for a special occasion. When Gambetta mentioned a ceremony to mark the return of the National Assembly from Versailles to Paris in June 1879, Léon wrote anxiously: 'But my dear sweetheart you leave me in a terrible state of uncertainty about what to wear! Will I have time, yes or no, to have this masterpiece created? I wanted to rush to my *artistes*; but the decision wasn't made quickly enough, time is short, and I am delaying that step until tomorrow, all the more so since you will [then] have given me the [precise] date.' A good relationship with one's *artiste* was imperative – perhaps explaining why Gambetta sent theatre tickets on at least one occasion to Léon's 'most esteemed seamstress'.[13]

Léon had expensive tastes. The short astrakhan cape paired with an astrakhan-trimmed skirt, reported by a particularly astute police officer in 1874, is a good example. Astrakhan was a luxury product, curly wool obtained from stillborn lambs of a particular species, and necessarily expensive. Kid boots were also the preserve of the bourgeoisie, like tortoiseshell hatpins, golden slippers, or the fur rug Léon asked Gambetta to help her choose in 1879. 'Here is another fantasy for tomorrow', she wrote. 'You will come and collect me in the carriage without a rug . . . you can choose between the two furs I have chosen from a hundred.'[14]

Although we have no records of Gambetta's shopping habits, photographs indicate his conformity to the fashions of the day: cravats, starched shirtfronts, and gentleman's dress coat.[15] Bourgeois men rarely shopped for themselves in this period, apart from the necessary visits to their tailors. Léon bought him presents like cufflinks, but his manservant probably took care of his shopping.

Neither Léon nor Gambetta was entirely comfortable with the vestimentary rules that prevailed in high society. Gambetta had been taken in hand by Juliette Adam at the beginning of his parliamentary career, when his breaches of the dress code, like his breaches of etiquette, were a source of amusement to the 'well-bred'.[16] The observant policeman thought Léon's clothes were 'flashy': 'she dresses like a streetwalker', he reported.[17] His comment reflects the contemporary anxiety to distinguish 'respectable' women, identified by their tasteful dress, from women of ill repute.[18] Léon adopted the fashion excesses essential for the courtesan, just as she crimped her hair in the latest style. Her fashion sense was shaped by the rules of sexual enticement, not the rules of elite decorum. Perhaps this was why she hesitated about purchasing a coat from the Louvre department store, which had a reputation for conservative and conformist style.[19]

Purchasing elaborate clothing played a particular role in the life of a courtesan, but it also allowed Léon to perform the first task that fell to all women as consumers in the nineteenth century, that of adorning themselves and marking their difference from men. Above all, Léon dressed to be attractive to Gambetta. She delayed her visit when awaiting a new outfit in May 1879, and warned Gambetta of a further delay if the weather proved unsuitable to wear it. 'It's an enormous matter to ensure that Sweetheart's eyes rest pleasantly on a harmonious outfit; one to which the greatest impatience of the heart must be sacrificed!'[20]

Flashy or not, Gambetta enjoyed Léon's sense of style. In early 1877, he looked forward to seeing the next creation produced by 'the wonders of your imagination and of Madame Tridon combined'. 'Tomorrow evening we'll make arrangements for this premiere and the apparition of this shimmering purple outfit', he wrote. Again, in 1879, he declared: 'I really want to tell you how beautiful and tender I found you yesterday, how divine and radiant in that exquisite apparition, in that diaphanous and fetching outfit which seemed to my eyes the image of the ideal flower picked for me in the Eden of our noblest love. I remained smitten the entire day, possessed by that intoxicating image.' He looked forward, also, to the pleasures of summer in 1880, with its 'many fine days, its beautiful, mad romps through the fields, its bright and sparkling outfits (*toilettes*) to have made and to wear'.[21] Léon sought his opinion on her hats when she was uncertain, and he had some favourites: 'Don't forget to bring the pretty green beret with the gold clover-leaves', he reminded her in 1882.[22]

Furnishing a home for the couple was the second task that fell to women as consumers. But while a mistress might decorate the apartment provided by her lover, only a legitimate wife decorated the couple's home.[23] It was a mark of Gambetta's devotion and serious intent that he assigned Léon that task. In 1879, Léon made a gift to Gambetta of a fashionable Minton vase, an English brand based on the style of Sèvres porcelain, along with a stand specially made to display it. Gambetta announced three weeks later: 'I have received the delightful pedestal for my beautiful Minton vase. It is exquisite, harmonious, simultaneously Parisian and oriental, I couldn't stop myself from lauding your good taste to François and it is understood that you will be specially charged with furnishing our next home.'[24]

In 1882, Léon would oversee the preparation of the house on the rue Saint-Didier expected to become their shared home. Once again, she would purchase some items direct from small manufacturers. 'Praux came to install the two lamps', Gambetta reported. '[They] are in charming taste and, like all your purchases, cost a mere song.' But Léon also took advantage of the range of goods provided by the department stores, which had become very popular sites for shopping by the 1880s.[25]

Léon favoured the 'Grands Magasins du Louvre' (generally shortened to the 'Louvre') over its competitors. It was located on the rue de Rivoli, just 300 metres (330 yards) from her apartment. She had only to cross the Seine via the Pont du Carrousel and continue across the courtyard of the Louvre Museum, where the pyramid stands today. It was very convenient, then, when she was looking for trim for her collar in 1874. But when she was shopping for household items in 1882, it had the added advantage of being quite luxurious, having undergone a massive two-year renovation from 1875. The Louvre's clientele was clearly bourgeois: unlike stores catering to working people, it sold expensive goods and did not extend credit. Léon bought a table, an easel (the painting to be displayed is not identified), and a set of curtains.[26]

Like bourgeois wives, Léon assumed responsibility for creating a domestic style that would reflect her own tastes and also please Gambetta. If she rejected the Louvre's conservative style in dress, such conservatism perhaps became a guarantee of good taste as she set out to create a suitable home for herself and Gambetta and to replicate a conventional bourgeois lifestyle. Léon took charge, outlining the delivery arrangements and instructing Gambetta on items to be returned. 'Each supplier has been reminded to be punctual', she added.[27]

Gambetta deferred to Léon's decisions: 'They came from the Louvre to hang the curtains', he wrote on 6 March. 'I am suspending judgement until your inspection. The fabric is very nice but Paul ! [sic] doesn't think they are very well hung.'[28] The choice of a cushioned footstool – a popular form of seating for women encumbered by crinolines – may have seemed particularly Léon's to make. In any case, Gambetta remained non-committal, reporting: 'I didn't choose anything but I encouraged [the young man from the Louvre], reserving the final word for your superior competence.' However, he did take the decision on the design for a stand to display a Greek terracotta figurine: a purchase that reflected his interest in antiquity.[29]

By this time, Léon was agonizing over her own earlier choice: 'I am tormented by the thought that a little column covered in plush would have been better under the [Minton] vase, what do you think?'[30] Her indecision attested to the array of choices available to the bourgeois homemaker in that burgeoning consumer society. With limited access to bourgeois homes where she might have seen other people's choices, Léon's task of creating a home appropriate for Gambetta's position was particularly difficult.

The pleasures of entertainment

Evenings at the theatre were a favourite leisure activity of the urban bourgeoisie in the 1870s. In 1874, there were forty theatres in central Paris.[31] Like other Parisians, Léon and Gambetta were always enthusiastic about going to the theatre. 'Come on Tuesday', Gambetta wrote to Léon in November 1878. 'I have the *baignoire* at the Gymnase. We will go without fail, one act. That will relax us without taking too much time.'[32]

Gambetta and Léon chose the Gymnase for its generally light-hearted and cheerful offerings. They chose a *baignoire* – a ground-floor box set back under the balcony and equipped with curtains – rather than a *loge* (a box in the circle), preferring seclusion to the self-display that characterized bourgeois theatre going.[33] This choice may have reflected their status as an illicit couple. In a *baignoire*, they were safe from prying eyes and, in Léon's case, from the prospect of being snubbed by 'respectable' women.

An evening at the theatre remained an overwhelmingly bourgeois experience. Seats were expensive; boxes even more so. To rent a loge for the season cost about 45 francs per week. The cheapest seats at the Opera cost roughly the daily wage of a male worker, and more than that of a female worker. Even at less prestigious theatres, like the Palais-Royal, the Gymnase and the Vaudeville, seats still cost five francs or more for the evening.[34]

The need to outfit oneself appropriately added to the expense. The dress code dictated formal dress for opening nights, though on 'ordinary evenings' a 'simple' dress, with a silk stole and an elaborate hat, might suffice.[35] Small wonder that Léon made many visits to the dressmaker and the milliner, and that she required plenty of time to dress for the theatre. Anticipating an evening at the Opéra-Comique to see Mozart's *Magic Flute* one Friday in May 1879, for instance, Léon wrote to Gambetta: 'There will be a lot of magic flutes in a single day! Yes, [I'll arrive] between 2.30 and 3 o'clock but I cannot walk in the woods dressed for the theatre, and you'll have to let me come back to change.' Gambetta replied: 'Come at 2.30, we'll go walking and you won't have to dress for the theatre because, as you already know from this morning's letter, that will be on Saturday. I am keeping you for two days.'[36]

The couple's tastes in both theatre and music were popular rather than highbrow, favouring comedy over tragedy. Gambetta detested the famous Hugo tragedy, *Hernani*, revived by the Comédie-Française in November 1877. 'I finished my evening at the play by Hugo', he wrote to Léon. 'Rarely have I seen a more puerile show. Fortunately there was a good actor, some great lines, and a good crowd. I know your holy horror of tragedy [*le drame*] and I am quite close to sharing it.' He promised to take her instead to 'the premiere of the Augier play' which was due to open: 'That will be more cheerful and more alive for there is nothing more sepulchral, more fossilized than this frenzied romanticism of 1830.' Indeed, Augier's *Les Fourchambault* – a comedy about marriage making, seduced young women, and illegitimate children – was a hit when it finally opened in April 1878. The *Annales du Théâtre* reported: 'Four performances per week are not enough to satisfy the impatient curiosity of the public, attracted to the booking office every day in large numbers by the fuss surrounding this new show.'[37]

Like most of the audience, Gambetta and Léon generally went to the theatre to be distracted from the worries of daily life. This was why they often chose the Théâtre du Gymnase for a night's entertainment. Since the 1840s it had been at the forefront in developing more natural acting and staging. Scenes were arranged to imitate life, and actors spoke to each other in a conversational style, rather than addressing the audience directly in the declamatory style that was the hallmark of the French classical tradition.[38]

The repertoire of the Gymnase in this period aimed to suit popular tastes, hence its preference for works on contemporary themes. According to journalist and critic Charles Monselet, it focused on 'the analysis of exceptional emotion'. It specialized in portraying 'the illicit, the shocking'; in presenting 'compromising situations, cold turpitude, calculated effrontery'. And its shows employed every available dramatic device to seize the imagination of the audience: 'Its comedies shrink neither from pistol shots, nor sobbing, nor agonies' of every kind, he wrote.[39]

The three one-act plays performed there in November 1878, when Gambetta invited Léon to join him in a *baignoire* for an evening, were exactly in this vein and were panned by the critics. Writing in Gambetta's *République Française*, Jean Bertrand condemned Henry Becque's 'The Shuttle' (*La Navette*) as a 'pornographic fantasy'. The *Annales du Théâtre* vowed to 'pass over it without stopping', but then stopped long enough to express disgust: 'It displays the morals of the gutter . . . The characters that *La Navette* presents have no names in polite language; we have to turn to the catechism of vulgarity [*catéchisme du poissard*] to find their vocabularies.' Bertrand condemned Edmond Gondinet's 'The Cascades' (*Les Cascades*), as a torrent of 'gutter slang'. Paul Parfait's 'The Captain's Boots' (*Les Bottes du Capitaine*) was inoffensive by comparison, dismissed simply as 'a banal vaudeville' by the *Annales*. Nevertheless, the audiences for these plays apparently enjoyed such titillating subject matter. While a number of shows at the Gymnase in 1878 survived only one or two performances, these were all performed more than twenty times.[40]

Above all, Gambetta and Léon enjoyed the Palais-Royal – the 'joyous theatre' in the words of theatre critic Émile Abraham – which specialized in lighthearted comedy. In the 1860s the Palais-Royal came to be renowned for its operettas, especially those that combined the talents of leading librettists Henri Meilhac and Ludovic Halévy with the music of Jacques Offenbach.[41] Meilhac and Halévy also wrote some highly popular comedies. Their four-act comedy 'The Debutante's Husband' (*Le Mari de la Débutante*), which premiered at the Palais-Royal on 5 February 1879, was a hit. It portrayed a young woman, won in a game of whist between rival suitors, who turned the tables on her petit-bourgeois husband by becoming an operetta star. Seats were hard to come by for weeks after it opened. It was 'hearty merriment', reported Juliette Adam, attracting absolutely everybody.[42] She asked Gambetta to obtain a ticket for her; he succeeded only on his third attempt.[43]

Three weeks after the premiere of 'The Debutante's Husband', Gambetta explained to Léon: 'Alas! We don't have a ticket for the Palais-Royal [tomorrow evening]. It's a fever, a crush of the rue Quincampoix, you have to put your name down well in advance. They've promised to keep our little corner for us on Tuesday.' If they did go on Tuesday, they went a second time the following Monday: 'I still expect you

Monday without fail, come and meet me [at Versailles] . . . We'll return arm in arm, and in the evening we'll go and laugh . . . [sic] at the Palais-Royal.'[44]

Outings to the Palais-Royal were always portrayed in their letters as opportunities to laugh: opportunities that took on different nuances with the fluctuations of political life. The sheer pleasure of 'The Debutante's Husband' suited Gambetta's cheerful optimism barely a fortnight after he had been installed as President of the Chamber of Deputies on 5 February 1879.

Laughter was also the remedy when the parliamentary contest was at its most difficult. The couple's outing to see the comedy 'M. Blondeau's Lodgers' (*Les Locataires de M. Blondeau*) in June 1879 was no doubt a moment of welcome relief after the tumultuous parliamentary sessions that preceded it, when the Right attacked Gambetta fiercely.[45] Having reported on the day's 'battle' on 17 June, Gambetta added: 'I will be at your place at 2.30 or 3. We will go strolling if the weather permits; in the evening, *baignoire*. We will go and laugh at the new show at the Palais-Royal.' After another day of 'incoherent tumult' in January 1880, they would 'go and laugh' at another comedy by Meilhac and Halévy, 'The Hot-Water Bottle' (*La Boule*). They enjoyed it so much that they saw it again in June.[46]

Many of these plays had in common not only their farcical style, but also their social themes. Marriage and its misadventures were frequently the source of their humour; perhaps not surprising at a time when arranged marriages were increasingly being challenged by love matches, and when the reintroduction of divorce was being hotly debated. In 'The Hot-Water Bottle', the errant husband who mistrusted his wife and sought a divorce finally came to his senses. 'The Debutante's Husband' parodied the vows of marriage and exposed its financial underpinnings by presenting it as a game of chance. The husband soon repented of his jealousy, consoling himself with his wife's wealth while she consoled herself with the Vicomte de Champ-d'Azur.[47]

So common was marriage as a subject for farce that farce became the ready referent for marriage. Gambetta used that analogy to describe a marriage ceremony to which he was invited in 1880: 'Yesterday I attended the civil marriage of [General] Gallifet's daughter . . . Such scenes are always captivating and when they are played in real life by actors from high society the show is quite delightful. The ceremony was well conducted by the Mayor, the audience was perfect for the civil contract that is so criticized and so little respected by [the play-wright] Victorien Sardou.' Sardou's hit of 1880, 'Let's Get Divorced!'

(*Divorçons!*), played for a record nine months without a break at the Palais-Royal, perhaps because it was topical; divorce was finally legalized in 1884.[48]

The couple also favoured lighthearted musical entertainment over serious works, just as they favoured lighthearted theatre. They found opera unappealing. In December 1880, Gambetta declined invitations to *Les Huguenots,* Meyerbeer's masterpiece, and *Comte Ory,* one of the ever-popular Rossini's two French operas.[49] Occasionally, though, he was forced to attend such events in his official capacity. He had to go alone because Léon was not his legal wife, and he went unwillingly, describing it as his 'forced labour [*corvée*]'. The re-opening of the Théâtre-Lyrique as a second venue for opera in 1876 was one such event. This gala evening was presided over by Mme MacMahon, wife of the President, and Gambetta was a guest of the Commission of Fine Arts. The programme featured *Dimitri,* a grand opera in five acts and seven scenes by Henri de Bornier, set in sixteenth-century Russia. Gambetta found the event quite tiresome. 'I couldn't stop yawning and left in the second act', he wrote to Léon.[50]

Of the operatic repertoire, only Mozart's *The Magic Flute,* with its comic and bawdy elements, appealed enough to make them desire to see it. Comic opera, which dispensed with sung dialogue, interspersing song with spoken dialogue instead, was more accessible. Gambetta apparently felt some obligation when he accepted an invitation to the Opéra-Comique in March 1882: 'I couldn't turn down Carvalho [the Director] a third time, that would have been too much', he wrote to Léon, who was reluctant to leave her sick dog. But the show, *Galante Aventure,* resembled the farces he so often enjoyed at the Palais-Royal: Captain Urbain de Bois-Baudry discovered, to his dismay, that the woman with whom he had had a nocturnal adventure was none other than his beloved fiancée Armande.[51]

Galante Aventure was well reviewed. And Marie Van Zandt was making a name for herself in Paris, even before her leading role in Delibes' opera *Lakmé* the following year.[52] Gambetta nevertheless gave Léon a very negative report of the evening: 'The show was extremely boring, and performed by the ugliest specimens of the strong sex. The little Van-Zandt . . . sings well, but that isn't enough to make me enjoy the theatre, the rest of the troupe is odious to see.' Gambetta seemed to fear that Léon might interpret his decision to go alone as an infidelity. He emphasized the ugliness of the largely male cast, and pointed out that his colleague Eugène Étienne had accompanied him to and from the show. In the same letter he offered an olive branch, foreshadowing an evening of vaudeville together: 'When [the dog] Fidès is up and about, we will take a real revenge at the Variétés and applaud *Lili* for all we're worth.'[53]

If their preference for comedy and farce was clear, both Gambetta and Léon occasionally ventured to a show that was well reviewed, even if it was not in their normal repertoire. Despite his dislike for *Hernani*, for instance, Gambetta decided to see another Hugo tragedy, *Ruy Blas*, which was a hit at the Comédie-Française in 1879. He wrote to Léon: 'In the evening we'll go to see and hear *Ruy Blas*. People are saying that the performances of the actors are marvellous and they are talking about an apotheosis like that of Voltaire for V[ictor] Hugo in the fifth act.'[54] Similarly, Léon's interest was piqued by rave reviews of the diva Adelina Patti, who toured with an Italian opera company in 1880. Patti was 'cheered ecstatically, called for an encore after each act' of Verdi's *La Traviata*, which opened on 14 February. 'Nothing but these performances was talked about in Paris for several months', according to one commentator. Gambetta promised to find out about the show for Léon, but whether they attended a performance we do not know.[55]

There was one form of serious theatre that Gambetta adored, however, and that was Molière, whose works formed part of his own library. Admiration for Molière took Gambetta and Léon to the Comédie-Française, France's most prestigious theatre company, which specialized in seventeenth-century classical drama in verse.[56] On 15 January 1878, they attended the annual celebration of Molière's birthday at the Comédie-Française. The programme featured a five-act play, *The Misanthropist*, sandwiched between *The Forced Marriage* (a one-act comedy-ballet), and *Les Précieuses Ridicules* (a one-act farce). Gambetta revelled in the 'divine language' of Molière's rhyming Alexandrine couplets: 'Two words in haste to embrace you, to thank you for the delightful evening yesterday. I savoured at my leisure the pleasure of listening to a divine language beside the most seductive, the most delicate, the most adorable woman of my day, and I really enjoyed the secret pleasure of being sole possessor of a treasure, without having to fight all the abductors [*ravisseurs*] of court and town for her, like Alceste [the hero of *The Misanthropist*].'[57]

Among other works of tragedy, the one play that the couple truly appreciated was Henri de Bornier's work, 'Roland's Daughter' (*La Fille de Roland*), which opened at the Comédie-Française on 15 February 1875.[58] 'Roland's Daughter' was immensely popular, thanks partly to its renowned cast: Sarah Bernhardt – 'the extraordinary Sarah', as Léon described her – played the lead to great acclaim opposite

Mounet-Sully, the pre-eminent male actor of the day.[59] The subject of the play was also riveting for Gambetta and Léon – indeed for the entire audience. It was based on a medieval poem, 'The Song of Roland', which depicted events in the reign of Charlemagne. Republished in a new translation in 1872, 'The Song of Roland' began to make its way into republican iconography, thanks to the efforts of Ernest Lavisse and Jules Michelet.[60]

'The Song of Roland' had particular resonance in the context of the recent Franco-Prussian war as a study of treachery and honour. Reviewing the premiere in the *Petit Journal,* Thomas Grimm stated: 'the public has only wanted to see and has only seen the indignant protest of the poet against traitors to the fatherland'. As the character Ganelon confessed, 'I have sinned. I have betrayed my country to destroy those I envied; and I had no remorse', the names of suspected traitors of 1870 were being muttered in the audience.[61]

'Roland's Daughter' no doubt summoned up echoes of Gambetta's own efforts in 1870 to defend national honour. He read the play, and praised its patriotic themes to Juliette Adam, inviting her to share a *loge* presented to the *Republique Française*.[62] Gambetta probably took a discreet *baignoire* to see it with Léon. They were both deeply moved: 'Who is the sceptic', Léon wrote to Gambetta, 'who denies that one can be stirred by Roland? Were we not quivering and sobbing proofs to the contrary, thanks to M. de Bornier?' They were not alone. Grimm's review – which was the paper's lead story the morning after the premiere – quoted the lines that most moved the audience: 'Oh France! Sweet France! Oh my blessed France! Nothing will exhaust your strength and your genius!' Grimm noted: 'This public that people claim is devoted and even addicted to operetta and parody, gave free flow to its patriotic emotion.'[63]

La Fille de Roland was 'serious' theatre. It met the criterion that republican theatre should be morally uplifting, an argument defended in the pages of Gambetta's own *République française*: 'The true theatre with which the Republic must concern itself is that which inspires heroic thoughts, generous sentiments, in the people, that which celebrates the great moments of our national history, or which . . . sets in motion noble examples or fertile lessons.'[64] But 'serious' theatre was not always what was required. As this report also noted: 'We will certainly not proscribe theatre where one laughs, where one sings, where one dances: all forms of art have a right to their free expression.' Gambetta and Léon certainly loved theatre 'which inspire[d] heroic thoughts'. They wept at tragedy and were uplifted by stories of heroism. More often than not, however, they went to the theatre simply to laugh and enjoy themselves.

The pleasures of nature

The city offered thrills and excitement, but the stresses and strains of urban life were believed to cause exhaustion and ill health. The restorative powers of 'nature' were seen as the cure, health benefits adding moral justification to the sheer pleasure of immersing oneself in the natural environment. The city's parks and gardens provided a domesticated experience of nature for urban dwellers. If the boulevards of Paris had become 'outdoor salons', its parks had become 'green boulevards', attracting the crowds too.[65] Like many others, Gambetta and Léon enjoyed strolling in the city's green spaces. The gardens of the Tuileries Palace were just across the river from Léon's apartment on the rue Bonaparte. She loved to 'take the air' there, as the elites had done since Louis XIV first opened them to the public, and as the popular classes had done since the French Revolution.[66]

The Tuileries Gardens had been designed by Louis XIV's landscape architect, André Le Nôtre. He had also designed the gardens of the former Palace at Saint-Cloud, 12 kilometres (7.5 miles) west of Paris, where Gambetta sometimes went walking.[67] Orderly, symmetrical and manicured, these 'French' gardens allowed visitors to enjoy their splendour only from the confines of well-kept paths. But Gambetta and Léon also adored the more romantic 'English' gardens, which came into vogue in the eighteenth century. 'English' gardens offered an array of different pleasures, with their dense plantations, ponds, pavilions, temples and ruins.

Most famous of Paris' 'English' gardens was the Bois de Boulogne. Napoleon III and Haussmann had transformed this arid expanse, once famous only for 'duelling and suicides' according to a guide book of the day, into Paris' equivalent of London's Hyde Park.[68] The Emperor personally oversaw the construction of its lakes, grottoes, and waterfalls, its carriageways and walking paths, which were so extensive that Gambetta was able to take 'a five-hour promenade on foot' there in November 1879.[69] It had the added advantage that Gambetta and Léon could enjoy the pleasures of this 'countryside' without leaving the city; they could even take refreshments, city-style, in its cafés and restaurants.

Excursions to nearby forests offered the illusion of encountering nature in all its wildness and glory. Gambetta and Léon shared the popular taste for such excursions, embracing the beneficial pleasures of walks in the forest as relief from the stresses of urban life. In the early years of their relationship, Léon's responsibility for her son limited her freedom of action. Similarly, Gambetta's exhausting electoral campaigns, his constant rounds of public meetings, and the demands of the parliamentary schedule limited his availability for rural adventures.

In later years the couple had considerable freedom of action, particularly during parliamentary recesses. They were able to take excursions during the week, rather than joining the Sunday crush. They enjoyed 'wandering under the oaks, glistening in their spring foliage'. In summer, they found refuge from the heat in some 'cool and shady place' in the forest; 'in an adorable wood perfumed with honeysuckle, heather and eglantine!'[70] As winter approached, Gambetta encouraged Léon to 'take advantage of the sun'. 'Remember especially that [it] is going to become more and more rare, more and more miserly with its favours', he wrote in October 1874, 'let's profit from the last fine days and go and mock the stupidities of the septennialists [the monarchists who wanted a seven-year term for the president] among the bushes of Fontainebleau'.[71]

Léon and Gambetta savoured the forest as a place of beauty and grandeur: a sensibility evoked by the romantics of the late eighteenth and early nineteenth centuries. But they also found it an emotional refuge, a place of escape from the pressures of politics and daily life. This vision of the forest reflected the new environmental sensibilities emerging in the mid nineteenth century. It inspired those arguing for forest preservation, as well as painters and writers, all of whom emphasized the spiritual rejuvenation that the forest offered.[72]

For Gambetta, walking in the woods, strolling under the oaks, seizing the chance 'to roam, to forget, to love', provided a restorative to the political pressures that weighed on him. With Léon by his side, a visit to the forest assured his revival. He wrote to her in 1877: 'You know very well that you are my joy, my strength, the constant renewal, the eternal spring of my life. What a beautiful day, how readily one can forget external events with you and savour only the pleasure. We will return under these great trees, in the green solitude that you love, that you fill simply by the radiance of your grace.' 'I am going to try to free myself on Tuesday', he wrote again in 1879, 'so that we can go and find in the woods those delightful sanctuaries where the beauty of my goddess seems more triumphant, more luminous than in our cold corridors [*galeries*].'[73]

Gambetta and Léon visited a number of the forests on the outskirts of Paris. The forest of Meudon was only 4 kilometres (2.5 miles) from the city, making it possible to 'roam under [its] fragrant foliage' and return to Paris for an evening at the theatre. Gambetta went walking alone in the forest near Argenteuil, 15 kilometres (9 miles) north west of Paris. But in doing so he recalled an earlier visit to Argenteuil with Léon, and 'that pretty Pointu that we climbed together'.[74] The couple also explored the former royal hunting forest of Saint-Germain-en-Laye, about 20 kilometres (12.4 miles) west of Paris: 'I will collect you at rue Bonaparte', Gambetta wrote in August 1876. 'We will leave straight away for Saint-Germain, so that we can take a nice excursion in the forest . . . Prepare for the heat of four in the afternoon.'[75]

On this occasion, they had a carriage accident. 'I am black and blue but happy to know that you are better', wrote Gambetta two days later. 'I spent the day stretched out on my bed, anointing myself with camphorated alcohol and other remedies . . . I am looking after myself in order to put back together these pieces which, after medical investigation, seem serviceable for some time to come.' Léon replied the following day: 'I too am on my bed very injured also, the foot is less swollen but covered in bruises.'[76] For days afterwards they were reporting on the healing of injured ankles and knees.

Enjoying nature became an essential part of the modern metropolitan lifestyle in the nineteenth century, but 'nature' was often carefully constructed to profit from city-dwellers' desire for escape and to minimize the dangers they might face.[77] This was certainly true of the forest of Fontainebleau, 60 kilometres (37 miles) south-west of Paris. Fontainebleau was the most popular site for the urban encounter with nature; it was also Gambetta and Léon's favourite walking spot. Formerly the greatest of the royal hunting forests, its 18,000 hectares (45,500 acres) of woods had attracted the Romantic poets of the early nineteenth century, as well as the new school of landscape painters, who based themselves at nearby Barbizon in the 1840s. These creative spirits imagined the ancient oaks of Fontainebleau as a remnant of France's distant past as the land of the Gauls. Théodore Rousseau, a Barbizon painter whom Gambetta admired, lauded Fontainebleau as 'the only living souvenir that remains of the heroic times of the Motherland from Charlemagne to Napoleon'.[78]

Little more than an hour from Paris by train, Fontainebleau became accessible to those unable to afford a private carriage when cheap excursion fares were introduced in 1850, and it became a regular Sunday tourist spot for the multitudes. Fontainebleau's popularity, however, was not spontaneous. It was actively assisted by Claude-François Denecourt, whose guidebooks charted forest walks for eager readers and whose promotional works advertised its attractions. His guidebooks were the first to outline detailed walking trails, which he then signposted in the forest using colour-coded arrows. Gambetta and Léon benefited from these guides. 'It is agreed that we will go and visit our beautiful rocks at Fontainebleau on Tuesday', Gambetta wrote in 1877, 'to recall our sweet and tender impressions of the fairy pond and the little amphitheatre of old druidic oaks.' The Fairy Pond and a majestic old oak named Clovis (after the first Christian king of the Franks) featured on Denecourt's 'red' walk.[79] On each of his five walks, Denecourt identified and named features like these, directing visitors to particular sites, establishing the meaning of what they saw, and constructing a romantic Fontainebleau for them.[80]

Denecourt's guidebooks built on the tradition that associated Fontainebleau with the ancient Gauls. The walks he outlined had their natural features named for Dryads and Druids, as well as for the historical figures of the ancient past, Vercingetorix and Veleda. But Denecourt accentuated the Gallic link by altering the landscape. He excavated caves to turn them into 'grottoes' and cultivated mosses to add to the romantic effect. The 'Druid's Cavern' – one of the highlights of the Gorges de Franchard on the green walk – was manufactured in this way.[81] Gambetta himself invested Fontainebleau with mystical significance, exactly as Denecourt intended. After returning by train from Nice to Paris, he wrote to Léon: 'When I travelled through the forest of Fontainebleau I achieved the sublime hallucination and I tasted with the vividness of reality the most intoxicating sensations that I have experienced under the great oaks of the valley of the druids.'[82] Despite the souvenir stalls and cafés that had mushroomed at Fontainebleau by this time, Gambetta chose to remember it as a magical place that had particular significance in his love affair with Léon.

Forest streams offered Gambetta the opportunity to go fishing. He would share his catch with Léon, although she drew the line at eel: 'Eel leave me cold; I prefer them under their rocks.'[83] Gambetta also took advantage of the increasing democratization of the formerly aristocratic privilege of hunting, a pleasure he shared with male friends and colleagues. Sometimes he only caught cold, but when the hunt was successful, he sent Léon 'the first fruits of his bag', the pheasant and rabbit which were plentiful in the forests around Paris.[84] Gambetta liked to think of himself as king of the hunt, but noted in September 1880 that his form had declined. 'After a long day's hunting and walking', he wrote from Forges, ' I returned to the abode, without having too large a number of victims on my conscience. I didn't have last year's success, I saw myself reduced to second place and my conqueror is indeed the most intrepid old man of the nineteenth century; it's M. Fd [Ferdinand] de Lesseps himself [engineer of the Suez Canal]. He shoots like Saint Hubert [the patron saint of hunters] and seems to have thunderbolts in his fingertips.'[85]

Purchasing a country house at Ville-d'Avray in August 1878 was the culmination of the couple's embrace of nature and the outdoors.[86] Holidaying in picturesque villages had become fashionable for the bourgeoisie, and the word *villégiaturer* was coined in 1860 to describe the practice.[87] Acquiring country houses not only enabled the urban bourgeois to follow in the footsteps of the landed aristocracy, but also became a new Parisian way of enjoying nature. Properties were marketed for their views and panoramas, their gardens and greenery, and for the private encounter with nature's pleasures that they offered.[88]

Gambetta and Léon knew the village of Ville-d'Avray from their carriage rides back to Paris from Versailles. Ville-d'Avray was half way on the most direct path, and hence a logical place to stop and take refreshment. The village was surrounded by forests, making it ideal for a couple who loved walking. Moreover, the train from Paris to Versailles stopped at Ville-d'Avray, putting it only half an hour from Paris by that route. And the house they found there was perfectly located, only a three-minute walk from the station and 300 metres (330 yards) from the edge of the forest.

Gambetta first rented a small house in Ville-d'Avray, perhaps (as his coachman recalled) 'on the advice of the doctors his friends Testelin and Nord'. Gambetta first mentioned Ville-d'Avray in July 1878, inviting Léon to join him the following evening: 'tomorrow . . . we will *dine in Paris* and . . . we will leave for Ville-d'Avray until Monday (travel by night and without the moon)'. Gambetta purchased les Jardies a few weeks later.[89]

Les Jardies had formerly been the country retreat of the author Honoré de Balzac, who lived there from 1837 to 1840 and gave it its name. Gambetta initially acquired only a small portion of that property, with a modest seventeenth-century dwelling that had housed Balzac's gardener. Gambetta and Léon made this house their 'nest' and Gambetta subsequently enlarged his property several times, acquiring the remainder of Balzac's former estate and the house he had lived in, in 1882 (Figure 5.1).[90]

Les Jardies provided Gambetta and Léon with a secluded haven, a 'sweet nest'. Its romance, as well as its solitude, had been one of its selling points. Alone there in July 1878, Gambetta described to Léon 'ris[ing] as quickly as possible to roam in the woods and find the places chosen for our next walks': 'How I love the pleasures – new for me – of

Figure 5.1 Les Jardies: Gambetta and Léon's country house, 1884 (Edmond Marie Petitjean, *Les Jardies, maison de Gambetta à Sèvres*, oil on canvas, 10 January 1884; Collection Musée de l'Île-de-France, Sceaux. Photo: Pascal Lemaître)

solitude, this great and beneficial silence, these wonderful wooded refuges, these calm and sleepy waters at the foot of perfumed heaths, and above all the voluptuousness of reflecting, of thinking, of meditating at one's ease, without hubbub and recriminations from outside!'[91]

From their 'nest' at Ville-d'Avray, the couple could wander across the countryside with their dogs, picking lily of the valley and hyacinth in the fields and meadows. In the woodlands surrounding the cottage they could enjoy the sylvan pleasures otherwise provided by visits to forests like Fontainebleau. A year after purchasing the cottage, Gambetta wrote from les Jardies: 'This morning I recommenced my walks in the woods, under a splendid sun which gleamed through the branches as though through the immense arches of a never-ending and limitless Gothic Church.'[92]

At les Jardies, Léon and Gambetta also shared the contemporary passion for gardening. Their property did not boast a greenhouse, as many did, but it nevertheless offered the leisure space and sensory delights of a floral garden.[93] Gambetta was proud of helping to design it, likening his gardener to the creator of the Tuileries Garden. Apologizing one day for being late with his letter, he noted that 'my gardener, my architect, my Le Nôtre in fact, has kept my head in the plans since this morning, and I have just left him quite delighted with his combinations and my own'.[94]

Léon had grown to love the garden at Fontenay-aux-Roses, where she lived with her mother and son from 1875 to 1879. As she and Gambetta recovered from their carriage accident in August 1876, she had written to him: 'This morning I was able to drag myself into the garden; the storm has made everything green again and I noted with infinite regret that all my *belles de nuit* are red and opening without perfume; so the pleasure of getting you to breathe the scent of this intoxicating flower is delayed until next year, that's a very long settlement date for such a pleasure!'[95]

The couple's enjoyment of les Jardies was enhanced by sharing a garden of their own. 'We will go and water our roses, watch our seeds sprouting, and plant more of them', Gambetta wrote on the eve of a visit there.[96] But the garden also provided rich metaphors of love with which both delighted in adorning their letters. 'Despite the tin-grey sky, the forget-me-nots and hawthorn are flowering', Léon wrote in 1879. 'I'm sending them to my Sweetheart with all the flowers of my soul which blossom in the burning sun of his tenderness.' Gambetta likewise found in the lushness of the garden an evocation of the mysteries and pleasures of their love: 'I will show you a tree in the garden, more sacred, more prophetic than those which once made famous the garden of Dodona' where, in ancient times, an oracle was believed to speak in the rustling of the oak leaves.[97] In their own 'sweet nest' with its verdant surrounds and floral delights, the romance of the forest was domesticated as a private experience for this urban couple.

Bourg-la-Reine, Thursday [1872?][1]

Dear Léon,

So who realized why I was standing mysteriously at the door of [the Assembly], the Temple of that divinity which contends with me for your heart???? [sic] *By what right, my beloved, would I display ill will because of your lateness; have I not given you absolution in advance, for all the delays caused by politics; and, besides, don't I owe you many indulgences for having given my life, hitherto empty and monotonous, the passionate interest in admiring you and cherishing you [which enables me] to pardon you with all my heart for having made me spend a boring evening?*

If I didn't write to you yesterday when I arrived, it's your fault, or at least the fault of the book you lent me. When one finds oneself in touch with the memory of that infinitely gracious creature who possessed to such a high degree the precious gift of pleasing and of being loved, it is impossible to detach oneself from it before having exhausted the account of her pure and steadfast friendships. Your note of this morning, a touching attention, which was appreciated as it deserved, and what you had told me the previous day of your situation had completely reassured me. I await without anxiety the hour of battle; hoping that the master [Thiers] has finally understood that you alone can offer him serious support; and persuaded that the obstacles which your enemies plant on your road will be for you new opportunities to demonstrate your great political astuteness, the strength of the party which you dominate, and the justice of the cause you defend.

What a beautiful and noble nature this M. Renouard [a republican politician] must be; here is eloquence worthy of serving your cause. Would he not be an excellent minister of justice? Is it true that changes in the ministry are afoot?

I don't know anything about my return to Paris. I know only that all the hours spent far from you are centuries of discouragement and suffering.

See you soon, my dear ray of happiness; tell me of your health.

I am always yours

Léonie

6
'We will proudly put our heads together in books'

Léon and Gambetta enjoyed sharing the delights of urban living and the pleasures of the outdoors. But their life together was also shaped by their interest in intellectual and cultural pursuits. They enjoyed visiting museums and galleries, together and separately. They had strong views on art, so their visits to the Salon, the annual art exhibition hosted by the Academy of Fine Arts, provided opportunities for both pleasure and criticism. Léon also attended lectures at the French Academy, a sign of her intellectual curiosity.

Above all, however, Gambetta and Léon enjoyed books and reading. They reported in their letters on books they had read or wanted to read, on books borrowed from each other, on books advertised and serialized, on books to be disposed of and books newly acquired. Their letters stand as testimony to the intensifying 'mass culture of print', as reading became more deeply embedded in French society and as 'the industrialization of the book' made books cheaper and more readily available.[2]

'I dream of bibliomania'

The pleasure that both Gambetta and Léon derived from reading reflected their social backgrounds. If French peasants and workers became universally literate during the nineteenth century, Gambetta's 'new social stratum' – the aspirational bourgeoisie from which they both came – became increasingly educated. Education, for men, was one passport to bourgeois status, as Gambetta's rise from shopkeeper's son to lawyer and politician attested. Ownership of books reinforced that status. Education did not open doors to the professional bourgeoisie for women in the 1870s. It might provide a better class of husband, but it might also (as in Léon's case) provide entry to the ranks of the courtesans.[3] The ability to converse intelligently on diverse subjects was essential for a courtesan, but that alone does not account for the deep interest in books and reading that is evident in Léon's correspondence.

Léon claimed to possess 'a curious, enquiring mind which, if it were free of worries, would wander at leisure through the vast fields of the arts and literature'.[4] An avid reader with broad literary tastes, she found in 'the arts and literature' an absorbing set of interests. Reading was the iconic pastime for bourgeois women in the late nineteenth century. The image of the woman reader, someone with the time and leisure for intellectual pursuits, even served as one marker of social status in many paintings of the day.[5] In Léon's case, reading was ideal for filling periods of separation from Gambetta. But the letters between Léon and Gambetta confirm that he was a great reader also; he even kept notes on his reading.[6] The couple's mutual enjoyment of books and reading was yet another link reinforcing and expressing their love.

Léon suggested that her own collection of books – 'what I glorify with the title of library' – was small. She burned the collection of military books inherited from her father after inviting Gambetta to take any that interested him. At the time of her death in 1906, however, she owned a modest personal library. Two sets of bookshelves in her bedroom contained 'about 600 bound volumes – history, literature, novels'. Another eighty volumes of memoirs and history were shelved in a second bedroom.[7] Unfortunately, the titles of these volumes were not recorded.

The lovers began to share books almost immediately their relationship began. 'If I didn't write to you yesterday on arriving home it's your fault, or at least that of the book you lent me', Léon wrote in an early letter. She found it 'impossible to tear [her]self away' from it.[8] She and Gambetta continued to exchange books throughout their relationship, sometimes organizing the process by letter. 'I will bring back the book, with a recommendation to keep the next volume for me', Léon noted on one occasion. 'Don't forget the second [volume of] Panizzi', she reminded him on another.[9]

Gambetta wrote to Léon in 1875: 'I dream of bibliomania, we will proudly put our heads together in books [*bouquiner*]'.[10] But since each knew what the other was reading, they did not need to name those books in their letters. Only rarely did they leave clues to the specific volumes. In 1881, for instance, Léon simply asked: 'what time [tomorrow]? We will finish the Mérimée and then what?' It seems likely that they had been reading Mérimée's recently published letters to Antonio Panizzi, since Gambetta recommended them a week later to the Marquise Arconati-Visconti: 'they are charming, very witty, full of depth'.[11]

The literary tastes of Gambetta and Léon owed a great deal to their education and background. The lovers' familiarity with the cultures of ancient Greece and Rome, cultures revered as pinnacles of Western civilization, reflected their bourgeois status. Works of the admired authors of antiquity dominated the education of bourgeois boys. They encountered the great myths of Western culture by reading Homer's *Iliad* and *Odyssey* and Virgil's *Aeneid*.[12] Gambetta's library included works on Roman history, and a copy of Julius Caesar's *Commentaries on the Gallic and Civil Wars*, which he had studied for the baccalaureate in 1856.[13] His letters are sprinkled with references to historical figures like Caesar and Decius, to Homer and the *Odyssey*, and to many myths and mythological characters.[14] Friends later recalled him declaiming Cicero's third Catiline oration over dinner when he was a student, or reading Aristophanes' comedy, *The Clouds*, in Greek.[15] His enjoyment of the writers of antiquity remained with him for life.

Léon did not have Gambetta's systematic introduction to the ancient world, but she knew the myths and legends of the Greek and Roman worlds along with some ancient history. The little 'summary of mythology' produced by the Louvencourt Sisters for their pupils provided an introduction to that world: it outlined the major and minor gods and their roles, the main characters in ancient fables, and the leading figures in Homer's account of the Trojan Wars. Perhaps Léon had also encountered some of the collections of extracts specifically intended to introduce female readers to Homer, Herodotus and Aristotle.[16] Her references to the ancient world are brief and schematic, mainly likening Gambetta to gods and mythical heroes like Ulysses, Jupiter and Oedipus, or likening herself to Penelope, Homer's heroine.[17] But her intent was not to demonstrate great erudition; rather, she drew on a common fount of classical references in order to cement her relationship with Gambetta. The literature of antiquity, with its accounts of heroes and goddesses, offered a language through which the couple could express their devotion to each other.

The letters also demonstrate that Gambetta had received a broader and more systematic education in classical French literature than Léon. Without knowing the titles of her 680 volumes, the scope of Léon's reading in the French classics remains uncertain. She cited Blaise Pascal, regarded as one of the greatest thinkers of the seventeenth century, and she certainly read Rousseau's *La Nouvelle Héloïse*, a novel that retained its great popularity into the nineteenth century.[18] When Léon quoted the French classics in her letters, however, she generally appealed to the sorts of works that were extracted in collections. In her first letter to Gambetta, declaring her love but trying not to frighten him away, she quoted the *Reflections* of La Rochefoucauld: 'We can no more account for the duration of our sentiments than for that of our life.' On other occasions she cited La Fontaine's *Fables*, pithy 'maxims' by Vauvenargues, and verse by Benserade: all were well known authors in her day.[19]

In contrast, Gambetta's education had immersed him in the French classics.[20] He owned many works by the major French authors of the sixteenth and seventeenth centuries: Montaigne, Racine, La Fontaine, Bossuet, Rabelais, Molière and Pascal. He often referred to them in his letters, along with other classics like Alexander Pope's *Rape of the Lock*, and Tasso's *Jerusalem Delivered*.[21]

Gambetta also owned works by the renowned 'enlightenment' figures Rousseau, Voltaire and Diderot. At a society dinner, he reputedly recited passages from Voltaire's *Candide*, and declared Diderot the 'true leader' of the movement. Whilst travelling to Nice in January 1874, Gambetta read 'the magnificent preface by d'Alembert to the Encyclopedia dictionary'. 'It is a very beautiful philosophy, humane and rational', he wrote to Léon, 'expressed in admirable language that resembles the profundity of Blaise Pascal, with the clarity of Voltaire, and the gracious and mocking half-smile just right for [d'Alembert,] the person who so loved Madame de Lespinasse.'[22]

Gambetta was particularly familiar with the works of Molière, whose plays he loved to read as much as he loved to see them in the theatre. The humorous and clever verse of Molière's farces delighted him, enabling him to send up delicate or ridiculous situations. Considering the stance that France should adopt in response to friction among the major powers in 1875, for instance, Gambetta suggested: 'Our role is to be everybody's friend, like Molière's Sosie [the servant in Molière's *Amphitryon*], free in our movements, and ultimately deferring the final clash for as long as possible.' Again, considering the international situation in 1878, he was reminded of Molière's most famous play, *The Bourgeois Gentleman*. In one renowned scene, the philosophy teacher takes a declaration of love – 'Beautiful Countess, your wonderful eyes make me die for love' – and searches for effect by playing with the word order. Gambetta likened this farcical moment to diplomatic exchanges: 'It's always the same telegram people send from every point in Europe, with variations, like the famous phrase of the grammar master in *The Bourgeois Gentleman*.'[23]

'These Academic delights'

Léon's interest in literature may have sparked her regular attendance, well before she met Gambetta, at the public lectures of the French

Academy. Founded in 1635, the Academy is made up of the forty most prestigious living authors, who are elected by their peers and wear distinctive gold-braided green jackets. In the nineteenth century, lectures at the Academy were major society events frequented by the elite. Women attended in large numbers and played a key role in sponsoring candidates, although they themselves, as women, could not be elected to the Academy.[24]

How did Léon gain access to this exclusive gathering? Perhaps her entrée came originally through Hyrvoix. Perhaps she attended the Academy as a courtesan, hoping to meet potential clients. In the early 1870s, Léon's sister Émilie attended the Academy of Fine Arts, another of the five academies which comprise the Institut de France. Léon substituted for her sister at one of their meetings in November 1873.[25]

The lectures at the Academy may have been society events, but they also addressed serious literary and cultural topics. Information about Léon's visits to the Academy is patchy, but the subjects of a number of the lectures, and the identities of those delivering them, are likely to have appealed to her. Perhaps she was interested, for instance, in hearing Emile Littré's address to the Academy at his reception on 5 June 1873, given his prominence as editor of the great dictionary that bears his name. The reception on 8 January 1874 of Louis de Loménie, successor to the Romantic novelist Prosper Mérimée, saw a discussion of the merits of Mérimée as a writer. Since Léon had recently been reading Mérimée, she would certainly have been interested in that event.[26]

Léon scheduled her time with Gambetta to accommodate her visits to the Academy. Gambetta asked about her plans to attend the Academy in his first letter, as he tried to arrange to see her again. And she explained to him in an early letter why she would see him only on Monday the following week:

> There will be meetings of the Institut on Wednesday and Friday; it is absolutely essential that one of us [Léonie or her sister Émilie] attend, and I admit that I won't ever have the courage to renounce an hour of your divine company to fulfil this intellectual duty. I will return to the country on Tuesday for dinner, and my sister will come as soon as I return to plunge herself into these academic delights.[27]

If Léon was keen to reassure Gambetta in this early letter that she would not put the Academy before him, she was less adamant in 1873: 'I cannot promise the whole day Thursday', she wrote in September, 'the Academy is on and I may have to go and spend an hour there.' But when she stood in for her sister at the Academy of Fine Arts in November, she was glad of the opportunity afforded by her extra visit to Paris, for she also found time to 'talk politics at our leisure' with Gambetta.[28]

Léon's dedication to attending the Academy became a subject of repartee between the couple: 'And the Academy?' Gambetta asked late in 1874. 'I see that you quite enjoyed yourself under the dome . . . Did you miss me even for one minute amongst all those green-suited idlers?'[29] Sometimes the speeches Léon heard there were highly amusing and she shared the joke with Gambetta. The reception to the Academy in 1875 of the novelist and playwright, Alexandre Dumas *fils*, was one such moment. The reply was delivered by the comte d'Haussonville, embodiment of good breeding and political conservatism, with several multi-volume works of serious history to his credit. His speech was filled with irony as he welcomed this author of potboilers to the intellectual elite. 'There are entire passages of some of your comedies', said Haussonville, 'where, from the stalls or the boxes, the spectators could if necessary prompt the actors.' This was a compliment about Dumas' popularity, but also a suggestion that his work was vulgar; that he was popular among the ignorant. Gambetta wrote that evening: 'Did you enjoy yourself at the Academy? Haussonville's speech seems exquisite and merciless. We'll read it together on Saturday.'[30]

'I've been reading novels'

As well as reading the classics, Gambetta and Léon read a variety of contemporary works. In some respects, their reading preferences echoed the gender stereotypes that differentiated between works suitable for men and for women. But Gambetta and Léon often confounded the stereotypes. While they did not necessarily share identical tastes in literature, their reading often overlapped, enabling them to exchange reactions and literary allusions.

The lovers shared an admiration for Victor Hugo, the grand old man of republicanism, regarded by many as the greatest poet of the century. Léon adored the 'sublime lines' of Hugo's celebrated attack on the Empire, *Châtiments*, quoting them to Gambetta.[31] Gambetta was not always a fan of Hugo, as his reaction to Hugo's *Hernani* suggests. But he admired Hugo's epic poem, *La Légende des Siècles*, which depicted humanity's moral and spiritual evolution from the Garden of Eden to the present and beyond. Sent a copy of part two by the author when it appeared in 1877, Gambetta responded: 'I received it, I read it, I lived it. I don't want to add another word to this: I admire and adore

Hugo!'[32] Indeed, he placed a portrait of Hugo in the dining room at Ville-d'Avray.[33]

Léon quoted the Romantic poets Alfred de Musset and Alphonse de Lamartine in letters to Gambetta.[34] But if their sentimentality and emotional tenor appealed to her more than to Gambetta, she quoted without giving the source, confident that Gambetta had read them and would recognize her references. She quoted Lamartine's lines on the beauty of Sorrento, for instance, believing that he would share her nostalgia for a place they had visited.[35] The wistfulness of the Romantics seemed, to Léon, particularly appropriate amid the political frustrations that beset Gambetta during 1881. 'Till tomorrow then', she signed a February letter, 'I am returning to Musset to savour those disappointments that used to move me.'[36] Musset's disappointments, she implied, were as nothing compared to those she now shared with Gambetta.

The couple also read a diverse range of published correspondence and memoirs, which were popular reading at the time. The memoirs of the duc de Gramont, in Léon's acerbic evaluation, revealed only the 'superficiality' of the eighteenth century. Those of Prince von Metternich, one of the most important European statesmen of the early nineteenth century, were of greater interest and Léon passed them on to Gambetta. Occasionally, too, the couple's interest in a work may have been sparked by its author rather than its subject matter. This may have been the attraction of Abel-François Villemain's *History of Gregory VII*, the Pope renowned as the defender of Papal supremacy. The work was published posthumously by Villemain's daughter, Geneviève, wife of Gambetta's friend and colleague, Henri Allain-Targé.[37]

Léon had a particular interest in the memoirs of society women and salon hostesses. Frustrated by her inability to fulfill her own 'aspirations in society and politics', she perhaps enjoyed reading about other women who were more successful.[38] She suggested to Gambetta, for instance, that they read together the biography of the courtesan, Fortunée Hamelin, friend of Napoleon I and the Empress Josephine. She 'absorbed' the memoirs of Mme de Rémusat, former lady-in-waiting to the Empress Josephine, which were serialized by the *Revue des Deux Mondes* in 1879, and she admired those of Mme Vigée-Lebrun, the eighteenth-century painter.[39]

Léon took particular delight in the *Souvenirs* of Caroline Jaubert, published in 1881. They helped her to 'forget [her] neuralgia and everything else!' Jaubert, born into the high society of the First Empire, ran a salon attended by such figures as the duc de Morny, the socialist Louis Blanc, and the poet Alfred de Musset. Her memoirs, filled with anecdotes about such famous writers and political figures, proved irresistible: 'Thank you for the book', she wrote to Gambetta, but 'I am enjoying Madame Jaubert too much to put it down before completely finishing it.'[40]

Memoirs, as a genre, offered a glimpse into the recent past, shaped by events and identities that were still familiar. Gambetta enjoyed them too. He had by his bed in 1877 a book by Marie d'Agoult, author, historian, salon hostess, lover of Franz Liszt and mother of Cosima Wagner. It was probably her *Souvenirs*, which had just appeared, and which recounted both her own personal history and the dramatic political developments in France from the Restoration to 1848.[41]

The publishing vogue for such memoirs demonstrates their broad popularity as a genre. They chronicled a period and a career, rather than being works of personal introspection and self-exploration.[42] Memoirs were usually 'a good read', too, revealing the secrets of the rich and powerful. The memoirs of writer and salon hostess Hortense Allart, for instance, which Léon read in 1873, provoked a scandal by discussing her affair with the celebrated Catholic poet François René de Chateaubriand.[43] In reading such works, Léon and Gambetta shared the curiosity and literary tastes of the age.

The couple's interest in novels and newspapers – the mass-marketing successes of their day – identified them as 'modern' readers. Indeed, Léon's taste for reading novels, and novels serialized in newspapers, marked her as a modern *female* reader by the standards of the day, since women's emotional nature was believed to attract them to this form of fiction. Serials, in particular, were aimed primarily at a female readership. But while women did form an important segment of the market for novels, and hence an important target group for authors, the fan mail sent to authors indicates significant male readership of novels as well.[44]

Gambetta was one such male reader. He had read the eighteenth-century classic, *Robinson Crusoe*, as popular in France as in England. Léon assumed he had read *Around the World in Eighty Days*, Jules Verne's 1873 best seller, when she reminisced about their having 'played Phileas Fogg' on their travels in 1876. And when Léon mentioned Don Quixote in her letters, she did so assuming that Gambetta was familiar with Cervantes' famous novel.[45] Gambetta also read some of the novels written by his powerful patron Juliette Adam, though his tactful comments suggest he did so from a sense of duty.[46]

When commentators lamented women's taste for novels, they were not referring to works by Defoe or Verne. They generally had in mind the romance novel, the nineteenth century equivalent of 'pulp fiction'. They feared that women might be seduced by the novel's escapism, becoming dissatisfied with their lives, like Mme Bovary in Flaubert's scandalous best seller. Léon certainly enjoyed the escapism of romance novels and drew comparisons with her own life. 'How have you spent these two long holidays? Sleeping?' she asked Gambetta early in 1876. 'I've read novels, the lives of others are happier than my own.'[47]

Life struggled to match fiction for Léon, particularly when she dwelt on the mistakes of her past and their longstanding consequences. She commented ruefully on Mario Uchard's *My Uncle Moneybeard* (*Mon Oncle Barbassou*), a lengthy account of a young man's search for true love, with a happy ending, which was serialized in the *Revue des Deux Mondes* in 1876: 'I shed a tear for the trials and tribulations of [the hero] and gave a good mark to Mario Uchard for this moral ending, unfortunately there are some situations in which an Uncle Moneybeard is missing.' But the ardour of such novels [*romans*] also provided a metaphor for the thrill of Léon's romance with Gambetta: 'Try as I might to take the story [*roman*] back to its very first hour', she wrote, 'there were never any [hours] more divine than those of yesterday, and that's always true of the last one that brought us together. Will our souls always have new and secret gestures of love to reveal to each other?'[48]

Despite enjoying escapism, Léon did not confuse fiction and fact as the moralists feared. She was a critical reader of novels, holding many of the same views as Gambetta. If Gambetta labelled one unnamed novel 'as stupid as it is pretentious', Léon dismissed others as 'stupid', or 'second-rate'. But even a poorly written book could be a good read: 'I'm finishing [the story of] my lovers', she wrote. 'It's quite faulty and very badly translated, but evidently interesting since I've read it in one sitting!' And rather than being carried away by excessive literary emotion, Léon was quietly amused by it. 'Give me the news on the Swedish novel and the floods of maternal feeling that you have mopped up', she wrote to Gambetta in July 1879.[49] Overall, Léon's romance novels provided her with a degree of entertainment, like the farces she enjoyed at the theatre, but she did not mistake them for portraits of real life.

Words were Gambetta's tools of trade. Reputedly the greatest political orator of his time, he manipulated words skillfully and admired that talent in others. Perhaps he found that talent in Honoré de Balzac, whose *Contes Drôlatiques* formed part of his personal library in the study at les Jardies[50] (Figure 6.1). Its witty wordplays and neologisms no doubt appealed to Gambetta, like Molière's 'exquisite lines'. Léon apparently conformed to 'feminine' stereotypes in adoring the emotional power of Balzac's prose, which was second only to that of Gambetta, she declared lovingly. Léon was keen to share an unnamed Balzac work with

Figure 6.1   Les Jardies: Gambetta's study, *c.*1884 ([*Sèvres: Les Jardies: pavillon*], photo, black & white, Collection Musée de l'Ile-de-France, Sceaux)

Gambetta in 1876: 'I return to Balzac. This morning I read several moving pages, do read [them]!'[51]

When the couple shared further pages from Balzac in 1882, Gambetta also admitted the 'magnificence' of Balzac's prose. Like Léon a decade earlier, however, he also declared that the author's depiction of love failed to match their personal experience. 'I am returning that magnificent page of Balzac', Gambetta wrote, 'noting that it is true of the two of us, for the two of us, and that it is indeed this perfect harmony of our souls, a harmony that he [Balzac] has been able neither to possess nor to attain, which creates the excellence – inaccessible to others – of our divine communion.'[52]

Léon's tastes in reading were more sophisticated than the contemporary image of the sentimental woman reader would suggest. In contrast to her passing comments on romance novels, she reflected at some length on Ivan Turgenev's novel, *Smoke,* published in 1867. It recounts a brief reunion between former lovers who had been prevented from marrying by family considerations. Léon observed to Gambetta: 'Smoke was indeed the appropriate name for this fast-moving and beguiling study, which flits before the mind, captivates it and disappears, carrying into space the memory of an hour of emotion!' But rather than indicating what critics deplored as a 'feminine' tendency to wallow in sentiment, Léon's response to the novel was shaped by the verisimilitude of the plot. She read *Smoke* as a depiction of 'real' Russian aristocrats and their failings, a depiction which gave the story its emotional power: 'It is a very accurate account of the state of decomposition of the Russian aristocracy', she wrote. The author depicted the lack of 'intelligence, strength, initiative, elevation of soul', which was responsible for 'retard[ing] the progressive movement in Russia'.[53]

Gambetta and Léon neglected a number of famous authors. The highly popular George Sand, the greatest female Romantic author, appears only once in the letters: 'On the article of G. Sand', Gambetta wrote in 1878, 'will I be disappointed? I would like to be since the pedant who wrote it exasperates me so much.'[54] A strong and forthright woman like Sand was not to Gambetta's taste. Neither Flaubert nor Zola appears in the letters, though they are frequently seen as the iconic authors of the Third Republic. Flaubert's cynical realism and Zola's sharp-edged and sometimes brutal 'naturalism', portraying the harsh realities of life with all their apparently inevitable and gloomy consequences, may not have appealed to Gambetta and Léon.[55] Their choice of novels reflected a more optimistic viewpoint, and especially the desire to find pleasure and entertainment in books, as at the theatre.

'The only diversion is reading the newspapers'

The couple also read widely in the newspaper and periodical press. They shared each issue of the *Revue des Deux Mondes,* the leading periodical of the day, which combined political analysis with features on literature, the arts, science, the economy and finance. Indeed, Gambetta had been reading and making notes on articles in the *Revue* since the 1850s. Reading the *Revue*, along with the other leading periodical, the *Journal des Débats*, provided a way of staying in touch with a broad range of ideas.[56]

Léon regularly read the *Revue's* serials, and both digested its serious content, especially its articles on contemporary politics.[57] Léon read closely its extracts from Charles de Mazade's *Fifty Years of Contemporary History*, for instance, noting that the author had 'taken his courage in both hands' in discussing Adolphe Thiers.[58] The December 1881 issue of the *Revue* was 'full of interest', too. It contained articles on Thiers and Bismarck, and essays by Victor Duruy and Gambetta's friend, Ernest Renan.[59]

Similarly, both Gambetta and Léon were keen readers of the daily newspapers, though Léon commented on their reportage more than Gambetta did. The number of newspapers increased rapidly in the 1870s, thanks to technical improvements in printing and to the rapid spread of information via the telegraph and the railways. By 1880, Paris' sixty dailies had a circulation of almost two million copies. Léon observed that 'they are creating more newspapers than readers'.[60] Newspapers were defined as 'male' reading at the time, given their attention to politics and finance. But Léonie Léon defied the stereotype, finding in the daily press her lifeline to politics and to Gambetta's world.

Léon commented on reading 'lots of newspapers' in a single day and mentioned ten different dailies by name. Gambetta occasionally sent her papers he thought would be of interest, including foreign ones.[61] It is likely that many of her comments on public affairs and political events refer to items gleaned from the newspapers, even if that is not indicated.

Léon's selection of newspapers included *Le Petit Journal*, whose new formula attracted the widest readership. A small-format paper selling for five centimes, it was not a 'political' paper but a 'news' paper, combining stories about prominent people with current affairs, *faits divers*, and serialized novels: perfect for attracting both male and female readers. Its circulation reached 700,000 by 1882.[62]

But most of Léon's reading was in the 'serious' newspapers. Gambetta's *République Française* was, of course, at the top of her list. She read it carefully, praising Gambetta's 'masterpieces' of journalism and his shrewd political tactics. She commended his 'magnificent and persuasive eloquence', recognized his moments of discouragement, and even corrected him: 'An error in your newspaper: *Fabiola* is by Cardinal Wiseman and not by Saintine.'[63] Only once did she refer to Gambetta's second newspaper, *La Petite République Française*, a small-format paper, selling for five centimes, intended for a rural and working-class readership.[64]

Léon's extensive perusal of the papers reflected an intelligence that had few outlets: 'The only diversion that I can bring to my boredom', she wrote in 1873, 'is to devote myself frenetically to reading the newspapers.'[65] She carved out a role as volunteer press attaché, keeping Gambetta up to date with commentary and reportage that he lacked the time to pursue himself. Léon read newspapers of every political stripe. She reported to Gambetta the views promoted in the Catholic and Bonapartist press,[66] and sent him clippings of interesting or important articles.[67]

While it was useful to know what this array of newspapers was publishing, however, their opinions carried little political weight. *Le Figaro*, by contrast, a Legitimist newspaper, strongly opposed to the Republic, was the most successful serious newspaper of the day. Léon was thus understandably angry when *Le Figaro* reported at length on Gambetta's poorly judged purchase of the palatial 'mansion' to house the *République Française* in 1876. The fact that she had argued so strongly against the move no doubt added to her displeasure: 'I am very upset to see *Le Figaro* publishing in full this irritating story of the *hôtel*, so is there no way to avoid this interference by the public in our private affairs? This is very annoying.'[68] Even when the reportage was negative, however, reading the newspapers served the couple's political interests, enabling them to keep up to date with current affairs, and to gauge public opinion on a variety of issues.

'We can go to the Salon on Tuesday morning'

Léon and Gambetta also shared an interest in art, although he wrote about it more often than she did. They had no need to correspond about art they saw together, but Gambetta's trips enabled him to visit distant galleries and he reported his impressions in detail to his lover. Gambetta was never a collector, but he enjoyed both painting and sculpture. He was particularly enthusiastic about art that portrayed ordinary people and places in recognizable ways, or that celebrated the Republic and its social ideals. His views on art resembled those of many republicans of his generation, who believed in the moral and educative value of art, who appreciated the 'romantic' style of the Barbizon school, and who were not yet ready to embrace the radical art of the Impressionists.[69]

According to Alphonse Daudet, who knew him as a young lawyer, Gambetta learned about art as a student, visiting the Salon and the Louvre with the critic Théophile Silvestre.[70] Gambetta came to share Silvestre's appreciation of Flemish art. Visiting Belgium as a young man of twenty-seven, he praised Jan van Eyck's 'Madonna with Canon Van der Paele'. This was a highly stylized religious painting, but Gambetta was enraptured by its vivid representation of the Canon, particularly its life-like depiction of his face.[71]

His early fascination with the life-like soon became a passion for 'naturalist' or 'realist' works depicting contemporary life.[72] This is evident in letters from October 1874, when Gambetta travelled to Belgium and Holland with friends. He was retracing a trip he had made with Léon a year earlier, when the Rembrandts particularly impressed them.[73] Having written to Juliette Adam from The Hague in praise of 'The Bull', by seventeenth century Flemish painter, Paulus Potter,[74] Gambetta wrote a long letter to Léon from Brussels about an exhibition of landscape painting.

The exhibition featured works by English painters J. M. W. Turner and John Constable, whom Gambetta described as 'the inaugurator of the new naturalist school in painting'. Constable had abandoned 'all the conventions, the false contrivances, the depictions of supposedly Greek or Roman countryside', becoming 'the first to use his own eyes, to see, to feel for himself, to admire the grass, the water, the trees in their striking and natural beauty'. According to Gambetta, Constable attempted to represent those objects as they actually were, with 'all the strength of their tones, the imprecision of their shapes, the variations of shade'.[75]

Gambetta also credited Constable with rejuvenating French landscape painting, a view espoused by Silvestre. Without Constable, he declared, French painters might still be influenced by those 'lovers of Greek temples hidden in the midst of trees of zinc and cardboard'. This barb was aimed at the Academy of Fine Arts, which regarded 'classical' subjects as the only suitable subjects for great art.[76] Gambetta enthused about works by 'the three great representatives of the contemporary French [Barbizon] school' at this 1874 exhibition: Jules Dupré, Théodore Rousseau, and Jean-François Millet. He praised the 'vigour and boldness' of Dupré's landscapes, and Rousseau's images of the 'immortal forest of Fontainebleau', where he loved to walk with Léon. His comments illustrate Gambetta's admiration for art that captured its subject as he thought it really was. This suggested objectivity. Yet his claim that artists should 'see for themselves' also suggested the subjectivity of their work.[77] Gambetta never discussed the tension between these two positions.

Millet's renowned painting, 'The Angelus', attracted Gambetta's lengthiest comments.[78] He had seen this painting before, remaining proud of having 'caused a fuss' when it was displayed at the Salon of 1866.[79] Now, in 1874, he shared his appreciation with Léon:

> [This is] a masterly canvas where two peasants, bathed in the colours of the setting sun, bow down, filled with mystical sensations [*frissons*] at the sound of a bell which chimes the evening prayer at the monastery blurred on the horizon, which shimmers [*saphire*] and forces us to reflect on the still-powerful influence of religious tradition on rural populations. These two great silhouettes of the farmer and his maidservant rise up on the still-warm earth with such a combination of meticulous detail and impressive scale!

Surprisingly, Gambetta saw a 'farmer and his maidservant', not a peasant couple working the land in partnership. The social hierarchy he detected seems to be of his own making.

Millet's peasants appeared to 'count the strokes of the bell', he went on, 'as they did yesterday, as they will do tomorrow, in a pose too natural not to be customary'. Gambetta saw rural archaism, fatalism, and religiosity in the painting, reflecting his belief that 'the peasants are several centuries behind the enlightened portion of the country'. But this was the result of injustices, which he believed the Republic would remedy. He certainly saw an image of quiet perseverance, eternal rhythms and unchanging routine. But he also saw a life marked by hard labour, which he always admired, and indeed by beauty and serenity.[80]

Gambetta's reading of 'The Angelus' confirmed his commitment to the social role of art. He praised Millet for accepting his social responsibilities, for depicting 'the passions and problems of his time'. 'Understood like this,' he wrote, 'the painting . . . assume[s] a moralizing, educative role; the citizen enters the artist and with a great and noble painting we have a lesson in social and political morality'. Precisely what this lesson was he did not say, but the belief that the artist had a responsibility to paint as a 'citizen' would shape republican arts policies once they assumed control of government in the late 1870s.[81]

Gambetta's appreciation for works that depicted ordinary life also inspired his admiration for the work of Jules Breton, whose paintings of 'The Gleaners' (1859) and 'The Potato Gatherers' (1868) made him one of the most renowned painters of nineteenth-century rural life. Breton was also a poet, and Gambetta was deeply moved by *Jeanne*, a lengthy narrative poem published in 1880. This poem inspired his praise for Breton as both poet and artist. 'I cannot tell you', he wrote to Breton, 'whether the poet or the painter has more greatly moved me, upset me, won me over, delighted me!'[82]

Similarly, Gambetta admired Sir Joshua Reynolds' portrait of a widow and child, which he read as a 'naturalist' work, although it was painted a century before 'Naturalism'. In 1874, Gambetta hailed it as the 'pearl' of the Brussels exhibition.[83] His description sought to capture the emotion of the domestic scene. He described the baby, 'stretching out his fat little pink hand under the chin of his mother, who cannot, despite her mourning, refrain from smiling, like a flower blooming suddenly in the midst of a storm'. For Gambetta, this was not a portrait of a prominent woman by a society painter, but a Rousseauian image of motherhood, an image deeply embedded in republican ideology. 'It is impossible to offer a more perceptive and more elevated image of intimate life', he declared.[84]

Given Gambetta's preference for landscape and portraiture, defined by the Academy as 'minor' genres, he was frequently critical of the Salon, the annual exhibition at which painters displayed their work and competed for the prizes that would bring commissions. Gambetta and Léon were regular visitors to the Salon, but the works that won the Academy's eulogies were generally large-scale works on grand themes drawn from history, religion and mythology. Gambetta was scathing of the Salon of 1876: 'I was exhausted beyond measure by seeing the mediocrity of our fine arts', he wrote to Léon. 'Painting is absolutely worthy of the epoch, lacking ideas, lacking distinctiveness [*relief*], lacking grandeur, an appalling level of practical skill invariably combined with a sterility of ideas. French genius in marble and bronze is still evident, that is where the aesthetic renaissance of this country will come from.' This assessment echoed a widespread sense of national decline highlighted by the defeat of 1870 and reinforced by the Exposition of 1878, which many believed had confirmed a significant slide in French dominance of the fine arts.[85]

Léon's preferences in art, too, were at odds with those of the Salon. She visited the Salon of 1879 in search of the portrait of Sarah Bernhardt, rather than in search of moral edification. She did not find the portrait, but she made another discovery, reporting to Gambetta: 'I believe I found a painter, named Renouf, about whom none of the Salon crowd [*salonates*] has spoken! He has an old fisherman repairing his boat which reminds me of the heads of D and which I greatly admired.'[86] Officially titled 'Last refit, my poor friend', Émile Renouf's painting depicted a weathered old seaman lovingly sanding the hull of an equally weathered boat. It was one of a number of paintings on maritime themes submitted to the Salon that year, which the *Gazette des Beaux-Arts* suggested formed a new genre: 'seascape with figures'.[87] Léon was not the only one to see the merit of this painting. Its naturalist style and its unthreatening view of working people suited republican aesthetics, and it was acquired by the state for one thousand francs.[88]

Léon also looked to the Salon with an eye to promoting Gambetta's career. With her customary combination of decisiveness and deference, she wrote to him in an early letter: 'I forgot to say that I am basically very anxious that you should have your bust made for the next salon. We'll choose together the artist who will have the honour of bringing to life under his chisel the sublime beauty of my dear master.' Léon was well aware of the importance of publicity for a political figure. When Gambetta did not give the issue much attention, she chastised him: 'The more you efface yourself the less the world will want to see you. You must impose your personality on those who don't recognize it. If you had two busts or three portraits at the Salon, that would prove your popularity strongly and surely, which would convince many of the undecided ones; not to mention the effect produced by your perfect and seductive beauty!'[89] But Gambetta's image never appeared at the Salon. While he had his photographic portrait taken on a number of occasions, most if not all of the paintings and sculptures of Gambetta were created posthumously.[90]

In the 1870s, the 'new painting', as Philip Nord calls it – realism and Impressionism – was making its mark. Links between republicanism and the 'new painting' were strong, not because republicans necessarily had radical tastes in art, but because both groups opposed the reactionary programme of the Academy and its political defenders.[91]

Gambetta himself was part of this coming together between republicans and the art world. His links with the Manet family dated back to his days as a young lawyer, when Gustave Manet, brother of the painter Edouard, was a colleague. Jules de Jouy, who later employed Gambetta, was Manet's cousin. As Gambetta's political career took off, his regular presence at a number of republican salons strengthened his links in art circles. The salon presided over by Hippolyte Lejosne saw him rubbing shoulders with the artists Frédéric Bazille, Henri Fantin-Latour and Edouard Manet. At the salon of the publisher Georges Charpentier and his wife Marguerite, he mixed with Claude Monet, Auguste Renoir, Gustave Caillebotte, Edgar Degas and Alfred Sisley. Gambetta also crossed paths with many of these figures at the salon of Henri Cernushi. In addition, he formed friendships with republican art critics – particularly Philippe Burty, who wrote a regular column for Gambetta's *République Française* – and with arts curators.[92]

Gambetta's links with the 'new painters' were not reflected in his own modest collection. A Tanagra figurine was one of Gambetta's most prized possessions, given his passion for classical antiquity.[93] The few other works of art he owned were often given to him by their creators, generally reflecting shared political commitments. In 1873, the women of Thann (in Alsace) presented Gambetta with a painting by the Alsatian-born artist, Jean-Jacques Henner. Entitled 'Alsace: She waits', the gift was in recognition of his staunch defence of the 'lost provinces' during and after the Franco-Prussian war.[94] Gambetta also owned a number of busts of the Republic (one also a gift from the citizens of Alsace and Lorraine) by unnamed sculptors, as well as a bronze by Bartholdi, best known as creator of the Statue of Liberty.[95]

Gambetta did not, so far as we can tell, purchase paintings by the emerging 'Impressionist' painters, despite being well placed to do so. Nor is there any evidence that either Gambetta or Léon visited the independent exhibitions (the *salons des refusés*) organized by the 'new painters' as a response to their exclusion from the Salon, although Gambetta did intervene, following a personal request by Auguste Renoir, to advertise the independent exhibition of 1877 in the *République Française*.[96]

Gambetta may have shared the views of other republicans who were critical of the Impressionists for representing only the transitory, or for emphasizing the purely material qualities of their medium, ignoring the all-important ennobling ideal. It seems likely that Gambetta was left behind by the Impressionists' stylistic innovations. His tastes were not avant-garde, and there is no reason to think that Léon's were either. Rather, both seem to have remained attached to a naturalist style, unmoved by – or uncomprehending of – the Impressionists of the 'younger school', who were setting the aesthetic pace by the late 1870s.[97]

Dear Little Woman,

I've already been receiving solicitations for a long time and the procession gets longer every day. I really don't know which way to turn; I'm invaded, overwhelmed, besieged on all sides. I too have a great need for an armistice, for my supplies are running down. Fortunately I'm fighting fit, and the inner joy you give me keeps all fatigue at bay. This is the period of my life when I have the most work and the greatest happiness. I'm getting very interesting information from Italy, and it seems indeed that the new King won't repudiate the paternal policies and will seek a rapprochement with the Gauls, whom he was thought to detest when he was the crown prince.

There is in this House of Savoy a hereditary good sense, which transforms the ruling princes upon maturity and always facilitates the expansion and increase of their beautiful domains. This one won't betray his blood and I have the best assurances of this. It will just be a question of undertaking a skilful policy here and we [Italy and France] will be able to march together toward the common good.

Tomorrow I will go to mass despite my anticlerical repugnance; I am telling myself under my breath, to excuse myself, and without wanting to plagiarize [Henry IV]: Rome is worth a mass. I expect lots of mockery, but I've heard plenty in the past and such jeers would never frighten me or block my path. During the mass, I will read a pretty Provinciale *by Pascal,*[2] *on the art of hearing mass, in a little jewel of a volume, which I have kept since M. Thiers' death for occasions like this. How you've changed your Leon.*

I kiss you with all my strength.

L. Gambetta

7
'This religion satisfies my soul'

Gambetta is famous for the declaration, 'Clericalism! There is the enemy.'[3] But his correspondence with Léon suggests that he was a moderate anti-clerical by the standards of the day. While he had left his Catholicism comfortably behind and was determined to ensure the rights of a secular Republic over those of the Catholic Church, he was tolerant of others' beliefs. Moreover, he seriously entertained the possibility of an arrangement with a 'Gallican' Church, rather than a separation of church and state as the Belleville Programme demanded. Under different political circumstances, he might well have resolved the religious question less acrimoniously than was the case. Nevertheless, Gambetta could, and did, mobilize verbal violence against Catholic activists when necessary for his own political ends.

Léon and Gambetta were both inducted into the culture of Catholicism as children. Léon attended a convent school.[4] She never abandoned the religion in which she had been raised, although she struggled to live up to its demands. Gambetta attended religious schools until age thirteen, when his father moved him to the public secondary school in Cahors. But since instruction in the catechism was compulsory even in state schools until 1882, he continued to receive grounding in Catholic doctrine. He probably made his First Communion, like most children,[5] but he became a committed anticlerical in early adulthood, alienated by the Church's monarchist loyalties and its opposition to 'modern' ideas like democracy.[6]

Negotiating a path between republican anticlericalism and religious faith was not straightforward in the 1870s, and their personal struggles to do so left echoes in the couple's correspondence. As a moderate and a pragmatist, Gambetta tolerated Léon's ongoing if conflicted links to Catholicism. He adopted a playful attitude toward religion in his letters, far from the angry hostility that characterized so much anticlericalism. Léon responded in kind, sometimes critical of the Church but never abandoning religious practice completely, as Gambetta apparently did. While their attitudes to Catholicism were not identical, their shared Catholic culture continued to provide Gambetta and Léon with a common fund of images and ideas about the world, and a language in which to communicate in familiar terms.

'This religion satisfies my soul'

The couple's letters were sprinkled with Latin phrases from the Catholic liturgy, allusions to feast days and seasonal rites, and other references to the religion in which they had been raised. Gambetta was certainly irreverent. He mocked the penitential rites of the 'devotees of clericalism' at Lent,[7] and the intercessionary powers attributed to particular saints: 'If you know a saint as useful for the weather as your Saint Anthony of Padua is for finding lost objects', he jibed, 'add it to my deck [of cards], and you will have half-converted me.'[8] Gambetta's mode of commemorating the saint's day he shared with Léonie Léon would certainly have raised Catholic eyebrows. After thanking her for 'the rapture of yesterday evening', he noted: 'the calendar tells me it's the feast of Saint Leo today, we have celebrated it in a fitting manner'.[9]

Gambetta sometimes teased Léon about her attachment to religious practices. When she enquired about a medal she had lost, he seized the opportunity to claim a symbolic victory over her religiosity:

> I myself removed the ribbon and the medallion from that adorable and adored neck; it has remained with me as a sweet mark of triumph. I look at it every morning and every evening with a rapturous smile and await the return of the goddess who has left me a part of her finery.[10]

The saga of this medal, a mark of piety lost in an amorous encounter with her lover, symbolized the contradictions in Léon's life.

While religious practices and beliefs offered opportunities for witty repartee, most of the couple's references to religion were devices to express a truth or an aspiration about their relationship. Religion offered a range of metaphors to describe events around them and to articulate their love for each other. Gambetta frequently described Léon's beneficent role in his life in religious terms. She was his 'fountain of life', his 'beautiful Samaritan' or his 'good angel guardian'.[11] 'Hail Nini, full of grace', he addressed her, echoing the words of the *Ave Maria* (Hail Mary), the well-known Catholic prayer to the Virgin. He invoked her as 'Our Lady of Good Succour' or begged her to 'pray for us', alluding to the Litany of the Virgin.[12] And just as the faithful erected votive plaques to thank the Virgin or the Saints for their intercession, so Gambetta wanted to demonstrate his gratitude to Léon: 'I would like to place at your feet all the treasures of this world to make a thanksgiving plaque [*ex-voto*] worthy of you and of the marvellous cure that you have procured for your devoted worshipper.'[13]

The language of the sacraments also provided metaphors for Gambetta's relationship with Léon. He alluded to the sacrament of penance (or reconciliation) to 'seek her forgiveness' and 'expiate his faults', hoping to 'return to grace' through her mercy. He 'examined his conscience and reproached himself' for the number of times he had made Léon wait. But she had readily given him 'absolution in advance' for the same fault on another occasion.[14] Gambetta also likened Léon's revitalizing presence to the viaticum, the Eucharist administered to the dying. 'I especially want to tell you what consolation I find in the thought of our love at times like this', he wrote amidst his political trials in 1876, 'love is the viaticum.' Again, disgusted by politics in mid-1882, he reiterated: 'Together, we will triumph over ill destiny, and in every case our mutual love will be the viaticum for us, the life support.'[15]

After one particularly memorable day of tenderness, Gambetta assembled a collection of religious concepts to express what Léon meant to him: 'You transfigure me, you are perpetual rebirth, and I regard you as the very source of my strength and of my life, you are the true, the unique miracle in which I believe and in which I place my faith for ever. This religion satisfies my soul, but I call for the real presence of my goddess.'[16] Such an unwieldy amalgam of ideas suggests his ongoing, and perhaps frustrating, search for a telling metaphor. Ultimately, the greatest tribute Gambetta could pay to Léon was to assign her the status of personal divinity: 'Are you not my sole religion and the only support of my life?' 'I love you as my visible and ever active providence, and with piety I truly adore you.' 'I will love you above all things in this world', he declared, 'and in the next if there is one.'[17]

To a devout Catholic, many of the couple's allusions would have been offensive. To proclaim, for instance, as Gambetta did, that he held Léon's letters 'with the respect of a priest for the [sacred] host' would have been sacrilegious: in Catholic belief, the Sacred Host was truly the Body of Christ.[18] But Léon does not seem to have taken offence. Indeed, she herself made many religious allusions, some at least as playful as

Gambetta's. 'It is you, my love', she wrote early in their relationship, 'who are and who always will be my divinity, my cult and my life.'[19] She described Gambetta's political task in Biblical terms, likening it to Moses' long struggle to reach the Promised Land.[20] Moreover, Léon compared Gambetta's qualities to the supernatural qualities of Jesus. She likened her experience in Gambetta's presence to that of Jesus' disciples at the transfiguration, when a brilliant white light surrounded him and his face shone like the sun: 'I felt that you were so great, so sublime, that my passion surpassed what the imagination can conceive, I was at your feet, like the disciples on Tabor, fascinated, overcome with admiration and love!'[21]

On another occasion, Léon likened Gambetta's campaign for the Republic to the Sermon on the Mount, when a vast crowd followed Jesus onto the mountainside to hear his message:

> In spirit I followed you as you were preaching the truth under the shining sun, spreading to the four winds of heaven these treasures of eloquence . . . I pictured you in the midst of a true genre painting, surrounded by groups of villagers crowding around at your sides, gathered picturesquely in tiers up the mountainside, in order to better hear and see the new prophet who has come, as Christ once did, to teach love of duty, of family, of the fatherland, to make the chords of hearts not hardened vibrate.[22]

Léon even identified Gambetta with the Messiah: 'You are the resurrection and the life', she declared and, citing the prominent biblical scholar, Gambetta's friend Ernest Renan, she added: 'As Renan explains in his *Life of Jesus*, you work miracles simply by your will, your touch and your gaze!'[23]

For Léon to cite Renan's famous book places her, intellectually, among progressive Catholics and moderate anticlericals, sympathetic to the religious impulse yet critical of the official Church. Published in 1863, it pioneered modern textual criticism, seeking to write Jesus' life as one would write the life of any great man. Renan rejected the divinity of Christ, portraying Jesus sympathetically but as a human being, 'an incomparable man', who offered 'a pure worship, a religion without priests and external observances, resting entirely on the feelings of the heart'.[24] The book outraged the Church and was placed on the Index of Forbidden Books; indeed, it was one of the books that triggered the Syllabus of Errors. But it sold 60,000 copies in five months and has never since been out of print in French or English. Gambetta probably encountered the book soon after its appearance, when he was a young lawyer in Paris. In all likelihood, he introduced it to Léon. But Léon clearly read it and referred to it on several occasions.

Religious ideas and exaggerated religious images provided Gambetta and Léon with discursive tools to express their love. In the overarching concepts and superlative expressions of religious thought, they found the hyperbole and excess on which the love letter relied, in its struggle to describe the depth of passion that inspired it. Catholicism was a cultural language among many for Gambetta and Léon, perhaps their deepest shared language. They were both imbued with it; they both understood its nuances and symbolism; and they both mobilized it to describe their mutual love. If Gambetta wore his Catholicism lightly and playfully, Léon, too, was sometimes willing to join him in the game.

'Clericalism! There is the enemy!'

Religion was also, to be sure, a substantive issue for them, given its enormous political significance in French society in the 1870s. The Revolution of 1789 had seen the emergence of a bitter division between the Catholic Church and republicanism. That division remained strong in the nineteenth century and the culture of the Church remained strongly monarchist.

The Catholic Church did not speak with a single voice in the 1870s, but the dominant voice was that of the ultraconservative Pope Pius IX, who led the Church from 1846 until 1878. His Syllabus of Errors of 1864 condemned many republican ideas: the exclusion of the Church from temporal affairs, state control of education, belief in divorce and indeed all of 'modern' thought; the Syllabus castigated the belief 'that the Roman Pontiff can, and ought to, reconcile himself, and come to terms with progress, liberalism and modern civilization'.[25] This pronouncement posed a dilemma for moderate Catholics and became infamous among republicans; the word 'syllabist' was coined to denote an intransigent monarchist Catholic.

The Vatican Council of 1869–70 reinforced the Church's opposition to modern thought by establishing the doctrine of papal infallibility: the claim that the Pope could not err when making official pronouncements on matters of faith or morals. A small group of French bishops who argued against these ideas were in a minority at the Council. Decades ahead of his time, Bishop Maret had declared in 1852 that science and liberty were 'as divine as faith and religion'. He saw no reason to cling to the political forms of the past. Bishop Ginouilhac of Lyon and Bishop Gilbert of Bordeaux also defended 'modern civilization'. Having questioned the proposed doctrine of papal infallibility, they nevertheless accepted it, and Maret was forced to recant his earlier position. Progressive views within the Church were silenced.[26]

The declaration of Papal infallibility marked the triumph in the Church of 'ultramontanism': the belief that papal authority should prevail over the authority of governments and regional ecclesiastical authorities.[27] Some, like Bishop Freppel, maintained that the laws of the state should be based on canon law.[28] Even if only a small minority supported this ideal, it threatened the Republic.

Ultramontanism was, unsurprisingly, anathema to republicans. Its triumph challenged the spirit if not the letter of the Concordat between Napoleon I and the Pope in 1801, which in effect made the Catholic Church an established and state-funded Church in exchange for its acceptance of the secular regime. If the Church no longer accepted the regime, now that it was republican, republicans naturally questioned the regime's support for the Church. And since the main proponents of ultramontanism were the Jesuits, republican hostility to that religious order was particularly intense.[29]

While their views were not identical, French bishops in the 1870s were overwhelmingly monarchist. Indeed, as Jacques Gadille notes, 'the great majority' were 'hostile to any form of parliamentary democracy and proved to be advocates of an authoritarian regime'. They regarded monarchy as the only basis for a stable society and the only guarantee of the security of the Church. The few who believed that the alignment of the Church with a particular form of government dangerously conflated the religious and temporal spheres had been silenced.[30] That alignment led Gambetta to accuse the clergy of having 'ceased to be a great religious body and [having] fallen to the rank of a political faction'. It also contributed substantially to the rise of anticlericalism.[31]

The political and religious maps of France generally coincided in the nineteenth century: observant areas voted conservative; anticlerical areas voted republican.[32] In anticlerical areas, 'Free Thought' associations mobilized around issues like the right to a secular burial. In Paris, 25 per cent of burials were secular ceremonies by 1882. In Belleville, Gambetta's highly anticlerical electorate, 45 per cent of burials were performed without a priest by 1879.[33]

Not all priests were hostile to the Republic. Indeed, the curé of Léon's porter liked to attend the Chamber of Deputies, and she obtained tickets for him from Gambetta.[34] A staunchly monarchist priest, however, could fuel local anticlericalism if the parish favoured the Republic.[35]

So, too, could strong pronouncements on sexual matters. Jules Michelet, in 1845, had tapped a vein of male resentment at clerical interference in relations between husbands and wives when he thundered that 'our wives and daughters are raised, governed *by our enemies'*. This charge had enormous resonance among republican men; his book, *Priests, Women, and Families,* went through many editions.[36]

On the other side, the Church retained its opposition to family limitation despite the gradual shift to a less severe theology during the nineteenth century, and tension often remained, since such limitation was widespread by the mid-nineteenth century.[37] Gambetta appealed to a range of resentments when campaigning at Grenoble, ahead of the Senate elections of October 1878. He echoed Michelet: 'The elector must be asked', he declared, 'if he wants to be the master in his home, in his commune, in his school, in his local byways, in the choice of men who will represent his opinions, his interests . . . or if he prefers the tutelage of the sacristy to having his share of government and sovereignty in the commune.'[38]

One function of Gambetta's anticlericalism, therefore, was simply to connect with grassroots republicans. The Belleville Manifesto, drafted by Gambetta's constituents in 1869, listed 'separation of Church and State' as one of its goals. He pledged himself to that agenda on his election as their Deputy. Many of Gambetta's speeches, both inside and outside the Chamber, appealed to the anticlericalism of the republican electorate and inevitably drew wild applause from his audience. It was to this popular sentiment that Gambetta played when he famously proclaimed, 'Clericalism! There is the enemy!' As J. P. T. Bury puts it, he 'concealed' his moderation behind this 'verbal violence'.[39] In fact, Gambetta distanced himself from this slogan by attributing it to someone else: 'And I only translate the intimate thoughts of the French people in saying of clericalism what my friend Peyrat [father of his friend, the Marquise Arconati-Visconti] said one day, "Clericalism! There is the enemy".'[40]

Another sign that, compared to some of his colleagues, Gambetta was relatively moderate in his anticlerical views was his distance from freemasonry. Freemasonry was hostile to the Church, and Masonic lodges were condemned in return as fomenters of revolution. But while lodges often gave Gambetta their support, Gambetta himself never became an active freemason.[41]

In general, Gambetta escalated his anticlerical rhetoric when Catholic monarchism seemed to threaten the Republic. His speech at Romans during the election campaign of 1878, for example, was a response to the Catholic politician Albert de Mun, who had urged Catholics to rally to the counter-revolution in the forthcoming elections.[42] Gambetta, in reply, condemned 'the growth of a spirit which is not merely clerical but vaticanesque, monastic, congregationalist, and syllabist [shaped by monastic orders and religious congregations like the Jesuits, and by the Syllabus of Errors]'. These words produced 'Lengthy rounds of applause. Bravos and repeated cries of Long live Gambetta!' Similarly, he called for the removal of religious teachers from the classroom so that reason and science might shape children's intellectual development. This statement also produced 'salvos of applause and enthusiastic bravos'.[43]

Anticlericalism united republicans when other issues divided them. Gambetta thus found anticlericalism a useful device to distract more radical colleagues from pursuing troublesome issues. In mid-1876, for instance, the Extreme Left was irate about the republican government's failure to pursue a full amnesty for former Communards. Gambetta wrote to Léon: 'The government seems committed to a fatal course, on which it will be as difficult for us to stop it as to support it. We must find a diversion; I think I have one: the Affair of the rue des Postes.'[44] Students of a Jesuit school on that street allegedly knew the questions in advance of a public examination, giving them an unfair advantage. Gambetta's speech on the 'Affair of the rue des Postes' mobilized the anticlerical Left, effectively diverting them from the amnesty issue.

Gambetta's anticlericalism was nevertheless sincere and had a substantial intellectual basis. Like many republican law students in Paris in the 1860s, Gambetta had subscribed to 'Positivism', the philosophy of Auguste Comte (1798–1857), who held that knowledge should be based on the 'positive' data of experience, excluding religion and all metaphysical speculation. Gambetta called Auguste Comte 'the most powerful thinker of the century'.[45] He affirmed his commitment to Comte's philosophy in 1873, in a speech to honour Emile Littré, author of the famous *Dictionary of the French Language* (1873) and himself a leading positivist. Again in 1875, speaking at the initiation to freemasonry of Littré and Jules Ferry, Gambetta exhorted his listeners to 'fight the great fight of science against obscurantism, of liberty against oppression', but he added 'and of tolerance against fanaticism'.[46]

As a positivist, Gambetta was committed to freedom of thought. He objected not to the existence of the Church, but to its attempt to control knowledge and behaviour. He declared in a speech at Albertville in September 1872:

Let each person adore a god or not, that is an intimate question, for his heart of hearts . . . every one is free to believe or not to believe . . . Go to your temples, gather in your churches, believe, affirm, pray, that is of no concern to me [*je ne vous connais pas*]. What I ask is the freedom, a freedom equal for you and me, for my philosophy as for your religion, for my free thought as for your freedom to practise. [*Bravo! Bravo!*][47]

Gambetta reiterated his commitment to this freedom at Romans six years later: 'We are not the enemies of religion', he insisted, but 'the servants of freedom of conscience, respecting all religious and philosophical opinion.' Nevertheless, all beliefs were not equal. He drew a round of applause from his audience when he added: 'I have the right [either] to use my reason and to make it a torch to guide me after centuries of ignorance, or to allow myself to be lulled by childish religious myths.'[48]

Gambetta rejoiced in any evidence that undermined those 'childish religious myths'. He perhaps read Renan's *Life of Jesus* in that light; he certainly welcomed Renan's later work, *Ecclesiastes,* for that reason. Renan sent him the proofs in February 1882: one indication that, while Renan was slow to move to republicanism, they were good friends. 'It's delicious, exquisite', Gambetta wrote to Léon. 'I'll bring this delicate dish back to the rue Saint-Didier, when the sweet nest is ready[,] and we will taste it, savour it together.'[49] Renan's reinterpretation of the Old Testament Book of Ecclesiastes (one of a series he wrote on the origins of Christianity) reiterated some of the themes in his earlier *Life of Jesus:* 'Ecclesiastes reveals no established dogmatic power, no religious catechism, no priestly teachers, no concept of the prophets'; it shows 'no trace of messianism, nor of resurrection, nor of religious fanaticism.'[50] This explains why Renan's *Ecclesiastes*, too, found a broad anticlerical audience.

'To relieve my remorse'

If Gambetta wore his Catholic background lightly as an anticlerical republican, Léon remained attached to the religion of her childhood. Her mental world differed significantly, not only from that of Gambetta, but also from that of leading republican women like Juliette Adam, the Marquise Arconati-Visconti, Mme Arnaud de l'Ariège and the Kestner sisters. They had all received a thoroughly secular education, designed to instil in them the 'republican faith' rather than the Catholic faith. Some of them were not baptized and did not baptize their own children; some insisted on secular marriages.[51] These privileged women, tutored privately within staunchly republican homes, received an intellectual development that encouraged scepticism and made them just as anticlerical as their husbands.

Léon's experience was more typical. Many wives of republican men had been raised as Catholics. Her schooling was not without intellectual merit but emphasized spiritual development. While Gambetta's education in the cultures of antiquity was seen as a virtue in itself, for instance, in Léon's education it was subordinate to religion: as the 'Summary of Mythology' employed in her school noted, this knowledge 'is especially useful to reveal to us the errors man is capable of falling into when his reason is not enlightened by the insights of the true faith, and if he allows himself to be led by his passions; and this consideration must bring us to thank God who has allowed us to be born in a time and a country where He is fully known'.[52]

Republicans frequently lamented the intellectual gulf between husbands and wives. Jules Ferry declared in 1870: 'The most profound differences of opinions, of tastes, of feelings' separated husbands and wives. 'You must choose, citizens, either woman must belong to science or she must belong to the church.'[53] The republican refrain, repeated since Michelet's day, that gullible women had been captured by the priests, was part of a rhetorical battle among men for political control.[54] The 'profound differences' between the sexes were due to girls' limited education, not only to their religious teachers. But the republicans nevertheless believed that secular education would win girls for the Republic.

Léon became a committed republican, but she also remained attached to her religious faith. How deeply attached is impossible to say. We do not know, for instance, whether she attended Sunday Mass, but her son, Alphonse, attended a Catholic school and made his First Communion. According to some of Alphonse's former classmates, Léon was stunning in a dress of pale pink silk on that occasion.[55] But as a courtesan who had subsequently entered more than one liaison not blessed by the Church, Léon's relationship to the Church and to her faith must have been difficult. Indeed, her letters suggest considerable anxiety about her life, which affected her relationship with Gambetta.

Léon and Gambetta thought differently about religion, a talking point from the beginning of their relationship. In August 1872, Gambetta penned a scathing attack on a proposal by the Legitimist politician, Edmond Ernoul, to bring public primary schools under Church control. Gambetta condemned the attempt to spread 'clerical education', which was opposed to 'liberty, the search for legal equality, the aversion to privilege, the independent search for truth in science and history'.

'Let the clergy keep to their own schools, and their own churches', he declared, 'we have faith in reason.' Gambetta asked Léon for her reaction: 'what do you think about the newspaper, on the subject of clerical education? Were your conservative instincts quite offended, and did you think we went too far?'[56] Her response has not survived.

Given Gambetta's strong opposition to clerical education, Léon's decision to send Alphonse to a Catholic school must have displeased him. But he probably realized that any attempt to impose himself between mother and son would have been disastrous for their relationship and there is no suggestion in the letters that they argued about the matter. Indeed, he was enthusiastic about Alphonse's progress and discussed it with the Principal, Father Dubief, on at least one occasion. At Léon's request, Gambetta even invited Father Dubief to the grand reception he hosted, as President of the Chamber of Deputies, on 14 July 1879: 'Certainly yes, Dubief will be invited, that is indeed the least I can do for *la Chine* whom I never forget.'[57] Whether Father Dubief accepted the invitation to this republican celebration we do not know.

Léon's personal links with Catholic priests and nuns continued throughout her relationship with Gambetta, and beyond. She had a particular connection with the Dominican Sisters at Sèvres; they ran a school adjoining their convent as well as a nearby orphanage.[58] Léon visited her 'good sisters' [*religieuses*] quite often. Once the republicans were in power, she several times invoked Gambetta's assistance on their behalf. 'My sisters are making requests on behalf of a poor man in whom they have taken an interest', she wrote in early 1879, 'I will put the case to you.' Sometimes the sisters' requests were easily met and Gambetta was happy to oblige. 'Here is the photograph requested, and also the reply from the editor of the *Gaz* [*Gazette de France?*]. I hope that you'll be able to satisfy your good sisters and that that will earn me a sweet smile.' 'You perform your errands with such precision', Léon replied, 'that acknowledgement can only be expressed *tête-à-tête*.'[59]

Léon had affectionate ties to her 'good sisters' and appreciated the work they did. But her desire to help them was also motivated by the urge to make amends for her misspent life. She explained to Gambetta in July 1879: 'I accept the meeting for tomorrow, because I have to discuss men and women supplicants with you; my dear superior is one of them and she has to be given what she wants at once; this is to relieve my remorse, the only possible consolation for the irreparable loss that my heart and my life have suffered!'[60] Léon was plagued by guilt and self-reproach. They underpinned her bouts of depression, since she frequently alluded to her past when the 'black butterflies' overwhelmed her. Her life straddled two worlds: the anti-republican Catholic world of her childhood, and the anti-clerical republican world of her adulthood; the world of faith in which she had been raised, and the demimonde into which she had fallen.

Léon had a personal confessor for at least part of her adult life, another indication of her ongoing attempt to maintain Catholic practice. In 1878 her confessor was Canon Codant, the only one she named in her letters. It is unclear when her spiritual relationship with him began. Codant had been spiritual head of the Dominicans at Sèvres from 1861, so that Léon may have known him for some time. When he died at the end of 1878, the sisters at Sèvres gave Léon a souvenir of her 'good curé, the holy water font he had in his bedroom!'[61] This gesture suggests that they regarded Léon's relationship with Canon Codant as warm and supportive, though Léon's ability to channel patronage may also have shaped their thinking.

Léon's apparently warm relationship with the Canon suggests that he may have been sympathetic, rather than a harsh critic of her conduct. But however understanding he was, Léon's spiritual advisor could only have urged her to live a virtuous life. Perhaps Codant reminded her of the wages of sin. This was the message of his sermons at Saint Augustine's Church in Paris in November 1878: the month when Catholics commemorate the dead and pray for the souls in purgatory. His first sermon, on 'the benefit that the living should draw from the week of the dead', reminded the congregation: 'The expiation of every sin must be made through suffering, and the sufferings of purgatory surpass all human suffering.'[62] Indeed, Léon already saw her 'sufferings' as punishment for her sins. In 1872, she described the illness of her loved ones as 'expiation for the infinite joys' experienced with Gambetta.[63]

Léon's periodic qualms of conscience frustrated Gambetta. He wrote in 1876: 'I am counting on you for Monday without fail and I think that the rantings [*déclamations*] of your Jeremiah in a cassock won't make you delay by a single day the pleasure that I am promising myself.'[64] Gambetta's self-interested words ignored, or were intended to counteract, Léon's spiritual anguish. We might even speculate that some of Léon's many delayed visits to Gambetta were due, not only to family responsibilities and her mother's domineering ways, but also to Léon's struggle with her conscience. She recognized and agonized over the contradictions in her life, disrupting her relationship with Gambetta. Gambetta declared in 1878: 'I curse your scruples and your pride, which put so many obstacles between you and me.'[65]

'Our enemies would do well to be vigilant'

At least at the beginning, Gambetta preferred compromise to an all-out attack on clerical power. Republicans were wary of repeating the error of the 1790s, when the revolutionaries had attacked not only clerical abuses but also religion itself, thus alienating many devout Catholics.[66] The republicans' focus in the 1870s was on respect for the Concordat, which enabled them to oppose ultramontanist ambitions without opposing the exercise of religion. Gambetta called for a return to 'Gallicanism': belief in a strong national Church, operating within the terms of the Concordat and therefore subject to a degree of State control.

In a speech at Saint-Quentin in November 1871, Gambetta lamented the disappearance of 'a great clergy, faithful to its traditions of religious and national independence'. He asserted that ordinary priests retained 'Gallican' principles, while the Church hierarchy had become 'ultramontanist'. This dubious claim allowed him to praise the simple rural priest serving his community, whilst excoriating the political interference and lack of patriotism of the bishops. 'Far from being the enemies of the clergy', he continued at Saint-Quentin, 'we only ask to see them return to the democratic traditions of their elders in the great Constituent Assembly [of 1789–1791], and to associate themselves like the rest of the French people with the life of the republican nation.'[67]

The 'ultramontanist plots' of 1877 again stirred Gambetta to call for a return to Gallican principles within the Church.[68] The conflict between republicans and their monarchist and clerical opponents reached new heights at this moment. President MacMahon's choice of Catholic monarchists, like the duc de Broglie, to head his Ministries fuelled republican anticlericalism. So did the actions of Pope Pius IX, who was at loggerheads with the Italian government over new laws against militant priests. These laws would actually be struck down in May by the Italian Senate, but by then the damage had been done.[69] In March 1877, Pius IX appealed for international protests against these laws. Catholic Action committees immediately began campaigning across France. They were promptly banned, but a number of French bishops and Legitimist politicians continued to agitate in support of the Pope.

As the issue festered during April, Gambetta foreshadowed an attack in the Chamber of Deputies when it resumed its sessions on 1 May. 'I'm back in harness on the budget', he wrote to Léon on 24 April, 'and for the first session I've obtained an excellent report on the religious question [*les cultes*] that should cause the clergy to reflect, if there are still a few men of good sense and patriotism voting in their ranks.' The President of the Council of Ministers, the conservative republican Jules Simon, tried to pacify both sides when the Catholic agitation was discussed on 3 May. Gambetta was scathing about his approach: 'Simon was odious. It's either a collapse or a betrayal.'[70]

Gambetta took the podium himself the following day to condemn the 'ultramontanist intrigues' and the government's weak response. He drew applause from both the left and the centre of the Chamber when he insisted that this was not a religious matter but a political one, an attack by ultramontanist Catholics on the Republic: 'the same men who . . . lead the assault on the institutions, on the Revolution of 1789, on its conquests', he claimed, are 'at the head of the Catholic committees, the Catholic circles, the Catholic associations.' They 'make all these associated ideas a lever, indeed a battering ram, raised against the citadel of the State'. He attacked their 'submission' to the Syllabus of Errors, and linked their political activities to the proclamation of Papal infallibility: 'when Rome has spoken, all, without exception, priests, curés, bishops, all obey'. At the end of Gambetta's speech, the Chamber voted overwhelmingly to condemn 'ultramontanist demonstrations' and to call on the government to 'use all the legal means at its disposal to repress this antipatriotic agitation'.[71]

This vote was a major cause of the constitutional crisis that saw an irate President MacMahon dismiss Simon's government and dissolve the Chamber: the so-called 'coup' of 16 May 1877.[72] It provoked widespread outrage in republican circles, as Gambetta reported to Léon:

> Revealing information is reaching us from all quarters, proving that the display of disapproval [for MacMahon's actions] by the two chambers has spread throughout the country . . . businessmen, urban-dwellers, workers, peasants, are agreed on this point: that it is an act of aggression by the clerical party: it's all the fault of the priests, they are saying in the countryside.[73]

'The priests' had certainly played a part. Several bishops, including Dupanloup, had joined other conservative leaders in pressuring the President to sack Simon. Other bishops congratulated Cardinal Guibert for his involvement. In response, Jules Dufaure, Simon's replacement as Head of the Council of Ministers, would veto Dupanloup's elevation to Cardinal in May 1878.[74]

Gambetta suggested to Léon that an international clerical conspiracy lay behind these events: 'it seems impossible to believe that our adventurers had in view only a campaign in the interior [of France]; they have secretly entertained the dream of a Catholic League in Europe and won't draw back from a general conflagration, either to remain in office, or to obey the promptings of the Vatican'. Gambetta read the results of the elections in October, which gave the 'clericals' a few more seats, as confirmation of his conspiracy theory: 'this proves clearly for the country and for Europe that the true inspirers and beneficiaries of the coup d'état of 16 May are indeed the agents and servants of the Roman Curia'.[75] Like most conspiracy theories, this one appears unconvincing with hindsight, but it highlights the gulf of understanding and sympathy separating Catholics and republicans.

'We can hope for an arranged marriage with the Church'

Gambetta's anticlerical oratory helped shape the republican victory in May 1877. With the republicans holding the upper hand, however, he again demonstrated that his preferred approach to dealing with the Church was conciliation, not confrontation. Gambetta again proclaimed his own moderation, as well as his pragmatic tolerance of religious practice, in a letter to Léon in January 1878. The King of Italy had died, and Gambetta was keen to keep his successor friendly to the French Republic:

> Tomorrow I will go to Mass despite my anticlerical repugnance; I am saying to myself quietly to excuse myself, and without wanting to plagiarize [Henri IV]: Rome is worth a Mass. . . . I will read . . . a pretty *Provinciale* by Pascal, on the art of hearing mass, in a little jewel of a volume, which I have kept since M. Thiers' death for occasions like this. How you've changed your Leon.[76]

Perhaps Léon did reinforce Gambetta's moderation on religious matters. But he had long been a political pragmatist rather than an ideologue, and he was still prepared to negotiate his way to a settlement with the Church if that were possible.

The death in February 1878 of the ultraconservative Pope Pius IX, and his replacement by the more liberal Leo XIII, opened the real possibility of 'reconciliation with the Vatican', as Gambetta was quick to note:

> They have named the new Pope; it's the elegant and refined Cardinal Pecci, bishop of Pérouse . . . the name Leo XIII that he has taken seems to me to be a good omen. I welcome this very promising

development. He won't break openly with the traditions and declarations of his predecessor; but his conduct, his actions, his relationships will count more than speeches, and if he doesn't die too soon,
we can hope for an arranged marriage with the Church.[77]

Gambetta was still excluded from the ministry, so he had no direct
opportunity to foster this 'arranged marriage'. But his efforts to have
Léon's confessor, Canon Codant, appointed a bishop in 1878 are suggestive of his intentions.

Bishops were nominated by the State under the terms of the Concordat
of 1801.[78] Until 1880, when the republicans began to exercise firmer
control over these appointments, officials of Church and State agreed
on the desirable candidate for each See. There was much politicking
behind the scenes.[79] In early 1878, at Léon's request and perhaps at the
prompting of the sisters at Sèvres, Gambetta approached the Minister
for Education and Religious Affairs, Agénor Bardoux, to seek Codant's
appointment as Bishop.

Gambetta was always happy to grant Léon favours, but he believed
that Codant exhibited 'a nature suited to the politics that we want to
have govern the new relations between Church and State'.[80] This suggests that Codant was a man of moderate views; perhaps he was even a
republican sympathizer, which would have made him unusual for the
time. That Gambetta sought to name such men as bishops, and that he
sought 'an arranged marriage' with the Church at all, point again to
the moderation of his anticlericalism. His Belleville constituents, and
the Extreme Left republicans, had far more radical ideas.

In March and April, Gambetta was confident of success, to the delight
of both Codant and Léon. Codant had indicated that he would accept a
position at Bayonne, where the elderly incumbent had recently retired.
But the matter dragged on, despite Gambetta's appeals to the Minister.
Gambetta suspected that the Papal Nuncio opposed the move. But even
after May 1878, when the role of the Papal Nuncio in such appointments was reduced, Codant was still not elevated.[81]

The reasons for his rejection are unclear. Perhaps he was just regarded
as unsuitable. Perhaps the fact that he was not a Jesuit disadvantaged
him, given that the Bayonne diocese had a strong Jesuit presence.[82]
Perhaps political factors won the day. Léon had reported in 1876 that
an unnamed priest had been disciplined for associating with her: 'My
relations with the curé have been incriminated, from the political point
of view you understand, and he has been advised to suspend them
for the time being.'[83] If Gambetta regarded Codant as a sympathetic

figure in 1878, the bishops may have regarded him as too 'political', or too close to the republican government. Moreover, given Gambetta's prominent role in anticlerical politics, his sponsorship was probably not helpful to Codant's cause. Many Catholics had been offended, during the debates of May 1877, when Gambetta questioned Catholics' loyalty to France. In late July 1878, therefore, Gambetta's efforts on Codant's behalf had still not been successful. Gambetta asked the Minister again: 'Tell me it's arranged . . . or at least that you are naming [Codant] to Saint Denis with the rank of titular bishop [*évêque in partibus*].' [84] But Codant died suddenly in December without having been elevated to the episcopacy.

It seems that the sisters sought Léon's intervention to secure a posthumous decoration for Codant. Gambetta was pleased to report the following July: 'I finally have the decoration and you can tell your good friends that with certainty.' 'In this as in everything', he added, 'it never costs me anything to satisfy you.' A few days later, he continued: 'You can tell your religious whatever you like . . . I will take pleasure, on every occasion, in doing all the good that I can in your name; I have only one request, that you resolve to make use of your friend and husband.'[85] Gambetta's hostility was reserved for those members of the Church who used their religion as a political weapon.

In the late 1870s, the balance of power in the Chamber of Deputies moved to the left and more radical voices prevailed on the religious question. If Gambetta had hoped to negotiate a settlement with the Church, the Republican Left and the Extreme Left were determined to establish a thoroughly secular State. Their secularization campaign began with a series of education laws – collectively known as the Ferry Laws after Jules Ferry, Minister for Public Instruction and the Fine Arts – passed between 1879 and 1882. These 'free, compulsory and secular' laws in France were not a republican aberration; their introduction coincided with that of similar laws across the Anglo-American world.

Gambetta did not play a major role in the passage of this legislation, but he supported it and attempted to use his influence when the first Bill stalled in the Senate in July 1879.[86] When that Bill was finally passed in March 1880, however, it was amended to remove Article 7, which prohibited members of non-authorized religious congregations from teaching.[87] The fallout from this amendment saw republicans mobilize to expel from France a number of religious orders known for their anti-republican activities.

Some of the education laws, especially one requiring all teachers to have a teaching certificate, affected female congregations in particular.[88]

When Léon foreshadowed another request from her 'sisters' in December 1881, therefore, they were anxious about their own future.[89] This would explain the wording of Léon's letter to Gambetta on their behalf: 'The good sisters beseech Esther to plead with Assuerus once again, the details later.'[90] The Book of Esther in the Old Testament tells how Queen Esther, a Jew, risked death by approaching King Assuerus to plead for the lives of her people, who were to be slaughtered throughout the kingdom on a given day. This may have seemed, to Léon's 'good sisters', like a metaphor for their own position. Gambetta had already shown some sympathy for them, writing to Léon as the expulsion of male religious got underway late in 1880: 'P.S. Today we execute the monks and little monks [*moinillons*] – if there was [*sic*] alarm at Sèvres[,] reassure your good women; they won't be touched.'[91] What they asked of Gambetta in 1881 we do not know, but Gambetta's reply to Léon's letter again sought to allay her fears and those of her 'good women'.[92] Gambetta remained sympathetic to these 'good women' who posed no threat to the Republic.

Gambetta was a non-believer and a committed anticlerical, then, but he was not a zealot who wished to make war against all believers. He was a pragmatist, who accepted that some people – even his beloved Léon – would maintain their religious faith in the foreseeable future. Léon was a believer but she was also a republican. This was unusual in the 1870s when very few republicans were practising Catholics.[93] Not until the 1890s, when Pope Leo XIII urged Catholics to accept the authority of the republican government and pursue their interests within its parliamentary framework, did the phenomenon of the Catholic republican become more commonplace.

Had Léon not been smitten by Gambetta, she may not have become a republican in the 1870s either. But smitten by him she was. This confirmed her dedication to the Republic he championed, despite its conflict with the Church to which she remained attached. For this couple at least, love triumphed over intolerance.

Part III
Years of Frustration, 1877–1882

My adored master,

It's you who are great and not the [electoral] triumph! What glory to have single-handedly, in just a few years, created a new France full of promise for the future, by the force of your eloquence, your will, your genius! And you love me and the memory of me overrides all that exhilaration! Darling, it is too much happiness! When will I be at your feet to cover them with kisses and tears of gratitude?

Till tomorrow, and yours
Léonie

P.S. The letter didn't arrive until 5 o'clock yesterday after mine had left!
6 January 79

8

'What glory, to have created a new France'

The elections of October 1877, which gave the republicans a majority of 119 in the Chamber of Deputies, sealed the victory for which Gambetta and Léon had struggled since 1872. The Republic had triumphed and monarchism would never again pose a serious threat. Gambetta had been pivotal to this triumph. He led the largest republican faction in the Chamber: roughly one hundred of the 326 republican Deputies were aligned with him. Nevertheless, President MacMahon not only refused to appoint him to lead a government; he even refused to include him in the ministry.[2]

Léon remained, as always, Gambetta's comfort in his political frustrations. But her periodic bouts of melancholy continued to trouble them both. Moreover, rumours of his affairs began to multiply as Gambetta's fame increased, providing new causes for sorrow. The couple's emotional upheavals added to the political frustrations that beset them. Both their political and personal aspirations remained tantalizingly out of reach.

'Tell me your feelings, which are always so insightful'

Gambetta shared the pleasure of victory with Léon as the Chamber of Deputies reassembled and the republicans rubbed salt into the conservatives' wounds. Gambetta's confrontation on 1 February 1878 with Eugène Rouher – formerly President of the Emperor's Council of State – was a personal triumph. Gambetta again likened the confrontation to a duel, construing it as a personal contest of strength between male adversaries:

> It is one o'clock and I've just returned from Versailles where I had an oratorical duel with Rouher in which I like to think that the

Vice-Emperor was crushed. I hadn't felt such force and eloquence since the Baudin affair. . . . The battle was provoked by a rash and cynical statement from this *auvergnat*, I took the opportunity to be done with him and I am satisfied.

He relied on Léon, again, to acknowledge and affirm his achievement: 'You will read these speeches the day after tomorrow, if they have been recorded accurately, and you will be happy.'[3]

Deprived of a ministerial portfolio, Gambetta was free to exercise his talents as he chose. He threw himself into foreign affairs, in which he had a longstanding interest. Immediately after the elections, therefore, he assumed the task of promoting the French Republic in Europe.[4] Gambetta exchanged lengthy letters with Juliette Adam on international relations, outlining a broad view of France's place in the world.[5] Léon, on the other hand, was Gambetta's intimate sounding board. She had his complete confidence as he evaluated specific courses of action and sought advice, even though he did not necessarily take that advice.

Gambetta turned his attention first of all to Italy. After a lightning visit in January 1878, he concluded that the Franco-Italian relationship was strong. With the accession of the more liberal Pope Leo XIII, he was also optimistic about improving France's relations with the Vatican.[6] Gambetta was even more hopeful of improving relations with Germany, which still bore the scars of the war of 1870. The republican government made several gestures of goodwill to Germany immediately on assuming power. Chancellor Bismarck's speech to the Reichstag in February 1878 seemed to offer an olive branch to France in return.

Bismarck referred to 'the friendship that, happily, unites us to most of the European States, at this moment I might even say to all'. His customary suspicion of Bismarck relieved, Gambetta wrote enthusiastically to Léon: 'I am delighted, enchanted; that's exactly what I wanted, what I had been waiting for, without daring to hope for it.'[7] His pleasure at this modest gesture reflected his deep-seated mistrust of the ambitions of 'the Monster' (as the couple nicknamed Bismarck). Now, however, Gambetta outlined his hopes for a 'new order' in Europe in which France would have its place.

Independent as ever, Léon disagreed with Gambetta's analysis, apparently arguing that Bismarck's conciliatory words were aimed at Russia, not at France. This was a reasonable view, given that Bismarck delivered the speech when tackling the 'Eastern Question': the question of territorial conflict, and Russia's ambitions, in Eastern Europe. Gambetta replied in detail to her arguments, although he 'persist[ed] in [his] first impressions.' The discussion continued for several days. Whether Gambetta persuaded Léon to his point of view is unclear, but he insisted that she should not hesitate to disagree with him: 'No, no, you must always express your opinion freely, I need that, it is the most reliable, the most shrewd check on my own thinking.'[8]

Gambetta also interpreted Bismarck's speech in a second context: that of a plan he and Léon had been hatching for a personal meeting between Gambetta and Bismarck to iron out Franco-German differences. It is difficult to establish precisely when Gambetta began to consider such a meeting. He cautioned that it was 'better to talk about [these matters] than to write about them', and delicate political discussions between the couple mainly took place face-to-face.[9] Perhaps the 'very serious diplomatic affair' he had 'launched' in April 1876 referred to this proposed meeting. Léon's letter of early June was more suggestive still: 'I don't despair of the success of our plan, since you call it that. For the monster, it will have the appeal of a new combination that he hadn't been able to consider seriously, not knowing whether it was possible to meet with us other than armed to the teeth, and on diplomatic ground.' Two weeks later, she speculated, 'How dramatic it would be if he [Bismarck] found himself face-to-face on one of his morning excursions with the only intelligence that could match his own!'[10]

Gambetta had held no hope of undertaking such a mission in 1876.[11] But from October 1877, when the republicans held the reigns of power, the possibilities for rapprochement between France and Germany began to improve. It was not only Gambetta who thought so. Immediately following the republican victory in the legislative elections, Prussian Count Guido Henckel (later Prince von Donnersmarck) wrote to Bismarck offering to arrange a meeting with Gambetta. Henckel was a cousin of Bismarck. With his wife, known as La Païva, he hosted an exclusive salon in their fabulous mansion on the Champs Élysées. Gambetta had attended the salon since about 1875. But Bismarck rejected Henckel's October offer, and another in December, as premature.[12]

In early 1878, therefore, Léon and Gambetta were discussing two difficult issues concerning 'the Monster'. As well as debating whether France should attend Bismarck's proposed Congress, which was to take place in Berlin in July, they were also considering whether Gambetta should pursue the idea of meeting with Bismarck in person in the hope of advancing rapprochement. These two issues were intertwined in their correspondence, and given the couple's sometimes elliptical exchanges, it is not always easy to disentangle them.

At the beginning of March, despite what he saw as Bismarck's olive branch, Gambetta was adamant that France should not attend the Congress of Berlin. This decision was not his to make since he was not the Minister, but he nevertheless promoted his own strong views. A 'rigorous, hermetic neutrality would make everyone feel the void created by France's absence from the governance [*traitement*] of European affairs', he argued to Léon, and would also prevent alienating possible allies. France should concentrate on military reorganization, building its preparedness for the future. 'Meditate on the subject and tell me your feelings, which are always so insightful and so certain', he urged Léon.[13]

Léon's correspondence on the subject has disappeared but she must have disagreed strongly. The following day Gambetta acknowledged 'the electric effect' of her 'harangue', which revived his 'perplexities'. By 6 March he was persuaded to her view: 'I surrender arms to wise Minerva', he wrote, 'your latest words have overcome my final hesitations, and if people are gathering in Berlin under the presidency of the Monster, we must go, especially if the invitation comes from him.' On 11 March he again confirmed, 'It's done, we will go there with all sorts of precautions, safeguards [*lisières*].'[14]

Perhaps Gambetta was persuaded to her point of view because the views of others now coincided with hers. The Minister for Foreign Affairs, William Waddington, reported to Gambetta the advice of his foreign policy experts that France's interests in Egypt and the Middle East might be jeopardized if France were not represented at the Congress. France should attend, therefore, but seek guarantees in advance that French interests in the region would not be subject to negotiation. These were presumably the 'safeguards' that Gambetta mentioned to Léon.[15]

Sometimes Gambetta's references to 'going to Berlin' referred to France's presence at the Congress, therefore, not necessarily to his own presence. But 'going to Berlin' also referred to the couple's plans for a personal meeting between Bismarck and Gambetta. This was the 'daring' move that Gambetta attributed to Léon's inspiration and good judgement: 'The most daring, and probably the most fruitful endeavour of my career was the product of your inspiration and the clarity of your intelligence. Everything that is happening and evolving in this regard shows that you have judged soundly.'[16]

With agreement on the international Congress having been reached among the European governments, Bismarck himself now thought a meeting with Gambetta worthwhile and asked Henckel to make the arrangements. On 23 April 1878, Gambetta reported to Léon that a date was fixed: 'I have seen, I have promised. The Monster is returning [from his country house] to meet me, and I need to see you; so till Thursday, it's essential.' He clearly wanted to talk it over with Léon. But the following day he gave his excuses to Henckel, citing a major parliamentary debate that he could not miss.[17] Word had leaked to the press and his colleagues were dismayed at the move, which would severely damage both his reputation and that of the Republic. Public opinion was still strongly in favour of 'revenge' against Germany, not reconciliation.

If Léon's advice was accepted in March when it coincided with that of leading republicans, it was now overturned because it was at odds with those views. No letters survive discussing this outcome. But Léon apparently did not succumb quietly to superior force. She suggested again the following March that Gambetta should let it be known that he planned to travel in the next parliamentary vacation: 'the Monster will be informed, and we will see'.[18] But nothing came of the idea.

Gambetta's political adversaries later used this projected meeting with Bismarck to accuse him of a lack of patriotism.[19] But the return of Alsace-Lorraine was probably his motive. Since France had no hope of recovering the territory by force of arms, Gambetta perhaps considered negotiating that return directly with Bismarck, in a gentlemanly fashion. Once he accepted that this idea was illusory, a meeting with 'the Monster' lost its main justification.[20] But his dedication to Alsace-Lorraine remained: 'My name will go down in history [est inscrit au Panthéon]', he wrote to Léon in 1879. 'It's an account on which I must still pay what is owing. I undertake to do that and you know what price I want to put on it. The Monster defeated and the frontier redrawn. V.L.R.F. [Long live the French Republic].'[21] Léon, convinced of the formidable power and persuasiveness of her 'great man', continued to believe that, if Bismarck were to come face to face with 'the only intelligence that could match his own', the outcome would inevitably be in France's favour.

'Blinded by an old idol?'

Léon began her letter to Gambetta on 24 March 1877, asking him, 'are you allowing yourself to be blinded by an old idol?'[22] She may have heard rumours that Gambetta's high public profile had led his former mistress, Marie Meersmans, to seek him out again. Juliette Adam claimed in her memoirs that Meersmans was seeking money in exchange for potentially damaging documents. They included a photograph of Gambetta that he had supposedly inscribed, 'To my little Queen whom I love more than France!' Adam claimed to have purchased those documents in October 1877. Adam's claims invite caution, but undercover police did report rumours, in December 1877 and January 1878, that money had changed hands for compromising materials.[23] If Meersmans had reappeared, Léon's anxiety about this former mistress would certainly have been acute.

That there was tension between Gambetta and Léon over this issue was evident in Gambetta's note as he left for Italy on his unofficial diplomatic mission in late December 1877. Assuring Léon of his fidelity, he promised 'to return, like the pigeon in the fable, *with all my feathers,* without having sought anything outside except food and shelter, disdaining *"the rest"* with all the force of my love [emphasis orig.]'. [24]

It would have been easy for Gambetta to become distracted from single-minded devotion to Léon at this time. He was lionized by society and sought after by prominent social hostesses. Edmond de Goncourt noted in January 1878, in his often spiteful diary: 'Right now, the bourgeois woman has an appetite for Gambetta. She wants to have him in her home, she wants to serve him to her friends, she wants to show him, sprawled [*échoué*] on a silk sofa, to her guests.'[25] Gambetta's lack of breeding was always a talking point in high society. Goncourt used the word *échoué* – meaning run aground, or beached – to connote Gambetta's increasing size and lack of the expected social graces; he contrasted his implied vulgarity and appetite with the elegance of silk. But Goncourt had a point: Gambetta was invited everywhere, particularly by wealthy republican hostesses.

It was not surprising, then, that rumours spread during 1877 and 1878 of Gambetta's affairs with or plans to marry various society women. These rumours concerned women whose salons Gambetta frequented; women who were both beautiful and wealthy. The women named, with one exception, were fervent republicans. While society women competed for Gambetta's presence at their salons and dinners, Léon was excluded. Few of Léon's letters from this period survive to indicate what she heard and how she reacted.

One wave of rumours concerned the strikingly beautiful and fabulously wealthy Marquise Arconati-Visconti. Daughter of Alphonse Peyrat, the Radical Republican Senator, Marie Peyrat shared her father's republican convictions. Having married the Marquis Arconati-Visconti in 1873, she was widowed in 1876 at the age of 36 and inherited a vast fortune. She became a major figure in Parisian high society, holding weekly salons on art (Tuesdays) and politics (Thursdays). Gambetta attended regularly, and rumours soon spread that the Marquise was

Gambetta's mistress.[26] Those rumours have long been given credence, despite the Marquise's protestations.[27]

Some of the surviving letters from Gambetta to the Marquise might, at first glance, suggest an affair in 1877. Warm and playful, they are sprinkled with terms of endearment in often-faulty Italian, exhibiting a mutual delight in their shared Italian link. The Marquise also showered Gambetta with expensive gifts: 'You're too kind, dear [*Tout beau, mignonne*]', he replied, 'I'm collapsing beneath the flowers and the books, and the bronzes, and I'm as happy as I am overwhelmed to find myself at such a party.'[28]

But these letters are quite different from Gambetta's letters to Léon or to Meersmans. They never refer to passion or desire, still less to the body, as his letters to his lovers do. The kisses that Gambetta sent the Marquise were *baci* – kisses between friends, pecks on the cheek – not passionate kisses between lovers.[29] Their letters were letters of friendship and their relationship was largely epistolary: the letters never fix times to meet or dine. As Carlo Bronne notes, 'nothing in this epistolary banter permits one to conclude that they were united by more than an amorous friendship, cerebral rather than sensual'.[30] This friendship nevertheless sparked rumours and, if Léon heard them, they would certainly have disturbed her.

In 1878, too, Gambetta's long-standing friendship with Mme Arnaud de l'Ariège was embroidered with rumours of romance. Like the Marquise, Mme Arnaud was the daughter of a republican notable; her husband, Frédéric Arnaud, was a leading republican who had served in the Revolutionary Assembly of 1848, and a friend of Gambetta. The wealthy couple provided funds for Gambetta's newspaper *La République française,* and when Mme Arnaud inherited an immense fortune from her uncle in 1878, she settled on Gambetta an annual subsidy of 100,000 francs, a princely sum.[31]

Gambetta was a regular at Mme Arnaud's salon and visited the couple at the Chateau des Crêtes, on the shores of Lake Geneva, every autumn from 1872.[32] When Gambetta visited Mme Arnaud in October 1877, however, she was an available widow: her husband had died in May that year. Rumours flew of his impending marriage to the republican heiress and Gambetta wrote to Juliette Adam to deny them. Mme Arnaud also wrote to Adam: 'we know too well that Gambetta is fixed to attach any credence to the news of his marriage, unless it's with Mlle L'.[33]

While none of Léon's letters for 1878 has survived, Gambetta's visit to Mme Arnaud in 1879 sparked a bitter quarrel between the couple. 'You must be held by very tight bonds, or captivated by especially fascinating pleasures, if it matters so little to you that I suffer without consolation, or more to the point without seeing you', Léon wrote. 'Your eloquence is cruelly persuasive, and your indifference mortal!'[34] Nothing suggests, however, that Gambetta and Mme Arnaud had a sexual liaison. Four extant letters from Gambetta, all dated 1882, are formal and correct, as befitted letters to his patron. All are addressed 'Dear madam and friend'. They often contain exchanges about Mme Arnaud's son, whom Gambetta made his personal secretary when he became President of the Chamber of Deputies.[35] But Léon's reaction suggests that she had heard the gossip about Gambetta's women friends, and that she feared it was true.

That both Gambetta and Mme Arnaud protested to Juliette Adam highlights Adam's role in spreading rumours about Gambetta's personal life. Adam was implicated, too, in reporting yet another supposed affair: in August 1878, word spread that the 'beautiful and seductive' comtesse de Beaumont was 'very prettily occupied in the arms of our illustrious leader'.[36] The comtesse was not just any society hostess; she was the sister-in-law of Marshal MacMahon, still President of the Republic.

Gambetta may have been invited to one of the comtesse's monthly society dinners, and she may have been, as Adam put it, 'wildly enthusiastic' for Gambetta. But the charge that there was an affair rests on very flimsy evidence: one letter whose author has never been revealed, and Adam's claim that the President had come upon Gambetta and the comtesse walking in a park, 'apparently on intimate terms'.[37] Perhaps Gambetta offered the comtesse his arm, as social convention required. Even if the comtesse de Beaumont was eclectic in her guest list, however, she remained a royalist. It seems highly unlikely that she would have shared her bed with a republican politician, a grocer's son. It seems equally unlikely that Gambetta would have taken up with an aristocrat and monarchist, thereby jeopardizing his political career, and that he would have done so in public. Nevertheless, President MacMahon apparently believed these rumours (one historian even asserts that the comtesse 'was known to be a woman of loose morals').[38]

It is not surprising that rumours about Gambetta's personal life multiplied from 1877. He was the most prominent political figure of the day, personifying the newly secured Republic to both friends and opponents, and he was unmarried. Both the Marquise and Mme Arnaud were recently widowed. It was widely assumed that they would want to remarry, and since they were both committed republicans, Gambetta would have been the perfect match. But both women were apparently content with their independent lives as wealthy widows. Both remained Gambetta's devoted friends until his death. They enjoyed the company of this charming and intelligent man, and regarded their financial support for him as a contribution to the republican cause.

Juliette Adam, however, widowed in June 1877, may have aspired to marry Gambetta. When he visited her at the beginning of 1878 for his now-customary New Year's holiday, he found himself the sole guest. Their relationship seems to have deteriorated from this time. By 1879, it was in ruins. Adam broke publicly with Gambetta over his policy of rapprochement with Germany, and moved to an authoritarian patriotism.[39]

Some suggest that the tone of Juliette Adam's memoirs indicates that she had an affair with Gambetta. But the memoirs were written many years later, and her comments on Gambetta reflect their bitter falling out.[40] Perhaps unrequited love explains the tone of the memoirs, as well as the breakdown of that relationship. Gambetta's letters to Juliette Adam had never been love letters, and he had begun to address her as his 'sister' even before Edmond's death, perhaps as a precaution. Adam had written to her husband: 'his [Gambetta's] love life is fixed, if not his fidelity'.[41] The fact that his fidelity appeared in doubt, however, was due in no small measure to the rumours spread by Juliette Adam.

Despite the gossip and innuendo that swirled around Gambetta linking him to other women, then, there is little evidence for Gambetta's philandering. His colleague, Auguste Scheurer-Kestner, later recalled: 'Gambetta was not what one calls a "ladies' man" . . . but he greatly enjoyed their company and knew how to make himself adored by them, in a positive and honourable way.'[42] Gambetta may have flirted with other women, but his love for the one he called 'my goddess, my all, my own universe, my Léonie' reigned supreme.[43]

Contrary to the rumours, in 1878 Gambetta was exploring ways to spend more time with Léon. His purchase of les Jardies, the country house at Ville-d'Avray, was the culmination of this plan. On 11 August, he wrote jubilantly to Léon: 'the contract is signed, the money paid, and here we are sole masters of les Jardies'. There he could try to ful-fill the promise he had made to Léon in May: he would, he told her, 'encircle you in my arms to make you believe that you are safe from the bitterness and the cruel anguish of your inner life [intérieur]'.[44] Les Jardies was a haven from the troubles of daily life, from rumour, social opprobrium, and prying eyes. It offered a space to create the domestic happiness that was to become increasingly important as Gambetta's political career began to falter.

'The force of your eloquence, your will, your genius'

The opening of the Universal Exposition in Paris on 1 May 1878 provided an opportunity for the Republic to celebrate its triumph. Although he did not have a ministerial portfolio, Gambetta's high public profile at home and abroad assured him a key role in what would be the most successful Exposition to date, attracting 16 million visitors. On 24 May, he addressed representatives of the foreign delegations at a dinner hosted by the republican Cercle National. The Republic's agenda was 'a politics entirely of peace', he declared, and he proposed a toast to 'peace and industry' [*le travail*].[45]

The reception of Gambetta's speech convinced him that suspicions about an aggressive Republic had been allayed. 'It is a powerful and glorious day', he wrote exultantly to Léon that evening: 'all these representatives of the world who were present at our table will carry back to their peoples the echo of our words, the impressions of justice and progress that they have formed, and the cause of Republican France will thus be strengthened, acclaimed, blessed'. He attributed this triumph to Léon: 'What a star your love has placed on my forehead and what a stream of sovereign inspiration flows from your beautiful lips, I owe to you the peace, the strength, the happiness that sustained me and enlivened this evening.'[46]

These sentiments affirmed Gambetta's commitment to a partnership with Léon defined in political as well as amorous terms. But Léon's role, as woman and especially as mistress, was to inspire behind the scenes while Gambetta publicly implemented the vision. This gender division is highlighted in retrospect by Léon's apparent disinterest in the first women's rights congress, held in conjunction with the International Exposition at which Gambetta triumphed. The press reported the controversy when one delegate to the congress, Hubertine Auclert, was prevented by the organizers from raising the question of women's suffrage. Even the few feminist militants of Léon's generation feared that such a wild notion would brand them as extremists. Barred from the Congress, Auclert published a pamphlet with the provocative title, 'The Political Rights of Women – A Question that is Not Treated at the International Congress of Women.'[47] While Léon, in particular, followed current events closely, neither she nor Gambetta mentioned this controversy. Like most people of the day, she could not even imagine women as political actors, so deeply rooted were the gender structures of her day.

This division of labour was highlighted again in September 1878, as Gambetta campaigned for the Senate elections due in January 1879. Crowds turned out exultantly as he travelled down the Rhône Valley.

They cheered and threw flowers; they feted him with triumphal arches and tricolour flags while bands played the *Marseillaise*. This was the republican family rejoicing in the victory that had gradually unfolded since 16 May 1877. They shouted 'Long live the Republic!' but they also shouted 'Long live Gambetta!'[48]

Léon shared Gambetta's triumphs only vicariously and from afar. He reported on his progress, and on the toll that constant travel and dozens of speeches took on his health. During a brief respite in late September at the chateau of Mme Arnaud, he reported: 'I am recovering, but quite slowly. The weather is beautiful, I wander all day along the banks of the lake under a blazing sun and thanks to the warmth of its rays I can feel my voice returning.'[49]

Léon reported her own ongoing health problems and Gambetta again urged her to seek treatment, this time from Jean-Martin Charcot, the leading neurologist of the day. Charcot was renowned for his work on hysteria at the Salpêtrière asylum, which became the leading centre for the treatment and study of neuropathological disorders. In his private practice, Charcot treated patients suffering from 'melancholy' (or 'melancholy and a bit of hysteria'), his case notes recording their 'black thoughts', and their vague references to dying. His recommended treatments included hydrotherapy, drugs, electrotherapy and the 'vibrating chair'. Gambetta was so impressed by Charcot that, on forming a government, he created for him a Chair in maladies of the nervous system at the Paris School of Medicine: the first of its kind.[50]

Gambetta had met Charcot in late 1877, just after returning from that earlier gruelling campaign tour. He found Charcot very genial company, and benefited from his medical treatment: 'my throat is improving a bit, I believe that the visit to and the evening spent with Charcot has brought me real relief'. Charcot's expertise seemed particularly appropriate for both Léon's neuralgia (a nervous disorder) and her 'melancholy'. Gambetta urged her to consult him: 'I am really sorry to hear that you have been gripped again by your sorrows and I beseech you to go and see Charcot; I assure you that nothing you could do would give me more pleasure. He would be very happy to treat you given the friendship [with me] that he wants to strengthen, and I do not doubt that in his hands you would be cured.' Whether Léon took Gambetta's advice is unclear. But his electrotherapy did provide her with an analogy to describe the effect of Gambetta's love on her: it was like a 'galvanic bath, strong enough to overcome the world!'[51]

Popular adulation followed Gambetta into the Savoy region, and only two days after leaving Mme Arnaud's chateau he again wrote to

Léon: 'I'm snowed under, it's a real campaign that I have undertaken across this fine country . . . I hardly have time to embrace you. I can hear under my windows the acclamations of delegates from the mountain cantons [electoral districts] and I am about to go to a meeting. Ah! My beautiful Mimi, what a country and what people. How simple [*naïf*] and good they are.' In Grenoble and surrounding towns, banquets, brass bands, and bouquets were again the order of the day.[52]

Gambetta was quick to warn enthusiasts 'that we must beware of the prestige of personalities and that there is nothing more dangerous than making a man into an idol'. But Gambetta's own popularity caused some of his colleagues to fear that it was a platform for his own ambition.[53]

The Chamber resumed for the autumn session on 28 October 1878. Back from his triumphant campaign tour, ahead of elections scheduled for January, Gambetta put his popularity to good use addressing meetings in Paris, as well as dedicating himself to the Commission for Budgets. His lethargy had gone with the resumption of the Chamber, he wrote Léon, and he begged her to leave her mother and come to Versailles: 'Hurry back and escape the malevolence of your jailer.' He sent her tickets and sketched the agenda for forthcoming sessions. Mindful of the dazzling spectacle presented by the female spectators in the gallery, he noted: 'I hope you won't be too stunning so that you don't distract the attention of our honourable members.'[54]

The proximity of the elections added bite to the parliamentary session, and highlighted once again Gambetta's pivotal role in the republicans' domination of the Chamber. He had emerged victorious from a confrontation with the Bonapartist Eugène Rouher in February; now, in November, he clashed with Oscar Fourtou, formerly Interior Minister in the government installed in the so-called 'coup' of 16 May 1877.[55] When Fourtou accused him in the Chamber of having 'declared war' on non-republicans in France, Gambetta called him a liar, a term unacceptable in parliament. Gambetta withdrew the term, but refused to meet Fourtou's other demands. The result was a duel, not oratorical but with pistols, fought on 21 November 1878.

This was not an unusual event in the early Third Republic. Some 800 duels were fought annually as men defended their 'honour', and politicians employed the duel to prove both their personal and political mettle.[56] Gambetta wrote nonchalantly to Léon the evening before the encounter:

Tomorrow morning, I am going to stroll over by Châtillon, near the Bois de Vincennes, to settle an outstanding account with a certain fellow from Périgord. It seems that this Gentleman wants to test my skills with a pistol; he will be satisfied. So don't worry at all, the event will occur quite near your place and under your protection.

Gambetta was delighted by her brave response: 'What pride and joy fill my heart!' he announced. 'That is the language of my proud and gentle companion whom heroism costs nothing, her character being naturally noble enough for every ordeal.' When the encounter passed uneventfully, with neither party injured, he sent her a telegram: 'nothing untoward [*pas de résultat*]; am very well'.[57] Following this incident Gambetta nevertheless began practising his shooting, perhaps anticipating more dangerous challenges.

Some newspapers were scathing that neither party exposed himself to injury: their seconds had negotiated conditions that virtually ensured this. But the real contest was political, and Gambetta's popularity soared as a result of this duel.[58] That a politician should defend his political honour, and display manly courage by duelling, was not only accepted but expected.

The elections to replace a third of the Senate, scheduled for 5 January 1879, were a critical test of Gambetta's gamble in accepting an undemocratically elected Senate. During his tour through central and South-Eastern France at the end of 1878, Gambetta had taken every opportunity to stress the importance of the choice of Senators, given that many of the mayors and councillors who greeted him were members of the electoral colleges. He singled out the rural delegates, exhorting them to use their vote to 'democratize' the Senate: 'I want the Senate, created in a spirit of reaction against universal suffrage . . . to become . . . the veritable citadel of the Republic', he declared, 'to such an extent that one would pay homage to the Senate of the Republic as one did to the Senate of Rome.' Gambetta predicted a majority of twenty seats, but the republicans won sixty-six seats to the conservatives' sixteen, giving them a majority of forty-eight in the Senate. It became and remained a 'citadel of the Republic', as Gambetta had hoped.[59]

Léon was ecstatic as the election results came in, and Gambetta presented the victory as a victory for their love. 'This triumph will only have its full rapture for me in your arms . . . This willpower, this obstinate perseverance . . . are entirely the fruits of your gentleness, of that genius for patience that you have inspired in me and that is your personal triumph.' Léon, too, exaggerated her lover's role in this achievement: 'It's you who are great, not the triumph! To have singlehandedly created a new France full of promise, in just a few years, by the force of your eloquence, your will, your genius, what glory! And you love me . . . ! My beloved, it is too much happiness!'[60]

'You judge severely what has been accomplished'

The Republicans now controlled both the Chamber of Deputies and the Senate, although they remained divided on factional lines. But Marshal MacMahon's term as President had two years to run. The republican ministry of Jules Dufaure, which MacMahon had grudgingly appointed in 1877, was increasingly caught between a President for whom republican policies were anathema, and an increasingly confident and demanding republican legislature.

The showdown between the President and the Assembly unfolded over two weeks, beginning in mid-January 1879. Gambetta was in the thick of it. Léon was caring for her son, who was confined to bed with measles; she and Gambetta exchanged lengthy letters about the emerging political crisis. 'Our difficulties have begun', Gambetta informed Léon on 11 January. 'The Ministry is groping and floundering. The [republican] majority is tossing and turning without deciding anything, I am trying in vain to make them accept a common set of rules.'[61]

Gambetta had threatened to withhold the support of his Republican Union for Dufaure's government if the Ministers of War and Foreign Affairs were not republicans.[62] The appointment of the Minister for War (who had charge of the army) was critical to head off the possibility of a coup. But President MacMahon flatly refused to concede on the War ministry and Dufaure yielded. Gambetta wrote angrily to Léon, railing against the ministry – 'impotent, passive, blind, incompetent' – and MacMahon, who was 'pigheaded, impervious and reactionary, avid for power and fearful of losing it but doing nothing that would be necessary to keep it'. With Léon urging him on, Gambetta declared: 'I have absolutely decided, I will cast my vote for the death of the cabinet.' He optimistically enclosed a ticket, hoping against hope that her son would have recovered, and that Léon might come to see the 'execution'.[63]

Both Léon and Gambetta clearly hoped that Gambetta was on the verge of heading a government. Léon asked what would happen once the government fell, and queried the likely support Gambetta would have to form a ministry. She advised him to consult Louis Martel, the President of the Senate. 'It's not that I place the least hope in the talent of M. Martel; it's simply his intercession with the old soldier [MacMahon] that I believe useful, in order to underpin your ministerial combination with the authority that his post brings.' Gambetta agreed. 'Your advice is good, I will see the President of the Senate and acquaint him with my thoughts on the reconstitution of the ministry.'[64]

Gambetta was optimistic that MacMahon would invite him to form a government, adding: 'I am reflecting on the little speech that I might have to make to the old soldier if the inspiration took him to call on me. Think about it from your point of view and give me your impressions. I won't and can't accept governing as a subordinate. Take that as your starting point and write from the heart.'

'What the old soldier fears is to be dominated', Léon responded, 'and he will be if he invites you to advise him.' But she seems to have mistaken the President's attachment to monarchism for an attachment to power. Léon suggested to Gambetta: 'assure him of your keen desire to see him retain his post until the end [of his mandate], perhaps beyond', so long as he is prepared 'to conform to your views', and be sure to add 'a few flattering words'. Far from 'charming' the President, as Léon believed, such a speech would probably have had disastrous effects.[65]

In the event, Léon's advice was irrelevant. Gambetta wrote that same evening: 'We are defeated, the ministry is defeated, the majority is divided, the programme is in ruins, and I am happy because I didn't dip my toe in this mess, not finding the time right to deliver the decisive blow.' The Senate's republican majority, persuaded by elder statesmen Jules Grévy and Jules Simon, had baulked at voting no confidence in Dufaure's republican ministry. But Gambetta reasserted: 'He will only last as long as I let him, and that won't be long.'[66]

Explaining this turn of events to Léon, Gambetta claimed that the Republican Union had abstained in the vote in order to allow people to reach the realization that change was necessary, but they did not have the numbers in the Senate to enforce their will. Perhaps Gambetta had taken the advice of some associates who urged him to wait until after MacMahon's term expired before seeking to head a government. By coming power too soon, they argued, he risked being used up in a frustrating battle, making limited gains and leaving republicans disappointed. But Gambetta's misery was evident as he appealed to Léon: 'I love you with all my soul and I am grieving at not seeing you any more. Sweetheart, sweetheart help! I am withering on the vine, I await you, I throw myself at your knees. When? Tell me quickly.'[67]

Léon was equally despairing at being separated from Gambetta by Alphonse's illness. She wrote the following day: 'I must see you! I am suffering, discouraged, nervous!' The political crisis and the crisis over her son's health combined to create a state of intense anxiety, and she switched almost imperceptibly from one problem to the other as she confided in Gambetta:

> The child is better, but cannot leave his bed, under pain of complications, nor contemplate going out for six weeks! What a trial on top of so many others! Till Thursday or Friday, my heart cannot wait any longer than that. Evidently I am wrong, but if there must be a crisis, I would prefer that it took place immediately, rather than see this state of uneasiness, disunity, uncertainty prolonged for several more weeks; it profits nobody and could damage the Republic. Uncertain situations must be as damaging for institutions as they are cruel for individuals![68]

The political uncertainty was not to last long. When President MacMahon's new appointee as Minister for War proposed to change certain military commands, MacMahon refused to sign them. Was this the news in Gambetta's telegram of 29 January that put Léon on tenterhooks? She wrote back, 'things are hotting up, play your cards close'.[69] On 30 January 1879, President MacMahon resigned.

That evening, a joint sitting of the Chamber and the Senate elected the republican Jules Grévy as the new President of the Republic. The last barrier to the survival of the Republic had fallen. Gambetta wrote to Léon immediately: 'Be reassured, things went very well, Grévy is elected, but I am taking his place as you advised, tomorrow I will be elected President of the Chamber [of Deputies], an excellent post for observation and influence.' But Léon's response to this momentous news was cool. Despite his invitation, she did not go to Versailles for his election: she thought his letter 'did not exhibit a very keen desire for [her] presence'.[70] There was a more substantive issue behind her absence, however, as Gambetta indicated in his next letter:

> It seems to me that, from a distance, you judge severely, bitterly what has been accomplished. Tenderness clouds your view and that is why I so wanted to see you in order to outline the serious reasons for rejoicing and the proof that I had chosen the good part, the superior part. It won't take long for you to be convinced after the briefest explanation . . . I will now be able to pass to the second programme, action abroad, and hold myself above and outside the parties, to choose my hour, my way, my means.[71]

Gambetta and Léon had expected Dufaure to be installed as President. His colleagues, Charles de Freycinet and Auguste Scheurer-Kestner, were both certain that Gambetta was dismayed when Dufaure refused to put his name forward.[72] Léon noted in one of her letters: 'If we had foreseen the retirement of Dufaure, we wouldn't have inclined ourselves so readily to the satisfaction of our fantasy.'[73] Under Dufaure, Gambetta might well have been asked to form a government as leader of the largest republican contingent in the Chamber. Grévy, however, disliked Gambetta: the reserved northerner felt an 'instinctive aversion' for the jovial southerner, according to one assessment.[74]

President Grévy now persuaded Gambetta that, despite his support within republican ranks, the time was still not ripe for him to form a government. He appointed William Waddington to head the ministry instead. Grévy suggested that Gambetta stand for the position of President of the Chamber of Deputies, and he was elected by an overwhelming majority. Whether he accepted this role enthusiastically, as he tried to persuade Léon, or whether his enthusiasm was a way of saving face and preserving republican unity, is difficult to determine.[75] But it was to take another week before Léon accepted Gambetta's positive interpretation of the outcome. This brought him great relief. 'Finally, I have found you again', he wrote on 9 February. 'I have regained the confidence of this heart for which I have lived, fought, breathed for seven years.'[76]

Dear adored woman,

Where is the mortal in time, in history, who ever tasted these sublime ecstasies? If pride in surpassing other men is measured especially by the possession of a treasure without rival, without precedent, I am sure that I will never feel envious of anyone; I have possessed the incommunicable; I have been dizzy with pleasure, I have really experienced, attained the upper limit of ineffable voluptuous pleasure, and I still haven't descended from those heights, I have barely regained possession of my reason and my eyes are still filled with the unforgettable clarity of elevated spheres. An instant, a second more and my life would have unravelled in a spasm from which there is no recovery, I felt the sensation of the endless abyss of pleasure from which one doesn't return, I will retain the memory and the imprint until my last breath. I owe to you, oh unique source of these ecstasies, a moment's experience of the nature of the gods, and I swear to you that my love will preserve the unchanging and religious stamp of the infinite; I adore you, oh goddess, you will admit that these bedazzlements had ill disposed me to understand the vulgar and confused noises that rose today from the depths of the parliament. I listened without hearing, I heard without understanding. The report you know about was read, it seemed to me emptier than the first time, besides it had a mediocre impact which will continue to diminish from now until the discussion which is set for Thursday at 2 p.m. precisely. I don't believe the indictment, I have seen the government, it is perfectly trained, determined, it will triumph. I am beginning to believe that it won't even be necessary to give it a prod. In any case we will see.

I still await you Monday without fail, come and get me, it [the debate] will still be the merchant navy, don't hurry, come as you did the other day, I will wait for you till 5.30. We will come back arm in arm, and in the evening we will go and laugh . . . [sic] at the Palais-Royal.

In the meantime I kiss you as I love you, without restraint, without rest, without measure.

Always and entirely yours,
Léon Gambetta

9
'Triumphant and full of regrets'

By persuading Gambetta to accept the Presidency of the Chamber of Deputies, President Grévy had shrewdly sidelined him. Despite the public profile of the position, it offered little scope for advancing a political programme. Gambetta's frustration was intense as he watched a succession of colleagues, each commanding fewer votes in the Chamber of Deputies than he did, appointed President of the Council of Ministers.[2] His career seemed blocked.

Dreams of domestic bliss with Léon provided solace for these political disappointments, more so now that, having tasted the pleasures of fatherhood through his relationship with Léon's son Alphonse, Gambetta thought of the three of them as a family, an 'indestructible trinity'. Marriage to Léon and living a family life became passions for him. But Léon, more attuned than Gambetta to the problems that marriage would present for them, never brought herself to consent, despite Gambetta's chorus of appeals.

'Under the influence of your good star'

As President of the Chamber of Deputies, Gambetta moved into the official residence at the Hôtel de Lassay in Paris. Mindful of Léon's criticisms of his 'upstart's mansion' on the rue de la Chaussée-d'Antin just three years previously, Gambetta pointed out that it was not 'a luxurious or even elegant Palace', but 'a hall, without taste, facilities, or grace'.[3]

Gambetta was soon fully engaged in a world of meetings, soirées and receptions where Léon could not venture. She kept away from Paris, seeming to 'hold the Presidency in horror'. Almost forty-one, she expressed anxiety about her 'age and the burden of time'; about the possibility that Gambetta would succumb to the trappings of power and abandon her. He was indignant, but responded to the appeal underpinning her words: 'What is more serious, more disturbing for me, is to feel behind all these lines that you are still mournful, suffering and anxious. Believe me, the true remedy is to come and find me, for us to love each other as in the past.'[4]

Léon was indeed suffering from a recurrence of her melancholy and was unable to grasp the reassurance he offered. Instead, she apparently wrote a harsh note, which Gambetta returned: it was 'too cruel, too unjust'. To return a letter signified serious pain or displeasure, and Léon then apologized. But she emphasized her insuperable sorrow; her feeling of being 'just a weak woman' weighed down by 'destiny'; forever doomed to be only a spectator to the happiness of others. Dwelling on past injustices and their ongoing impact, she was unable to appreciate the good things she had in the present. Still, Léon vowed in this same letter: 'Expect to find me changed'.[5]

If Léon's anxieties and black thoughts disrupted the couple's meetings, Gambetta's new duties also disrupted their letter-writing pattern. Gambetta suggested a new arrangement: 'you write in the evening, I'll receive your letter the following morning[.] I will reply before eleven o'clock, you'll receive it about 4.30 in the afternoon and we'll be able to resume our amorous dialogue with a sense of security.' But two weeks later he was pleased to report that a new postal system at the Palais Bourbon would enable him to send Léon her customary early morning letter, and with it '[his] affection, the news, [his] plans and above all the enthusiastic expression of an ever-growing love'.[6]

On 20 February, Gambetta sent Léon a permanent entry card for the Chamber, anticipating her regular presence at its sessions. Léon had already written: 'I've been thinking a lot about your politics; I don't believe that you should remain a simple spectator . . . On Friday we'll make some plans.'[7] As President of the Chamber (equivalent to Speaker of the House in the Anglo-American system), Gambetta was effectively a 'spectator' to the events over which he presided. He had lost his main political weapon: his oratorical domination of his opponents. Léon recognized the problems that this posed for Gambetta's political ambitions.

Since 1872, Gambetta's cautious political strategy had been dictated by the need to retain the support of conservative republicans and the Centre-Right (the Orleanist monarchists) in the Chamber. But by 1879 the strength of the Extreme Left was growing. Gambetta was in danger of losing ground to more radical republicans. He had already been approached by a delegation from his Belleville electorate, politely but firmly demanding action on a republican agenda. They wanted confirmation that he would walk 'prudently, firmly and surely, on the path of political and social, intellectual and moral progress, which is the necessary consequence of the establishment of the Republic'. Gambetta gave an undertaking that he would work to create a 'fruitful Republic, a Republic that would put things right [*réparatrice*], a Republic animated by the spirit of justice and progress'. But he emphasized that reforms would be carefully studied and gradual: he was not about to be pushed into action by the Extreme Left.[8]

Gambetta immediately set out to secure the return of the legislature to Paris. It remained at Versailles under the terms of the 1875 constitution, reflecting the conservatives' fears of the Parisian populace. To return it to Paris would be a major symbolic gesture of the Republic's triumph. But the move required a constitutional amendment, and this meant securing the support of the Senate.

Gambetta associated Léon with every stage of the amendment campaign. Initially confident of success, he wrote on 22 March: 'Today under the influence of your good star everything proceeded wonderfully in the Chamber. We finally took a bold step towards Paris.' Léon penned a seductive reply in which amorous and political aspirations coalesced: 'If you achieve the return to Paris it will be a grand victory, making a great impression on the world, and we will celebrate it in a thousand intoxicating ways that I am already dreaming about!'[9]

When the Senate finally approved the measure in mid-June, Gambetta shared his delight with Léon: 'Paris is returned to us, that is where the Republic should have its headquarters and it's from there that she must remake France, the old France, greater than that of the monarchy, prouder than that of the Empire, freer than that of the Revolution, the France of the Republic.'[10] Once again, both Gambetta and Léon represented this political victory as a triumph for their love. It strengthened Léon's affection for 'the sweetheart and the President [of the Chamber] . . . that I alone know in all his gracious and intoxicating aspects'. It reflected, for Gambetta, the influence of Léon's good star, which had watched over him since 'that 27 April, when we met, were smitten by each other, gave ourselves to each other'.[11]

Gambetta wanted to mark this important political moment with a grand celebration. He chose 14 July 1879 for the event: a reception and concert, with lavish refreshments, in the ballroom of his official residence at the Hôtel de Lassay. Only the following year did 14 July become the official national holiday, but this date – anniversary of the capture of the Bastille in 1789, as the French Revolution began – was highly symbolic. It linked the Chamber of Deputies with the revolutionary and democratic tradition from which it emerged, another powerful gesture to the republican electorate.

If Léon was enthusiastic about relocating the Chamber to Paris, however, she was highly critical of this celebration, reminiscent of the pomp of dynastic regimes: 'Such reminders of the great days of the empire were not part of my plan for your future', she declared.[12] Léon emphasized her own investment in Gambetta's career and in his triumphs; she did not face his political pressures so she could stand on principle, ignoring the symbolic and tactical considerations that motivated him.

The celebration on 14 July brought together representatives of the military, the diplomatic corps, the university, the law, the press, the business community, and the artistic community, who were all welcomed at the Hôtel de Lassay by Gambetta himself. He was at the high point of his career (Figure 9.1). The event was part of his plan to wed French institutions to the Republic, establishing the solid allegiance that would make the Republic the default regime. But only men were invited, except for the singers and dancers who were part of the evening's entertainment.[13]

Some republican women objected to their exclusion, no doubt conscious of their financial and other contributions to the cause.[14] 'I'm being politely abused for hosting a banquet for men only', Gambetta observed. 'It's a storm from start to finish. But I am holding firm and scoffing at all these feminine outbursts because I have the consent of my sweetheart and I hope I can count on being rewarded by her.'[15] Léon's surviving letters offer no hint that she associated herself with the women's complaints. As with the women's rights congress a year earlier, she gave no sign that she regarded women's exclusion from this political celebration as contentious. Perhaps she preferred that all women be excluded since she herself could not be invited, but her acceptance nevertheless suggests that she was deeply imbued with the gender norms of her day.

She continued, however, to criticize the event, and Gambetta had to work hard to end their disagreement. Speaking of her as 'Minerva', he acknowledged 'the excellence, the sublimity of her precepts and her counsels' and even conceded that he might have made a mistake, but he did not retreat: 'It may have been better not to embark on such a venture but there is no more time for regrets and I want to extract myself as soon as possible and on the best possible terms from this difficult position.'[16]

Throughout the first half of 1879, the Bonapartists in the Chamber of Deputies waged a campaign of disorder and personal insult in an effort to undermine Gambetta's authority. The death in June of the Prince Imperial,

Figure 9.1 Léon Gambetta: the statesman, *c*.1880 (Bibliothèque Historique de la Ville de Paris; Roger-Viollet)

their 'heir apparent', took the wind out of their political sails, as Gambetta noted: 'The death of this unfortunate henceforth hands the future to us, removes an obstacle, takes from our foreign enemies their best card for disturbing our internal affairs.' 'It's prodigious and almost frightening the extent to which everything succeeds for you!' Léon replied.[17] Gambetta still had the fractious Extreme Left to contend with, however, so his role as President of the Chamber remained stressful and difficult.[18]

'Our indestructible trinity'

Gambetta and Léon increasingly included Alphonse in their activities. Gambetta was beginning to contemplate marriage, and he wanted to show Léon that her son could be integrated into their family life. His affection for Alphonse seems by now to have been quite genuine. He followed his health and schooling closely, and increasingly acted as a father figure in Alphonse's life.

Gambetta celebrated the new year of 1879 by sending gifts to both his darlings. 'For the first time in my life I have had a good New Year', Léon wrote in reply, adding of Alphonse: 'The poor little thing, whom I was wrong not to forewarn, excuses himself for his timidity, which prevents him from expressing all his joy and gratitude.' There was further excitement a few days later, when Alphonse was declared first in his class. Gambetta proposed to Léon that they meet at two o'clock 'to run in the woods. . . . In the evening, we will celebrate the success of *la Chine*, whom I entrust you to kiss on both cheeks.'[19]

When Alphonse came first in geography in March, Gambetta declared to Léon: 'I will be first in geography too, I mean in [studying] the map of the heart [*la carte du tendre*].' He sent Alphonse a gift and expressed his deep affection: 'I felt the noblest and most tender emotions . . . I sealed our indestructible trinity, and I was rewarded for that immediately by the child's joy, by the voice of my conscience, and by the discreet emotion of my sweetheart. I am happy, and I can never be so again except at that price.' 'Tell me what words came to *la Chine*'s lips', he concluded, and 'embrace him for me'.[20]

Alphonse had produced 'an effusion of written gratitude', Léon replied, '[but] I suppressed what he wrote, in accordance with my customary moderation and I am taking it on myself to express his emotion, which was very intense and infinitely happy'. Gambetta replied, 'it's enough to know that my *Chine* wanted to write and did write'. 'It is high time that I show openly that I have understood all the tenderness this little darling gives me.'[21]

The school prize-giving in April brought further testimony of Gambetta's growing sense of family. Caught in a wave of paternal affection, he emphasized his joy in 'loving you both simultaneously with the same fervour and in the same embrace'. By supporting Alphonse, he declared, he wanted to prove his 'invincible attachment' to Léon.[22] Alphonse was the gateway to Léon's heart, and Gambetta surely knew that Léon would only accept marriage if Alphonse were included in their plans for the future.

Gambetta also arranged for Alphonse to 'make his debut in the parliamentary world' at this time by visiting the Chamber of Deputies. 'The enthusiasm, the joy, the gratitude of *la Chine* are inexpressible!' Léon reported the following day. 'You are happy, you want to say so, my soul is aglow and quite proud', Gambetta replied. 'As for the joy of *la Chine*, I savour it paternally, which only pricks my desire to triumph over the prevarications of nature. And I will triumph with you and through you.'[23] Gambetta continued to insist that the boy was henceforth 'inseparable from their joys'. In August, inviting them both to his 'nest' at Ville-d'Avray, he reiterated: 'I've checked the cage, it's pretty enough for my two rare birds. I want them and I kiss their most beautiful feathers.'[24]

Alphonse had turned fourteen in February 1879. He graduated from the junior college at Fontenay-aux-Roses in July, again winning prizes for his achievements. 'Embrace our prizewinner, our victorious child', Gambetta wrote, proudly asserting paternal affection. A few weeks later, as Gambetta distributed the prizes in the *Concours général* (the competitive examination for admission to the elite universities, the *Grandes Écoles*), he reflected again on Alphonse's future. Alphonse was due to enter the fourth form at the prestigious Collège Sainte-Barbe in Paris in October. Gambetta saw the Principal of the school at the prize-giving and apparently learned that Alphonse had been accepted into the special stream, where boys were groomed for the competitive examination and hence for an important career. Gambetta was 'happy, thrilled': 'I crowned the two winners of the *prix d'honneur* and in the depths of my soul I was trembling with joy, thinking that one day I would place the same crown on a head which is, after yours, the dearest to me in the world.'[25]

'When you say yes, I will be ready'

As 1879 unfolded, Gambetta poured all his epistolary skill into persuading Léon of his enduring love. The effort he put into his love letters, and the delight they elicited from Léon, show just how important their correspondence remained to them. Gambetta expressed his love in poetic phrases, emphasizing the joy that marriage would bring. Marriage could be imagined, in a letter, without the practical difficulties and mundane realities that loomed so large for Léon. But while none of Léon's responses to Gambetta's proposals of marriage has survived – did she destroy these letters? – her need for, and delight in, Gambetta's repeated declarations of undying attachment were always evident.

Gambetta wrote in March 1879: 'there are still summits to climb, sublimities to attain and . . . the more we move forward in time, in love, the more we make flames and lightning burst out beneath our footsteps.' A week later, he asked: 'where is the mortal in time, in history, who ever tasted these sublime ecstasies? . . . I have possessed the incommunicable; I have been dizzy with pleasure, I have really experienced, touched the upper limit of ineffable voluptuous pleasure.'[26] Léon looked to his letters for such reassurance: 'how many tears are forgotten, their painful tracks erased by such a marvellous letter', she replied. Another letter from Gambetta was 'the most moving letter that you have ever written; you have finally found the path that leads to the most profound and most sensitive fibres of my heart'.[27]

Given the crucial role that letters played in their romance, Léon still jumped to conclusions if a letter failed to arrive as expected. Her readiness to leap from adoration to accusation was a sign of her fragile emotional state, and perhaps a device for tying Gambetta more securely to her. On 20 April 1879, when Gambetta was due to leave for a brief holiday, she received no letter in the first two mail deliveries: 'I began to think that you had left, or were going to leave without warning me, without saying goodbye', she wrote. 'I ran in panic to send you a telegram.' But when she returned home, she found his letter, 'so calm, so protective.' A month later, Léon suffered another moment of anguish: 'I no longer think, I no longer breathe! All the deliveries have gone by without bringing me a letter.' But in a post-script, she spoke of the 'late arrival of a letter divine in its tenderness'.[28]

Léon's anxious wait for Gambetta's letters was linked to her fears about his fidelity. She imagined Gambetta with other women, perhaps those whose married status protected them from scrutiny. Leaping from supposition to accusation, she wrote: 'I believed you lost forever, when it was only a letter delayed as a result of an evening prolonged with some seductive sinner shielded by the impunity afforded our bourgeois institutions'; someone who 'despite a thousand conjugal or other infidelities, enjoys the one good that reigns supreme over all others, even over love, respect'. The fact that she herself was not a 'respectable' woman once again came back to haunt Léon, and the injustice of her situation filled her with resentment. Gambetta's reply ignored the charge in a tender message of love.[29]

Léon's reliance on Gambetta's letters may have been excessive, but Gambetta became anxious, too, when Léon's letters failed to arrive. He wrote in August: 'I spent a bad moment not having any news from you, I was attributing your silence to all sorts of misfortunes, I thought you were ill, I feared I was to be disappointed . . . my heart was beating as though it would burst, I was feverish.'[30] Both Léon and Gambetta regarded the letter as a vital part of their relationship; its absence was as painful as the absence of its writer. But whereas Gambetta read an epistolary silence as a sign of Léon's need for his support, she interpreted that silence as a sign of Gambetta's lack of need for her; a sign that he found consolation elsewhere. Léon's emotional insecurity and her tendency to depression ensured that she interpreted even minor events in a negative light.

An incident in April 1879 highlighted her sensitivity. Gambetta was aware of the 'wound' that Léon suffered as a result of her 'fall',[31] her sexual history, but he inadvertently touched on that 'wound' during a discussion of Rousseau's epistolary novel, *Julie, ou la nouvelle Héloïse* (1761). Léon wrote: 'I would like to know what was in the depths of your heart [last night] when your lips were so cruel? And I would like to say why and how much I suffered.' Léon had been reading the section of the novel where Julie confesses to Claire that she has 'given herself' to Saint-Preux, and Claire consoles her for her 'disgrace' by reminding her of her virtues. Gambetta's loving reply consoled Léon, though it condemned women in general:

> I said and I repeat, I was quietly savouring a double pleasure, noting the bitter truth applied to women in general and enjoying in the most secret realm of my being the happiness of having chosen so well, of finding you so unlike the others, of being the only one among my contemporaries as well as my predecessors, to possess the love of a woman as noble, as superior, as disinterested, as faithful, as passionate, and as devoted as you.[32]

Despite Léon's outbursts of anxiety, Gambetta was looking to the future. He stepped up his efforts persuade her to marry him. In a long August letter, he sought to allay the fears of his 'Dear Adored Wife' about the consequences of such a move: 'I love you and you love me, we can defy everything, the elements, the people, the false social conventions and everything else if there is anything else', he wrote. 'You can, as soon as you wish and when you wish, erect with a wave of your hand an impassable barrier to these ridiculous assaults of worldly convention. When you say yes, I will be ready and everything will be consecrated.' Gambetta painted a tempting picture. Léon could escape the 'domestic hurt and anguish' of life with her mother for life with him: 'I will always be your adoring darling at your feet like yesterday, intoxicated, blinded, happy, triumphant; using the force that I find in you to tame the world.'[33]

But if Gambetta could dismiss social convention 'with a wave of [his] hand', Léon could not. She was the one who could not be received in respectable homes or receive guests in her own. And she may have become more uncomfortable with her illegal situation now that Alphonse was growing up. Three days after Gambetta's loving appeal for Léon to 'say yes', he went off to les Jardies for ten days. Léon and Alphonse visited him but did not stay there.[34]

Despite Léon's anxiety about marrying Gambetta, however, the fact that she was not his wife meant that she continued to be excluded from society. She wrote in mid-August 1879: 'the summer which brings you nearer to me by emptying your salons, will soon be over; you will leave in autumn'.[35] Gambetta did leave in autumn, heading for his annual visit to Mme Arnaud in her Swiss château. Mme Arnaud had made a generous financial settlement on Gambetta. He may have felt a sense of obligation to make this annual pilgrimage, though a holiday at the château was undoubtedly a pleasure. Léon could not be received, either at these salons or at the château.

This visit caused an exchange of unhappy and angry letters between Gambetta and Léon that lasted for a fortnight. On his arrival at the château, Gambetta had written back happily about sightseeing and walks in the mountains, but almost immediately he began receiving distressed letters from Léon. 'I left, thinking that all was explained, believing that all was organized', Gambetta wrote, 'and five days after all this beautiful orchestration, for unforeseen reasons you change your mind'. He could not return immediately, he noted, because the renovation of his apartment would not be finished until 20 October, which had always been his intended date of return.[36]

According to Léon, however, Gambetta had intended 'to spend a *week*, unwillingly, and from pure *politeness!* [emphasis orig.]' with Mme Arnaud. Léon accused him of having extended his stay 'by another month', hinting at infidelity and blaming him for 'indifference'. Perhaps she had heard the rumours about Gambetta's relationship with Mme Arnaud. Gambetta tried to defuse the situation, suggesting Léon come to meet him in Lausanne or Geneva: 'you know I'm prevented from accepting', she replied, unable to abandon her family responsibilities.[37]

There are no extant letters revealing how the dispute was eventually resolved. In late October, Léon had still not forgotten 'the abyss of sorrow dug by that cruel absence'.[38] Gambetta's declarations of unfailing love did not compensate for the fact that he could leave her for weeks at a time, especially when he left to stay at the home of another woman. But Léon was also jealous of Gambetta's freedom of movement and resented her own inability to receive such invitations. At every turn, her status as a 'fallen woman' cast its irreparable shadow over her life.

In October 1879, when Alphonse enrolled at the Collège Sainte-Barbe in Paris, Léon and her mother left Fontenay-aux-Roses for an apartment on the rue Soufflot, close to the school. They almost certainly had Gambetta's financial assistance. The rent of 2050 francs per year was more than Mme Léon's annual pension and Léon still had to pay the rent for the rue Bonaparte, which remained a refuge for the lovers, a place of rendezvous. Gambetta even enjoyed visiting the 'sanctuary' of his 'goddess' in her absence.[39]

Léon's relationship with her mother, nicknamed 'the rhinoceros' in the couple's correspondence, had not improved. Léon complained about her mother's bad moods, which 'paralysed all the sweet words [mignonneries] stirring in my heart'. 'So this nasty rhinoceros is incurable!' Gambetta declared. 'Don't you have some way of confining her in a distant zoological garden?'[40] Gambetta tried to convince Léon that marriage was the solution to both her domestic problems and her social isolation. 'Consider, dear wife, and come back some beautiful day . . . to tell me, "Yes, I agree"', he wrote on 10 November 1879. 'I have the secret certainty', he continued three days later, 'that our wishes will be crowned by success and that you will begin your life anew under the auspices which ought to have inaugurated it.'[41] She would, he believed, become his wife.

Kingbreaker and kingmaker

President Grévy had chosen William Waddington rather than Gambetta as President of the Council of Ministers in January 1879. While Gambetta approved Waddington's republican agenda, he nevertheless complained that the ministry was 'indecisive, irresolute, divided, lacking in direction and already without authority'. Léon attributed those problems to President Grévy himself: 'I was opposed to trying Grévy and this unhappy beginning justifies my fears. . . . it is absolutely essential to restore some spirit, some initiative, some prestige to this ministry.'[42]

By-elections in April that saw gains for the Extreme Left alarmed Léon further: 'Too many intransigents, far too many intransigents!' Gambetta agreed. Indeed, he was soon planning to replace Waddington: 'You can count on the fact that I won't allow another day to pass without contemplating the best means to consign this Englishman [Waddington] and his Yankee [wife] to the obscurity they should never have left. We'll discuss that often, until the day of victory.'[43] The fact that Gambetta used his influence behind the scenes to shape political outcomes – his 'hidden power' – became a major theme in his opponents' attempts to discredit him.

As tensions between Greece and Turkey threatened to unleash war, Gambetta was highly critical of Waddington's handling of the Foreign Affairs portfolio. He complained to Léon: 'it is urgent that we join forces with Italy and England. I'm receiving letter after letter from Rome to conclude [arrangements] as soon as possible and no one here seems to have budged. 'The day that [destiny] strikes W[addington]', Léon replied soothingly, 'it will be justice for his having so sorely tried your patience.'[44]

An attempt by Gambetta's Republican Union to defeat Waddington failed in early December. With Léon's encouragement, Gambetta redoubled his efforts: he would 'arrange a thorough cabinet reshuffle' with the Head of State before the New Year holidays.[45] Again, Gambetta suggested that ministries were his to make and unmake, though the results suggest that he overestimated his own power.

Gambetta's strategy was to replace Waddington with Freycinet. But even when Freycinet finally agreed to accept the job, President Grévy refused to accept Waddington's resignation. Gambetta broke the news to Léon in the early hours of 23 December: 'There is no Freycinet cabinet, no Brisson or Floquet cabinet, we have returned purely and simply to the Waddington cabinet.' He added: 'there wasn't the faintest gesture from the Élysée [the presidential palace] to find out my thoughts on the situation'.[46] Like MacMahon before him, Grévy was not about to do Gambetta's bidding and was determined to keep him out of power.

The struggle continued, Gambetta trying to force an outcome and Léon encouraging him. Waddington was 'clinging to his rock with the tenacity of a crustacean', and the contest for positions was fierce: 'never did the hunt at [the forest of] Méry have more indefatigable devotees than these hunters of portfolios'. When Waddington resigned again on

27 December, Grévy accepted his resignation. Gambetta claimed credit for forming the new ministry:

> Once again I was able to put the broken crockery back together, Frey[cinet] is steadier in the stirrups, and he has promised to present to the venerable Mikado [Grévy] the list of the new ministerial Sanhedrin. He reverted to my first idea of taking the portfolio of foreign affairs, a combination that greatly appealed to him, that you had approved and that was actually very decisive in every respect.[47]

Gambetta named the proposed ministers, promising to look over the list with her tomorrow. Léon replied: 'I am a great fortune-teller, but above all I am a woman greatly in love who will go to sleep very happy feeling that your mind is at ease.'[48]

'The festival of tenderness'

Léon's first extant letter for 1880 – one of only two to survive from that year – was a joyful one, concluding, 'All my adorations in remembrance of the most divine evening that could occur on earth.' Gambetta, too, was in high spirits. 'I cannot tell you and repeat often enough how adorable you are; your letter of yesterday evening brought the sweetest tears to my eyes, and if I had had you near me, I would have gone mad from the pleasure of kissing the hands that wrote those beautiful lines of love and tenderness.' He also believed that Léon would soon agree to be his wife: 'I feel a growing confidence in the depths of my soul that our two lives will be united increasingly closely and that we are approaching the blessed moment when you will say the holy and decisive word. Oh! Darling, dear heart, what a happy man you could make [me] with a word, a simple gesture. When "perhaps" becomes certainty.'[49]

1880 was punctuated by visits to their little house at Ville-d'Avray. This had indeed become their sanctuary from the stresses of political life and from Léon's domestic tensions. They made repeated visits in February and early March, until chimney sweeping and the construction of Gambetta's study in the garden (since demolished) brought a halt to their escapades. Visits resumed in the summer. Sometimes Gambetta went by himself, but he 'suffered badly to be alone there', he wrote in March, after 'the festival of tenderness that we had given each other'. In June, Léon joined him there for a day or two, which they spent gardening, but construction work resumed at les Jardies in the autumn, disrupting their visits again. Léon would only be set up in her own apartment shortly before Gambetta's death.[50]

Visits to les Jardies were generally made as a family, 'with *Chine* and the dogs' (this makes a nice word play in French: *'avec Chine et chiens'*).[51] Alphonse was often in Gambetta's thoughts. He noted in March: 'I hope *Chine* has done well [at school] and that Sweetheart is less demanding of him!' When the June report was a good one, Gambetta sent his congratulations and kisses. He assured Léon: 'I take too strong an interest in him ever to be tired of him.'[52]

In the bucolic setting of les Jardies, Gambetta and Léon lived their fantasy of a bourgeois married life. The best picture of this life comes from the coachman's recollections and from an 1880 report by the police, who had been assigned to protect Gambetta from possible assassination. Two police agents disguised themselves as Parisian bourgeois seeking to retire to the country. They installed themselves in a neighbouring property and made friends with Gambetta's servants.

The agents noted that the couple arrived, along with Alphonse, on 20 June 1880. Two days later the valet, the cook, his wife and his assistant arrived. Gambetta walked around the property in the mornings, they reported, and often practised shooting his pistol. The three lunched around 11.30 a.m. In the afternoons, Gambetta sometimes went to Paris on official business (he was still President of the Chamber); sometimes colleagues came to pick him up for political dinners. On other days, Gambetta and Léon went for daylong carriage rides. They dined about 7.30 p.m., after which the valet informed the police, Gambetta worked in his study until one or two in the morning, rising again at six. He took the liberty, he added, of scolding his master for working too hard, to which Gambetta responded, 'You see, my friend, I don't tire myself because I keep growing stouter!'[53]

The coachman's recollections broadly tallied with that account. He noted the couple's daily carriage excursions, with frequent stops to pick wildflowers. He remembered fishing on the Villeneuve pond at Garches. On one trip Gambetta 'even lost a ring of great value that slipped off his finger', the copy of Saint Louis' ring, one of the pair that he and Léon had exchanged in 1874. The coachman remembered the couple reading in the library, and lunching at noon. And he remembered Gambetta's penchant for shooting: he 'prepared a box of a dozen bullets' and shot his pistol in the mornings. 'In the afternoon during their customary promenade he always had a small-calibre pistol in his pocket with which he shot birds in the bushes, resting the gun on my shoulder'. Sometimes Gambetta 'shot and without ever getting out of the carriage', and he did not hesitate to shoot 'M. Grévy's pheasants [i.e. pheasants protected by the law of the Republic] even though the hunting season was over'. The coachman was convinced that 'the president gave the order to the [forest] guards to let him continue'.[54]

Neither the police nor the coachman detailed Léon's comings and goings, but the cook gossiped at length with the police agents, explaining that Gambetta would not receive anyone when Léon was there: 'The President of the Council [of Ministers] himself might come and he wouldn't be received. A few days ago, M. Gambetta refused to receive his own secretary. I think he would refuse to receive his father, if he turned up and one can understand that: M. Gambetta is a man and he's not married. I can tell you, just between us, this person [Léon] who is here and who is passed off as his relative is not a relative. So, you see, he can't receive anyone, and he couldn't care less what people might say about him.'[55]

The cook made quite clear that this was an illegitimate relationship: Gambetta was not married, and this 'person' was 'not a relative'. The wording suggests disapproval, at least of Léon. The report conveyed the whiff of scandal that surrounded this domestic idyll. Léon was the beneficiary of the practice of 'not receiving' at les Jardies, whereas normally she was the victim. But 'not receiving' served only to keep the elite at bay; it could not prevent the servants' gossiping. The cottage at Ville-d'Avray was as close to privacy as a bourgeois couple could hope to get. But despite their best efforts, Léon's privacy could not be completely protected, and her reputation could not be restored.

'It's useless to discuss politics'

The stalemate in Gambetta's political career, with its attendant frustrations, was one factor leading him to seek escape at Ville-d'Avray. President Grévy remained obdurate in his resistance to a Gambetta-led government. But in light of the growing strength of the Extreme Left, Gambetta may have been quite happy to see Freycinet assume the challenge of government instead.

The Extreme Left had been strengthening at the polls for some time. Despite the Freycinet government's energetic republican programme, they continued to press for more, disrupting the Chamber as a tactical manoeuvre. Gambetta reported on 22 January: 'It's useless to discuss politics. One can hardly dignify with that name the incoherent tumult to which the diverse fractions of the Left [devote themselves]; it's like delirium tremens, something like Saint Vitus' dance . . . I'm waiting until all these dervishes are exhausted in order to intervene and try at last to construct something which could play the role of a majority.'[56]

Political differences among the republicans were highlighted in February and March 1880, when Jules Ferry's bill on 'freedom of instruction', stalled in the Senate since July 1879, was finally debated. Its anticlerical focus (especially Article 7, which prohibited unauthorized religious orders from teaching) was extremely popular with most republicans, particularly on the Left. But republican elder statesmen Jules Dufaure and Jules Simon joined the attack in the Senate, and Article 7 was defeated. As protests and counter-protests unfolded over the education reforms, Gambetta feared that Freycinet's resolve was weakening. 'He wants out; the escape path matters little to him', Gambetta wrote. He 'dreads the enormous difficulties of 30 June', when the decrees expelling unauthorized religious orders were due to come into effect.[57]

The issue of an amnesty for the Communards (Paris radicals who had fought against the government in 1871) also returned to divide republicans, pitting Gambetta against Freycinet. The Chamber had rejected an amnesty decisively in May 1876. The Extreme Left had continued to introduce bills for total amnesty: Waddington's partial amnesty in 1879 did not placate them. In January 1880, they introduced yet another bill for complete amnesty, which again failed to win a majority.

Gambetta had resisted total amnesty in order to keep the support of Centre groups in the Chamber. But in June 1880, he himself promoted the measure. This was his response to attacks on his 'opportunism' by the radical press, whose vehemence had prompted the government to place the police guard on his house at Ville-d'Avray. The Extreme Left had also developed the tactic of electing Communards to vacant seats, despite their ineligibility, in order to press the amnesty issue. On 1 June 1880, Gambetta's electorate at Belleville chose a Communard still in exile as its candidate for the Municipal elections. The message was clear, and Gambetta took it. He urged Freycinet to sponsor a complete amnesty for all Communards still in prison or exile.[58]

Gambetta was forced to work hard, however, to get the new amnesty Bill through the Chamber of Deputies. It required another oratorical tour de force, as Gambetta again descended from the Presidential chair to speak in the debate. He shared his feelings with Léon that evening: 'I am sorry and happy, triumphant and full of regrets. The amnesty came up today; . . . Cassagnac launched into some lies [*infirmations*] about me that forced me to descend from my perch and I spoke! . . . The amnesty is through [*fait*].'[59]

Gambetta could not speak in the Senate, however, where opposition remained solid. His resolute exterior concealed the despondency that he revealed only to Léon. 'I am being dragged by 4 horses and I am feeling the pleasure of being torn apart by my closest friends. Ah! How much I will need your advice and your sweet caresses.' He resigned himself to defeat in the Senate, which amended the bill to exclude those convicted by military tribunals of arson or murder. It was not a total amnesty at all. Gambetta was furious at the 'ridiculous outcome': 'thanks to the cowardice of the cabinet, [the Senate] has succeeded in depriving the measure of its worth and political significance'.[60]

Gambetta's tussle with Freycinet over the amnesty law was exacerbated shortly afterwards, when news broke that Freycinet had entered secret negotiations with the Vatican about the law affecting the religious congregations. The proposed compromise would require the congregations only to abjure political links, rather than to declare their loyalty to the French Republic and seek authorization. When this was leaked by the Catholic press in late August, anticlerical republicans, as well as anti-republican Catholics, were outraged. Gambetta made no effort to defend Freycinet. Elections were due within a year. Radicals had already disrupted political meetings in Belleville in June, and Gambetta's parliamentary seat would certainly have been in danger had he supported Freycinet's measure. When President Grévy supported Freycinet, two ministers resigned. Two days later, on 22 September 1880, Freycinet himself resigned. The following day, President Grévy appointed Jules Ferry to head the ministry.[61]

'The infallible consolation of your love'

Many believed that Gambetta should have been called; even Ferry believed that was the appropriate outcome. But Grévy remained hostile and Gambetta may have been wary of trying to govern with such an ill-disciplined republican majority.[62] Nevertheless, some in Gambetta's Republican Union were unhappy with Ferry's appointment, and only Gambetta's intervention prevented Ferry's resignation. Gambetta wrote to Léon on 10 November: 'After three hours of meetings, I finally got to bed at 2am . . . This morning I saw Ferry, just now I've paid a visit to Cam[byses: Grévy], heads are cooling down and I hope that yesterday's broken porcelain will be mended this evening.'[63]

As 1881 began, the Chamber energetically pursued republican reforms ahead of the elections due in mid year. As well as Ferry's remaining education measures, they passed 'a law of freedom and liberty' for the press, by far the most liberal press law in Europe before 1914. Indeed, Léon objected that it was 'distorted to the point of license'.[64] But Léon was in good spirits in early 1881. She wrote early in January: 'How heroic I was to abandon to politics this entire day which might have been so sweetly spent at your feet, expressing to you in all the languages known to us the gratitude which has so profoundly penetrated my soul this time that it is for ever unwavering in its faith.' She even wished Gambetta well as he headed off to one of his many formal evenings, while she settled down to read his latest speech.[65] She was not always so sanguine about her exclusion.

Gambetta began campaigning to replace the district-based electoral system (*scrutin d'arrondissement*) for the Chamber of Deputies with a multi-member list system (*scrutin de liste*). The new system was intended to break the hold of local elites on parliamentary seats and raise the calibre of representatives. Gambetta's slipping grasp on the radical seat of Belleville may have increased his enthusiasm for the measure. But the proposal reflected Gambetta's growing conviction that stable government, and perhaps his own chance at leading a government, required a disciplined republican majority. His enemies again warned of dictatorship.[66]

When the list system had last been a significant political issue, in 1875, both Jules Grévy and Jules Ferry had supported it. Now, in 1881, Gambetta's campaign pitted him against both the President of the Republic and the head of the ministry. Gambetta kept Léon abreast of the bill's fate, and sought inspiration beside her: 'We are launched at top speed into the parliamentary unknown', he reported on 17 March. 'Positions are taken, orators chosen, I've spent the evening training my people, tomorrow I'll reflect on my own account while strolling with you, my true, my only inspiration.'[67]

He was confident after the first skirmish, when 'having set out to do battle, swords high, banners unfurled, [our opponents] stopped dead at the first line of our defences . . . I foresee better and better things for my dear *scrutin* [*de liste*].' Again, he descended from the presidential chair to add his voice to the debate in a powerful speech on 19 May, and the bill passed the Chamber with a comfortable majority the following day. But the Senate, recalcitrant again, rejected the measure on 11 June.[68]

The first round of the legislative elections was scheduled for 21 August 1881 and Gambetta now threw himself into election mode. On the eve of his departure for Tours, he wrote a good-bye note: 'Did you not feel, my dearly beloved, that in speaking of these compensations [*rachats*] of the life of the orator, I was thinking of the infallible consolation of your love?' He wanted to 'affirm louder than ever that you are the rest, the hope, the support of my entire life'. Gambetta was to need her consolation as the campaign unfolded. His Belleville seat had been divided as the population grew, and while he still had many friends in Belleville itself, he was abused and heckled by malcontents in the new seat of Charonne. A later letter by Léon suggests that he was jaded by these attacks: 'I didn't agree, I admit, that you should resign after the Senate vote; but *never* did you express in my presence the idea of not standing in the elections!'[69]

Gambetta's prediction that the republicans would have a good victory was nevertheless accurate. His Republican Union remained the largest group in the new Chamber, although the balance was moving gradually leftward and the Extreme Left now outnumbered the Centre Left. While Gambetta won the seat of Belleville outright, he could not carry Charonne and withdrew before the second round in favour of a more radical candidate. 'We won with difficulty', he informed Léon. 'I was prepared for worse, I accept the mediocre and I am confident of extracting an almost habitable world from all this chaos.' Léon affirmed him once again: 'The result is better than I predicted, we will draw out all its consequences tomorrow.'[70]

'Our indissoluble union'

On 1 January 1881, Gambetta had written a New Year letter that constituted yet another proposal of marriage: 'Dear Adored Wife', he began: 'Yesterday evening after leaving you I found the letter which you must have written to me during the day, thank you for having kept your promise and for having written what you quite unintentionally didn't want to say.'[71] Gambetta's words are confused, but he apparently meant that Léon took advantage of the letter to express thoughts that were difficult to express face to face; to write what she 'didn't want to say'. Léon's letter has disappeared, but Gambetta's response is one of the few moments when the traces of Léon's rejection of marriage are visible, if only indirectly.

Gambetta's letter highlights Léon's fixation on the past and its ongoing consequences. He sympathized with her 'bitterness'; with her sense that an 'evil star' had irredeemably blighted her life. Léon well knew that her past would be in the spotlight if she were to marry Gambetta. But Gambetta assured her that marriage would solve her problems and relieve her sufferings. 'Don't lull yourself with unattainable goals, take the sure, sweet, efficient, definitive path, we must be united with all the legal formalities and seek in this regularization relief of your pains and security for my tenderness . . . just say yes as I ask and we will finally get the better of your evil star.'[72]

Gambetta's letter also indicates that Léon found Alphonse's adolescent presence a problem, perhaps an obstacle to marriage. Acknowledging her sufferings, he added: 'I would never have believed that they would receive a new and cruel augmentation because of the inevitable curiosity of the young man.'[73] Alphonse turned sixteen in February 1881. Gambetta chose on this occasion to abandon the nickname, *la Chine*, a feminine term, and acknowledge that Alphonse was entering manhood.

Alphonse's 'curiosity' was understandable: Gambetta's role in his own life as well as in Léon's was unclear; he had grown up thinking Léon was his aunt. Alphonse's 'curiosity' was no doubt linked, too, to his emerging sexuality. He must have known that Gambetta and Léon were not married, and that this made intimacy socially unacceptable. But on 'family' visits to Ville-d'Avray it would have been difficult to conceal such intimacy. Les Jardies was a small house and 'lovers' trysts' would have remained secret only with great ingenuity. On the other hand, a move towards marriage would have highlighted Léon's hitherto unmarried status. These considerations may explain why Alphonse spent much of 1881 at school in Dresden learning German. Gambetta and Léon visited him there in mid-October.[74]

Marriage between Léon and Gambetta presented yet another problem, raised in subsequent letters: would they be married 'before heaven' or simply in a civil ceremony? It would have been virtually impossible for Gambetta to accept marriage by a priest, given his own anticlericalism and that of many republicans, not least in his seat of Belleville. For Léon, already guilt-ridden about her past, a civil marriage perhaps offered further cause for spiritual anxiety. From a Catholic point of view, a civil marriage lacked divine sanction. Perhaps to overcome her scruples, Gambetta urged Léon in February: 'We will find in ourselves what might be missing in heaven.' But there was no doubt it would have to be a civil union: 'You only have to say a single word, make a single sign, before the Mayor it is true', he admitted, adding, 'we will enter the Promised Land'.[75] Religious metaphors could not resolve the problems they faced.

During 1881, stays at les Jardies were frequent, if generally short. Burdened by political difficulties, Gambetta sought every opportunity to escape, to 'take the air, to talk', to bring back 'gaiety and spiritedness', even if only for a day. When Gambetta wrote at seven o'clock one February morning wanting to whisk Léon away, she replied 'How could

I refuse?' 'Bring my woollen scarf, and don't forget your hat.' Gambetta always wrote of freedom, of escaping from constraint, when planning visits to les Jardies with Léon: 'we will go and see our plantings and wander at our ease'; 'we will philosophize completely at our ease under our shady trees'. When parliament rose in April, Gambetta was eager to 'run away to the country' at the first opportunity.[76]

Political pressure, and the winter weather, took its toll on the couple's health. Their letters had long been punctuated by reports on their head colds, influenza and bad throats. Such minor ailments were common, but the lovers always feared that they heralded more threatening conditions. Moreover, concern for the other's health was an expression of love; a means for reasserting that the body of the beloved was treasured. Now Gambetta promised Léon: 'I will pamper you so well that you will be cured immediately [of your cold].' Apparently he could not keep that promise, because a few days later he sent Dr Siredey to visit her.[77] Similarly, Léon was concerned about Gambetta's lungs, as well as his 'spirit'. As Gambetta's cold got worse, he sent Louis (the coachman) to collect his 'love doctor [*amour médecin*]': 'Come, we will share our infirmities, which fortunately are passing ones.'[78]

Despite the treatment that Léon may have received over the years, she was far from cured of her melancholy. Her 'black thoughts' continued, and she tried unsuccessfully to chase away 'all the clouds in me and around me'. She was painfully conscious of her tendency to see the world in black:

> I am so happy, so embarrassed, so grateful for your love, that the memory of my moody moments weighs heavily on my heart! Will there never come a day when I will be able to give you the full measure of this tenderness so infinite that all imaginable effusions only render it very imperfectly. This inadequacy of language brings me back to the other impossibilities and my poor nerves troubled by a very bad night begin to suffer again.[79]

In March Léon complained of a 'frightful sadness that nothing can dispel'; in June of 'an irremediable and ever increasing sadness, justified by so many physical and moral pains and grief accumulated on one single head'. Again, in November, she repeated: 'The physical and moral weakening persists despite all the gracious things that you say or write'; she was, she concluded, 'in a state of absolute prostration'.[80]

If Léon sometimes seems a hypochondriac, her physical symptoms were undoubtedly a response to the troubled situation in which she found herself, not to imaginary misfortunes. Her past, which she could not undo, continued to taint the present. Her home life with her mother was intolerable, yet she could not leave because she wanted to be near her son. As Gambetta's political career stalled and began to falter, her investment in that career also seemed wasted.

Gambetta's response to Léon's troubled spirits was, as it had long been, to surround her with his love. No woman was ever more loved than she, he proclaimed. It was 'towards his darling' that he turned from Le Havre in October, 'to send her my evening prayer which is merely a long cry of love. I kiss her hands, her eyes, her lips . . . Believe that my thoughts are always with you and that I am thinking only of being at your feet, in body and soul.'[81]

'Triumph or defeat?'

The new Left-leaning Chamber assembled for the first time on 28 October 1881. Gambetta refused to accept nomination as President of the Chamber. Perhaps he anticipated an even more challenging task; perhaps he wanted to be available to form a government if (or when) Ferry fell. But as the correspondence shows, the couple realized that being President might be fraught with danger for Gambetta in a parliament where the Extreme Left held ever greater sway.

Controversy raged in the Chamber over the Ferry government's actions in Tunisia. France had established a 'protectorate' over the area in May and, following an insurrection in June, Ferry sent 50,000 troops to pacify and occupy Tunisia. The Extreme Left was irate that Ferry had engaged France in an unauthorized war; they ignored or dismissed his arguments about the national interest.[82]

After an 'odious' day on 8 November, when the Extreme Left attacked Ferry remorselessly, Gambetta was disgusted. For several months he had been considering abandoning politics: 'There is still time, if you want to leave and let this ghastly world tear itself apart as it pleases, I am ready to save *us*. A word, a yes, a simple yes and we will be free forever.'[83]

Léon was tempted: 'Dear, be quiet and don't lead me into the temptation of conniving with this enticing salvation!' She continued on a more serious (and prophetic) note:

> But one might well ask, with an anxious soul, where the true path lies, when it's a matter of compromising one's health, amidst incessant tumult, and perhaps of compromising one's prestige, to reach a goal that is quite problematic given the current state of minds and

things! At such a moment hesitation is certain proof that it is impossible to foresee whether one is heading for triumph or defeat as one throws oneself into the parliamentary fray; and that means asking oneself whether this dedication is useful or dangerous?

She nevertheless closed her letter 'good night dear Minister', probably realizing that, despite his momentary disgust, Gambetta would seize the opportunity for leadership if it arose.[84]

Indeed, Gambetta overcame his disgust, not by resigning, but by shaming the Chamber into what he regarded as an act of national pride. While he and Ferry had recently been at loggerheads over the voting system, he supported Ferry's aims in Tunisia. A staunch colonialist and defender of French international prestige, he was aware of the power struggles in the region and did not want to see France left behind. After hours of tumult in the Chamber on 9 November, Gambetta made yet another compelling speech, and a motion approving the government's actions in Tunisia passed with a large majority (but nevertheless with 124 abstentions). That evening, Gambetta explained to Léon: 'After eighteen successive votes on motions each more obsequious [*plat*] than the last, a feeling of indignation pushed me to the tribune. I couldn't tolerate such an abasement of republican France in the face of Europe and I intervened. In a few minutes I made them ratify a politics of action [*exécution*] and of national pride.'[85]

His speech had, in effect, saved Ferry from defeat in the Chamber, and the implications were clear. Gambetta therefore added, 'I don't know what will happen, but I need to see you . . . We will discuss how to proceed. My good angel guardian don't refuse me your magic influence, I place myself under your protection and I love you as the light of my life.'[86] The following day, 10 November 1881, Jules Ferry resigned. President Grévy finally called on Gambetta to form a ministry.

Paris, this 28 May 1882[1]

Dear adored darling,

I have just left the Palais-Bourbon, I conscientiously (ouf!) discharged my duty, between a conversation of nauseating banality and a dinner worthy of a suburban boarding house. I have nothing to say about the service or about the masters, one sees these things only in Molinchard![2] *ah! dearest how harsh is republican austerity; it's enough to send one off to the court of the Great Mogul; the details for tomorrow, if they can amuse you a bit.*

I will be there around three o'clock promising myself to make a tour of the Chamber to see the faces of our master idiots of diplomacy. The news from Egypt gets worse and worse; here we are back to the Arab dictator and our leaders to Turkish intervention.

Twelve years after Sedan,[3] *we are prostrated even lower, we are at the point of begging the protection of the Turks! I don't dare to think that this assembly of eunuchs will be satisfied just to be thought worthy to guard the harems of the Khedive [titular ruler of Egypt]. I feel terrible anger in the depths of my soul and I have a violent desire to mount the tribune one of these days to spit all my scorn, all my disgust on their faces, and to leave this sewer, shaking the dust from my sandals, never to return there. What shame or rather what an ocean of shame.*

Poor France, memorable Republic, I had dreamt other dreams for both, but they were only dreams. My sister, it's time to end.[4]

I embrace you with the supreme energy of the man who feels that he no longer has any refuge and any passion in this world but his wife, yours always and exclusively,

Léon Gambetta.

10
'Poor France, I had other dreams'

As President of the Council of Ministers, Gambetta had the opportunity to implement his vision for the Republic. This was the goal for which he and Léon had struggled for a decade. But he faced a 'coalition of jealousies, threatened interests, frustrated ambitions, wounded pride, of the cautious, the mediocrities'.[5] His letters reveal that Gambetta was fully aware of this hostility even before taking office and that, rather than approaching office with bravado, he felt a sense of frustration and discouragement.

The hostile coalition did indeed frustrate his plans; it overturned his ministry early in 1882, after less than three months. Gambetta's political dreams evaporated. The death of his mother and the life-threatening illness of Léon's son threw both Gambetta and Léon further into turmoil. If Léon was frequently overcome by the burdens of life, Gambetta, too, was at times overwhelmed by despondency. Separated and distressed, the couple relied more than ever on the comfort of their epistolary relationship.

'Will it be possible to achieve good and great things?'

Gambetta had dreamed of creating a 'great ministry', one which would assemble all the talent in the republican Chamber. That dream vanished rapidly. He wrote defiantly to Léon as he struggled to form a government: 'Yesterday evening everything seemed fixed; this morning everything is collapsing. The lead horses in the team are heading back to the stable and I am forced to begin the puzzle over again today with mandarins of the second rank. Perhaps that will be better, but if I don't succeed this evening I will send the lot of them to the devil!'[6]

The 'lead horses' were probably Léon Say, Charles de Freycinet, and Jules Ferry, the high profile republicans whom Gambetta needed to give his ministry credibility. Say feared that Gambetta would not accept his conservative economic policies and refused the Finance portfolio. Freycinet, still smarting, no doubt, from his recent political conflicts with Gambetta, feared to associate himself with what seemed a fragile ministry and refused Foreign Affairs. Jules Ferry, on the other hand, was willing to join but was excluded by Gambetta's Republican Union colleagues because of his enormous unpopularity over the Tunisian affair. Without these prominent figures in the ministry, experience was limited.[7]

Léon shared Gambetta's frustration at this turn of events: 'The refusal of important figures seems to me a serious symptom, but it is indeed too late to retreat. After you everything will collapse! Who will be able to build on those ruins? Perhaps it would have been better to have saved yourself for that [rebuilding] project?' she wrote, referring obliquely to her warning, a month earlier, against undertaking a mission with an uncertain outcome. She nevertheless suggested 'Lannessan for Interior and the colonel for Police'. She adopted a self-sacrificial stance, noting her own anxieties but adding: 'what will it matter whether I have suffered or not if you succeed!'[8]

Finally, on 14 November, Gambetta reported to his 'dear little beloved woman' that the ministry was formed. 'I have left the shore for the high seas and the storms. Our lady of good succour watch over me.'[9] Rather than a 'great ministry' grouping all the leading republicans, Gambetta's ministry was a combination of trusted allies and promising but unknown younger men. Several had been Gambetta's associates in the Government of National Defence of 1870. Most were young – 35 to 40 years old – and Gambetta himself was only forty-three. But if the ministry was devoid of great names, Gambetta had chosen men of great potential. René Waldeck-Rousseau and Maurice Rouvier were future Presidents of the Council of Ministers; Félix Faure later became President of the Republic.[10]

Two new portfolios offer clues to Gambetta's vision for the Republic: a dedicated ministry for agriculture would wed the rural masses to the Republic; a separate ministry for the arts would both reflect his own interests and address contemporary concerns about France's declining international reputation. Gambetta's ideal was an 'Athenian Republic', in which the scientific and cultural elites would join with the political elite to create a shared national vision and purpose.[11]

Despite the innovative ideas he brought to government, and the talent of many in the ministry, however, Gambetta was overwhelmed by a sense of failure even before he took office. He turned to Léon for consolation:

> I have failed to put together the great ministry, I have formed a pha-
> lanx of young men that I am going to lead into the firing line, come
> what may . . . But good Lord, what a face Cambyses [Grévy] made in
> reading the list, I almost burst out laughing. But I'll keep the details
> for tomorrow evening, because I am really counting on you to come
> and dine with me . . . Don't send me a telegram declining, like yes-
> terday evening. I thirst to see you, to embrace you, to find life, joy
> and courage again.[12]

Gambetta's ministry received a cool reception in the Chamber on 15 November and was derided in the press. And just when he needed her support, Léon was critical too. Gambetta defended himself:

> You are perhaps too hard on me, I assure you that it's after serious
> reflection and through absolute necessity that I resolved to adopt
> the combination you criticize so severely . . . What you regard as a
> contradiction on my part is only the result of the defection of people
> who seemed about to support me and who are holding themselves
> back . . . There, sweetheart, is the very simple, if summary, explana-
> tion of my conduct. Like you, I feel all the perils that threaten me
> and I ask you to help me face them.[13]

Léon's aspirations had been dashed along with Gambetta's. She had seen him as the great leader who would loom over his century, the savi-our of the Republic. Now she asked despairingly, 'Will it be possible, despite all the ill will to achieve good and great things? The sacrifice would be too great, if it were to be without glorious results!'[14]

'Fortune will decide'

Gambetta's failure to seek the approval of the Chamber for his two new ministries had created considerable ill will; his legislative agenda was in trouble from the start. Only days after taking office, he admitted to 'the blackest thoughts': 'I feel neither faith nor courage'. He relied on the 'moral assurance', the 'counsel and tranquility of mind' that Léon brought him. 'You are an integral part of my being . . . I can no longer act, think, live unless convinced that you share equally in whatever I want, plan and strive for.'[15]

Gambetta's government survived its first big test on 1 December when the Chamber overwhelmingly approved funding for the 'protectorate' over Tunisia, left in abeyance by Ferry's fall. But Senate approval was not a foregone conclusion. 'Where are my thoughts?' Léon wrote on the eve of the vote. 'In the Senate; and at your feet which I no longer leave, since you so tenderly placed me there!' Gambetta responded warmly the following day, crediting her (as so often) with inspiring his oratorical victory over his old foe Broglie: 'Yesterday, and probably thanks to the magnetic influence of your thoughts fixed on the Senate, I had the first good day since the accursed day that I took this burden on my shoulders.'[16]

Victories were rare, however, and the reception of Gambetta's government was not what he and Léon had anticipated when they set out on their political adventure in 1872. Now, as both faced adversity, Léon struggled to maintain her equilibrium. Mired in unhappiness, she even complained about Gambetta's preoccupation with politics: 'I was forgetting that you have the time neither to read me nor to write to me!'[17]

Feeling neglected, Léon frequently compared her own 'restricted, humiliating, exhausting, inevitably prosaic' life with Gambetta's life in politics, which 'absorbs you, impassions you, dominates you, consumes you'. His life, she complained, had a significance that hers did not. Hers was 'without a glimmer on the horizon to enlighten the infernal path on which Destiny has so brutally cast it', she wrote, while he would 'leave his imprint' on the century; 'the future whatever it brings means glory, eternity for your name, your words, your deeds'.[18]

Léon's frequent comparisons between their lives clearly point to the different social expectations of men and women; they reflect the broader social context in which women's possibilities for self-fulfillment were very limited. Léon herself, however, never noticed that the difference between them was based on gender. Once again it is evident that the common sense of the age about men's and women's fundamental natures and roles was too deeply rooted in her psyche to be questioned.

The gloom of year's end had not lifted when the Chamber of Deputies reassembled on 10 January 1882. Gambetta was intent on constitutional revision. He aimed to create a more democratic Senate, and to introduce voting by list for the Chamber of Deputies in order to produce more coherent majorities and more stable government. Having fought the 1881 elections highlighting his intention, Gambetta claimed a mandate.[19]

Many Deputies met Gambetta's proposals with suspicion and hostility. In turn, he adopted a belligerent attitude, too battle weary or discouraged to mobilize the charm and persuasiveness that had so often smoothed his path in the past. 'The storm is gathering', he told Léon on 12 January. He would play 'double or quits . . . fortune will decide'. Léon was present, heart racing, as he introduced his bill for constitutional revision on 14 January, 'this day so decisive and so great for history'. But the parliamentary committee appointed to examine Gambetta's bill was resolutely hostile.[20]

Battle metaphors predominated as Gambetta prepared to face his opponents. He would 'see his enemies face to face', he told Léon. He would 'do battle in the full light of day' in 'a final and glorious combat'. Both Gambetta and Léon were resigned to defeat. 'In any case, I want a quick outcome', Léon wrote. 'Any solution is preferable to the alternative!' Again, she made a virtue of feminine self-sacrifice: 'I am deliberately suppressing everything that concerns me, except the affirmation of my ever-deepening, ever more ardent, ever more enthusiastic, ever more devoted feelings for my dear great Sweetheart, whom I embrace.'[21]

Gambetta insisted repeatedly that life with Léon was now his priority; this may have helped him steel himself for defeat. He had already written on 19 January: 'If I win, I will have them, if I lose I regain myself and this time I will keep myself forever for you and our dear projects.' That sentiment grew stronger as the day of reckoning approached. On 23 January he declared: 'Without you nothing matters to me anymore . . . Apart from you . . . I feel only the emptiness and the insuperable vanity of the things of this world.' Léon's presence at the debate would sustain him, come what may: 'you will be there, I'll do battle under your eyes, that will suffice and I couldn't care less about the rest'.[22]

The 'battle' occurred on 26 January. Gambetta passionately defended his proposal, as well as his longstanding contribution to the republican cause. 'Who could be persuaded that I would use whatever moral and intellectual authority I have to harm you, to discredit you, to hinder the common task, begun twelve years ago?' he asked the Chamber.

> I have shared with you in the full light of day the struggle against the adversaries of the Republic, whom I have opposed . . . because . . . their triumph was incompatible with the liberty, the prosperity, the grandeur of modern France.

'We have overcome our enemies', Gambetta continued. 'It remains for us to govern ourselves, to struggle against the incessant causes of division that besiege us, to divest ourselves of personalism and focus only on the country.'[23]

'Personalism' – personal hostility to Gambetta – was the only factor uniting the disparate group of Deputies opposing the bill, which was the pretext for Gambetta's colleagues to overthrow his government. It was not surprising that the 76 conservatives in the Chamber voted against the bill; nor was it surprising that the Extreme Left did so. But 137 republicans from several mainstream factions also voted against the government. Gambetta and his ministry resigned immediately.[24] Impatient for change, determined to push his own agenda without cultivating support for it, Gambetta had played 'double or quits' and lost.

'At least one consolation'

After finally attaining the position to which he had so long aspired, Gambetta had lost office after less than three months. He turned to Léon, repeating his desire to marry her. He had already written on 19 January, in response to a distressed note: 'It's not three times a week and on the run that I want to console you, spoil you, cure you, it's every day and all day long.' And marriage would bring him 'at least one consolation . . . the tenderness and the indissoluble company of my dear adored wife'. A few days later, he returned to the theme: 'remember the magic ring I gave you, it contains the motto of my life ['outside this ring, no love'] and the symbol of my passion, not to mention the secret of my most daring ambitions. I no longer want to exist but for you, through you, in you alone.'[25]

Gambetta now chose to view the defeat of his government as 'deliverance' and its timing as propitious. 'It is indeed 27! January 1882', he wrote to her the day after his resignation. The exclamation mark recalled 27 April, anniversary of their first encounter: 'This date was indeed promised and blessed for deliverance. I felt the liberating date coming, I welcomed it, and I beg sweetheart not to protest about stupidity or human ingratitude, everything that happens must happen, as a lesson for the future.' Léon replied reassuringly, if insincerely, 'Things have indeed turned out for the best.'[26]

Gambetta dated his last letter on official stationery 'the last day of prison'. But it was perhaps symptomatic that on leaving 'prison' he had no home to go to, because the house on the rue Saint-Didier was not yet ready. A vacation helped to solve the accommodation problem, and in the interim he accepted Mme Arnaud's invitation to use her Paris mansion to receive the many callers who came to offer their sympathies. Léon's apartment on the rue Bonaparte sufficed for a final lovers' rendezvous before Gambetta departed on 1 February.[27]

Gambetta was absent for nearly three weeks, travelling in Italy. On the way, he stopped at Nice to see his father, who had retired there. He wrote to Léon, 'I can't avoid the sweet thought that you should be with me.'[28] Perhaps Léon preferred not to go, since a visit to Gambetta's family would have been awkward. And perhaps Gambetta did not press her to accompany him: it was a 'sweet thought', a gesture of affection to invite her, but a family reunion was no place for a mistress. In Gambetta's absence, Léon threw herself into completing the redecoration of his new house.

Writing to Léon from the family home in Nice, Gambetta reported that he had broached the question of marriage: 'He [father] was wonderful, I will tell you everything, such things demand to be said with a kiss.'[29] Gambetta made no reference to his mother's views. It was his father's approval that he dearly wanted to obtain. And he no doubt hoped that reporting his father's support would reassure Léon.

In his frequent letters home, Gambetta reiterated his love for Léon and his dream of life with her in the 'sweet nest' under preparation. 'I am ready, more than ready to return to you', he wrote on 7 February, 'tomorrow it will be eight long days without Nini, that's too many, far too many.' He would soon return 'never to leave [her] again', 'to build our life together'. He also declared that his return date was Léon's to decide. 'A little word from you and I am ready to take the train north', he wrote on 4 February. 'When will you call me back and what day will I be with my beautiful and good magician in the sweet nest cushioned [capitonné] for the two of us?' he asked two days later.[30]

But these statements were not meant to be taken literally. Having written on 8 February: 'I am anxious to return to my place, to our place, near my dear wife who will be my wife forever if she so wishes', he added: 'From here I am heading to San Remo then to Savona and from there via Genoa to Turin.' The following day at San Remo he received Léon's 'delightful letter' telling him that the works were finished: supposedly the cue for his return. On 10 February, still at San Remo, he wrote: 'I am going to leave and take every shortcut to be in Paris, in the sweet nest, on Wednesday 15 February', but on 18 February he was still in Genoa, arriving in Paris only the following weekend.[31] Gambetta wrote to his father: 'Here I am back, alas, much sooner than I would have wished from that beautiful land of Italy and [am now] half installed rue Saint-Didier . . . Were it not for the annoying crowd of visitors I would still be with you.'[32]

Neither Gambetta's tardy return, nor Léon's apparent failure to call him back, indicated a lack of love: his letters were genuine in their passion; she lavished her time on decorating his – or their? – home. But words of regret and anticipation smoothed the path of absence and held out the reassuring promise of return. When he did return, however, Gambetta moved alone into the house on the rue Saint-Didier. Léon continued to live with her mother and son. Their relationship continued as in the past. They saw each other every few days – 'three times a week and on the run', as Gambetta had put it – and they wrote letters every day.[33]

Gambetta reiterated his desire to marry, but Léon remained all too aware of the likely consequences. In November 1881, as Gambetta was assembling his ministry, the republican newspaper *Le Siècle* had warned him against selecting men whose private lives were tarnished. It imagined a situation in which a minister's colleagues, or foreign diplomats, might 'refuse to enter a house whose master could see his name linked to financial scandals, and whose wife, the hostess, has a past that prevents honest women from entering her home'. The story targeted Maurice Rouvier, Minister for Commerce, who had married his former mistress, Marie-Noémi Cadiot (the sculptor 'Claude Vignon'): Mme Rouvier was indeed shunned at the official reception at the Élysée Palace.[34] Léon surely envisaged her own ostracism too.

Gambetta decided to confront the problem of Léon's social exclusion directly. In February 1882, playing cards with Mme Pellet and her mother, Mme Scheurer-Kestner, Gambetta suddenly asked, 'If I marry, will you receive the woman who has long been my companion [*ma compagne de toujours*]?' His 'companion': there was no word in polite speech to describe Léon's position. The women assured him that they would receive Léon, and that Mme Kestner and Mme Arnaud (close to the Kestner family) would do so too. These women of the Republican elite could afford to shrug off criticism, and their willingness to ignore social protocol suggests the deep loyalty that Gambetta inspired. That willingness, however, was limited to a few close friends. Jules Ferry's wife, Eugénie (Mme Pellet's cousin), was obdurate: she would never receive Léon.[35]

Léon probably worried, too, about the effect of their marriage on her son Alphonse. Marriage would bring intense, sometimes hostile, press scrutiny. There was a very real danger that close investigation would expose as fiction the claim that she was Alphonse's aunt. Such a possibility must have filled her with terror.

From May to November 1881, Alphonse studied German in Dresden.[36] He returned to Paris just as Gambetta became President of the Council of Ministers, but it appears that he did not return to school. Gambetta had alluded to a problem concerning Alphonse in a letter from Italy in February 1882. In March, replying to another letter from Léon, he wrote: 'You did well to say no to Dubief [principal of Alphonse's former school] since that is your opinion, but it is essential to obtain *a good certificate of studies.* That is very necessary.' Gambetta added: 'I will set to work and place him somewhere else, we have time to think about that. So calm down now.' But there is no trace of Alphonse in school records elsewhere.[37] Despite his earlier academic achievements, it seems that he did not obtain his baccalaureate. Perhaps he was too sickly to undertake the necessary hard work. Perhaps the seventeen-year-old had simply decided to resist his mother's high expectations.

Léon and Gambetta found Alphonse's presence awkward as they arranged their lives in 1882; presumably Alphonse found the situation difficult too. The happy threesome when Alphonse was a boy had now become the problematic threesome of a man, his mistress and her adolescent son. The 'intruder' was sometimes sent to a restaurant for his meal when Léon dined with Gambetta 'in the nest' at the rue Saint-Didier. What Alphonse thought of that arrangement we do not know.[38]

When Gambetta deplored Léon's 'domestic hell' in March 1882, he wrote in the plural, indicating that domestic conflict with Léon's mother was now exacerbated by conflict with Alphonse: 'I am impatient to snatch you away from this odious domestic hell. What dreadful people they are not to adore you, to kiss the imprint of your footsteps, after all the boundless affection and the sacrifices you have made for them. Happily there will soon be an end to all this.' Gambetta suggested marriage as the solution to Léon's problems, signing off as 'your very loving little husband'.[39]

Less punctilious about his political duties than in the past, Gambetta had time on his hands. He took long walks. He visited les Jardies to see how renovations were proceeding. He attended republican dinners and salons. He went hunting. Still he was bored and lonely. 'You must return to your poor lover who doesn't know what to do without your sweet presence', he wrote to Léon in April.[40] But if he was missing her, he was also missing the full life he had lived when deeply engaged in a promising political project.

Poor health was also taking its toll. Gambetta was exhausted from a decade of constant toil, and he struggled to 'shake off the physical torpor that is spreading through all my old limbs'.[41] Léon's 'sufferings' continued to be more emotional than physical. Gambetta felt helpless to do anything to comfort her. 'I cannot tell you how haunted and troubled

I am by your anguish', he wrote in May. 'I want so much to put a little honey in this cup of absinth.' A few days later he repeated: 'sweetheart, I am ready to do anything, whatever you like, to put an end to your sufferings'. He no doubt hoped she would take up his offer of 6 April, when he had written: 'you too often forget that somewhere there is a man always ready to receive you in his arms, to give you his name and to remove you from the fate which weighs on you'.[42] Marriage remained his hope, but Léon continued to elude him.

'With France lost, the rest of the world disgusts me'

Gambetta had claimed, on leaving office, that he was henceforth 'indifferent' to politics: 'the few lines of politics that you trace in your letter of today seem to me to come from beyond the grave', he told Léon in February.[43] For two months after his fall he avoided the Chamber and the offices of the *République française*. He had 'the pleasant feeling of a man escaping from a nightmare', and was 'really enjoying [his] freedom'. As spring moved toward summer, Gambetta continued to profess indifference to 'the men and the things of politics'.[44] But he could not abandon politics so easily, and the crowds who had greeted him in southern France when he travelled there after his defeat showed that he still retained enormous popular appeal. He was soon drawn to the political contest again, and perhaps even hoped that he might be recalled to power.

At the end of March, Gambetta admitted to Léon that he had joined the commission on the army: 'I couldn't leave such important matters in the destructive hands of this crowd.' Noting that people had been 'moved' by his decision, he added: 'their emotions are only beginning, time will tell'.[45]

Gambetta had already tabled a bill to reduce military service to three years; he was now elected to head the parliamentary committee considering this proposal. He wanted to end all exemptions and the special treatment of the wealthy, creating a national army in which all men would serve for three years. He 'wanted to see, all together in the barracks, the blouses [of workers], the vests [of bourgeois] and the jackets [of peasants]'.[46]

Gambetta also took a passionate interest in Egypt, where France's colonial problems next erupted. Egyptian patriots were in revolt against the Ottoman Emperor's Viceroy of Egypt, the 'Khedive', who was being supported by France and Britain. France was already struggling to subdue Tunisia and Indochina (today Vietnam; Gambetta's brief government had sent an expedition to capture Hanoi, which led to France's protectorate). Freycinet, who had replaced Gambetta as President of the Council, shrank from yet another military operation. Even when riots in Alexandria killed some fifty Europeans in June 1881, he declined to act. Britain acted, however, establishing British hegemony over Egypt.

For Gambetta, this abandonment of French interests (as he saw it) verged on treachery. His disgust dominated his letters to Léon throughout May and June: 'I am nauseated by what's happening. There's no shame we haven't undergone.' France had fallen 'lower than the Greeks and the Bulgarians'. 'Poland died in battle', he added, 'we will die on our knees of fright without defending ourselves.' *'Finis Galliae* [the end of France]', he announced on 23 June. 'We are ripe for slavery . . . which province tempts Bismarck? It can be had without effort.' 'How they must laugh in Berlin, how they must despise us in London!' he lamented.[47]

Gambetta's frustration at losing control of policy on vital matters accentuated his desire to make Léon the centre of his life. 'I've an immense desire to flee and at times I wish I no longer had a Fatherland, for with France lost, the rest of the world disgusts me', he wrote on 7 July. Léon remained his 'sole and eternal consolation', his 'only love', now that he claimed to have none for France. Again he dreamed of marriage: 'whenever you wish, we will put to use the inventions of our Civil Code [civil marriage] here or beyond the frontiers'.[48]

In mid-July, Freycinet was sufficiently concerned about the situation in Egypt to ask the Chamber for credits to support the French fleet. On 18 July, despite his personal anguish (his mother lay near death), Gambetta made his first planned speech in the Chamber since losing office. He criticized government inaction but supported credits. France had to send troops to Egypt – 'it's for the French nation'– but in co-operation with Britain. 'Never break the English alliance', he concluded. This was to be Gambetta's last speech in the Chamber.[49]

'I no longer know where to find the strength to bear all these misfortunes'

Gambetta's mother had arrived in Paris on 11 July, feeling unwell. The next morning, she suffered a stroke. 'Misfortune overwhelms me', he wrote to Léon. 'I ran to her, I'm choking with tears, at first she didn't recognize me at all . . . I'm mad with grief.' The following day (13 July) he had received no word from Léon: 'this silence increases my anxieties and leaves me defenceless against the terrible anguish that assails me'. 'May I find in returning home a word, a single word in your hand, I need it.'[50]

Léon had written a letter, but then tore it up as 'untimely': perhaps she had initially underestimated the seriousness of the situation. The following day she wrote a kind and loving letter: 'Your sorrow breaks my heart . . . may the assurance of my infinite tenderness, which increases with your suffering, bring you some solace!' But she added: 'My first thought was to come to you; but you don't ask for it, and I await your orders!'[51]

Writing from his home that evening, Gambetta made no reference to receiving any letter. 'I'm broken', he began simply. 'I want to see you, I beg for you.' His mother was now comatose. The following day, Gambetta reached new depths of despair: 'I can't go on, this struggle against the inevitable is breaking me, my tender mother is doomed, it's only a question of hours.' And he was still without his lover: 'I beg you to be home at five o'clock and wait for me there.' Without Léon's letters, there is no explanation for her unavailability at this painful time, but a meeting was finally arranged for Sunday 16 July.[52] Gambetta's mother rallied briefly, and then died on 19 July.

Gambetta took his mother's body back to Nice. He wrote to Léon on 22 July, 'Alone, I am going to accompany my mother to her resting place.' For Pillias, this wording – 'alone' – was a reproach.[53] But Léon could not have attended the funeral as his mistress, only as his wife. This event increased Gambetta's desire to persuade Léon to marry him.

Gambetta wrote to Léon again on the evening of the funeral: 'I've a truly great need to rejoin my tender friend, and my dear consoler.'[54] But the return to Paris brought new woes. Alphonse was seriously ill with typhoid fever. For several weeks, Léon was totally occupied in nursing him. The consolation that Gambetta had hoped for on his return would be provided only by letter, and by a lover preoccupied with the health of her son. Writing to Léon on black-bordered mourning paper, Gambetta found it 'impossible to contain [his] anguish'. 'I've received nothing from you neither letter nor telegram and I fear that the state of our dear *Chine* has worsened.' Grieving for his mother, bereft of Léon's comfort, Gambetta had reached a low ebb. 'It's too many blows at once, and I no longer know where to find the strength to bear all these misfortunes.' He pleaded again for news, concluding, 'Dear soul, a word to revive me and tell me if you will come tomorrow at the usual time.'[55]

Gambetta soon realized that the 'usual' arrangements with Léon would not resume immediately. Letters were to be their only link. He offered her support and encouragement. 'I am with you with all the strength of my heart . . . I implore you, dear light of my life, to turn to me, to remember from the depths of your torments that I belong wholly to you and as soon as you call me, I will run to you.' In return, he sought consolation from her letters: 'Your good letters sustain me and allow me to bear the cruel grief of a doubly-sorrowful separation.' If he received no news, he worried that Alphonse's condition had worsened, or that Léon herself had caught the disease. He emphasized his unselfishness, reassuring Léon that he, too, regarded Alphonse's recovery as the top priority: 'I can resign myself, and it would be too selfish to call for you when the cause keeps you away.'[56]

Still, he could not help asking: 'Come now baby [*bébé*] when can I see you, even if only for an hour, enough time to put a new provision of light in your eyes? Of courage? Of hope??' A few days later, he wrote again: 'I have lost my soul [*âme*] since I no longer see you . . . Is it true that I cannot come to rue Soufflot to get some news? Why not?' 'If only I could press you against my heart for one minute I would be stronger, and I believe without being vain that you yourself would more assured.' Gambetta's pleas to be allowed to support Léon do not conceal his deep need for her support.[57]

This period of separation once again heightened Léon's concerns about her age (they were both forty-four, but this was old for a mistress). If this was a plea for reassurance, it brought a passionate response: 'Don't torment yourself, dear angel, remember that my love rests on many supports other than youth, that it is entirely composed of admiration for the nobility of your spirit, for that moral beauty in you that nothing can hide and which binds me forever to my idol. I love you as the incarnation of the Ideal and I adore you in spirit and in the flesh.'[58]

Alphonse's illness did not produce a truce in Léon's domestic warfare with her mother. She contemplated moving out, not to the rue Saint-Didier with Gambetta but perhaps to a country house. Gambetta offered to rent an apartment she had liked on the avenue d'Iéna, and tried to cheer her up: 'As for the rhinoceros [Mme Léon], I agree that you should . . . make a present of it to someone, perhaps the director of the Zoological Gardens.' Gambetta's good humour on 8 August was almost certainly due to the fact that a rendezvous had been arranged for 8.30 the following evening. He was finally able to 'dream of the moment when he would see [Léon] again'.[59]

'Poor France, poor Republic'

Léon had advised Gambetta to seek 'distraction in politics' during their forced separation. But political and personal discouragement were closely intertwined in Gambetta's correspondence. Having expressed his anguish about Alphonse's condition on 27 July, he wrote: 'I don't have the courage to speak to you about politics, this Chamber, this government every day extends the limits of national shame.' Two days later, before the confidence vote that would bring down the Freycinet government, he added. 'I'm off to the Chamber for the burial of old French honour. It's over, and as they say in the old tragedies, "Exit Gallia." . . . I appeal to the future, if there is still to be a future for this degenerate nation. I have lived too long.'[60]

Gambetta's last action in the Chamber was uncharacteristic inaction. Freycinet was finally proposing limited military intervention in Egypt to protect the Suez Canal. Gambetta was 'nauseated': 'I walked in the hallways so as not to give way to a surge of emotion that might have led me to break the law of silence I had imposed on myself.' Gambetta did not intervene and the Chamber rejected Freycinet's proposal, 400 votes to 75. For Gambetta, the removal of Freycinet from office was the only positive feature of the crisis.[61]

In late July and early August, Gambetta presented Léon with scathing reports on efforts to form a new government. Each proposal was 'more ridiculous, more impotent' than the previous one. Blaming President Grévy for the debacle, Gambetta feared it might provide an opportunity for the Bonapartists: some people were 'ready to throw themselves at the feet of a saviour'.[62] Pessimistic and depressed, he feared seeing a decade's work in establishing the Republic undone.

Politics had literally become a postscript in Gambetta's letters, ceding prominence to his efforts to reach out to Léon. Irony became his refuge as he reported daily on attempts to form a ministry: 'Today it's the Leblond ministry', he announced on 3 August, adding that Leblond was 'an old remnant from 1848 that everyone thought had been dead since time immemorial'. The following day he noted that 'the ineffable Tirard is to be president of the council. It's enough to make one resign as a Frenchman.' On 5 August, he declared in disgust, 'they are offering power to people passing in the street'. 'Poor France, memorable Republic', he added, 'I had dreamt other dreams for the one and the other, but what use are dreams?' Finally, he informed Léon that a new government had been formed: 'We've reached the most farcical, the most inane combination, a Duclerc ministry. It's the news of the day, it will be the non-event of tomorrow.'[63]

Irony then gave way to despair. 'These men are all incompetents, intriguers or idiots. This ministry is a precursor to the final catastrophe that will finish off France, the State and the Republic.' Once people saw that 'neither merit, nor talent, nor past service' was of any account, they would 'welcome any other regime which would rid them of this one'.[64]

Gambetta's bitter political assessments had a personal edge. He was aware of Grévy's role in frustrating his ambitions and undermining his government. In criticizing the rise to power of nonentities, he was surely remembering both his own popularity, undimmed by his fall from power, and his long contribution to the establishment of the Republic.

But there are also hints that Gambetta saw the ministerial crisis as a harbinger of his own political resurrection. Reporting on efforts to form a new ministry, he observed: 'As for me, I watch, I listen, I push gently for dissolution, I refuse to take the least part in ministerial combinations and I wait.' And should anarchy and dictatorship descend, Gambetta noted: 'It will be up to us to see where we stand.'[65] The police were reporting that Gambetta's supporters, and even some who had voted against his ministry, were expecting his imminent return to power. Nevertheless, Gambetta envisaged a return, not as the 'dictator' some accused him of being, but thanks to 'the secret of universal suffrage'.[66]

In late October, Gambetta was looking forward to the new parliamentary session. He wrote to his father that he was 'very rested in body and spirit, and ready to take on the parliamentary harness again'.[67] The elderly Duclerc, who replaced Freycinet as head of the ministry, had little authority in the Chamber, presenting an opportunity for Gambetta to impose himself on the Chamber as he had in the past. He did not attempt to do so. Despite his cheerful report to his father, he was in poor health. The Deputy Francis Charmes noted that, at the last hearing of the committee on conscription reform, on 22 November, Gambetta was exhausted after speaking for 15 minutes: 'He was swimming [in perspiration] . . . I was struck by the difficulty of his breathing and by the weariness he was experiencing.'[68] For some time, too, Gambetta had been experiencing bouts of severe pain in the abdomen, signs of the appendicitis that would eventually lead to his death.

'Yes to tomorrow, to Sunday, to forever'

With Alphonse on the mend in late August, and his relationship with Léon restored to its normal pattern, Gambetta's spirits lifted. Léon had written of lifelong love, producing effusions of hope that she would marry him. Léon's letter has not survived, but Gambetta quoted it in his reply:

The last line of your letter produced in me the sweetest emotion that I have felt for a very long time; I cannot tell you what feeling of dazzling hope filled my heart when I read those few words written in your hand, ['] I want to live my entire life, which really does have its rewards, for you alone. ['] It seemed to me that I had won you a second time never to lose you again.

Gambetta was sure that he would 'change [Léon's] life and make it what it should never have ceased being, beautiful, good and happy'.[69]

Léon was even considering moving to the rue Saint-Didier, which would have marked a major step towards a life together. 'You can regard this house as your own, to use and abuse', Gambetta wrote. 'Truly, I can't imagine why the future might make this decision delicate. If it pleases you it thrills me.' Léon's hesitation was again due to Alphonse. Gambetta reassured her: 'Our two lives are intermingled forever, the presence of *la Chine*, even permanently, would not trouble or disturb them in any way.'[70]

Only days later, however, Gambetta was back on the emotional roller coaster. Léon sank into renewed despair and Gambetta did so too, frustrated by his inability to overcome her melancholy. He insisted: 'it is always possible to remake one's life, when two people do it together, loving and adoring each other'. But he added, 'I cannot express the sorrow that your desperate and despairing letters cause me, I am quite black in heart and soul.' When Léon's mood brightened a few days later, Gambetta's spirits rose accordingly.[71] Perhaps he briefly believed that their marriage was imminent. The remnant of a lost letter might suggest as much: 'Thus, dear well beloved wife, courage and constancy for a few more hours and you will be happy and I will be the most radiant of husbands, to tomorrow at the agreed time and always more adoring.'[72] But that belief was short-lived.

On 7 September, Gambetta sent Léon a 'morning kiss, saying au revoir and courage during my absence'. He was off for his annual visit to Mme Arnaud at her Swiss château. He left Léon 'the keys for the rue Saint-Didier' – obviously she had not moved in there – and added, at Ville-d'Avray, 'everything is open'.[73]

A cheerful letter from Léon awaited Gambetta on his arrival at the château, accompanied by his father, on 11 September. But in Paris, Léon's spirits had plummeted: 'you can't judge the state in which your absence has left me'; she wrote of 'this horrible solitude of a soul which only the sight of you retains in this world'. 'I haven't slept since your departure, and my fever doesn't abate!' Unaware of Léon's state, Gambetta was seeking his father's active support in persuading her to marry him. He quoted his father's rapturous praises of Léon, and concluded: 'repeat well to her, [Father] added, that my prayer, my wish [*voeu*] is joined with yours to invite her to agree as soon as possible'.[74]

Léon apparently made a brief visit to Switzerland at this time – a sign, perhaps, of her desperation – since Gambetta noted the 'condolences I have received on your departure'. Was she presented to Joseph Gambetta, or received by Mme Arnaud herself ? That would have marked a major social breakthrough. It seems unlikely.[75]

Gambetta returned to Paris about 24 September, a few days after Léon. 'I'm counting on your already being installed at Ville-d'Avray', he had written, where 'you will be . . . mistress of the household, a prelude to the definitive role which awaits you'. Marriage seemed to be rapidly approaching: 'I am so impatient, as the greedy man that I am', Gambetta wrote, 'to enjoy unceasingly, without interruption, at every minute of the day and night, the treasures embedded in the sanctuary that is my wife'.[76]

Léon was moving house, too, and it seems she was planning – again – to move in with Gambetta. She gave notice to the owner of 7, rue Bonaparte on 15 October.[77] Gambetta continued, however, to write to her throughout October and November: she did not yet reside with him on the rue Saint-Didier.

In an effort to clear the way for marriage, Gambetta was also 'trying to smooth everything out' for Alphonse's future. He wrote to a contact in Hamburg, and to an old friend employed by the State Railway Company in Vienna, about 'a certain young man of eighteen years . . . very interested in locomotives, whom I would very much like to see placed in one of the many sections under your charge in Austria'. In October, Gambetta approached Émile Crozet-Fourneyron – former Deputy for Saint-Étienne and member of Gambetta's Republican Union – whose family ran a foundry in Le Chambon-Feugerolles.[78] Gambetta outlined Alphonse's 'aptitudes for locomotives, his bizarre passion for everything that concerns railways' and Crozet-Fourneyron offered to interview him. 'Advise *Chine* to respond only to his questions, to speak of his plans and his desire to enter the industry', Gambetta suggested to Léon, hoping that soon 'la *Chine* will be safely tied to the Forge'. But nothing came of this.[79]

Despite rumours circulating during October, Léon had not yet agreed to marry Gambetta. 'I have not yet triumphed over her scruples and her resistance', he confessed to his father. Friends later recounted that Léon consented in November and that the banns were to be announced in early December, when Gambetta's accident cut everything short.[80] Gambetta's letter of 19 November, his last, might suggest as much: 'Ah!

How impatient I am to end this disjointed life, used up running one after the other', he wrote. 'I console myself in thinking that we're reaching the end and that soon we will never again leave each other.'[81] But he had often expressed such hopes in the past. There is no evidence that marriage was imminent when Gambetta and Léon made what was to be their last trip to les Jardies, on Saturday 25 November 1882.

'Our poor leader still has some fever tonight'

Shortly before eleven the following Monday morning – ironically, it was the 27th, a day which recalled their first meeting on 27 April 1872 – Gambetta picked up his revolver, apparently to put it away. Noting that it was not fully closed, he pushed on the butt, setting off a bullet that was still in the chamber. The bullet entered the palm of his hand, travelled through his wrist and out his arm, slamming into the door.[82] Two local doctors arrived within half an hour and bandaged his wounds. Léon sent the coachman to Paris to find Gambetta's friend, the surgeon Odilon Lannelongue, who arrived around one that afternoon.[83]

Lannelongue prohibited all visits and prescribed absolute immobility to protect the hand. He called in Gambetta's regular doctor, Siredey, and a longtime friend of Gambetta, Dr Fieuzal, 'who knew his habits and medical history'. Lannelongue also assigned two interns to stay by Gambetta constantly. Other friends and admirers from the medical world soon became involved, including Charcot, the famous neurologist, and Cornil, the anatomist, both of whom owed their chairs to Gambetta. In all, seven doctors attended officially and signed the clinical notes.[84] Others came as friends but also offered medical opinions. The extraordinary number of doctors fed rumours that the wound was very serious. Moreover, his medical friends were virtually Gambetta's only visitors; as his doctors, they were sworn to confidentiality, so no eyewitnesses were available to attest publicly to what was happening.

Gambetta's political opponents immediately used the incident to attack him through Léon. The royalist newspaper *Le Gaulois* sparked the rumours with a front-page story claiming a cover-up: the presence of so many eminent doctors proved that Gambetta was seriously wounded; it was probably the result of 'private vengeance'. The next day, *Le Gaulois* declared that the person who shot Gambetta was 'Mme L . . . [*sic*], the mother of the child whom M. Gambetta is having raised in Leipzig, under the name of Léon Massabie [Gambetta's mother's maiden name]'. During a stormy scene, the article continued, 'Mme L picked up a revolver. "Be careful", cried Gambetta, "it's loaded!" At the same time, he instinctively extended his arm and the gun went off.' The nationalist Henri Rochefort then pursued the story in his newspaper, *L'Intransigeant*. The rumours took off, stoked by the press of the emerging new right.[85]

There was no basis to these rumours. All those present at the time gave the same account of the accident.[86] If Léon had feared that public knowledge of her relationship with Gambetta would see her victimized in the press, however, this development proved her right. She was never to live down the rumours.

. Léon was the only person at Gambetta's bedside apart from the doctors. Both Siredey and Charcot were almost certainly aware of her role in Gambetta's life; others probably knew that she was neither wife nor blood relation. Lannelongue's intern, Charles Walther, noted that Gambetta sought to legitimize her presence by showing her 'respectful tenderness' and always addressing her as 'Madame'. Léon was granted acceptance as Gambetta's life companion. The republicans later acknowledged her as such and even included her in the semi-official painting of Gambetta on his deathbed, surrounded by his doctors and friends.[87]

Ten days after the accident, the wound had nearly healed. On 8 December, Fieuzal wrote to tell the family that Gambetta would regain full use of his hand, but that they would confine Gambetta to bed for another ten days. On that very day, the doctors reported symptoms – including severe abdominal pain and a mild temperature – that, to modern medical eyes, mark the onset of appendicitis. A diagnosis of 'appendicitis' did not exist in 1882, however, and the doctors paid little heed to these complaints.[88]

Gambetta had suffered from what were probably appendicitis attacks since the age of eleven. He also suffered chronic intestinal complaints and constipation, and for over a year had suffered frequent 'abdominal malaises' and 'overwhelming' pain, for which he regularly drank Pullna water, a commonly used laxative.[89]

Gambetta's severe abdominal pain still persisted on 10 December, when Jean-Martin Charcot visited him. Charcot's prestige was immense, but while he was a pioneering neurologist, his thinking on matters of internal medicine followed established doctrine. Symptoms like Gambetta's were diagnosed as 'typhlitis', an inflammation of the bowel caused by constipation; the remedy was thought to be laxatives and enemas, which Charcot duly prescribed. Gambetta's doctors were acting in accordance with the science of their day. Only after Gambetta's death, in 1886, did Reginald Fitz show that most cases of typhlitis proved, on surgery, to be inflammation of the appendix and coined the term 'appendicitis'.[90]

On 15 December, Gambetta had another abdominal crisis that left him suffering badly. The doctors nevertheless allowed him to go out in the carriage with Léon the next day, but he took cold and began to shiver. That evening, his temperature rose sharply. He had almost certainly suffered a ruptured appendix. Gambetta now suffered high night-time temperatures, fever and vomiting. His abdomen was swollen. Lannelongue feared possible ulceration of the large intestine.[91] He concluded that an operation to drain any pus and repair any perforations was the only hope, but could not persuade Charcot and other eminent attending doctors to agree.

Gambetta's faith in Charcot never wavered. He asked to see him again and, on 23 December, Charcot diagnosed 'perityphlitis', an inflammation of the lining of the large intestine. The doctors again prescribed laxatives and an enema, as well as a poultice on the abdomen: blisters on the skin were believed to reduce the swelling. But those blisters may have led to a new crisis. On 27 December, Gambetta's temperature rose sharply. This was due to erysipelas, which appeared on his abdomen two days later. Erysipelas – also known as Saint Anthony's Fire – is a very serious streptococcal infection, treatable with massive doses of penicillin. Erysipelas is normally introduced from an external source and penetrates the body through a small cut or abrasion. The blisters raised by the poultice may well have enabled the entry of the bacteria.

It is almost certain that erysipelas, rather than peritonitis, was the immediate cause of Gambetta's death. The doctors do not seem to have regarded it as a major factor, however, and historians have paid no attention to it. The autopsy would reveal that Gambetta's peritonitis was confined to the appendix and adjacent portions of the large intestine. It is possible to recover from such a localized infection. Without the erysipelas, Gambetta may have been winning the battle against the intestinal infection and on his way to recovery.

On 30 December, with the full onset of erysipelas, the doctors noted that Gambetta's condition 'had deteriorated considerably'. They now sought only to 'support the patient's vital forces'. Knowing that he had asked for the newspapers that morning, and hoping 'to prevent M. Gambetta's experiencing any anxiety', they issued a reassuring statement: 'The local inflammatory state is moving toward resolution. The general condition is satisfactory.' This statement was published in the *République française* on the day of Gambetta's death, further feeding rumours of a cover-up. The 'local inflammatory state' may well have been easing, but Gambetta was dying.

The young Algerian deputy Eugène Étienne, future leader of the colonial party, became a constant visitor during the last days and kept other friends up to date. His letters show how Gambetta's circle was lulled into false optimism. At one in the morning of 31 December – the day Gambetta was to die – Étienne wrote that the doctors 'are waiting for the right moment to operate and are now without fear about the result'. At nine that evening, he reported that 'our poor leader still has some fever tonight', but added that Lannelongue 'had no anxiety, a few days of serious treatment will cure the ill'. At 10 p.m., however, Étienne admitted to being 'very anxious': 'Lannelongue still says that his state is the same, I find that his forces are diminishing visibly. I can't keep my fears silent.' Étienne then tried to alert other members of Gambetta's circle, sending notes to their homes and clubs, but most were out celebrating New Year's Eve.[92]

Étienne's fears were justified. Gambetta remained conscious until 10.45 p.m., when he murmured his last words, 'Léon, Léon'. Perhaps he was trying to say Léonie's name. At five minutes to midnight Gambetta died, gently, 'without a tremor'. Étienne, Spuller, Fieuzal, Paul Bert, and Léon were at his side; the other members of Gambetta's circle arrived too late.[93]

No one was prepared for this tragic end. Had Gambetta thought of death as a possibility, he would surely have made a will to protect Léon. Instead, the coachman recalled, around seven that evening Gambetta discussed the household accounts and chatted happily until the doctors arrived.[94] Léon later wrote that 'the terrible moment which broke my heart and my life' was 'absolutely unforeseen'. She felt great regret 'not to have warned our Illustrious Dead One of the danger, which he would surely have averted by that force of will which had already accomplished so many prodigious things'.[95]

Gambetta's friends and many historians later concluded that the doctors had failed to operate for fear they might be blamed if Gambetta died under the knife. Years later, Paul Bert was quoted as saying, 'if it had been my gardener, he would have been cured'.[96] The appendicitis diagnosis and the appendectomy procedure, unknown in 1882, became routine by the 1890s. Gambetta's friends later wrongly assumed that they must have been available at the time of his death. Lannelongue, haunted by Gambetta's death, admitted in 1905 that what he had envisaged in 1882 was a procedure to drain infection, not an appendectomy, which was still unknown.[97] Gambetta received the best care available at the time.

That a forty-four-year-old man should die while so many eminent doctors were saying he was doing well nevertheless surprised people

222 A Political Romance

and fed conspiracy theories. Gambetta's death became proof that the wound was more serious than was admitted, that it directly caused his death, and that Léon was responsible, a claim still made today on some Internet sites. The servants' accounts, and Lannelongue's daily clinical notes, signed by all seven attending doctors (including five famous professors of medicine) leave no room for doubt: Léon was not involved in the wound and the wound did not cause death.[98] To believe, in the absence of any evidence, that Léon shot Gambetta and that so many persons of repute lied to cover up this 'crime of passion', requires absurd conspiracy theories.

Léon was 'overwhelmed by grief'. She probably knew that Gambetta had died without a will, and that, as his mistress, she had no legal standing. She certainly knew that Gambetta's sister Benedetta would arrive shortly. Benedetta would inherit and Léon would be excluded from les Jardies and from the rue Saint-Didier, the 'nests' she had shared with Gambetta. She had no choice but to return to the troubled household on the rue Soufflot to live with her mother and son. She spent the night putting affairs in order and paying the servants. Shortly before dawn, Étienne and Strauss accompanied her to the carriage, which drove her, alone, to the rue Soufflot.[99]

Dear adored wife,

You would like to be with me at the ends of the earth and I want that too! And if you like, without a thought of returning; I am not a man to retreat like the suitors of one of your women friends who fled at the first prospect of becoming entangled. Let us choose on the map of the world a country privileged by heaven, let's agree on it and set off for the promised land. Eve will never be betrayed. I'll do better than that, the world begins and ends for me in your beautiful eyes. Put your sweetheart to the test and we are saved forever.

You will have no more worries, tribulations, no more lodgings to visit, no more quarrels to settle, we will live in endless harmony and we will die together so that there will be no regrets for the survivor.

[2 lines excised]

Léon Gambetta
P.S. Tomorrow Sunday 9am.

11
'People are weeping for the patriot, the orator'

'A saint for the Republic?'[2]

'Democracy has lost a good servant, the tribune an incomparable orator, France a great citizen.' So began the front-page obituary of the conservative *Le Temps*. Around the world, Gambetta's death was cause for sadness; as far away as New York, the flags at City Hall flew at half-mast on the day of his funeral. In Paris, his death unleashed a torrent of public grief. Despite his recent eclipse, he remained 'the patriot' in the eyes of the vast majority of the population.[3]

On New Year's Day 1883, some 3,000 people visited les Jardies, filing up the tiny staircase to his bedroom to pay their respects. Police intelligence reported that everywhere there was 'very great, very profound and general emotion'. At Belleville, even radicals hostile to Gambetta were 'frightened at his death, which they considered disastrous for the Republic'. Elsewhere, 'grief is profound'. In wealthy neighbourhoods, from the left bank around the Palais Bourbon across the Champs-Élysées to the Gare Saint Lazare, 'the emotion seems even keener than anywhere else. People are weeping for the patriot, the orator.' 'The bourgeoisie, and even many workers who were hostile to him', explained the police chief of the wealthy sixteenth arrondissement, 'saw in him the defender of order.' Such was Gambetta's accomplishment: the Republic, which once had inspired fear akin to contemporary fears of communism or terrorism, was now widely accepted as the guarantor of stability.[4]

An autopsy was performed the next day in Gambetta's bedroom at les Jardies. The brain and heart were removed and weighed at the local pharmacy. The brain ended up at the museum of the Society of Anthropology. The heart ended up with Gambetta's friend, Paul Bert. Cornil took the bowel and appendix. After his investigations, he left them in his office for Lannelongue to collect; we do not know where they ended up. The journalist P.-B. Gheusi later claimed that, when Gambetta's body was transferred to a more elaborate tomb in 1909, even more was missing: Lannelongue, he claimed, had taken an arm and Fieuzal the entire skull. Gheusi is unreliable, but some body parts were certainly missing. Léon herself later complained to Scheurer-Kestner that 'the remains of our poor great man [were] scattered among various chemists'.[5] Despite their anticlericalism, Gambetta's republican medical friends could not escape the Catholic tradition of venerating relics or the body parts of saints. They may have had a 'scientific' interest in certain body parts, but science also served to cover their desire to preserve relics of their saint for veneration.[6]

After the autopsy, what remained of the body was placed in a closed casket in the bedroom at les Jardies. The next day, 4000 mourners passed to show their respect. That evening, the casket was transferred to the Palais Bourbon, where Gambetta had presided. Directly across the Seine from the Palais Bourbon, on the Place de la Concorde, the statue of Strasbourg was shrouded in black, symbolizing the German occupation of Alsace. The Palais Bourbon itself was draped in an enormous black crepe veil, to great dramatic effect. Its ceremonial hall was turned into a *chapelle ardente,* a candlelit shrine, though all religious signs had been carefully removed. Jules Bastien-Lepage, the noted artist, and Charles Garnier, architect of the Paris Opera, worked with others to decorate the improvised *chapelle*. On 4 January, an estimated 150,000 mourners filed past the coffin; more visited the following day.[7]

The government immediately began planning a huge state funeral, but Joseph Gambetta insisted that the body be returned to Nice for burial in the family vault. This would have made a state funeral impossible, because there could be no funeral without the body. A veritable *Who's Who* of the Republican elite tried to persuade Joseph Gambetta, or 'Father', as all now addressed him, to relent. 'In the name of our great dead one, I beseech you, to leave his body to our worship', wrote Scheurer-Kestner, making explicit the religious undercurrent. 'Leave your son to Paris', wrote Victor Hugo. Although deeply impressed by Hugo's approach – 'If there is one voice to which I might have ceded, it was certainly yours' – Joseph insisted that his decision was 'irrevocable'. Finally, however, he acceded to Léon's request that the body be interred 'provisionally' in Paris, making the funeral possible.[8]

'The funeral will be the greatest since the body of the First Napoleon was taken to the Invalides' in 1840, predicted the Paris correspondent of *The New York Times,* and he was right. Gambetta's casket was surrounded by more than 5000 bouquets and wreaths. Some 1500 delegations participated in the funeral procession. They represented not only Paris and national organizations, but also every town that Gambetta had addressed. Those from Alsace and Lorraine led the cortege, which left the Palais Bourbon at 10 a.m. on Saturday 6 January, to the sound of cannon fired from the nearby Invalides, a monument to the Army to which Gambetta had been so attached.[9]

The cortege crossed the Seine to the Place de la Concorde, where some 150,000 people waited for a glimpse, and then proceeded to the Place de la République. Using the telegraph to keep track of the procession, the police estimated that 800,000 people followed the casket; the number of spectators was 'incalculable'. The cortege finally reached Père Lachaise cemetery at 4 p.m. The numerous speeches – by parliamentarians, ministers, generals, Gambetta's local political committee, the 'lost provinces' of Alsace and Lorraine, even the Paris bar – had already begun. The official delegations then filed past and placed flowers on the tomb, followed by regiments of infantry, artillery and cavalry. Cannon fired interminably.

It was dark when the coffin was dropped into the vault by torchlight, along with a bag of soil from Lorraine. It was inscribed (in Latin): 'Lotharingia [the old name for the Duchy of Lorraine] remembers, violated not dominated.' The ceremony thus commemorated 'Gambetta the defender of France', rather than the architect of the constitution and leader of the government toppled less than a year before. Gambetta's newspaper, however, declared that it was impossible to separate the republican from the patriot.[10]

Gambetta spent only six nights in this 'provisional' tomb. After a last unavailing attempt to persuade Joseph Gambetta to leave the body in Paris, the casket was taken to a special train on 12 January. Loaded with friends and dignitaries, the train stopped at many towns before arriving in Nice twenty-four hours later. There, another secular ceremony was held and, late on Saturday, 13 January, Gambetta was placed alongside his mother in the modest family tomb.[11]

'So alone in this world so empty of him'

Léonie Léon was excluded from all these ceremonies. But she was not forgotten. On 6 January, Joseph Reinach published an account of Gambetta's illness and death that ended with an eloquent tribute:

> And now there remains for us a supreme duty to accomplish . . . One woman, faithful, devoted, indefatigable in goodness and affectionate

care . . . stood guard for 34 terrible nights at the bedside of the man whose heart had such enormous love for her . . . This broken soul imposes on all who knew and admired Gambetta a profound sympathy. Far off, in the shadows, we vow to her our discreet gratitude for the rays of joy that she spread upon this great life, for the consoling tenderness with which she cushioned his death.[12]

Gambetta's friends rallied around Léon, treating her as though she were his widow and offering her both practical assistance and friendship. Léon welcomed a sympathy note from Armand Ruiz, inviting him to express his sentiments in person 'whenever it pleases you'. Ruiz aided Léon in a variety of ways, and they remained in correspondence for many years. Similarly, an unannounced visit on 5 January by Mme Marcellin Pellet (Jeanne Scheurer-Kestner) was to initiate a long correspondence between the two women.[13]

Mme Pellet did not know Léon, 'having barely glimpsed her, occasionally, at the Chamber'. In visiting Léon, she was fulfilling – in an unexpected way – the promise she had made to Gambetta in February 1882 that she would 'receive' Léon once the couple married.[14] Indeed, most of the republicans who now supported Léon had not previously met her. This was true of Auguste Scheurer-Kestner (Mme Pellet's father and Gambetta's colleague), as it was of Armand Ruiz. Similarly, Joseph Reinach, who had made his public appeal on Léon's behalf and with whom she would conduct a lengthy correspondence, had not met her, even though he had dined at les Jardies only a few weeks before Gambetta's death: 'She was there. I never saw her. She stayed in her room.' The exceptions were Eugène Spuller and Eugène Étienne, whom Léon had met at Gambetta's deathbed and with whom she also remained in touch. Léon's anonymity was testament to the extreme privacy with which the couple had surrounded their relationship. But Gambetta's bereaved friends now expressed their loyalty and devotion to him by supporting Léon. Ironically, Gambetta's death integrated Léon more fully into the republican family than had been possible while he was alive.[15]

The most immediate problem facing Léon was financial. Gambetta had died intestate, so Léon had no claim on his estate. Alexandre Léris, Gambetta's brother-in-law, checked that Alphonse had no claim either, by verifying with Léon that Gambetta was not his father. According to Pillias, who knew many surviving Gambettistes personally, a group of Gambetta's friends, with Ruiz as treasurer, immediately began providing Léon with the sum of 500 francs per month. She could now afford to visit Gambetta's grave. 'Thanks to all of you', she wrote to Ruiz from

Nice, 'I can take flowers [to the grave] each morning and it's only here that my gratitude has acquired a magnitude that I beg you to express to your generous colleagues.' The monthly payments continued until 1894, when they were transformed into a life pension of 3000 francs per year. Mme Arnaud and Camille Depret (who had lent Gambetta money to enlarge les Jardies) each contributed around 10,000 francs to the investment. Etienne, Ruiz, Reinach and the composer Georges Koechlin also offered significant sums. Auguste Scheurer-Kestner rounded up the total with 11,000 francs.[16]

Other financial arrangements were put in place as well. When Gambetta's estate was settled in June 1883, the Léris settled a sum of 60,000 francs on Léon, which was invested for her by Ruiz. This produced about 3600 francs per year. To this was added the income from a small tobacco shop on the rue des Petits-Champs, obtained through the intervention of Gambetta's former Minister for Colonies, Maurice Rouvier (and exchanged in 1891 for another on the rue du Faubourg du Temple). It probably brought Léon less than 1000 francs per year: licenses for outlets more profitable than that were awarded by a special Commission in a highly competitive process.[17] Léon was also awarded a State pension, another sign that Gambetta's former colleagues treated her as his legal widow. The combined income from these sources enabled Léon to live quite comfortably. On 17 May 1883, she and her family left the rue Soufflot for a house at 2, avenue Perrichont, in the upmarket Auteuil neighbourhood of the 16th arrondissement.[18] This remained her home until her death.

Gambetta's sudden death took from Léon the only person – apart from her son – to whom she was deeply attached. She never fully recovered from that loss. Three months before his death, Gambetta had written to Léon about his hopes for their future: 'We will live in endless harmony and we will die together so that there will be no regrets for the survivor.' Instead, Léon was to survive another twenty-four years that were filled with regret; regret for Gambetta's death, but also regret for her own decisions: 'I wanted to become a wife and I wasn't asked, and after having been begged, I resisted due to a scrupulousness which was a complete deception, because it created misfortune for everyone!' 'How will I bear life', Léon asked Mme Pellet, 'forever deprived of this exchange of a tenderness so infinite that no expression ever seemed adequate to describe exactly what we were feeling; his letters testify to that!' Two years later, she again wrote: 'I feel so alone again in this world so empty of him, that he filled with his name, just as he filled my heart with his love!'[19]

Léon had long been accustomed to living an epistolary life with Gambetta. His death deprived her of both his physical presence and the daily letters that were integral to their relationship. After Gambetta's death, Léon created new epistolary relationships with some of his republican friends, especially Mme Pellet. These letters kept her in touch with the world, particularly with the republican world, at a time when she had few opportunities for social contact outside her extended family. They provided a vehicle for expressing her grief, which was extremely important given her unsympathetic relationship with her mother. More than that, they enabled her to be acknowledged as Gambetta's beloved. By corresponding with Léon in the shadow of Gambetta's death, his friends acknowledged her identity as his 'companion', if not his wife; the person with privileged access to his person, his ideas and his affection. Most importantly, these correspondences affirmed Léon's role as Gambetta's confidante and political collaborator, not just his mistress. Léon sought this recognition above all.

The compassion and friendship Léon received from Mme Pellet helped her to survive, especially in the first difficult months. '[I am] truly grateful for the treasures of exquisite goodness that you spread with such grace around my sorrow', she wrote in March 1883. She thanked Mme Pellet for 'taking pity' on her, and begged her for 'long letters' when she was away.[20] Sharing her memories of Gambetta was Léon's one consolation. She recalled his 'marvellous eloquence', which 'adorned every subject that stirred him'. She remembered 'so many wonderful improvisations aroused by a view, a work of art, something he read, a piece of history; such eloquence and charm [*séductions*] dispensed for me alone!'[21]

The present constantly evoked the past. The Pellets' move to Naples reminded her of Gambetta's love for Italy and for its camellias and daphne, which she had successfully acclimatized at les Jardies. The Exposition of 1889 reminded her of that of 1878, when Gambetta had been a rising star devoting his triumphs to her. She was, she wrote, trying to record her memories: 'I write numerous pages that I then tear up . . . finding my pen quite inadequate to retrace so many memories, to which he alone could have given the vividness of reality . . . Only a few loose sheets . . . will convey to posterity a hazy sketch of what this love was like.'[22]

'Altars of the religion of the fatherland'

Léon's attempt to record her recollections of Gambetta was her way of preserving Gambetta's memory for posterity. The republicans, too, were intent on memorialization. Only days after Gambetta's death came the first suggestion: 'the place where the great patriot died must become a sacred place where those who remember will henceforth go in pilgrimage'.[23]

But the fate of les Jardies – where Gambetta had died – had yet to be decided. Gambetta's sister Benedetta and her husband, Alexandre Léris, were quite unprepared to become custodians of his legacy. They were not political and seem to have had little contact with Gambetta, although they lived in Saint-Mandé, on the edge of Paris. Besides, in inheriting les Jardies they inherited a debt as well as an asset. Camille Depret's original loan to Gambetta of 40,000 francs may have been repaid, but the 100,000 francs Gambetta borrowed from him in 1882 to purchase more land was still outstanding, and this must have weighed on a couple of modest means. Léris reimbursed the loan in June 1883. Only in 1887 did the family agree to give the house to the state, keeping the gardens, which were sold the following year. In 1889, 225 square metres of land (some 2400 square feet) for a monument to Gambetta were also transferred to the State.[24]

Léon was distressed by the threatened loss of les Jardies, although for her it was primarily a personal memorial. She wrote to Ruiz: 'Save, save whatever you can of that estate [*terre*] that was so dear to him and that he lovingly called the nest of delights, his Villa of Roses, never foreseeing that it would be his tomb!'[25] Gambetta had devoted enormous effort to acquiring the land around the house, some 6300 square metres (1.5 acres). At the time of his death it boasted a residence for servants, a stable with a pigeon loft, and a pavilion in the garden that Gambetta had constructed as his study (see Figure. 6.1). Following the sale, all were demolished to make way for suburban development.[26]

Even before it was purchased by the State, les Jardies spontaneously became a memorial site. In 1884, more than a thousand people made what *La République française* termed 'a pious pilgrimage' there on the anniversary of Gambetta's death. The term 'pious pilgrimage' was adopted semi-officially to describe what became annual events.[27] In 1900, the police still counted more than 800 participants.[28] The house was by then so well known that a successful cutout and construct version had even been published.[29]

A small house in what was fast becoming a suburb of Paris was nevertheless an inadequate memorial for the 'great patriot'. Calls for a monument – indeed, more than one – soon surfaced. The town of Cahors, Gambetta's birthplace, quickly raised funds by a national subscription. Falguières, who had taken Gambetta's death mask, was engaged to produce a statue. But which Gambetta would the monument celebrate: the patriot, the leader of national defence in the Franco-Prussian War, or the founder of the Republic, the architect of the Constitution of 1875? Cahors chose the patriot. Falguières depicted Gambetta in defiant stance, his right hand on a cannon. The pedestal was inscribed with Gambetta's 1870 proclamation calling on the nation to rise up against the invader. This monument was inaugurated on 14 April 1884.[30]

Plans for a monument in Paris were underway within weeks of Gambetta's death. This one, too, was funded by subscription. Spuller headed a fundraising committee, which included the Presidents of the Senate and of the Chamber and, until his death in 1885, Victor Hugo. Some 250,000 subscribers raised 360,000 francs, making it the most expensive monument ever built in Paris.[31]

This monument sought to commemorate both the patriot and the republican. It took the form of a narrow truncated pyramid, 23 metres (75 feet) high, incorporating an array of symbolic tributes to the Republic and to Gambetta's role in creating and defending it.[32] Atop the pedestal was not Gambetta, but an allegorical female figure in bronze, 'Democracy', riding a lion and holding the 'Rights of Man'. An immense stone statue on the front of the pyramid commemorated Gambetta the patriot: it portrayed him simultaneously, if improbably, leaning on a cannon, holding a sword, supporting a 'citizen' about to fire a rifle and protecting a group of children. An array of secondary sculptures jostled on the sides of the pyramid, along with symbols of France and representations of republican virtues. The result was less an artistic creation than 'an altar to the Republic', representing its shared values and texts.[33] Indeed Spuller, inaugurating the monument on 13 July 1888, called it one of 'the altars of the religion of the fatherland', 'a monument of grateful piety and immortal glory'.[34]

The placement of monuments in Paris was always symbolic. Gambetta's was built in the Carrousel courtyard of the Louvre, near where I. M. Pei's glass pyramid now stands. It was thus at the beginning of Paris' most famous vista, the axis running through Napoleon's small Arc de Triomphe du Carrousel up the Champs-Élysées to the grand Arc de Triomphe nearly seven kilometres (more than four miles) away. Its placement in the Louvre courtyard carried a clear political message. The Louvre, begun in 1190 as a royal palace, had a clear association with the monarchy. Erecting the statue of Gambetta in this space claimed it for the Republic, as Eugène Spuller declared at the inauguration: 'In the midst of the architectural splendours of the monarchy, the stone erected to the glory of this plebeian is in its rightful place, at the centre of our history and our city.'[35]

A simpler monument to Gambetta, far from the city centre, was inaugurated three years later, in 1891, to celebrate Gambetta's defence of the 'lost provinces' of Alsace and Lorraine. Scheurer-Kestner (an Alsatian) again led the fundraising committee. But a suitable site was difficult to find and the government feared that Germany might take umbrage if the monument were too prominent. It was finally erected at les Jardies, thus commemorating the hero at the popular pilgrimage site and avoiding a crisis with Germany.

The committee engaged the renowned sculptor Auguste Bartholdi, whose *Liberty Enlightening the World* had just been inaugurated in New York. Bartholdi's statue showed Gambetta atop a high pedestal, 'holding to his chest a torn tricolour flag on a broken staff', his right arm outstretched, 'seeking', as Scheurer-Kestner declared at the inauguration, 'to reverse destiny'. Beneath the pedestal were sculpted an Alsatian woman and a Lorraine woman, each protecting a child.

This was more than a monument; it was a shrine. Léon alerted Scheurer-Kestner that Paul Bert's widow still had Gambetta's heart, preserved in alcohol. Encased in metal, then in a box of Alsatian wood, it was placed inside the statue and sealed on 6 November 1891, two days before the monument was inaugurated. Today, on a narrow street in a suburb of small villas, the enormous monument looks absurdly misplaced. But, in 1891, with a monument containing the heart of the patriot, the relic of the saint, les Jardies truly became a worthy shrine for the annual pilgrimage.[36]

'Our dear Republic'

The memorials to Gambetta were 'shrines' to the Republic to which, as the inaugural speeches inevitably declared, Gambetta had devoted his life. These speeches often called for national healing and unity, as Spuller's did in 1888: 'Frenchmen, republicans who are listening to me, forget your discord and your passing hatreds . . . unite for the fatherland and for humanity.'[37] But after Gambetta's death the sources of division amongst the republicans continued to multiply. Some were drawn towards a rampant authoritarian nationalism, others to issues of social justice. Léon was buffeted by these currents.

Without Gambetta, Léon felt out of touch with politics. She relied on the *République Française* for her information, 'but that's not much when you have been the confidante of all State secrets!'[38] 'I no longer know how to see or to foresee', she observed, 'it was devotion and passion that refined my political insight.'[39] Léon's comments on politics after Gambetta's death were partly an expression of her grief, since politics and personal affection were so enmeshed in their relationship. But she also regretted losing her role as political counsellor; the loss undermined her sense of identity. Moreover, Léon was convinced that Gambetta's death had left a political void; that no one could replace him. Considering France's ongoing problems in Indochina (today Vietnam) in 1885, for instance, she observed: 'It's at hours of crisis [like this] that one can measure the full extent of the genius of the Great Man, as well as the crime of those who ignored it!' She remained bitter about those who had opposed him, whom she held responsible for his death. News of the death of Jules Grévy in 1891 brought only one regret: 'If that miser had died fifteen years ago', she wrote to Mme Pellet, 'neither you nor I would be where we are now!' The wound that had killed Gambetta, she wrote, was 'the wound to the heart made by the ungrateful republicans who took power from him, when He [*sic*] could see clearly that he alone could establish his dear Republic on foundations that would be forever unassailable!'[40]

This was the judgement of the bereaved lover. But Léon's letters leave no doubt about her republican convictions throughout the 1880s, even if they place her toward the right of the republican spectrum. She took an intense interest in the republicans' electoral fortunes. When the first round of the legislative elections in October 1885 went badly for them, for instance, she was 'overcome, as if my poor friend were still involved in them', and was greatly relieved when 'our dear Republic' was saved by a strong republican vote in the second round.[41] Léon worried, as Gambetta had, about the instability created by the fragmented republican majority and by disagreements over major issues like colonial policy. The Ferry government was overturned for its handling of this issue in March 1885; the Brisson ministry fell in January 1886. Léon noted to Mme Pellet as Charles de Freycinet was then appointed to head a new cabinet: 'I was awaiting the formation of this new ministry with a certain anxiety. I cannot stop being interested in these matters, which occupied such a large place in my life.'[42] Writing about them to Mme Pellet provided some compensation.

At the behest of Clemenceau's Extreme Left, General Boulanger was appointed Minister for War in Freycinet's cabinet. Boulanger appeared to be a republican general – a rare phenomenon – making him an attractive political choice. His avowed commitment to 'revenge' against Germany gave him enormous popularity, but he used it to unleash an authoritarian challenge to the Republic.[43] The Boulanger Affair was a litmus test distinguishing genuine democrats from those attracted by authoritarian and neo-nationalist politics.

Léon clearly aligned herself with the republican position. She observed to Mme Pellet as the Boulanger Affair began to unfold: 'You have read, as I have, the enthusiastic applause for the young Minister for War. The country asks only to follow his white plume[d helmet] all the way to . . . Berlin [*sic*]!' She feared that France did not really possess the democratic impulse. Commenting on people's attraction to a flamboyant leader (and offering a perhaps unintended insight into herself), she added that France 'must be treated like a woman! – dazzled, charmed, seduced and dominated!'[44]

Léon shared the republicans' growing alarm in 1887, as Boulanger's sabre-rattling brought the threat of war with Germany. Her thoughts turned to Gambetta: 'where is the politician skilful enough, with enough authority to avert and remove [the danger]?' Relieved when Maurice Rouvier sacked Boulanger in May, Léon approved the stance of Rouvier's new ministry: 'it has set a path slightly to the right, which I think is the only good one'.[45]

In September 1887 the Boulanger Affair intersected with a major corruption scandal involving Daniel Wilson, President Grevy's son-in-law, who was accused of taking bribes to ensure appointment to the Legion of Honour.[46] His actions carried graft and corruption to the heart of the Republic. Léon well remembered that Wilson had been a bitter opponent of Gambetta, active in bringing down his ministry. Léon wrote, outraged, to Joseph Reinach: 'It seems to me essential to get rid of this stupid old man [Grévy] for the honour, the good reputation of the Republic.' She suggested Flourens for President, adding: 'This combination would definitely postpone the bid [for power] of the daring soldier [Boulanger].'[47] Léon could not resist the temptation to try to influence politics, even without Gambetta.

Léon was scathing of the so-called patriotism of the Boulangists: theirs was not 'that sublime sentiment of national honour', she stated, only 'a mask for the vilest ham actors'. And as the political threat fizzled with Boulanger's departure from France in 1889, Léon criticized the Extreme Left who had unleashed it: 'the blundering politicians who wanted to give him a greater part in the serious and important affairs of government than his capricious brain was capable of brought [the nation] to the edge of the abyss'.[48]

Léon's comments on politics in the 1880s suggested a keen sense of the loss of her political soul mate. Mme Pellet became the recipient of opinions and outrage that Léon would otherwise have offered to Gambetta. Her comments also lamented the loss of Gambetta's political legacy. Her effort to preserve that legacy focused on the preservation of his papers, which she urged should be assembled and protected as a matter of national interest. Gambetta's papers, in her view, would verify his place in history.

Léon appealed first to Joseph Reinach, asking him to work with Eugène Spuller 'to resolve this question of the dispersed papers of M. Gambetta!' 'There are some *significant* historical documents, the loss or dispersion of which would be irreparable . . . along with some interesting notes, a certain number of my letters, Paul Bert tells me, of which I would dearly love to regain possession.'[49]

In 1888, Léon turned to Mme Pellet, hoping that she might influence Jules Ferry (whose wife was Pellet's cousin) to intervene. Again, she worried about these 'papers dispersed in so many hands': 'Couldn't you interest M. Ferry in their fate?' She was anxious 'to know that historical documents of the greatest importance had been placed in our national archives'. Not until 1896, when Scheurer-Kestner took up the question, was Léon reassured.[50]

Gambetta's legacy also included his letters to Léon, and she planned to ensure their security as a republican inheritance after her own death. In May 1891, Léon informed Mme Pellet that the letters from Gambetta – 'my precious relics' – were safe in a 'pretty little strong box', until 'they pass into the hands of your dear husband'.[51] In July, she drew up a will leaving 'all the letters and writings of Gambetta in my possession' to Marcellin Pellet, 'authorizing him to publish them when he deems it appropriate'. A separate will created on 1 August 1891 left her other possessions to Mme Pellet.[52] By the time of Léonie Léon's death in 1906, however, her sentiments had changed.

'We must believe, we must hope'

Léon wrote in 1889, 'I had devoted my life to a great cause and a great man; it was a life of abnegation, of toil, of sacrifice, but it had a purpose, a goal, a consolation; today my strength and devotion are wasting away in emptiness, uselessness, abandonment! Besides, I have always regarded life as an evil [*mal*] for which death is the only remedy.'[53] Léon struggled to give meaning to her life without Gambetta. This struggle gradually led her back into the Catholic fold, rupturing her relationship with the republicans.

Léon's views throughout the 1880s were those of a sceptic. She wrote in August 1886: 'Isn't life itself a comedy in which the parts are badly distributed by Destiny, and where, unlike in the theatre, treachery always prevails and virtue remains unrewarded!' The death a few months later of Gambetta's colleague, Paul Bert, reinforced her 'indignation at the supreme injustice that governs the things of this world, striking the most useful, the most loved, in preference to the rogues who corrupt society'.[54]

The death of Léon's son in 1891 was to heighten her despair. When Alphonse became seriously ill in January, doctors treated him for a nervous complaint. His tuberculosis was quite advanced before it was diagnosed and he died at home on 3 June, aged twenty-six. Alphonse's slow and painful death was devastating for his mother. Still, his death certificate named his parents as 'Auguste Léon', who never existed, and 'Marie Émilie Léon', Léonie's sister. Alphonse was buried, not in the Léon tomb at Montparnasse with his grandfather and aunt (his supposed mother), but in a distant village near Montreuil-sur-Mer, with relatives of his maternal grandfather. Léon's desire to keep secret her maternal link to Alphonse continued into death.[55]

This second tragic loss accentuated Léon's grief, anger, guilt and self-pity. Her mother brought Léon no consolation. She was barely on speaking terms with 'the horrible creature who has tortured my life and that of so many others'. Léon blamed herself for not having procured better treatment for Alphonse; for having neglected the living Alphonse in her obsession with the dead Gambetta.[56]

Alphonse received the sacraments before death and was buried in a Catholic ceremony. This may have been his choice. But Léon left a bequest for prayers to be said for his soul every Sunday in the village church. She also made a bequest in his name to the Collège Sainte-Barbe, where he had been a student. Around this time, too, she began to consider visiting Rome.[57]

Léon was apparently returning to the Catholicism of her youth, which she had never entirely abandoned. But she was still searching for faith. 'One must be very happy to be able to believe in the supernatural', she wrote in July 1892, but happiness did not describe her state of mind: 'I can no longer bear a sorrow for which there is no remedy. I have so many bitter regrets for having badly managed my past life that it is impossible for me to rebuild another.'[58]

Léon's visits to Rome in the 1890s marked a gradual change in her outlook. Her first extended visit began in December 1892, but while dazzled by the splendour of Rome's churches and monuments, and the beauty of its religious services, Léon nevertheless maintained a critical eye: 'it is too retrograde, too medieval and I imagine that a young and progressive Pope would suppress the whole [theatrical] production'.[59]

It was in Rome – probably in January 1893 – that Léon met a Dominican priest, Father Henri Didon, who 'brought me some relief for my sorrows by his wise consolation'. A few months later, having arranged to see him in Paris, she remarked: 'Why didn't I know him sooner? He was exactly the great energy and the enlightened guide I needed!'[60] Expressions of grief by no means disappeared from her subsequent letters, but now they were interspersed with sentiments of resignation. In October 1893, for instance, Léon wrote to Mme Pellet, whose mother had died in August: 'We must turn our thoughts above [*plus haut*] and place our hope in a justice which is beyond our understanding, but on which it is our duty to rely in order to bear courageously to the very end the heavy burden of our sorrows.' Again, she wrote in 1894: 'If all these misfortunes were not the trials needed to prepare us for a more perfect state, what would these continual physical or moral sufferings signify? We must believe, we must hope so as not to bash our heads against the wall!'[61] Léon's sense of the 'supreme injustice' of life had been replaced by a fragile faith in a higher order of meaning.

If Léon had regained something of the faith of her youth, however, she had not turned her back on the Republic. True, the French Church and the Republic were at loggerheads throughout the 1880s. When Pope Leo XIII exhorted French Catholics in 1892 to 'rally' to the Republic, he was met with sullen resistance in many circles. Indeed, Léon attended a Papal audience with a group of French Catholics in 1896, where the elderly Pope reminded them, Léon tell us, that 'if they were good pilgrims in Rome, they should also be very good citizens on their return to France'.[62] His message needed repeating.

Gambetta had believed it was possible to work with progressive Catholics, and Father Didon was one such figure. Didon sought to reconcile the Church to modern times and to the Republic. His 1880 Lenten sermons on that subject had seen him silenced by his Superior and sent to Corsica.[63] Didon's progressive views enabled Léon to reconcile faith and republicanism: something she had struggled to do since the death of Father Codant.

Few sources remain on the last decade of Léon's life. Pillias notes that her mother died in February 1895, leaving her with no immediate family. But although Léon had complained of ill-health for decades, she remained robust until 1904, when Dr Lannelongue operated on her for breast cancer. From that point, Pillias argues, Léon lived in seclusion, visited only by Dominican religious and by the republicans Georges Pallain and Mme Pellet. She died on 14 November 1906, aged 68. After a funeral service at the church of Notre Dame d'Auteuil, she was buried alongside her father, mother and sister in the Montparnasse cemetery. Only Alphonse was missing from the family grave.[64] Despite Léon's return to the Church, her republican friends were stunned to discover that she had made a new will in 1900, leaving all her possessions to her cousin, Marie-Eugénie Gavoille. Her friendly, if intermittent, correspondence with Mme Pellet had continued until 1904, yet the new will implicitly criticized the Pellets: 'This will cancels those that I have formerly left in the hands of persons whose conduct has not been satisfactory.'[65] Pillias argues persuasively that this change of heart was due to two inter-related factors: the Dreyfus Affair, and Léon's more intense immersion in Catholicism.

There is no direct evidence of Léon's response to the Dreyfus Affair, the case of a Jewish Army officer wrongly convicted in 1894 of having sold military secrets to the Germans. Léon's surviving letters mention this matter only once, shortly after the initial charges were laid: 'There is no connection, I like to believe, between the accused captain and our friend [the deputy, Ferdinand Dreyfus]?'[66] The matter only became an 'Affair' in mid-1897, when it was revealed that the evidence against Dreyfus was forged, and that the forgery had been concealed by the Army. This revelation unleashed a massive conflict. Republicans constituted virtually all the Dreyfusard camp; anti-Semites, nationalist zealots, militant Catholics and other opponents of the Republic made up the anti-Dreyfusard camp. Dreyfus was granted a retrial in May 1899, but the military court reconvicted him. On 19 September 1899 he was pardoned by presidential decree. In 1906, he was cleared of any wrongdoing and restored to his rank in the Army.[67]

Pillias states that Léon appealed several times to Mme Pellet to have her father (Scheurer-Kestner) change his stance on the matter. No trace of those appeals remains in the correspondence, but there are few letters after 1894 and Léon may have stated her case in person. She may have been attracted to the anti-Dreyfusard camp by her strong sense of patriotism and her loyalty to the Army. She was, after all, the daughter of a Colonel. Gambetta had been a champion of the Army and had many friends amongst the military: he was the 'great patriot'. Whereas Léon had condemned General Boulanger as a fake patriot in 1888, therefore, she may have been persuaded – like many others – that the honour of the Army was at stake in 1897.

Léon's resurgent Catholicism probably helped to place her in the anti-Dreyfusard camp, too, even though she aligned herself with more progressive elements in the Church. The Dreyfus Affair sharpened the divide between republicans and Catholics. After Dreyfus' pardon in

1899, the republican government set out to curb the activities of the religious congregations, some of which had played leading roles in the Affair. Debate began in November 1899 on what became the 1901 Law on Associations, championed by Gambetta's protégé, Waldeck-Rousseau, now President of the Council of Ministers. The Law required the congregations to obtain authorization to operate in France. In January 1900, the Assumptionist Fathers were expelled from France because of their prominent role in anti-Semitic and anti-government agitation. The Left's victories in the partial Senate elections that month saw the proposed law strengthened, which in turn unleashed a campaign from the pulpit against the government's measures. When Léon wrote her new will in September 1900, therefore, conflict between Church and State was again rampant. Pope Leo XIII's objections to the proposed Law perhaps confirmed her decision; she greatly admired this progressive pope.[68] Instead of leaving her worldly goods to her republican friends and benefactors, she now left them to her Catholic cousin, Marie-Eugénie Gavoille.

Léon was close to that cousin in her later years. Gavoille brought to Léon's deathbed another Dominican priest, Father Marie-Albert Janvier, well known for his annual Lenten sermons at Notre Dame.[69] In the 1930s, Pillias confirmed with Father Janvier that the priest had spent half an hour daily with Léon for the last three weeks of her life, and that she received 'all the sacraments'. She died a Catholic, even if she had struggled to live as one.

In her will, Léon left money to the nun who cared for her in her final illness. It served, according to Janvier, 'to support the little Paris convent during the expulsion', that is, during the exile from France suffered by religious orders which refused to accept the Republic and seek authorization, as the Law on Associations required. The expulsions, along with the formal separation of Church and State in 1905, were the culminating acts of the republicans' anticlerical campaign. While Léon's financial support for the sisters was consistent with her long-standing appreciation of the work of women religious, it also marked her distance from the republican camp by the time of her death.[70]

Janvier noted that, in her latter years, Léon was very pious, 'visibly trying to redeem her past for which she was remorseful'. Was she remorseful for her relationship with Gambetta, or for not having sanctified it? Her self-admonition in 1894 suggests the latter. Rather than regretting the joy and happiness that marriage might have brought, she now wrote: 'What an inexplicable sin I committed in delaying what it was my duty to hasten, how criminal all my hesitations appear today!'[71]

By delaying marriage, she now thought, she had continued to live a sinful life, and had been an 'occasion of sin' to Gambetta as well. Her thinking now confused respectability with Catholic theology. Gambetta could only have accepted civil marriage, but marriage without the sacrament would not have sufficed in the eyes of the Church.

Janvier reported with amusement, too, that Léon disdained courtesans. He was aware that she had been a courtesan herself and she had admitted to him that she had borne a son. Léon had allowed Janvier to read Gambetta's letters to her and thus to witness the passion she had shared with Gambetta. Janvier pointed out to Pillias that he did not return to Léon's bedside once she fell into a coma, not wanting to 'have his name linked to hers'.[72] Even for her confessor, Léon remained a 'fallen woman', and perhaps worse, lover of Léon Gambetta, founder of the anticlerical Republic.

'Sleep content, Gambetta!'

The events and conflicts of the 1890s and the early 1900s that had taken Léon away from the republican camp served, by contrast, to enhance Gambetta's reputation as a 'saint for the Republic'. The number of annual pilgrims to les Jardies began to grow.[73] In another wave of monument building, Gambetta's legacy was summoned to instill the republican message in the hearts of the citizenry; to mark the republican victory over clericalism and to ward off the new ultra-nationalist threat.

Bordeaux led the way in 1905 with a huge monument sculpted by Dalou. He set Gambetta alone, atop a three-metre pedestal, in a pensive mood. The images on the pedestal highlighted the eternal vigilance of Gambetta the patriot, and the placement of the monument emphasized national defence: it stood in front of Bordeaux's famous Grand Théâtre, where the Assembly had met in 1871. Paul Doumer, President of the Chamber of Deputies, outlined the lessons that the monument would present to those who saw it: 'The statue . . . will tell them that they must cultivate the virtues that create the useful man, the enlightened citizen, the watchful soldier; that they must be attached to liberty, to the republican regime that assures it for everyone; that they must love the fatherland before all and above all.'[74] In the presence of the President and nine ministers, the famous composer and friend of Gambetta, Camille Saint-Saëns, himself conducted the premiere of a patriotic cantata he had composed to his own text during the Franco-Prussian War.[75]

In April 1909, Nice raised a monument to the Great Patriot who was buried there, at the same time replacing his tomb with one 'more worthy of the eminent statesman'. A huge pedestal four metres high was surmounted by a much taller but narrower pedestal, around which were grouped weeping women and soldiers grasping a huge flag. Atop this second pedestal was an enormous statue of Gambetta in full rhetorical flight. At the inauguration, Georges Clemenceau called on the people to continue Gambetta's struggle; he called for vigilance against 'the enemies' of the Republic: against 'the reactionary, who wants to return to superseded [*déchues*] forms of government, and the demagogue . . . who will make use of hard-won liberties to dragoon sections of the population who are not sufficiently enlightened and launch them on violent enterprises'.[76]

Victory in the Great War of 1914–1918 brought the 'lost provinces' back to France, completing Gambetta's historic mission. When French troops entered Strasbourg in triumph on 9 December 1918, one house displayed a banner reading, 'Sleep content, Gambetta! Finally the proud dawn of the day you dreamed of has risen for us.'[77]

Victory also led to a national tribute to Gambetta. On 28 March 1920, the President of the Republic proceeded to les Jardies, accompanied by the past Presidents of the Republic, the Presidents of the Senate and Chamber, the Prime Minister, ten ministers, Marshal Joffre, several generals, and old companions of Gambetta. The President took a French flag captured by the Germans in 1870 and recaptured in 1918. He climbed the stairs to Gambetta's room, knelt, and deposited the flag on his deathbed.[78]

Gambetta reached his apotheosis later that year, as the Republic's commemoration of its saints underwent a great transformation. The government decided to celebrate the fiftieth anniversary of the Republic on 11 November, the date of the armistice concluding the Great War that had restored the 'lost provinces' to the Republic.[79] How better to celebrate such an anniversary than to invoke Gambetta? The Chamber of Deputies decided to transfer Gambetta's heart to the Pantheon or, as one Deputy put it, making the religious aspect explicit again, to remove 'the relic from the reliquary'.[80] The Pantheon had passed between religious and republican hands several times since its construction in the eighteenth century until the republicans resumed it as a resting place for 'the great men of the fatherland' in 1885 in order to inter Victor Hugo there. Placing Gambetta's heart in the Pantheon, alongside Hugo's body, would enshrine it with the Republic's sacred relics.

The Republic also decided to canonize a new republican saint at this time: an Unknown Soldier representing the new patriots who had followed in Gambetta's footsteps. The Soldier would be buried, not in the Pantheon – too closely identified as republican for conservative tastes – but at the Arc de Triomphe.[81] The ceremony of his burial was linked to the transfer of Gambetta's remains to the Pantheon, the double ceremony taking the Republic's veneration of the relics of its heroes to new heights.

At 11 p.m. on 10 November 1920, Gambetta's heart – 'the heart of a patriot, this heart which beat so strongly for the fatherland'– was removed from the monument at les Jardies and taken in procession to Paris, to the Place Denfert-Rochereau. This site was named for the Governor of Belfort, the only city that had withstood the siege and remained undefeated during the Franco-Prussian War. There, the casket was placed in a *chapelle ardente* while the official party left to welcome the train from Verdun carrying the body of the Unknown Soldier.[82]

The next morning, the casket containing Gambetta's heart in a glass-sided reliquary, and the coffin of the Unknown Soldier, were each placed on a catafalque, to the strains of the *Marseillaise* and of Saint-Saëns' *Marche héroïque,* part of his 1870 patriotic cantata. The President of the Republic, accompanied by Raymond Poincaré (President in 1914), Marshals Joffre, Foch, and Pétain, and numerous generals, led the cortege to the Arc de Triomphe, where the relics of the heroes remained on display all afternoon. A huge crowd filed past to pay their respects.[83] That evening, the body of the Unknown Soldier was transferred to the hall in the top of the Arch to await its final burial in January. Gambetta's heart was taken to the Pantheon, where it remained on display in its reliquary for three days. A year later, it was finally laid to rest in a porphyry urn, where it remains to this day.[84]

Decline and fall

The national mood soured in the 1920s. Nearly half the men of France had fought in World War I and three-quarters of these men had been killed, wounded or taken prisoner. In 1921, there were a million fewer men than women.[85] In the light of such trauma, 'victory' could seem hollow and patriotism less glorious. The Republic, too, seemed less glorious. The economic and political crises that saw the rise of Communism and Fascism gradually polarized France as they did other nations. Respect for the Republic declined, and veneration of Gambetta, the patriot and the founder of the Republic, declined with it.

In the 1930s, the cult of Gambetta was maintained only by a declining band of Gambettistes and committed republicans. The fiftieth anniversary of Gambetta's death in 1932 passed with little official pomp.

No official or popular events marked the hundredth anniversary of his birth in 1938. To be sure, Émile Pillias curated an extensive exhibition of Gambetta iconography and memorabilia at the Bibliothèque Nationale. And, with the distinguished historian, Daniel Halévy, he edited a collection of Gambetta's letters, which remained definitive until the unpublished letters emerged.[86] But Gambetta had largely disappeared from popular memory. The dramatic German defeat of France, the consequent fall of the Republic Gambetta had founded, and the resulting triumph of the authoritarian right – the spiritual descendents of his monarchist opponents – completed the definitive eclipse of Gambetta's reputation.

The fate of Gambetta's monuments reflected this history. In 1919, press surveys had voted his monument the ugliest in Paris. No tears were shed when, in 1942, German occupying forces removed the statue of Democracy – Gambetta's credo – along with the other bronzes, to melt them down for cannon. The Bordeaux and Nice monuments suffered the same fate, leaving only bare pedestals. (The stone monuments at Cahors and les Jardies escaped destruction.)

Léonie Léon's memory suffered over these years, too, largely as a proxy for her lover. In the 1920s, the old lies that made her responsible for Gambetta's death were given a new twist to suit the interests of authoritarian nationalists, intent on destroying Gambetta's reputation and that of the Republic for which he stood. To the initial claims of a 'drama of feminine jealousy', they added a new element: Léon was a German spy, engaged to seduce Gambetta and weaken his thirst for revenge; having truly fallen in love with him and fearing that he would learn of her treachery and leave her, she tried to shoot herself; Gambetta was wounded trying to stop her. This story was meant to undermine Gambetta's standing as the great patriot, and indeed as a great man, by implying that a woman had compromised his patriotism and sapped his virility.

This fabrication formed the plot of 'The Drama of the Jardies', published in 1924 by Léon Daudet, renowned writer and leading member of the far right *Action française*. According to Daudet's wife, Juliette Adam (who lived until 1936) supplied information for the book.[87] Daudet called the story 'a novel', but Gambetta and Léon appear under their real names, with their portraits on the cover. Versions of Daudet's story were re-circulated by far right sources at moments when attacks on the Republic were in full swing. In 1966, for instance, Pierre Dominique reused the title of Daudet's book and his 'spy' plot for a chapter in an anthology aiming to discredit the Republic.[88]

Daudet's story gained credence within the mainstream Right. In 1968, André Beauguitte – conservative politician, amateur historian and member of the Académie française – published 'The Secret Drawer'. It recounted Daudet's fantasy as though it were history, but without any sources. The conservative historian Jacques Chastenet, also a member of the Académie, wrote a preface to Beaugitte's work.[89]

Pillias wrote his 1935 biography of Léonie Léon to redeem her memory and thus defend Gambetta, but it failed in its aim. Even her tomb in the Montparnasse Cemetery, which Pillias photographed in 1933, was obliterated after the war by the cemetery administration when it was left untended for ten years.[90]

Resurrection?

The first scholarly biography of Gambetta was not by a French Republican but by an Englishman. J. P. T. Bury maintained interest in Gambetta all his life, publishing the first volume of his trilogy in 1936 and the last in 1982, forty-six years later. After Chastenet's 1968 biography there was little scholarly interest in Gambetta for several decades.

The election of François Mitterrand as the first Socialist President of the Republic in 1981 led to renewed interest in Gambetta. Mitterrand's Minister of Culture, the flamboyant Jack Lang, saw in Gambetta a kindred spirit. Lang subsidized a major exhibition at the prestigious Musée du Luxembourg to mark the centenary of Gambetta's death, with the title 'Homage to Léon Gambetta.' A stellar constellation of historians explained Gambetta's significance in the catalogue.[91]

Lang also provided the impetus for the restoration of Gambetta's Paris monument. The remaining pieces were reassembled and reconstructed, though without the pyramid on which the statue had rested, and, of course, without the bronzes melted by the Germans. This partial reassembly was erected in a picturesque, shady square in Belleville. It looks, as June Hargrove puts it, 'like an archaeological ruin', if a charming one.[92]

By the 1990s, les Jardies, too, had fallen into disrepair. Edouard Balladur's conservative government decided upon its restoration. The Archives départementales undertook a study in preparation for the restoration, producing another exhibition, of greater scope than Pillias' in 1938: 'Léon Gambetta: A Saint for the Republic?' Between 1994 and 2008 four scholarly biographies and two superb studies of Gambetta's politics appeared.[93]

Is this the precursor to a revival of Gambetta's public prestige? Gambetta led the successful struggle 'for the Republic, for Liberty, for

Secular Democracy, for a State of Right', as the distinguished historian Maurice Agulhon put it.[94] If any French statesman deserves the title 'founder of the Republic', it is surely Gambetta. His vision of a democratic, secular Republic, unified around progressive patriotism and universal (male) suffrage and supported by non-sectarian education, seems more relevant than ever today. His political achievements live on in the French Republic. The share of his devoted lover and companion in those achievements and the legacy of their passionate love lives on in their letters, as Léon had hoped.

[Léon to Joseph Reinach][1]
Sir

This moment of calm will perhaps permit you and M. Spuller, restored to the simple office of Deputy, to resolve this question of the scattered papers of Monsieur Gambetta! There are some <u>notable</u> [sic] historical documents, the loss or dispersion of which would be irreparable, and in the bags deposited at the Main Office [Caisse Centrale], along with some important notes, [there are] a certain number of my letters, so Paul Bert told me, of which I would dearly love to regain possession. Time passes, we will pass too; but the writings remain, and in the event of the death of certain persons, [they] might fall into hands unworthy to hold them, or at least incapable of using them. Please excuse my insistence Monsieur; but I feel as though I am spurred on by a will from beyond the grave, being the only one to know what price Monsieur Gambetta placed on that page of history which belongs to him alone, the history of the [government of] national defence.

Please accept, Monsieur, the expression of my most distinguished sentiments.

Léonie Léon

This 18 January

Epilogue: 'The writings remain'

'Time passes, we will pass too; but the writings remain.'[2] So wrote Léonie Léon to Joseph Reinach in 1885 of her correspondence with Gambetta. For many years, it appeared that Léon's expectations were wrong; that her correspondence with Gambetta had not survived. This was the conclusion reached in 1935 by Émile Pillias, whose fruitless search to locate the correspondence led him to conclude that it had been destroyed.[3] But Pillias was wrong. The writings did remain. How did they survive? And how much survived? Each side of the correspondence has its own remarkable story.

On Gambetta's death, Léon remained in possession of the letters she had received from him. She re-read them often for comfort, and even carried them with her on her travels. Her initial concern was to preserve them as part of the republican heritage, fearing, as she put it in her letter to Reinach, that 'they may fall . . . into hands unworthy to possess them, or at least incapable of using them'. They were testaments to Gambetta's greatness. More personally, they were guarantors of the meaning and significance of her own life, proofs of her importance to Gambetta and to their shared project of building the Republic and regenerating France. As hostile rumours periodically resurfaced, insisting on her nefarious influence and even accusing her of Gambetta's death, she feared that 'instead of . . . the moving and flattering memory of a hidden and disinterested partner, [posterity] will only know me in the false light of a vulgar old maid on the lookout for a husband'.[4]

The letters thus became instruments in Léon's quest for recognition, a quest which sprang from deep emotional sources and erupted intermittently in her letters. She had, as we have seen, long been frustrated at her inability to assume a visible role in Gambetta's life. She had sought seclusion to protect herself, but at the same time she resented that she

249

could not receive the acknowledgement that history accorded other women associates of male leaders.

Léon used Gambetta's letters, with their tributes to her role and their statements of his gratitude, to defend her reputation. She copied 104 letters she had received from Gambetta, made five sets, and distributed them to some of his colleagues. The copies were supposed to be returned, but two apparently remained with their unnamed recipients and at least one further copy was made from them.[5]

Léon thus initiated the distribution of Gambetta's letters and inadvertently facilitated their publication: no sooner had she died in 1906 than the letters she had copied were published by the *Revue de Paris*.[6] Only twenty-four of those published letters now remain in manuscript. Léon's copying thus saved some from destruction, but she removed personal content in the process: all references to her son Alphonse[7] and all of Gambetta's most passionate references – to covering her with kisses, to his 'open arms and trembling lips', and to the 'unspoken desire' that 'devoured' him.[8]

As Léon lay dying in 1906, reconciled to the Catholic Church and reviewing her life from a religious perspective, she sought Father Janvier's advice on how to deal with Gambetta's letters. He later told Émile Pillias that she gave him 'full power to keep, give away or burn them'. Janvier claimed to have 'skimmed them rapidly for want of leisure'. But he read enough to decide that they were full of 'vanity' and 'rather puerile' declarations of love.[9] Janvier declared that he had returned the letters to Léon, advising her to give them to Georges Pallain. Léon followed that advice and informed her notary, Maître Camille Tollu, of her wishes. On 16 November, two days after Léon's death, Tollu duly handed to Pallain a box containing forty-five packets of letters.[10]

Léon's alienation from the Dreyfusard Republic and her recent re-embrace of Catholicism had exposed the correspondence to people outside republican circles. But in leaving the letters to Pallain, Léon placed them in firmly republican hands. Pallain was a long-time friend of Gambetta, formerly chief of his personal staff.

Léon's instructions envisaged at least a partial publication of the letters to promote 'the glory of this great and illustrious figure', after a lapse of thirty or forty years. Pallain, however, was devoted to preserving Gambetta's reputation. He wrote to Gambetta's nephew that 'publication of these letters of such an intimate character would add nothing to Gambetta's glory, and would have the grave drawback of arousing regrettable polemics'. He perhaps referred to rumours about Léon being a German spy that were gaining momentum in the 1920s, and to the fact that Gambetta's liaison with Léon would be a stain on the great man's character. The publicity surrounding the publication, in 1921, of Victor Hugo's love letters to Juliette Drouet sounded a warning. In the winter of 1921–2, therefore, a year before his death, Pallain and a friend burned the entire collection. According to his widow, the elderly Pallain believed 'that his duty was to protect a wholly intimate and confidential correspondence from all possible publicity'.[11]

Yet hundreds of Gambetta's letters to Léon appeared on the market in the 1970s and 1980s. How can this be reconciled with the above account? The investigations of the literary scholar Jacques Suffel led him to believe that Father Janvier had regained possession of Gambetta's letters, leaving them on his death to another Dominican, Father Avril. When Avril died, Suffel argues, they passed into the hands of an undisclosed Catholic organization.[12] Did Janvier or Pallain's associates deliberately mislead, declaring that the letters had been disposed of when they had actually been hidden away? The more likely explanation is that Janvier returned only some of the letters to Léon. After all, he insisted that she had given him the right 'to keep, give away or burn' them. In this case, Pallain would have received and later destroyed only some of Gambetta's remaining letters.

Suffel's conjecture was consistent with events. In 1975, it was indeed a Catholic organization – never identified – that approached a former Deputy, Michel Jamot, and asked him to sell them on its behalf. The President of the National Assembly authorized their purchase for the Assembly Library at a price of 20,000 francs. A typed copy of these letters, made by Jamot, was also included, but there were no letters for the years 1872 and 1874. In 1984, seventy-two letters from those years went to auction and were purchased by the Library for a further 20,000 francs. Only in 1984, therefore, did all the surviving letters from Gambetta to Léon pass into public ownership.[13]

Léon's letters to Gambetta took a different path to the Assembly Library. It was customary for letters to be returned to their sender at the end of an affair. But when Gambetta died, Léon was initially unable to retrieve her letters. She was still trying to recover them in 1888, as she noted to Mme Pellet: 'I would so much like to regain possession of my letters and prevent them from ending up as wrapping paper at the tobacconist's shop or worse.'[14]

It is unclear when the letters were returned to Léon, but she had them in her possession at the time of her death. Rather than being subject to special provision, like Gambetta's letters, they formed part of her estate and passed to her heir, her cousin Marie-Eugénie Gavoille. Georges

Pallain attempted to purchase these letters from Gavoille, but she replied that she, too, had consulted Father Janvier – although Janvier later denied all knowledge of these letters – and that he had advised her 'not to stir up this mud' by selling them. She also rejected Pallain's offer to donate money to charity in return for the destruction of the letters. Further investigations led Pillias to believe that these letters, too, had been destroyed.[15]

Again, however, that was not the case. In 1937, Gavoille's heirs sold Léon's letters to Gambetta to a Paris dealer, Emmanuel Fabius.[16] He offered them to the Library of the Chamber of Deputies (now the Library of the National Assembly). To help in their authentication, he had them transcribed and typed. In 1938 the President of the Chamber, Édouard Herriot, authorized payment of 150,000 francs for the original letters, with two typed copies.[17] Fabius added as a 'gift' a collection of documents from Léon's estate.[18]

Early in June 1940, with the German army advancing rapidly on Paris, the 'most valuable holdings of the Library' were sent for safekeeping to a strongroom of the Banque de France at Libourne, near Bordeaux. This region was occupied by the German army under the Armistice that came into effect on 25 June. Under its terms, all state assets, as well as private property, were subject to inspection and possible seizure. On 6 May 1941, representatives of the Devisenschutz-Kommando (Office of Currency Protection, an agency headed by Hermann Goering) appeared at the Libourne branch of the Banque de France. They demanded that the strongboxes of the Chamber of Deputies be opened for inspection. A bailiff was summoned hastily to keep a record of proceedings.

His report summarizes what happened: 'The lids of all the crates were removed and the contents . . . were unwrapped, taken out of each crate, summarily examined and then replaced in the crates by the representatives of the German authorities.' They found in one crate 'two packets, enclosed in wrapping paper tied with string, on which was written in blue pencil: "Letters from Léonie Léon to Gambetta".' 'At this moment', the report continues, 'the German authorities made ready to leave': they had apparently found what they were looking for.[19] A request by the Bank's representative that the documents remain in safekeeping was rejected, as was their right to verify or make notes about what was being removed.[20]

This theft is extremely curious. A soldier looking to line his pockets would have searched for valuables like jewellery or gold rather than for historical documents. And why these particular documents? Suffel argues that the theft was carried out at the behest of the German authorities, curious about rumours that Léon had been a spy for Germany.[21] It may be, too, that Gambetta's name was still potent enough to arouse interest and perhaps the hope of gain from selling the documents. After the war, the French government made strenuous efforts to recover the purloined documents, still invested with great significance. In 1950, the British authorities conducted an investigation in Hamburg on behalf of the French government, interviewing several former members of the Bordeaux branch of the Devisenschutz-Kommando. They denied all knowledge of the documents, which have never been seen since.[22]

There is, fortunately, a final twist to this saga. Hippolyte Ducos, Vice-President of the Chamber of Deputies in 1938, had taken a particular interest in Léon's letters. He borrowed the typed copies from the Library on 10 September 1938 and returned them on 23 February 1939, after delivering a lecture about them to the Cercle républicain. He borrowed them again on 9 March 1939 and they were still in his possession at the time of the Exodus in June 1940, when many Parisians fled before the advancing German onslaught. After the war, it was feared that the letters had been destroyed.[23]

In February 1947, the historian Adrien Dansette wrote to the Library, seeking confirmation that Léon's letters had been stolen. The Librarian replied with a report on the whole affair. On 28 March 1947, however, Hippolyte Duclos appeared at the Library and returned the volume of the typed copies intact. Had he heard that Dansette was looking for the letters? In any case, his extended loan fortuitously preserved the copies of Léon's letters; otherwise, they might have been stolen with the originals.

Thus, as Léon would have wished, her letters, or rather authenticated transcripts of her letters, are now housed alongside Gambetta's in a building frequented by Gambetta and visited regularly by Léonie Léon.[24]

Gambetta declared in 1876: 'If I had the pen of [Alexander] Pope . . . I would use it to tell posterity in the distant future about the mysteries of our love.' But after Gambetta's death, Léon lamented that 'Only a few loose sheets . . . will convey to posterity a hazy sketch of what this love was like.' Posterity would never know the 'grand and sublime emotions' that filled their hearts.[25]

In writing about the 'few loose sheets' and the couple who produced them, we have sought to evoke those 'sublime emotions'; to give voice to that 'mysterious' love, echoes of which still reverberate in the vibrant prose of their letters. We have sought to reveal Gambetta the lover, not merely Gambetta the politician; we have sought to reveal the little-known Léon, intelligent, witty, anxious, struggling to cope with the hand dealt her in life; we have sought above all to analyse their partnership, both personal and political. Mutual affection, need and desire united and sustained them, but they were not, as many contemporaries and biographers assert, on the verge of marriage when Gambetta died. They were trapped in a double bind by nineteenth-century gender and social norms: they could not live together unmarried because Gambetta, as a politician, had to receive people in his home, yet they could not marry because Léon, a fallen woman, could not receive others or be received by them, even if the couple did marry. Moreover, the threat of publicity and humiliation, and scruples about civil marriage, proved too much for Léon, while a religious marriage, even in secret, was impossible for Gambetta. They never overcame these constraints.

Nevertheless, Gambetta and Léon not only sustained a love affair, they also lived a political romance. While historians have assumed that Léon was only a sounding board for Gambetta, we have brought to light their continuing political dialogue and we have shown that it was at the heart of their relationship. This dialogue enabled Gambetta to evolve from flamboyant activist and war-time leader to long-term party leader and statesman, pursing the couple's shared goal, moderating his radicalism and anticlericalism while outflanking the monarchists and, above all, rallying the broad masses to the Republic. Perhaps Gambetta could have achieved this evolution alone, but in fact he achieved it with Léon. He depended on her throughout the decade of his political career for emotional support, political dialogue and tactical counsel. Their partnership was vital to the making of the French Republic.

Notes

Abbreviations

AD	Archives Départementales Hauts de Seine, Nanterre.
AN	Archives Nationales, Paris.
APP	Archives de la Préfecture de Police, Paris.
ASP	Archives d'histoire contemporaine, Centre d'histoire Sciences Po, Paris.
BAN	Bibliothèque de l'Assemblée Nationale, Paris.
BnF	Bibliothèque nationale de France, Paris.
Bury	[cited as Bury 1, 2, 3] J. P. T. Bury [1:] *Gambetta and the national defence: a republican dictatorship in France.* Westport, CT: Greenwood Press, 1971 [1936]; [2:] *Gambetta and the making of the Third Republic.* London: Longman, 1973; [3:] *Gambetta's final years: 'the era of difficulties', 1877–1882.* London; New York: Longman, 1982.
Chastenet	[cited as Chastenet 1, 2] Jacques Chastenet. *Histoire de la Troisième République.* 4 vols. Paris: Hachette, 1952. 1: *Naissance et Jeunesse*; 2: *Triomphes et Malaises.*
Discours	Joseph Reinach, ed. *Discours et plaidoyers politiques de M. Gambetta.* 11 vols. Paris: G. Charpentier, 1880–85.
Grévy, *La République*	Jérôme Grévy. *La République des opportunistes, 1870–1888.* Paris: Perrin, 1998.
H&P	Daniel Halévy and Émile Pillias, eds. *Lettres de Gambetta, 1868–1882.* Paris: Bernard Grasset, 1938.
Pillias	Pillias, Émile. *Léonie Léon, amie de Gambetta.* Paris: Gallimard, 1935.

Citation of letters between Gambetta and Léon

Most of Gambetta's letters to Léon are held in the BAN, though some were published in H&P; all of Léon's extant letters to Gambetta are held in the BAN. Unless indicated H&P, all letters cited are those in the BAN. Gambetta's letters to Léon (BAN Ms 1777) are catalogued by year and then by number, in the sequence for that year: 76.25/50 means the 25th of the 50 extant letters written in 1876; we cite them as 'Gambetta to Léon, date, number'. Léon's letters to Gambetta (BAN Ms 1777bis) are catalogued by number, consecutively through the ten-year period of the correspondence, from 1 to 495; we cite them as 'Léon to Gambetta, date, number'.

Preface

1 Léon to Gambetta, [undated], no. 2.
2 Sanford Elwitt, *The Making of the Third Republic: Class and Politics in France, 1868–1884* (Baton Rouge: Louisiana State University Press, 1975).
3 Cf. Jean Lhomme, *La grande bourgeoisie au pouvoir (1830–1880): essai sur l'histoire sociale de la France* (Paris: Presses Universitaires de France, 1960); Elwitt, *The Making of the Third Republic*; Philip Nord, *The Republican Moment: Struggles for Democracy in Nineteenth-Century France* (Cambridge, MA; London: Harvard University Press, 1995).

Introduction: 'What admirable pages!'

1 Gambetta to Léon, 11 May 1876, 76.25/50.
2 In 1876, four years into their ten-year relationship, Gambetta wrote that he had 'almost a thousand' of Léon's letters (Gambetta to Léon, 11 May 1876, 76.25/50); they continued to correspond in the same fashion during the remaining six years of their liaison, which would suggest a total of perhaps 2500 letters from Léon. In 1893, Léon wrote of 'three thousand letters' received from Gambetta (Léon to Mme Marcellin Pellet [Pillias, 267]).
3 There are 1165 extant letters between Léon and Gambetta, 495 from Léon and 670 from Gambetta. The BAN holds the 495 unpublished letters from Léonie Léon to Gambetta (BAN MS1777bis). The BAN holds 581 unpublished letters from Gambetta to Léonie Léon (BAN MS1777); in addition, 89 of the 113 letters from Gambetta to Léon published in H&P do not survive in manuscript, making a total of 670 extant letters from Gambetta to Léon. Suffel's count of 579 unpublished letters from Gambetta to Léon perhaps overlooks two additional letters in 1882 (82.74/73, and 82A.73): there are 75 letters for 1882, although the catalogue suggests there are 73. Cf. Jacques Suffel, 'Gambetta et Léonie Léon (Correspondance inédite)', *Bulletin du bibliophile* 4 (1987): 450–65. The BAN also holds 22 telegrams from Gambetta to Léon (MS1777).
4 See Epilogue.
5 Cécile Dauphin, Pierrette Lebrun-Pézerat and Danièle Poublan, eds, *Ces bonnes lettres: Une correspondance familiale au XIXe siècle* (Paris: Albin Michel, 1995).
6 Constant Mews, *The Lost Love Letters of Heloïse and Abelard: Perceptions of Dialogue in Twelfth-Century France* (Basingstoke: Palgrave Macmillan, 2001); *Abelard and Heloïse* (Oxford: Oxford University Press, 2005).
7 Alain Corbin, 'Intimate Relations', in *A History of Private Life*, 4: *From the Fires of Revolution to the Great War*, ed. Michelle Perrot (Cambridge, MA; London: Belknap, 1990), 497–502; John R. Gillis, 'From Ritual to Romance: Toward an Alternative History of Love', in *Emotion and Social Change: Toward a New Psycho-History*, ed. Carol Z. Stearns and Peter N. Stearns (New York: Holmes and Meier, 1988), 87–121; Lenard R. Berlanstein, 'The French in Love and Lust', *French Historical Studies* 27, 2 (2004): 465–79.
8 Cécile Dauphin, *Prête-moi ta plume: Les manuels épistolaires au XIXe Siècle* (Paris: Editions Kimé, 2000), 138–48.
9 Susan Foley, '"Your letter is divine, irresistible, infernally seductive": Léon Gambetta, Léonie Léon, and Nineteenth-Century Epistolary Culture', *French Historical Studies* 30, 2 (2007): 237–67.

10 Dauphin *et al.*, *Ces bonnes lettres*, introduction; Marie-Claire Grassi, 'Des lettres qui parlent d'amour', *Romantisme* 68 (1990): 23–32; Martyn Lyons, 'Love Letters and Writing Practices: *Écritures intimes* in the nineteenth century', *Journal of Family History* 24 (1999): 232–39. Cf. Mark Seymour, 'Epistolary emotions: exploring amorous hinterlands in 1870s southern Italy', *Social History* 35, 2 (2010): 148–64.

11 BnF, Naf 12701, Lettres de Mme Léonie Léon à Mme Marcellin Pellet, 1875–1887. Both envelopes and paper bore the monogram. For an example of Gambetta's monogram, see Gambetta to Léon, 24 Oct. 1880, 80.51/67.

12 Gambetta to Léon, 11 May 1876, 76.25/50.

13 Cf. Charles Sowerwine, 'Revising the Sexual Contract: Women's Citizenship and Republicanism in France, 1789–1944', in *Confronting Modernity in Fin-de-Siècle France: Bodies, Minds and Gender*, ed. Christopher Forth and Elinor Accampo (Basingstoke: Palgrave Macmillan, 2009); Françoise Thébaud, 'Le genre de la démocratie en France au XXᵉ siècle', in *De la différence des sexes: Le genre en histoire*, ed. Michèle Riot-Sarcey (Paris: Larousse, 2010); Pierre Rosanvallon, *Le Sacre du Citoyen: Histoire du suffrage universel en France* (Paris: Gallimard, 1992); *Le Moment Guizot* (Paris: Gallimard, 1985); Anne Verjus, *Le Cens de la famille: Les femmes et le vote, 1789–1848* (Paris: Belin, 2002); Michèle Riot-Sarcey, *La Démocratie à l'épreuve des femmes: Trois figures critiques du pouvoir 1830–1848* (Paris: Albin Michel, 1994); Laurence Klejman and Florence Rochefort, *L'Égalité en marche: Le féminisme sous la Troisième République* (Paris: Presses de la Fondation nationale des Sciences politiques/Des femmes Antoinette Fouque, 1989).

14 Chastenet gained access to the letters through his links to conservative Catholic circles; he says only that the letters are in a 'secure place' (*Gambetta* [Paris: Fayard, 1968], 8). He facilitated J. P. T. Bury's access (Bury 2: 472). Chastenet added little to Bury.

15 Daniel Amson, *Gambetta, ou, Le rêve brisé* (Paris: Tallandier, 1994), contains no new scholarship. Pierre Antonmattei brought not only exemplary scholarship, but also the insights of a practised politician to his *Léon Gambetta: Héraut de la République* (Paris: Michalon, 1999), complemented by Pierre Barral's *Léon Gambetta: Tribun et stratège de la République, 1838–1882* (Toulouse: Privat, 2008), which offers insight into Gambetta's oratory and political strategies. Jean-Marie Mayeur has provided an accomplished political biography in *Léon Gambetta: La patrie et la République* (Paris: Fayard, 2008). Two studies by Jérôme Grévy (*La République* and *Le cléricalisme, voilà l'ennemi: Une guerre de religion en France* (Paris: A. Colin, 2005) put Gambetta in a broader context.

16 Pillias, 268.

17 Camille Servan-Schreiber, 'Léonie Léon et Léon Gambetta: Les relations personnelles et politiques d'un couple au XIXᵉ siècle', Maîtrise d'Histoire contemporaine, Université de Paris X–Nanterre, 1994–1995.

1 'The unforgettable day of 27 April'

1 Gambetta to Léon, [Wednesday], 26 June 1878, *Revue de Paris*, 1 Jan. 1907, 60.

2 Susan Griffin, *The Book of the Courtesans: A Catalogue of their Virtues* (New York: Broadway Books, 2001), 79–80.

3 Pillias, 56–7; cf. Bury 2: 16.

4 Virginia Rounding, *Grandes Horizontales: The Lives and Legends of Four Nineteenth-Century Courtesans* (New York; London: Bloomsbury, 2003), 18–21.

5 ASP, 2 EP 2, Dr 2, sdr a: 'Léonie Léon': police reports, 5 and 18 Sept. 1873.

6 Coraboeuf saw the photograph of Léon in the press and requested a copy from Joseph Reinach in order to produce a portrait. See Christian Lasalle, Patrick Favardin, and Odile A. Schmitz, *Hommage à Léon Gambetta* (Paris: Musée du Luxembourg, 1982), no. 281. On hostile rumours about Léon, see Chapter 10, below.

7 On Meersmans, see ASP, 4 EP 3, Dr 3, sdr a: 'Marie Meersmans'; Pillias, 55–8.

8 Gambetta to Léon, 22 Mar. 1879, 79.33/111.

9 For a collection of photographs of Gambetta, see Lasalle, Favardin, and Schmitz, *Hommage à Léon Gambetta*, nos. 397–404. Gambetta's damaged eye was removed in 1867: De Wecker, 'Gambetta: Souvenir Opthalmologique', *Gazette Hebdomadaire de médecine et de chirurgerie paraissant tous les vendredis*, 30ᵉ année, 3 (19 Jan. 1883): 33–7.

10 Alexander Turnbull Library, National Library of New Zealand/Te Puna Matauranga o Aotearoa, Wellington, New Zealand, MS-Papers-4298-60: Jane Maria Atkinson to Margaret Taylor, Nelson, 24 Oct. 1870; 'Statesmen, no. 127: Léon Gambetta. He devoured France with activity', *Vanity Fair*, 19 Oct. 1872. We thank Marion and John Poynter for this image.

11 Bury 2: 56–7.

12 Pillias, 53–6, 58; Gambetta to Léon, 26 June 1878, H&P no. 383. Cf. Gambetta to Léon, 21 July 1879, 79.72/111: 'We will return [from Versailles] by our first path, that of 27 April, and you will see if anything has changed in this heart since then.'

13 ASP, police report, 5 Sept. 1873; cf. Pillias, 35.

14 Pillias, 19–25.

15 ASP, 2 EP 1, Dr 4, sdr a: 'Colonel Léon'; Pillias, 34–9.

16 Pillias, 63; Natalie Petiteau, *Lendemains d'Empire: Les soldats de Napoléon dans la France du XIXᵉ siècle* (Paris: La Boutique de l'histoire, 2003), 207–10; Roger Price, *The French Second Empire: An Anatomy of Political Power* (Cambridge: Cambridge University Press, 2001), 414.

17 Pillias, 38 and n. 4.

18 Chanoine Gustave Monteuuis, *Une Âme religieuse: Marie-Élisabeth de Louvencourt, fondatrice des religieuses des Sacrés-Cœurs de Jésus et de Marie, sa vie, ses œuvres* (Paris: V. Retaux, 1899), 294; Abbé C. de Laeter, *Discours prononcé à la Bénédiction de la Chapelle des Dames de Louvencourt, le 19 août 1847 à Dunkerque, rue des Sœurs-Blanches* (Dunkerque: Imp. de Vanderest, 1847). The records of the school were destroyed during World War I (Pillias, 40).

19 *Règles et constitutions des Filles des Sacrés Cœurs de Jésus et de Marie, dites de Louvencourt* (Amiens: Duval et Herment, 1846), 91–2; *Petit manuel des enfants de Marie* (Dunkerque: Imprimerie Vanderest, 1854), 9–11. A copy dedicated to 'Léonie Léon, enfant de Marie,' is held in ASP, 2EP 1, Dr 1, sdr a, 'La jeunesse de Léonie Léon'.

20 Léonie Léon to Mme Pellet, 3 July 1892, in Pillias, 241; Monteuuis, *Une Âme religieuse*, 260; *Règles et constitutions*, 93–4. Cf. *Tableau chronologique de l'histoire de France à l'usage des pensionnats dirigés par les religieuses des sacrés-cœurs de Jésus et de Marie, dites de Louvencourt* (Amiens: Imprimerie de Jeunet, 1859);

Principaux homonymes français, rangés par ordre alphabétique à l'usage des pension-
nats de demoiselles dirigés par les religieuses des sacrés-cœurs de Jésus et de Marie,
dites de Louvencourt (Amiens: Duval et Herment, 1847); *Abrégé de la mythologie à*
l'usage des pensionnats dirigés par les religieuses des sacrés-cœurs de Jésus et de Marie,
dites de Louvencourt (Amiens: Duval et Herment, 1847). Cf. Rebecca Rogers,
From the Salon to the Schoolroom: Educating Bourgeois Girls in Nineteenth-century
France (University Park, PA: Pennsylvania State University Press, 2005).

21 Pillias, 42–4; the pension increased to 2000 francs per year in 1878; cf. ASP,
2 EP 1, Dr 4, sdr a: 'Colonel Léon'.

22 Christophe Charle, *Social History of France in the Nineteenth Century,* trans.
Miriam Kocham (Oxford: Oxford University Press, 1994), 265.

23 Paul Gerbod, *La Condition universitaire en France au XIXe siècle* (Paris: Presses
Universitaires de France, 1965), 584–5. Cf. Marguerite Perrot, *Le Mode de vie*
des familles bourgeoises, 1873–1953, 2nd edn (Paris: Presses de la fondation
nationale des sciences politiques, 1982), 83ff.

24 ASP, police report, 18 Sept. 1873. The rent was 1200 francs per annum.

25 On the stigma of mental illness see Alain Corbin, 'Backstage', in A *History*
of Private Life, 4: From the Fires of Revolution to the Great War, 560–6, 618,
657. On the stigma of illegitimacy, see Rachel Fuchs, *Contested Paternity:*
Constructing Families in Modern France (Baltimore: Johns Hopkins University
Press, 2008).

26 Alain Corbin, *Women for Hire: Prostitution and Sexuality in France after 1850,*
trans. Alan Sheridan (Cambridge MA; London: Harvard University Press,
1990), 135.

27 ASP, 4 EP 2, Dr 4, sdr c, 'Hyrvoix'.

28 5, rue Bréa; see ASP, 2 EP 2, Dr 4: 'Le Receveur de l'Enregistrement à Monsieur
Pillias', 1 May 1934.

29 ASP, police report, 18 Sept. 1873. This report notes that the family had
been renting the apartment for 'about twelve years'. In 1865, Hyrvoix's will
noted that his son was living with his grandmother at that address (Pillias,
44, 47–8). Gambetta later referred to 'coming to be spoiled in your charming
mezzanine' (Gambetta to Léon [env. dated 7 May 1872], 72.2/18).

30 The latest possible date on which they might have met based on Léon's
subsequent pregnancy would be May 1864.

31 ASP, police report, 20 Jan. 1874.

32 'Hyrvoix, Alphonse Louis', in *Dictionnaire du Second Empire,* ed. Jean Tulard
(Paris: Fayard, 1995), 631–2. The courtesan Marie Colombier claimed that
Hyrvoix organized the Emperor's liaison with Margot (*sic,* for Marguerite)
Bellanger (Marie Colombier, *Mémoires,* 3 vols [Paris: Ernest Flammarion,
1898–1900], 1: *Fin d'Empire,* 130–1), 83ff.

33 Ferdinand Bac, *Intimités du Second Empire d'après des documents*
contemporains, 3 vols, 1: *La Cour et la Ville* (Paris: Librairie Hachette
[1931]), 33.

34 Tulard, *Dictionnaire,* 632; Pillias, 46: cf. *Papiers et correspondance de la Famille*
Impériale (Paris: Garnier Frères, 1875), 1: 93, 171.

35 Pillias, 42–9. Unwed mothers could not claim support from the fathers of
their children until 1912. See Anne Cova, *Maternité et Droits des Femmes*
en France (XIXe–XXe siècles) (Paris: Anthropos Diffusion Economica, 1997);
Fuchs, *Contested Paternity.*

36 Tulard, *Dictionnaire*, 632; Jean Autin, *L'Impératrice Eugénie ou l'empire d'une femme* (Paris: Fayard, 1990), 217–18.

37 ASP, 4 EP 2, Dr 4, sdr c: 'Hyrvoix': Note on his father's 'disgrace' by Albert Hyrvoix, June 1895.

38 ASP, police report, 20 Jan. 1874. Our research on *bureaux de tabac* in the Pas de Calais uncovered no reference to Léonie Léon, but she refers to correspondence with the Prefect at Arras (Léon to Gambetta, 30 July 1876, no. 207). Documents on Léon's *bureaux de tabac* were amongst those stolen with her letters in 1940. See Epilogue.

39 ASP, police report, 20 Jan. 1874; Bury 1: 12–13.

40 See André Chervel, *Les Auteurs français, latins et grecs, au programme de l'enseignement secondaire de 1800 à nos jours* (Paris: INPR/publications de la Sorbonne, 1986); François Picavet, 'Essai sur l'Éducation littéraire, philosophique et politique d'un grand orateur: Gambetta', *Revue internationale de l'Enseignement*, 15 Dec. 1905: 487–511; Susan Foley and Charles Sowerwine, 'Rousing, Dominating, Persuading: Léon Gambetta and the Construction of Male Democracy in France, 1868–1882', 'Oratory and Democracy' Seminar, University of Melbourne, 2009.

41 Mayeur, 13–22; cf. 'Discours prononcés le 26 septembre 1872 à Grenoble', *Discours* 3: 88–120 (101). His speech made famous the phrase 'une nouvelle couche sociale'.

42 Alphonse Daudet, *Souvenirs d'un homme de lettres* (Paris: C. Marpon et E. Flammarion, 1888), 145.

43 'Discours de M. E. Spuller à l'inauguration du monument de Gambetta, Place du Carrousel à Paris, le 13 juillet 1888', in *Gambetta et ses Amis*, ed. Émile Labarthe (Paris: Les Éditions des Presses Modernes, 1938), 253.

44 Cf. Juliette Adam, *Mes Sentiments et Nos Idées avant 1870*, 6th edn (Paris: Lemerre, 1905), 309–13.

45 Daudet, *Souvenirs*, 142–3.

46 Gambetta to his father, 9 Oct. 1860, in P.-B. Gheusi, *Gambetta par Gambetta: Lettres intimes et souvenirs de famille* (Paris: Ollendorff, 1909), 162. Daniel Amson accepts the 'dissolute' Gambetta as described in contemporary memoirs (*Gambetta ou le Rêve Brisé* [Paris: Tallandier, 1994], 58–65, 82–3). Others give more nuanced accounts: Jean-Marie Mayeur, *Léon Gambetta: La Patrie et la République* (Paris: Fayard, 2008), 23–30; Grévy, *La République*, 171–8; and Pierre Barral, *Léon Gambetta: Tribun et Stratège de la République (1838–1882)* (Paris: Privat, 2008), 25–31.

47 Mayeur, 31–43.

48 *Ibid.*, 48.

49 Nord, *The Republican Moment*, 193; *Le Figaro*, 15 Nov. 1868, 3; Adam, *Mes Sentiments et Nos Idées*, 317; Katherine Fischer Taylor, *In the Theater of Criminal Justice: The Palais de Justice in Second Empire Paris* (Princeton: Princeton University Press, 1993), 22–5.

50 Pillias, 51.

51 'Plaidoyer pour M. Delescluze prononcé le 14 novembre 1868 devant la sixième Chambre du Tribunal correctionel de la Seine', *Discours*, 1: 12–13, 17–18; Chastenet, *Gambetta*, 19–23.

52 Adam, *Mes Sentiments et Nos Idées*, 318–19.

2 'I want you to devote yourself to the Republic'

1 Léon to Gambetta, 'Friday' [1872], no. 1.

2 Léon to Gambetta, 15 June 1879, no. 335; Gambetta to Léon, 15 June 1879, 79.57/111.

3 Gambetta to Léon, [env. dated 1 May 1872], 72.1/18; Léon to Gambetta, [1872], no. 1.

4 Gambetta to Léon, 14 June 1872, 72.6/18; Léon to Gambetta, 'Sunday', no. 6; 'Sunday', no. 9; 'Monday', no. 10.

5 54, Grande-Rue, Bourg-la-Reine (Pillias, 76). Almost all of Gambetta's letters are addressed here until May 1877, when the family moved to the nearby suburb of Fontenay-aux-Roses. Cf. Pillias, 42–9, 76.

6 Léon to Gambetta, 'Tuesday', no. 30; [undated], no. 40.

7 Gambetta to Léon, [env. dated 2 June 1872], 72.5/18; Léon to Gambetta, 'Monday', no. 15.

8 ASP, 4 EP 3, Dr 3, sdr a: 'Marie Meersmans'. Cf. Pillias, 55–8. Juliette Adam, citing Émile de Girardin, claims that the affair lasted until 1876, but her testimony is unreliable (Après l'abandon de la revanche, 7th edn [Paris: Lemerre, 1910], 56). For Gambetta's extant letters to Meersmans, see H&P nos. 86, 88 (1870); 134, 135, 137 (1872); 582 (undated).

9 Léon to Gambetta [undated], no. 266; cf. 1, 2 Mar. 1879, nos. 292, 293; Gambetta to Léon, [env. dated 9 May 1872], 72.3/18.

10 Léon to Gambetta, 'Friday', no. 18; ASP 2 EP 2, Dr 2, sdr a: 'Léonie Léon': police reports, 20, 22 Jan. 1874.

11 Léon to Gambetta, 'Wednesday', no. 22.

12 Léon to Gambetta, 'Tuesday', no. 7; Gambetta to Léon, [env. dated 13 May 1872], 72.4/18.

13 Gambetta to Léon, [env. dated 13 May 1872], 72.4/18.

14 Alan Corbin, Women for Hire: Prostitution and Sexuality in France after 1850, trans. Alan Sheridan (Cambridge MA; London: Harvard University Press, 1990), 200, 201.

15 Liz Stanley argues that correspondence forms a 'parallel' relationship, not merely an extension of a physical relationship: 'The Epistolarium: On theorizing letters and correspondences', Auto/Biography 12 (2004): 201–35.

16 Gambetta to Léon, [env. dated 2 June 1872], 72.5/18; [env. dated 15 Aug. 1872], 72.8/18; Léon to Gambetta, 19 Oct. 1873, no. 94; [undated], nos. 8, 10. Gambetta was editor-in-chief of the République Française.

17 On the letter as a seductive strategy, see Danièle Poublan, 'Les lettres font-elles les sentiments? S'écrire avant le mariage au milieu du XIXe siècle, in Séduction et sociétés: Approches historiques, ed. Cécile Dauphin and Arlette Farge (Paris: Seuil, 2001), 141–82.

18 Léon to Gambetta, 'Friday' [1872] no. 1; Gambetta to Léon, [env. dated 1 May 1872], 72.1/18; [env. dated 7 May 1872], 72.2/18.

19 Léon to Gambetta, 'Friday', no. 20.

20 Léon to Gambetta, [undated], nos. 2, 4; Gambetta to Léon, [env. dated 2 June 1872], 72.5/18; [14 June 1872], 72.6/18.

21 Cécile Dauphin, Prête-moi ta plume: Les manuels épistolaires au XIXe siècle (Paris: Éditions Kimé, 2000), 144–6. On letter-writing strategies in this

correspondence, see Susan Foley, '"Your letter is divine, irresistible, infernally seductive"': Léon Gambetta, Léonie Léon, and Nineteenth-Century Epistolary Culture', *French Historical Studies* 30, 2 (Spring 2007): 237–67.

22 Léon to Gambetta, 21 Aug. [1873?], no. 71; [undated], no. 74; 16 Dec. 1873, no. 119; 21 Jan. 1879, no. 281.
23 Léon to Gambetta, 20, 25 Oct. 1873, nos. 95, 97; Gambetta to Léon, 24 Oct. 1873, 73.10/16.
24 Gambetta to Léon, 4 Nov. 1873, 73.11/16; Léon to Gambetta, 4 Nov. 1873, no. 102.
25 Gambetta to Léon, 28 Nov. 1873, 73.13/16.
26 Léon to Gambetta, 29 Nov. 1873, no. 114.
27 Jacques Chastenet, *Gambetta* (Paris: Fayard, 1968), 203.
28 Gambetta to Léon, 29 Nov. 1874, 74.50/55: 'J'étais furieux de m'être laissé gagné de vitesse, . . . J'ai joui même de la [*deleted*] momentanée que tu avais gagnée sur mon empressement.'
29 Virginia Rounding, *Grandes Horizontales: The Lives and Legends of Four Nineteenth-Century Courtesans* (New York; London: Bloomsbury, 2003), 307–8.
30 Léon to Gambetta, [undated; late Apr. or early May 1872], no. 2.
31 Léon to Gambetta, [undated], no. 9. Cf. Marie-Thérèse Guichard, *Les Égéries de la République* (Paris: Éditions Payot, 1991).
32 Léon to Gambetta, [undated], nos. 9, 44.
33 Camille Pelletan, *Le Théâtre de Versailles: L'Assemblée au jour le jour du 24 mai au 25 février* (Paris: E. Dentu, 1875), 4.
34 Anne Martin-Fugier, *Les Salons de la Troisième République: Art, littérature, politique* (Paris: Perrin, 2003), 44–7.
35 For a criticism of women's presence, see Jules Claretie, *Candidat!* [1877], quoted in Pierre Guiral and Guy Thuillier, *La Vie quotidienne des Députés en France de 1871 à 1914* (Paris: Hachette Littérature, 1980), 178–9.
36 Léon to Gambetta, 19 May 1876, no. 172.
37 Léon to Gambetta, 'Friday' [1872], no. 18; [undated], nos. 32, 61.
38 Léon to Gambetta, 17 Nov. 1873, no. 108. By-elections in four departments in October had produced republican victories, but had not overturned the conservative majority. See Bury 1: 166.
39 Léon to Gambetta, [undated], no. 60.
40 Léon to Gambetta, 'Sunday', no. 77.
41 Léon to Gambetta, 'Sunday', no. 11.
42 Gambetta to Léon, [env. dated 7 May 1872], 72.2/18; 13 May 1872, 72.4/18; Léon to Gambetta, [undated], nos. 5, 7, 13.
43 J. P. T. Bury and R. P. Tombs, *Thiers 1797–1877: A Political Life* (London: Allen and Unwin, 1986), 219, 223; *Moniteur universel*, 25 May 1850; Georges Valance, *Thiers: bourgeois et révolutionnaire* (Paris: Flammarion, 2007); Eric Cahm, ed., *Politics and Society in Contemporary France (1789–1971): a Documentary History* (London: Methuen, 1972), p. 82.
44 Léon to Gambetta, 'Friday' [1872], no. 1.
45 Gambetta to Léon, [env. dated 21 July 1872], 72.7/18.
46 Léon to Gambetta, [July 1872?], no. 21; [undated], no. 12.
47 Léon to Gambetta, 'Friday', no. 18; 'Monday', no. 15.
48 Léon to Gambetta, [undated], no. 8; [June 1872], no. 9.

49 Grévy, *La République*, 226–7.
50 Philip Nord, *The Republican Moment: Struggles for Democracy in Nineteenth-Century France* (Cambridge MA; London: Harvard University Press, 1995), 192–4; Léon to Gambetta, 15 Sept. 1872, no. 24.
51 Léon to Gambetta, 19 Sept. 1872, no. 27. In Greek mythology, Penelope waited faithfully for Ulysses during his twenty-year absence fighting the Trojan Wars. The nymph, Calypso, fell in love with the shipwrecked Ulysses and kept him prisoner on her island for seven years, until Zeus ordered her to release him.
52 Gambetta to Marie Meersmans, [Sept. 1872], H&P no. 137; Léon to Gambetta, 19 Sept. 1872, no. 27.
53 Léon to Gambetta, 16 Sept. 1872, no. 25. Gambetta's letters to Léon during this trip are lost.
54 'Discours prononcés les 22 et 24 septembre 1872 à Chambéry,' *Discours* 3: 10–64.
55 Léon to Gambetta, [undated], no. 19.
56 'Discours prononcés le 26 septembre 1872 à Grenoble,' in *Discours* 3: 88–120, (101).
57 Bury 2: 124–5; Gambetta to Léon, [env. dated 8 Dec. 1872], 72.17/18.
58 Léon to Gambetta, [internal references suggest Feb.–Mar. 1873], no. 38.
59 Judith decapitated the Assyrian leader Holofernes (*Apocrypha*, Judith 12–13). Charlotte Corday stabbed to death the radical leader, Jean-Paul Marat, during the French Revolution.
60 Léon to Gambetta, 'Tuesday, 7 am', no. 31. Bury argues convincingly (2: 358–9, n. 4) that the date attributed to this letter ('December 1872?') is incorrect; it is more likely May 1873.
61 Léon to Gambetta, [undated], no. 49.
62 Léon to Gambetta, [undated], no. 50.
63 Gambetta to Léon, 28 Apr. 1873, 73A (telegram); Bury 2: 140–4.
64 Léon to Gambetta, 21 Sept. [1872], 13 May [1873], nos. 28, 52.
65 'Discours prononcé au banquet commémoratif de la naissance du Général Hoche, le 24 Juin 1873 à Versailles,' *Discours* 4: 13–27, esp. 21, 22, 26.
66 Léon to Gambetta, 26 June [1873], no. 54; Broglie to the Comte de Paris, quoted in Bury 2:162.
67 Léon to Gambetta, 1 Aug. [1873], no. 67.
68 Léon to Gambetta, [undated], no. 48; 22 Sept. 1873, no. 84.
69 Léon to Gambetta, 24, 27, 30 Sept. 1873, nos. 85–7; Gambetta to Léon, 24 Sept. 1873, 73.8/16.
70 Léon to Gambetta, undated, 'Saturday', no. 59; 'Wednesday', no. 72; 'Tuesday', no. 75.
71 Léon to Gambetta, 'Saturday', no. 59; 'Wednesday', no. 72; 'Tuesday', no. 75; 2, 9, 25, 26 Oct. 1873, nos. 88, 90, 91, 97; 8 Nov. [1873], no. 98; 16, 17 Nov. 1873, nos. 107, 108.
72 Gambetta to Léon, 20 Nov. 1873, 73.12/16; Léon to Gambetta, 21 Nov. 1873, no. 111.
73 Léon to Gambetta, [undated], no. 137; 4 Sept. 1879, no. 363; Gambetta to Léon, 3 Nov. 1878, H&P no. 390.
74 Gambetta to Léon, [env. dated 3 Feb. 1873], 73.3/16; 29 Nov. 1873, 73.14/16; env. dated 7 May 1872, 72.2/18; Léon to Gambetta, 30 Nov. 1873, no. 115.

Cf. Pierre Larousse, *Dictionnaire complet de la langue française* (Paris: A. Boyer, 1870); Guichard, *Les Égéries de la République*.

75 Susan Foley, 'Vercingetorix meets Minerva: Gender, Politics and Classical Antiquity in the Letters of Léon Gambetta and Léonie Léon', *French History* (2012), doi:10.1093/fh/crr092.

76 Léon to Gambetta, 25 Oct. 1873, no. 97; 7, 16 Nov. 1873, nos. 104, 107; 19 Dec. 1873, no. 121; cf. Pillias, 80.

77 Léon to Gambetta, 20 Dec. 1873, no. 122. Cf. 'Tuesday', no. 75; 26 Oct. 1873, no. 98; 17 Nov. 1873, no. 108; 19 Dec. 1873, no. 121.

78 Gambetta to Léon, 21 Dec. 1873, H&P no. 169.

79 Gambetta to Léon, 20 Dec. 1873, 73.16/16; Léon to Gambetta, 23 Dec. 1873, no. 123.

80 Gambetta to Léon, 2 Jan. 1874, 74.1/55.

81 Guichard, *Les Égéries de la République*, 30–1.

82 Gambetta to Léon, 2 Jan. 1874, 74.1/55.

3   'Thank you for being my strength, my hope'

1   Léon to Gambetta, 27 Oct. 1873, no. 99.

2   Gambetta to Léon, 13 Oct. 1873, 73.9/16. Cf. Léon to Gambetta, 17 Sept. 1873, no. 82; 13, 14 Oct. 1873, nos. 92, 93.

3   Léon to Gambetta, 27 Oct. 1873, no. 99; 1 Nov. 1873, no. 101. Cf. 30 Oct. 1873, no. 100; 7 Nov. 1873, no. 104.

4   Philip Nord, *The Republican Moment: Struggles for Democracy, in Nineteenth-Century France* (Cambridge, MA; London: Harvard University Press, 1995), 192–7.

5   Léon to Gambetta, 25 Oct. 1873, no. 97.

6   Gambetta to Léon, 4 Nov. 1873, 73.11/16.

7   Jean-Pierre Rioux, 'Le Palais-Bourbon de Gambetta à de Gaulle', in *Les Lieux de Mémoire*, ed. Pierre Nora, vol. 2, part 3 (Paris: Gallimard, 1986), 487–516; Pierre Guiral and Guy Thuillier, *La Vie quotidienne des Députés, en France de 1871 à 1914* (Paris: Hachette Littérature, 1980), 244–6.

8   Camille Pelletan, *Le Théâtre de Versailles: L'Assemblée au jour le jour du 24 mai au 25 février* (Paris: E. Dentu, 1875), 165–6. Cf. Judith F. Stone, *Sons of the Revolution: Radical Democrats in France, 1862–1914* (Baton Rouge; London: Louisiana State University Press, 1996), 83. We have used Stone's translation in part.

9   Daniel Halévy, *La République des Ducs* (Paris: Bernard Grasset, 1937), 390, quoted in James R. Lehning, *To Be a Citizen: The Political Culture of the Early French Third Republic* (Ithaca; London: Cornell University Press, 2001), 28. On Gambetta's oratory, see also Susan Foley and Charles Sowerwine, 'Rousing, Dominating, Persuading: Léon Gambetta and the Construction of Male Democracy in France, 1868–1882', 'Oratory and Democracy' Seminar, University of Melbourne, 2009.

10 Léon to Gambetta, 16 Nov. 1873, no. 107.

11 Gambetta to Léon, 7 Jan. 1874, 74.3/55. Emphasis original.

12 ASP, 2 EP 2, Dr 2, sdr a: 'Léonie Léon': police reports, 5 and 18 Sept. 1873.

13 Alan Corbin, *Women for Hire: Prostitution and Sexuality in France after 1850*, trans. Alan Sheridan (Cambridge, MA; London: Harvard University Press,

1990); Louis Andrieux, *Souvenirs d'un Préfet de Police*, 2 vols (Paris: J. Rouff, 1885), 1: 27–31.

14 ASP, police report 20 Jan. 1874.
15 Léon to Gambetta, 'Friday', no. 18; Gambetta to Léon, 20 Jan. 1874, 74.4/55.
16 ASP, police report, 22 Jan. 1874; *Petit manuel des enfants de Marie* (Dunkirk: Imprimerie Vanderest, 1854), 10.
17 ASP, police report, 22 Jan. 1874. Cf. Anne-Marie Sohn, *Du premier baiser à l'alcôve: La sexualité des français au quotidien (1850–1950)* (Paris: Aubier, 1996); Laure Adler, *Secrets d'alcôve: histoire du couple de 1830 à 1930* (Paris: Hachette, 1983).
18 Gambetta to Léon, 23 Jan. 1874, 74.5/55; ASP, police report, 23 Jan. 1873 [*sic*, for 1874].
19 ASP, police reports, 24, 29, 30, 31 Jan., 1, 18 Feb. 1874; ' Feb. 1874', covering 19–23 Feb. 1874.
20 ASP, police reports, 20 Jan., 19, 22 Feb. 1874. Émilie was born in 1829, making her forty-five at this time. She had been committed to the asylum one month before this report.
21 Jacques Suffel, 'Gambetta et Léonie Léon (correspondance inédite)', *Bulletin du bibliophile* 4 (1987): 460–1, note 5, states that the document was written in pencil and unsigned but gives no location.
22 Adler, *Secrets d'alcove*, 115–17; Virginia Rounding, *Grandes Horizontales: The Lives and Legends of Four Nineteenth-Century Courtesans* (New York; London: Bloomsbury, 2003), 21–3.
23 ASP, police report, 23 Jan. 1874.
24 Gambetta to Léon, 4 Mar. 1874, H&P no. 175. Cf. [undated] 1874, no. 230.
25 Léon to Gambetta, [undated], nos. 127, 139.
26 Jean-Yves Mollier and Jocelyne George, *La Plus Longue des Républiques 1870–1940* (Paris: Fayard, 1994), 74–9; Bury 2: 175, 185–6.
27 Léon to Gambetta, 'Thursday' [Feb.–Mar. 1873?], no. 33; 'Tuesday', no. 63; 'Discours sur le projet de loi électorale prononcé le 4 juin 1874 à l'Assemblée nationale', *Discours* 4: 165–85; Bury 2: 200–1.
28 Gambetta to Léon, 12 May 1874, 74.16/55. Cf. 5 June 1874, 74.17/55.
29 Bury 2: 188–91; Gambetta to Léon, 12 June 1874, 74.18/55.
30 Grévy, *La République*, 51–3. He points out that these debates harked back to the constitutional debates of 1848.
31 Gambetta to Léon, 7, 16, 17, 18, 25 July 1874, 74.23/55, 74.25/55, 74.26/55, 74.27/55, 74.30/55.
32 Gambetta to Léon, 22, 29 Nov. 1874, 74.49/55, 74.50/55.
33 Gambetta to Léon, 29 Nov. 1874, 74.50/55.
34 Léon to Gambetta, [undated], no. 140.
35 'Chine', n.f., *Le Grand Robert de la Langue Française*, 2nd edn, 9 vols (Paris: Le Robert, 1986), 2: 572.
36 ASP, 4 EP 2, dr 4, sdr c: 'Hyrvoix': 2 letters from Hyrvoix to William (July 1856); letter from William to Hyrvoix (June 1859).
37 Gambetta to Léon, 2, 3 Nov. 1874, 74.46/55, 74.47/55; 13 Dec. 1874, 74.53/55.
38 Gambetta to Léon, 16, 18 July, 22 July 1874, 74.25/55, 74.27/55; 22 July (1 a.m.) 1874, 74.28/55; 28 Aug. 1874, 74.37/55.

39 ASP, 2 EP 2, Dr 1, sdr e: 'Bague donnée par Léon Gambetta à Léonie Léon'. The son of Georges Pallain (Gambetta's personal secretary) gave Pillias a note written by his father about these rings. Cf. Pillias, 81–2.

40 Guiral and Thuillier, *La Vie quotidienne des députés*, 95–6; Bury 2: 56–7; *Histoire générale de la presse française*, ed. Claude Bellanger *et al.*, 5 vols (Paris: Presses Universitaires de France, 1969–1976), 3: *De 1871 à 1940* (1972), 222. Pillias notes (74) that Gambetta's apartment on the rue Montaigne was on the mezzanine.

41 Christophe Charle, *Social History of France in the Nineteenth Century*, trans. Miriam Kocham (Oxford: Oxford University Press, 1994), 265; Marguerite Perrot, *Le Mode de vie des familles bourgeoises, 1873–1953*, 2nd edn (Paris: Presses de la fondation nationale des sciences politiques, 1982), 83ff.

42 Chastenet, *Gambetta*, 235–7. Cf. Gambetta to Léon, 2 Feb. 1875, 75.7/47.

43 Gambetta to Léon, 11 Feb. 1875, 75.8/47. Cf. Bury 2: 225–6. Marshal MacMahon and Napoleon III had been captured on the battlefield of Sedan in 1870, triggering the collapse of the Empire.

44 Bury 2: 229–37; Grévy, *La République*, 59–60.

45 Gambetta to Léon, 18 Feb. 1875, 75.10/47.

46 Gambetta to Léon, 24 Feb. 1875, 75.11/47; 4 Mar. 1875, 75.12/47.

47 Louis Blanc, *Histoire de la Constitution du 25 février 1875* (Paris: Charpentier, 1882), 152; Gambetta to Léon, 22 Apr. 1875, 26 Oct. 1876, H&P nos. 242, 290; 'Discours sur les lois constitutionnelles prononcé le 23 avril 1875 à Paris (XXᵉ arrondissement)', *Discours* 4: 299–340. Cf. Bury 2: 240–3; Léon to Gambetta, 26 Oct. 1876, no. 236.

48 Gambetta to Léon, 29 May 1875, 75.24/47; 29 June 1875, 75.25/47; 12 July 1875, 75.27/47; Bury's translation of 12 July (cf. Bury 2: 249–50).

49 Gambetta to Léon, 3, 4, 5 Dec. 1875, 75.37/47; 75.38/47; 75.39/47.

50 Gambetta to Léon, 12, 16, 27 Dec. 1875, 75.41/47, 75.43/47, 75.46/47; cf. Bury 2: 260-2.

51 Gambetta to Léon, 11, 31 Dec. 1875, 75.40/47, 75.47/47.

52 Gambetta to Léon, 13, 20 Jan. 1876, 76.1/50, 76.2/50. Marshal MacMahon's regime was known as the 'Moral Order regime'.

53 Gambetta to Léon, 13, 22 Jan. 1876, 76.1/50, 76.3/50. Cf. Léon to Gambetta, [undated], no. 141.

54 Cf. Bury, 2: 230–1; Grévy, *La République*, 234–5. We say 'groups' because political parties in the modern sense did not yet exist. People often belonged to more than one group, and there was no 'party discipline'.

55 Léon to Gambetta, 27 Jan. 1876, no. 146. Colonel Denfert-Rochereau, 'the Lion of Belfort', was a hero of the Franco-Prussian war. He later entered politics as a member of Gambetta's Republican Union. See Adolphe Robert and Gaston Cougny, *Dictionnaire des parlementaires français*, 5 vols (Paris: Bourloton, 1890), 2: 336–7.

56 Gambetta to Léon, 23 Jan. 1876, 76.4/50.

57 Léon to Gambetta, 1 Feb. 1876, no. 148. Cf. Bury 2: 269–71.

58 Gambetta to Léon, 14 Feb., 14 [16?] Feb. 1876, 76.6/50, 76.7/50; Gambetta to Juliette Adam, 22 Feb. 1876, H&P no. 269.

59 Gambetta to Léon, 16 June 1876, 76.31/50. Cf. Bury 2: 279; Chastenet 1: 11–13; *Dictionnaire des Ministres de 1789 à 1989*, ed. Benoît Yvert (Paris: Perrin, 1990), 234–5.

60 Gambetta to Léon, 10 Oct. 1874, 74.40/55; 27 Dec. 1875, 75.46/47. Origen was a Church Father reputed to have castrated himself to preserve his chastity.
61 Gambetta to Léon, 14 [16?], 29 Feb. 1876, 76.7/50, 76.9/50. Only two of Léon's letters survive for Feb.–Mar. 1876 (nos. 150, 151), one of which is damaged and almost illegible.
62 Gambetta to Léon, 5 Mar. 1876, 76.11/50. Cf. Bury 2: 281, 285: 'Fewer than 200 of the total of more than 500 had been members of the National Assembly.'
63 Léon to Gambetta, 6 Mar. 1876, no. 152.

4 'I am smiling at your triumph, at our love'

1 Léon to Gambetta, 30 Apr. 1876, no. 166.
2 Léon to Gambetta, 8 Mar. 1876, no. 153. Cf. Ernest Renan, *Vie de Jésus* (1863), and Chapter 7, below.
3 Bury 2: 285–6.
4 Gambetta to Léon, 9 Mar. 1876, 76.12/50.
5 Grévy, *La République*, 100–4, 107, 220; Gambetta to Léon, 5 June 1874, 74.17/55; 18 May 1876, 76.26/50.
6 Chastenet 1: 215; Bury 2: 288–95; Grévy, *La République*, 228–30.
7 See Gambetta's notes on finances reproduced in Joseph Reinach, *La Vie politique de Léon Gambetta, suivie d'autres essais sur Gambetta* (Paris: Félix Alcan, 1918), 173–91; Grévy, *La République*, 231–4; Léon to Gambetta, 5 May 1876, no. 168.
8 Gambetta to Léon, 23 Jan 1876, 76.4/50; 12 June 1876, 76.30/50; Grévy, *La République*, 108; Gambetta to Léon, 10 Aug. 1873 [1872], 72.7 bis/18.
9 Grévy, *La République*, 47–8; Bury 2: 299 & n. 3.
10 Léon to Gambetta, 27 Mar. 1876, no. 156; Gambetta to Léon, 27 Mar. 1876, 76.16/50; 18, 20 May 1876, 76.26/50, 76.27/50. Cf. Bury 2: 297–302.
11 Gambetta to Léon, 25 Apr. 1876, 76.21/50. Gambetta's 'additional power' came from his position as President of the Budget Commission.
12 Léon to Gambetta, 30 Apr. 1876, [undated], no. 167; cf. Bury 2: 303–10. Gambetta's letter is not extant.
13 Gambetta to Léon, 2, 11 May 1876, 76.24/50, 76.25/50; Léon to Gambetta, 18 May 1876, no. 171; 18 Oct. 1876, no. 234; 20 Dec. 1876, nos. 247, 252.
14 Gambetta to Léon, 16 June 1876, 76.31/50; Léon to Gambetta, 12 July 1876, no. 195. Cf. Bury 2: 318–9.
15 Gambetta to Léon, 19 Apr. 1876, 76.19/50; Léon to Gambetta, 21 Mar. 1876, no. 155. Cf. also 16 Mar. 1876, no. 154; [undated], no. 159.
16 Gambetta to Léon, 11 May 1876, 76.25/50; Cf. Introduction.
17 See Bury 2: 185, 345–6; Juliette Adam, *Après l'abandon de la revanche*, 7th edn (Paris: Lemerre, 1910), 9–12.
18 Léon to Gambetta, 5 June 1876, no. 178.
19 Gambetta to Juliette Adam, 17 Oct. 1876, H&P no. 289; Gambetta to Princess Lise Troubetzkoï, 24, 26 July 1874, H&P nos. 196–8; 'Saturday' [July 1874], H&P no. 198; 2, 3 Aug. 1874, H&P nos. 199, 201; 2, 6 Mar. 1876, nos. 272–3;

15 Oct. 1877, no. 343; Léon to Gambetta, 15 July 1876, no. 197. Juliette Adam described Troubetzkoï in *Après l'abandon de la revanche*, 10.
20 Léon to Gambetta, 18 May 1876, no. 171; 10 Aug. 1876, no. 211; 18 Oct. 1876, no. 234; 1 Nov. 1876, no. 238.
21 Gambetta to Léon, 11 Mar. 1876, 76.13/50.
22 Gambetta to Léon, 20 May 1876, 76.27/50.
23 Léon to Gambetta, 18 Oct. 1876, no. 234. Cf. Pillias, 34–8.
24 Léon to Gambetta, 20, 27 June 1876, nos. 185, 187; 9, 12, 28 July 1876, nos. 194, 195, 206; 10 Aug. 1876, no. 211; 3 Nov. 1876, no. 239. Cf. 16 Mar. 1876, no. 154; [undated], no. 159.
25 Pillias, 84–5 (137, Grande-Rue, Fontenay-aux-Roses); Léon to Gambetta, 12, 25 May 1876, nos. 169, 174.
26 Gambetta to Léon [env. dated 9 May 1872], 72.3/18. Cf. 11 Mar. 1876, 76.14/47; 12 May 1876, 76.25/47; 3 Sept. 1876, 76.40/47. Cf. Chapter 2, above.
27 Gambetta to Léon, 22 Mar. 1875, 75.16/47. Cf. 19 Mar. 1875, 75.14/47; 9 Mar. 1876, 76.12/50. Cf. Kathleen Kete, *The Beast in the Boudoir: Pet-keeping in Nineteenth-Century Paris* (Berkeley: University of California Press, 1994).
28 Léon to Gambetta, 4, 5, 12 June 1876, nos. 177, nos. 177, 178, 182; Gambetta to Léon, 10 June 1876, 76.29/50. The sex of the dog is unknown.
29 Gambetta to Léon, 12 June 1876, 76. 30/50.
30 Léon to Gambetta, 4 Aug. 1876, no. 210; 1 Sept. 1876, no. 224.
31 Léon to Gambetta, 22 Aug. 1876, no. 217; 17 Jan. 1882, no. 485. Cf. 5, 25, 30 June 1876, nos. 178, 186, 188; 24 Aug. 1876, no. 221; 20 Mar. 1880, 80.20/67; 9 Feb. 1881, no. 429.
32 See Judith Misbach and Henderikus J. Stam, 'Medicalizing melancholia: exploring profiles of psychiatric professionalization', *Journal of the History of the Behavioural Sciences* 42, 1 (2006): 41–59.
33 Gambetta to Léon, 30 Apr. [env. dated 1 Apr.] 1876, 76.17/50.
34 Gambetta to Léon, 30 June 1877, 77.36/70.
35 Léon to Gambetta, 25 June 1876, no. 186.
36 Gambetta to Léon, 30 June 1876, 76.33/50.
37 Léon to Gambetta, 9 July 1876, no. 194. Gambetta's letters for this period are not extant.
38 Léon to Gambetta, 12, 13 July 1876, nos. 195, 196.
39 Léon to Gambetta, 27, 28 July 1876, nos. 204, 206. Gambetta's preceding letter has not survived.
40 Léon to Gambetta, 25, 28, 30, 31 July 1876, nos. 202, 205, 207, 208. Cf. 24, 27 July 1876, nos. 201, 204.
41 Léon to Gambetta, 9, 12, 25, 27, 28 [two letters] July 1876, nos. 194, 195, 202, 204–6.
42 Léon to Gambetta, 25 June 1876, no. 186; 29 Nov. 1876, no. 246.
43 Léon to Gambetta, [undated], no. 159.
44 Léon to Gambetta, 5 June 1876, no. 178; 30 Sept. 1876, no. 226.
45 Gambetta to Léon, 29 July [env. stamped 30 June] 1876, 76.33/5; Léon to Gambetta, 30 June 1876, no. 188; Gambetta to Léon, 20, 29 July 1876, H&P nos. 282, 283; *Histoire générale de la presse française*, ed. Claude Bellanger *et al.*, 5 vols (Paris: Presses Universitaires de France, 1969–1976), 3: *De 1871 à 1940* (1972), 222–4; Pierre Guiral and Guy Thuillier, *La Vie quotidienne des*

députés en France de 1871 à 1914 (Paris: Hachette Littérature, 1980), 95–6; Bury 2: 307–10.

46 Léon to Gambetta, 2 Aug. 1876, no. 209; Gambetta to Léon, 30 [env. dated 21] Aug. 1876, 76.39/50.

47 Gambetta to Léon, 12, 13 Dec. 1876, 76.46/50, 76.47/50; Léon to Gambetta, 13 Dec. 1876, no. 250. The incumbent Minister, General Berthaut, was a Bonapartist. Cf. Bury 2: 372–3, 383.

48 Gambetta to Léon, 16 Dec. 1876, 76.48/50.

49 For examples see Judith F. Stone, *Sons of the Revolution: Radical Democrats in France, 1862–1914* (Baton Rouge; London: Louisiana State University Press, 1996), 238–9.

50 Gambetta to Léon, 21 Dec. 1876, 76.49/50; Bury 2: 385–7.

51 Gambetta to Léon, 27 Jan. 1877, 77.2/70; 18, 27 Apr. 1877, 77.10/70, 77.15/70; Bury 2: 388, 396, 399.

52 Bury 2: 396, 399.

53 'Discours prononcé le 16 mai 1877 à la réunion plenière des gauches', *Discours* 7: 1–10 (9); 'Discours sur la crise ministérielle du 16 mai prononcé le 17 mai 1877 à la Chambre des Députés', *Discours* 7: 11–24 (20); Gambetta to Léon, 17 May 1877, 77.24/70.

54 Gambetta to Léon, 12 June 1877, 77.32/70. Cf. 20 May 1877, 77.26/70.

55 'Discours sur la constitution du cabinet du 17 mai, prononcés les 16 et 19 juin 1877', *Discours* 7: 86–119 (104, 122, 139, 140). For a summary of the session and Gambetta's speech, see Bury 2: 409–11.

56 Jules Claretie, 'Notes et Souvenirs', quoted in Grévy, *La République*, 225.

57 Léon to Gambetta, 18 June 1877, no. 259.

58 Gambetta to Léon, 25 July 1877, 77.38/70; Gambetta to Mme Auguste Scheurer-Kestner, 23 July 1877, H&P no. 322.

59 'Discours prononcé le 15 août 1877 à Lille', *Discours* 7: 207–54 (229–30).

60 Gambetta to Léon, 27 Aug. 1877, 77.40/70; 5 Sept. 1877, 77.42/70.

61 Gambetta to Léon, 13 Sept. 1877, 77.44/70; Bury 2: 423.

62 Gambetta to Léon, 3 Sept. 1877, H&P no. 328; 23 Sept. 1877, 77.47/70. Cf. Bury 2: 425–9; Pierre Barral, *Léon Gambetta: Tribun et Stratège de la République, 1838–1882* (Toulouse: Privat, 2008), 149.

63 Léon to Gambetta, 14 Oct. 1877, no. 260. Cf. *The Times*, 17 Oct: 'There is not a Chamber in all Europe containing such a majority' (Bury 2: 434–5).

64 Gambetta to Léon, 15 Oct. 1877, 77.50/70; Gambetta to Juliette Adam, 15 Oct. 1877, H&P no. 342; Bury 2: 441.

65 Gambetta to Léon, 9, 11 Nov. 1877, 77.57/70, 77.58/70.

66 'Discours sur la proposition tendant à la nomination d'une commission chargée de faire une enquête parlementaire sur les élections des 14 et 28 octobre 1877, prononcé le 15 novembre 1877 à la Chambre des Députés', *Discours* 7: 328–73. Cf. Bury 2: 445–7; Pierre Antonmattei, *Léon Gambetta: Héraut de la République* (Paris: Michalon, 1999), 299.

67 Gambetta to Léon, 15 Nov. 1877, 77.59/70.

68 Bury 2: 447–52.

69 Gambetta to Léon, 25 Nov. 1877, 77.61/70; 10 Dec. 1877, 77.66/70.

70 Barral, *Léon Gambetta*, 147; Bury 2: 459–60; *Dictionnaire des Ministres de 1789 à 1989*, ed. Benoît Yvert (Paris: Perrin, 1990) 129–30.

71 Bury 2: 461.

5 'We'll go and laugh at the Palais-Royal'

1 Gambetta to Léon, 14 Apr. 1877, 77.9/70.
2 David P. Jordan, *Transforming Paris: The Life and Labors of Baron Haussmann* (New York: Free Press, 1995); David Harvey, *Paris: Capital of Modernity* (New York; London: Routledge, 2003), 125–40; Colin Jones, *Paris: Biography of a City* (London: Penguin, 2004), 345–52; David H. Pinkney, *Napoleon III and the Rebuilding of Paris* (Princeton: Princeton University Press, 1958).
3 Julia Csergo, 'Extension et mutation du loisir citadin: Paris XIXe siècle–début XXe siècle', in *L'Avènement des Loisirs 1850–1960*, ed. Alain Corbin (Paris: Aubier, 1995), 125–6, 132–8; Rebecca L. Spang, *The Invention of the Restaurant: Paris and Modern Gastronomic Culture* (Cambridge, MA: Harvard University Press, 2000).
4 ASP, 2 EP 2, Dr 2, sdr a: 'Léonie Léon': police report, 23 Jan. 1874; Gambetta to Léon, 11 June 1877, 77.32/70. Cf. Haejong Hazel Hahn, 'Du flâneur au consommateur: spectacle et consommation sur les Grands Boulevards, 1840–1914', *Romantisme* 134 (2006): 67–78; Christopher Prendergast, *Paris in the Nineteenth Century* (Oxford: Blackwell, 1992).
5 Pinkney, *Napoleon III and the Rebuilding of Paris*, 70–2; Jones, *Paris*, 362–3; *Illustrated Guide to Paris* (1884), quoted in Vanessa Schwartz, *Spectacular Realities: Early Mass Culture in Fin-de-Siècle Paris* (Berkeley: University of California Press, 1999), 17.
6 Gambetta to Léon, 20 May 1876, 76.27/50; 26 Sept. 1877, 77.48/70.
7 Gambetta to Léon, 15 Nov. 1878, 78.32/35.
8 For overviews of the vast literature on *flânerie*, see *The Flâneur*, ed. Keith Tester (New York: Routledge, 1994); Vanessa R. Schwartz, 'Walter Benjamin for Historians', *American Historical Review* 106, 5 (2001): 21 (electronic version); Gregory Shaya, 'The *Flâneur*, the *Badaud*, and the Making of a Mass Public in France, circa 1860–1910', *American Historical Review* 109, 1 (2004): 41–77.
9 On the evolution of promenading, see Laurent Turcot, *Le Promeneur à Paris au XVIIIe siècle* (Paris: Gallimard, 2007). Cf. Charles Baudelaire, *The Painter of Modern Life* (1859–60). Walter Benjamin's studies of Baudelaire's work, and his own extensive writings on the modern city, are generally credited with initiating the burgeoning interest in the study of *flânerie*. Cf. Walter Benjamin, *The Arcades Project*, trans. Howard Eiland and Kevin McLaughlin (Cambridge, MA: Harvard University Press, 1999).
10 On gender and *flânerie*, see Janet Wolff, 'The Invisible *Flâneuse*: Women and the Literature of Modernity', *Theory, Culture and Society* 2 (1985): 37–48; Anne Friedberg, *Window Shopping: Cinema and the Post-Modern* (Berkeley: University of California Press, 1993). Schwartz argues that Benjamin's *flaneûr* was an urban type, not a gendered individual ('Walter Benjamin for Historians', ¶28–9).
11 Léon to Gambetta, [undated], nos. 398, 422.
12 Gambetta to Léon, 3 Nov. 1877, 77.53/70. Cf. Judith G. Coffin, *The Politics of Women's Work: The Paris Garment Trades 1750–1915* (Princeton: Princeton University Press, 1996), 76–81, 132–3. There is some debate over when ready-made clothing for women became commonplace. Michael Miller suggests the 1880s (*The Bon Marché: Bourgeois Culture and the Department*

Store, 1869–1920 [Princeton: Princeton University Press, 1981], 50). Philippe Perrot links it to the rise of the department store from the 1860s (*Fashioning the Bourgeoisie: A History of Clothing in the Nineteenth Century*, trans. Richard Bienvenu [Princeton: Princeton University Press, 1994], 54–8).

13 Léon to Gambetta, 16 June 1879, no. 336; Gambetta to Léon, 21 May 1880, 80.25/67.

14 ASP, police report, 23 Jan. 1874; Léon to Gambetta, 16 Dec. 1879, no. 380. Cf. 29 Sept. 1879, no. 371; Gambetta to Léon, 28 Feb. 1882, H&P no. 528.

15 See Perrot, *Fashioning the Bourgeoisie*, 29–34.

16 Juliette Adam, *Mes Sentiments et Nos Idées avant 1870*, 6th edn (Paris: Lemerre, 1905), 309–14.

17 ASP, police report, 23 Jan. 1874; cf. Hahn, 'Du flâneur au consommateur', 71.

18 Perrot, *Fashioning the Bourgeoisie*, 167–70; Susan Hiner, *Accessories to Modernity: Fashion and the Feminine in Nineteenth-Century France* (Philadelphia; Oxford: University of Pennsylvania Press, 2010), 12–15, 25–31; Denise Z. Davidson, 'Making Society "Legible": People-Watching in Paris after the Revolution', *French Historical Studies* 28, 2 (2005): 265–96.

19 Léon to Gambetta, 15 Oct. 1876, no. 233; [undated], no. 414. Cf. Perrot, *Fashioning the Bourgeoisie*, 67.

20 Léon to Gambetta, 19 May 1879, no. 320.

21 Gambetta to Léon, 6 Nov. 1877, 77.55/70; [env. dated 9 Nov. 1877], 77.56./70; 9 Nov. 1877, 77.57/70; 13 July 1879, 79.69/111; 9 June 1880, 80.28/67.

22 Gambetta to Léon, 11 Mar. 1882, 82.23/73. Cf. Léon to Gambetta, [undated], no. 393; 28 Jan. 1881, no. 426.

23 See Leora Auslander, *Taste and Power: Furnishing Modern France* (Berkeley: University of California Press, 1996), 221–4; Bonnie G. Smith, *Ladies of the Leisure Class: The Bourgeoises of Northern France in the Nineteenth Century* (Princeton: Princeton University Press, 1981).

24 Léon to Gambetta, 28 Jan. 1879, no. 283; Gambetta to Léon, 19 Feb. 1879, 79.22/111.

25 Léon to Gambetta, 25 Feb. 1882, no. 488; Gambetta to Léon, 11 Mar. 1882, 82.23/73. Cf. Miller, *The Bon Marché*; Rosalind Williams, *Dream Worlds: Mass Consumption in Late Nineteenth-Century France* (Berkeley: University of California Press, 1982). On the gendering of consumer practices, see esp. Auslander, *Taste and Power*; Rachel Bowlby, *Just Looking: Consumer Culture in Dreiser, Gissing and Zola* (New York; London: Methuen, 1985).

26 ASP, police report, 23 Jan. 1874; Léon to Gambetta, 25 Feb. 1882, no. 488; Coffin, *The Politics of Women's Work*, 83.

27 Léon to Gambetta, 28 Feb. 1882, no. 489. See Auslander, *Taste and Power*, 290–2, 303–5.

28 Gambetta to Léon, 6 Mar. 1882, 82.20/73. Paul was the manservant, hence Gambetta's amusement that he had an opinion on the curtains.

29 Gambetta to Léon, 23 Feb. 1882, 82.17/71; 9, 11 Mar. 1882, 82.22/73, 82.23/73; Léon to Gambetta, 25 Feb. 1882, no. 488. Cf. Maurice Allem, *La Vie Quotidienne sous le Second Empire* (Paris: Hachette, 1948), 154.

30 Gambetta to Léon, 9 Mar. 1882, 82.22/73; Léon to Gambetta, 4 Mar. 1882, no. 491.

31   Christophe Charle, *Théâtres en capitales: naissance de la société du spectacle à Paris, Berlin, Londres et Vienne, 1860–1914* (Paris: Albin Michel, 2008), 25. Cf. Jean-Claude Yon, *Histoire Culturelle de la France au XIXe siècle* (Paris: Armand Colin, 2010).

32   Gambetta to Léon, 24, 25 Nov. 1878, 78.33/35, 78.34/35. Léon's letters for 1878 are not extant.

33   Self-display in the loges was part of the entertainment; dimming the lights during performances only became standard practice in the 1890s. See Anne Martin-Fugier, *Comédienne: De Mlle Mars à Sarah Bernhardt* (Paris: Seuil, 2001), 81; Yon, *Histoire Culturelle*.

34   Frédérique Patureau, *Le Palais Garnier dans la Société Parisienne 1875–1914* (Paris: Pierre Mardaga, 1991), 299 (1880 prices); Pierre Guiral, *La Vie Quotidienne en France à l'Âge d'Or du Capitalisme 1852–1879* (Paris: Hachette, 1976), 199.

35   Guiral, *La Vie Quotidienne*, 199; Michel Autrand, *Le Théâtre en France de 1870 à 1914* (Paris: Honoré Champion, 2006), 17.

36   Léon to Gambetta, 22 May 1879, no. 322; Gambetta to Léon, 22 May 1879, 79.48/111.

37   Gambetta to Léon, 21 Nov. 1877, 77.60/70; *Les Annales du Théâtre et de la Musique* (1878): 63–8; 78. This may have been the unnamed play that Gambetta and Léon attended in May 1878: Gambetta to Léon, 2 May 1878, 78.14/35.

38   Cf. Autrand, *Le Théâtre en France*, 19, 47–9; *Naturalism and Symbolism in European Theatre, 1850–1918*, ed. Claude Schumacher (Cambridge: Cambridge University Press, 1996), 68–9.

39   Quoted at www.theatredugymnase.com/theatre.html, accessed 7 Oct. 2009.

40   Jean Bertrand, 'Drame et Musique', *La République Française*, 25 Nov. 1878, 2; *Annales du Théâtre et de la Musique* (1878): 272–4, 281–2.

41   *Le Petit Journal*, 8 Feb. 1879, 3. See www.theatrepalaisroyal.com/historique-chapitre-6.html, accessed 7 Oct. 2009.

42   *Le Petit Journal*, 8 Feb. 1879, 3; Juliette Adam, *Après l'abandon de la revanche* 7th edn (Paris: Lemerre, 1910), 309.

43   Gambetta to Juliette Adam, 7, 9 Apr. 1875, H&P nos. 239, 240.

44   Gambetta to Léon, 27 Feb. 1879, 79.25/111; 8 Mar. 1879, 79.28/111. A 'crush of the rue Quincampoix': this street became synonymous with pressing hordes when John Law established his bank there and hordes of speculators jostled to get in (1715–20). Cf. Jean Bertrand, *La République Française*, 10 Feb. 1879, 2; Émile Abraham, *Le Petit Journal*, 8 Feb. 1878.

45   See Chapter 7, below, and Bury 3: 136–7.

46   Gambetta to Léon, 17 June 1879, 79.59/111; 22 Jan. 1880, 80.5/67; 9 June 1880, 80.28/67. Cf. Émile Abraham, *Le Petit Journal*, 15 June 1879.

47   *Annales du Théâtre et de la Musique* (1880): 361–2; *New York Times*, 23 Oct. 1904; *Le Petit Journal*, 8 Feb. 1879.

48   Gambetta to Léon, 21 May 1880, 80.25/67. See S. Beynon John, 'Victorien Sardou', in *The New Oxford Companion to Literature in French*, ed. Peter France, (Oxford: Clarendon Press, 1997), 741; www.theatrepalaisroyal.com/historique-chapitre-6.html.

49   Gambetta to Léon, 17, 18 Dec. 1880, 80.61/67, 80.62/67. Cf. Charles Beaumont Wicks and Jerome W. Schweitzer, *The Parisian Stage: Part 4*

(1831–1850), (University of Alabama Press, 1961); *Annales du Théâtre et de la Musique* (1880): 43–50. Léon's letters for 1880 have not survived.

50 Gambetta to Léon, 5 May 1876, H&P no. 277. Cf. *Annales du Théâtre et de la Musique* (1876): 291–5; *La Petite République*, 8 May 1876.

51 Gambetta to Léon, 31 Mar. 1882, 82.25/73. Cf. 22 May 1879, 79.48/111; Léon to Gambetta, 22 May 1879, no. 322; *La République Française*, 26 Mar. 1882, 2.

52 Marie Van Zandt, an American, made her French debut at the Opéra-Comique on 18 Mar. 1880. Cf. *Annales du Théâtre et de la Musique* (1880): 217–18.

53 Gambetta to Léon, 30, 31 Mar. 1882, 82.24/73, 82.25/73.

54 Gambetta to Léon, 3 Apr. 1879, 79.38/111. Gambetta apparently likens the apotheosis of Ruy Blas in Act 5, when he momentarily recovers after having taken poison, to the recovery of Voltaire in February 1778, when he had been on the verge of death.

55 Gambetta to Léon, 4 Mar. 1880, 80.17/67. Cf. *Annales du Thêâtre et de la Musique* (1880): 289–93.

56 AD Hauts-de-Seine, 2 Mi 41, 'Scellés après le décès de M. Léon Gambetta, 1er janvier 1883'. Molière's plays comprise nearly half those listed in the company's classical repertoire for 1878. Cf. *Annales du Théâtre et de la Musique* (1878): 49–53, 106–8.

57 Gambetta to Léon, 15 Jan. 1878, H&P no. 352. Molière's plays were written in verse, like all works in the French classical tradition.

58 Cf. Wicks, *The Parisian Stage* 4: 91; Autrand, *Le Théâtre en France*, 119–21.

59 Léon to Gambetta, [undated], no. 261.

60 Émile Faguet, *Notes sur le théâtre contemporain*, 3 vols (Paris: H. Lecène and H. Oudin, 1891), 3: 217–28; Wolfgang Schivelbusch, *The Culture of Defeat: On National Trauma, Mourning, and Recovery*, trans. J. Chase (New York: Metropolitan Books, 2003), pp. 142–7.

61 Thomas Grimm, 'La Fille de Roland', *Le Petit Journal*, 17 Feb. 1875, 1. Cf. Autrand, *Le Théâtre en France*, 72–5, 119.

62 Juliette Adam, *Nos Amitiés politiques avant l'abandon de la revanche* (Paris: Lemerre, 1908), 242.

63 Léon to Gambetta, 16 Aug. 1876, no. 214. Cf. Grimm, 'La Fille de Roland', *Le Petit Journal*, 17 Feb. 1875.

64 *La République Française*, 10 Feb. 1879, 1–2. These were the views of the newly-appointed Under-Secretary of State for Public Education and Fine Arts, Edmond Turquet.

65 Csergo, 'Extension et mutation du loisir citadin', 136, 139; José Santos, 'Réalité et imaginaire des parcs at des jardins dans la deuxième moitié du XIXe siècle', *Nineteenth-Century French Studies* 31 (2003): 278–96.

66 ASP, police report, 19 Feb. 1874. Cf. Davidson, 'Making Society "Legible"', 265–96.

67 Gambetta to Léon, 8 Mar. 1882, 82.21/73.

68 Pinkney, *Napoleon III and the Rebuilding of Paris*, 95; cf. Csergo, 'Extension et mutation du loisir citadin', 139–40; Nicholas Green, *The Spectacle of Nature: Landscape and Bourgeois Culture in Nineteenth-Century France* (Manchester: Manchester University Press, 1990), 69.

69 Gambetta to Léon, 11 Nov. 1879, 79.93/111.

70   Gambetta to Léon, 13 July 1875, 75.28/47; 26 May 1879, 79.50/111; Léon to Gambetta, 16 July 1876, no. 198.
71   Gambetta to Léon, 30 Oct. 1874, 74.45/55. Cf. Gambetta to Léon, 18 Oct. 1875, 75.33/47; 18 Feb. 1878, 78.9/35; 22 May 1878, 78.16/35; 26 May 1879, 79.50/111; Léon to Gambetta, 5 Oct. 1876, no. 227; 1 Jan. 1879, no. 272.
72   Caroline Ford, 'Nature, Culture and Conservation in France and her Colonies, 1840–1940', *Past and Present* 183 (2004): 173–98.
73   Gambetta to Léon, 29 June 1875, 75.25/47; 12 July 1875, 75.27/47; 19 Aug. 1875, 75.31/47; 18 Apr. 1877, 77.10/70; 29 June 1879, 79.63/111.
74   Gambetta to Léon, 23 Mar. 1879, 79.34/111; 21 May 1879, 79.47/111. He also refers to solitary walks near Bourg-la-Reine and Ville-Evrard: 14 Apr. 1879, 79.42/111; 13 Nov. 1879, 79.94/111.
75   Gambetta to Léon, 13 Aug. 1876, 76.36/50.
76   Gambetta to Léon, 15 Aug. 1876, 76.37/50; Léon to Gambetta, 16, 22 Aug. 1876, nos. 214, 217.
77   Simon Schama, *Landscape and Memory* (New York: Alfred Knopf, 1995), 559.
78   Quoted in Ford, 'Nature, Culture and Conservation', 181. On Gambetta's appreciation of the Barbizon painters, see Chapter 6, below.
79   Gambetta to Léon, 15 Apr. 1877, 77.9/70. Cf. Schama, *Landscape and Memory*, 546–59; Ford, 'Nature, Culture and Conservation', 180–6; Green, *The Spectacle of Nature*, part 4, and 213, n. 107.
80   Schama, *Landscape and Memory*, 553–7; Green, *The Spectacle of Nature*, 170; Françoise Cachin, 'Le Paysage du Peintre', in *Les Lieux de Mémoire*, ed. Pierre Nora, 2: 'La Nation', part 2 (Paris: Gallimard, 1986), 435–86 (459).
81   See *Guide des sentiers de promenade dans le massif forestier de Fontainebleau*, 6th edn (Fontainebleau: L'Association des Amis de la Forêt de Fontainebleau, 2006), paths 6, 7 and 8; Schama, *Landscape and Memory*, 553–4, 556.
82   Gambetta to Léon, 1 Jan. 1874, 74.1/55.
83   Gambetta to Léon, 5 Sept. 1879, 79.85/111; Léon to Gambetta, 6 Sept. 1879, no. 364.
84   Gambetta to Léon, 24 Nov. 1879, 79.97/111; 25 Nov. 1880, 80.58/67; 4 Dec. 1880, 80.59/67; 24 Dec. 1881, 81.32/36. Cf. Christian Estève, 'Le droit de chasse en France de 1789 à 1914: conflits d'usage et impasses juridiques', *Histoire et Sociétés Rurales* 21 (2004): 73–114.
85   Gambetta to Léon, 15 Sept. 1880, 80.43/67.
86   Gambetta to Léon, 11 Aug. 1878, 78.26/35.
87   'Villégiature, villégiaturer', *Le Grand Robert de la Langue Française*, 2nd edn, 9 vols (Paris: Le Robert, 1986), 9: 747.
88   Cf. André Rauch, 'Les vacances et la nature revisitée (1830–1939)', in *L'Avènement des Loisirs*, 92–4; Green, *The Spectacle of Nature*, 84–9.
89   Gambetta to Léon, 20 July 1878, 78.25/35. Many years later, Gambetta's coachman dated their first visit to 1877, but this seems mistaken (document n° 17, in Pillias, 286).
90   Centre des Monuments Nationaux, 'Maison des Jardies à Sèvres', pdf downloaded 27 Feb. 2010 from maison-jardies.monuments-nationaux.fr/en/; Véronique Magnol-Malhache, with Patrick Chamouard and Denis Lavalle, *Léon Gambetta: Un Saint pour la République?* (Paris: Caisse nationale des monuments historiques et des sites, 1996), 32; 48 (n. 14, 15).

91 Gambetta to Léon, 10 Feb. 1882, 82.15/73; 28 July 1878, H&P no. 385.
92 Gambetta to Léon, 20 Aug. 1879, 79.82/111. Cf. 25 May 1879, 79.49/111; 23 Feb. 1880, 80.15/67; 19 Jan. 1881, 81.5/73; 11 May 1882, 82.29/73.
93 Alain Corbin, *The Foul and the Fragrant: Odor and the French Social Imagination* (Cambridge, MA: Harvard University Press, 1986), 189–95.
94 Gambetta to Léon, 27 Jan. 1880, H&P no. 431.
95 Léon to Gambetta, 18 Aug. 1876, no. 215.
96 Gambetta to Léon, 4 June 1880, 80.26/67. Cf. 24 Feb. 1881, 81.6/36.
97 Léon to Gambetta, 7 Apr. 1879, no. 309; Gambetta to Léon, 21 Aug. 1879, 79.83/111.

6 'We will proudly put our heads together in books'

1 Léon to Gambetta, [undated], no. 12.
2 Martyn Lyons, *Readers and Society in Nineteenth-Century France: Workers, Women, Peasants* (Basingstoke: Palgrave Macmillan, 2001), 1–2.
3 Adeline Daumard, *Les Bourgeois et la Bourgeoisie en France* (Paris: Aubier, 1987), 114–16; Alan Corbin, *Women for Hire: Prostitution and Sexuality in France after 1850*, trans. Alan Sheridan (Cambridge, MA; London: Harvard University Press, 1990), 135.
4 Léon to Gambetta, 20 Dec. 1873, no. 122.
5 *La Liseuse* [The Woman Reader] was a genre established since the eighteenth century: Renoir produced at least four paintings under this title.
6 Joseph Reinach, *La Vie politique de Léon Gambetta: suivie d'autres essais sur Gambetta* (Paris: Félix Alcan, 1918), 159–64.
7 Léon to Gambetta, 23 June 1879, no. 340; 10 Dec. 1881, no. 475; ASP, 2 EP 2, Dr 1, sdr b: 'Les domiciles de Léonie Léon'. These appear to be Pillias' notes from the inventory of her possessions at her death.
8 Léon to Gambetta, [undated], no. 12.
9 Léon to Gambetta, 15, 16 Apr. 1876, nos. 162, 163; [early 1880], no. 389.
10 Gambetta to Léon, 22 Mar. 1875, 75.16/47.
11 Léon to Gambetta, 10 Feb. 1881, no. 431; Gambetta to Arconati-Visconti, 18 Feb. 1881, H&P no. 465. Cf. Prosper Mérimée, *Lettres à M. Panizzi, 1850–1870*, ed. Louis Fagan (Paris: Calmann-Lévy, 1881).
12 André Chervel, *Les Auteurs français, latins et grecs, au programme de l'enseignement secondaire de 1800 à nos jours* (Paris: INPR/publications de la Sorbonne, 1986).
13 AD Hauts-de Seine, 2 Mi 41, 'Scellés après le décès de M. Léon Gambetta, 1er janvier 1883'. Cf. Reinach, *La Vie politique de Léon Gambetta,* 159–64.
14 E.g., Gambetta to Léon, 29 June 1876, 76.33/50; 22 Nov. 1876, 76.41/50; 16 Dec. 1876, 76.48/50; 12 Feb. 1877, 77.4/70; 14 Feb. 1879, 79.20/111.
15 *Gambetta et ses Amis,* ed. Émile Labarthe (Paris: Les Éditions des Presses Modernes, 1938), 159, 157.
16 *Abrégé de la mythologie à l'usage des pensionnats dirigés par les religieuses des sacrés-cœurs de Jésus et de Marie, dites de Louvencourt* (Amiens: Duval et Herment, 1847). Cf. Lyons, *Readers and Society,* 82.
17 Léon to Gambetta, 30 Sept. 1873, no. 87; 11 Mar. 1879, no. 296; 5 June 1879, no. 332.

18 Léon to Gambetta, 1 Nov. 1873, no. 101; 2 Apr. 1876, no. 306; Gambetta to Léon, 3 Apr. 1879, 79.38/111.
19 Léon to Gambetta, 'Friday' [1872], no. 1; [undated], no. 37; 16 Dec. 1873, no. 119; [undated], no. 138. Cf. *Réflexions ou sentences et maximes morales de La Rochefoucauld* (Paris: Lefèvre Librairie, 1827), 17, no. 5.
20 Cf. Ralph Albanese, *Molière à l'école républicaine: De la critique universitaire aux manuels scolaires (1870–1914)* (Saratoga CA: Anima Libri, 1992); *Corneille à l'école républicaine: du mythe héroïque à l'imaginaire politique en France, 1800– 1950* (Paris: l'Harmattan, 2008).
21 Gambetta to Léon, 21 Apr. 1876, 76.20/50; 22 Nov. 1876, 76.41/50.
22 Ludovic Halévy, *Trois Dîners avec Gambetta*, ed. Daniel Halévy (Paris: Bernard Grasset, 1929), 16–17; Gambetta to Léon, 2 Jan. 1874, 74.1/55.
23 Gambetta to Léon, 18 Apr. 1877, 77.10/70; 5 June 1877, H&P no. 244. Cf. 12 Nov. 1881, 81.21/36; 6 June 1882, 82.38/73.
24 Anne Martin-Fugier, *La Vie élégante ou la formation du Tout-Paris 1815–1848* (Paris: Fayard, 1990), 250–6.
25 Léon to Gambetta, 12 Nov. 1873, no. 105.
26 Léon to Gambetta, 16, 17 Dec. 1873, nos. 119, 120. See www.academie-francaise.fr/immortels/.
27 Gambetta to Léon, 1 May 1872, 72.1/18; Léon to Gambetta, [undated], no. 8.
28 Léon to Gambetta, 24 Sept. 1873, no. 85; 27 Oct. 1873, no. 99. Cf. [undated], no. 8; 4 Nov. 1873, no. 102; 12 Nov. 1873, no. 105.
29 Gambetta to Léon, 28 Oct. 1874, 74.44/55. Cf. 11 Feb. 1875, 75.8/47. Meetings of the Academy are held at the Institut de France, renowned for its beautiful dome.
30 See Joseph d'Haussonville, 'Réponse de M. d'Haussonville au discours de M. Alexandre Dumas', available at www.academie-francaise.fr/, accessed 1 June 2009; Gambetta to Léon, 11 Feb. 1875, 75.8/47.
31 Léon to Gambetta, 15 Sept. 1872, no. 24; 28 July 1879, no. 352. Cf. Gambetta to Léon, 27 July 1879, 79.74/111.
32 Gambetta to Hugo, 26 Feb. 1877, H&P no. 301. Cf. Suzanne Nash, 'La Légende des Siècles', in *The New Oxford Companion to Literature in French*, ed. Peter France, (Oxford: Clarendon Press, 1997), 451. On *Hernani*, see Gambetta to Léon, 21 Nov. 1877, 77.60/70, and Chapter 5, above.
33 'Scellés après le décès de M. Léon Gambetta'.
34 Léon to Gambetta, [undated], no. 32; 10 Dec. 1881, no. 475; 28 Feb. 1882, no. 489. Cf. Lyons, *Readers and Society*, 106, 110–11.
35 A. de Lamartine, 'Le Premier Regret', quoted in Léon to Gambetta, 9 Nov. 1881, no. 463. Cf. Léon to Gambetta, 8 Nov. 1881, no. 461; Gambetta to Léon, 8 Nov. 1881, 81.19/36. Gambetta discussed Lamartine at a dinner with Eugène Yung, editor of the *Revue politique et littéraire*, in February 1881 (Halévy, *Trois Dîners*, 15–16).
36 Léon to Gambetta, 12 Feb. 1881, no. 434.
37 Léon to Gambetta, 10, 14 Dec. 1879, nos. 377, 379; 30 Sept. 1873, no. 87; Gambetta to Léon, 19 Jan. 1880, 80.2/67. On Geneviève Allain-Targé's authorship, see the catalogue of the Bibliothèque nationale de France.
38 Léon to Gambetta, 30 June 1879, no. 343.
39 Léon to Gambetta, 14 Nov. 1873, no. 106; 4 Sept. 1879, no. 363; Léon to Marcellin Pellet, Jan. 1892, quoted in Pillias, 239.

40 Léon to Gambetta, 9, 10 Feb. 1881, nos. 429, 430. Cf. *Souvenirs de Mme C. Jaubert, lettres et correspondances: Berryer, 1847 et 1848, Alfred de Musset, Pierre Lanfrey, Henri Heine* (Paris: J. Hetzel, 1881).

41 Gambetta to Léon, 14 May 1877, 77.23/70. Cf. Marie d'Agoult, *Mes Souvenirs* (Paris: Calmann-Lévy, 1877).

42 See Peter France, 'Autobiography and memoirs', in *New Oxford Companion to Literature in French*, 54–5; Philippe Lejeune, *On Autobiography*, trans. Katherine Leary (Minneapolis: University of Minnesota Press, 1989).

43 Léon to Gambetta, 14 Nov. 1873, no. 106. Cf. *Les Enchantements de Prudence par Mme de Saman* [Hortense Allart], 2nd edn (Paris: Michel Lévy frères, 1873).

44 Cf. Lyons, *Readers and Society*, 81–91,116–22; James Smith Allen, *In the Public Eye: A History of Reading in Modern France, 1800–1940* (Princeton: Princeton University Press, 1991), 55; 128–30; Table A 10.

45 Gambetta to Léon, 25 Apr. 1876, 76.21/50; Léon to Gambetta, 16 Sept. 1876, no. 225; 5 July 1879, no. 344.

46 Gambetta to Juliette Adam, 18 Mar., 23 Nov. 1878, H&P nos. 366, 395; 7 Apr. 1875, H&P no. 239; Gambetta to E. Pelletan, 10 July 1876, H&P no. 281.

47 Léon to Gambetta, 17 Apr. 1876, no. 164. Cf. Lyons, *Readers and Society*, 82–91.

48 Léon to Gambetta, 5 Oct. 1876, no. 227; [undated], no. 264.

49 Gambetta to Léon, 20 Aug. 1876, 76.38/50; Léon to Gambetta, [undated], no. 389; 19 July 1879, no. 348; 30 Sept. 1879, no. 372; 2 Mar. 1881, no. 439. Cf. Lyons, *Readers and Society*, 108, 114–15.

50 'Scellés après le décès de M. Léon Gambetta'.

51 Léon to Gambetta, 21 Aug. [1873?], no. 71; cf. 3 Nov. 1876, no. 239.

52 Gambetta to Léon, 21 Sept. 1882, H&P no. 564. Cf. Léon to Gambetta, 21 Aug. [1873?], no. 71.

53 Léon to Gambetta, 24 July 1879, no. 350. This time she did not assume Gambetta's familiarity with the novel, identifying it in a PS to her letter.

54 Gambetta to Léon, 18 Feb. 1878, 78.9/35. It is not clear to which article Gambetta refers; Sand had died in 1876.

55 See David Baguley, 'Naturalism' and 'Zola, Emile', in *New Oxford Companion to Literature in French*, 558, 864–5; Chantal Pierre-Gnassounou, 'Zola and the art of fiction', in *The Cambridge Companion to Zola*, ed. Brian Nelson (Cambridge; New York: Cambridge University Press, 2007), 86–104.

56 Cf. Joseph Reinach, 'Les lectures de Gambetta', in *La Vie politique de Léon Gambetta*, 157–217; Cf. Michael Palmer, '*Journal des Débats*' and '*Revue des Deux Mondes*', in *New Oxford Companion to Literature in French*, 416, 696; *Histoire générale de la presse française*, ed. Claude Bellanger *et al.*, 5 vols (Paris: Presses Universitaires de France, 1969–1976), 3: *De 1871 à 1940* (1972), 208–10, 391.

57 E.g., Léon to Gambetta [undated], no. 5; 9 Mar. 1879, no. 295; 4 Sept. 1879, no. 363; 18 Dec. 1881, no. 478; Gambetta to Léon, 15 Jan. 1879, 79.7/111; 16 Dec. 1879, 79.102/111; 13 July 1880, 80.38/67.

58 Léon to Gambetta, 18 May 1879, no. 319 (cf. *Revue des Deux Mondes* 33, 1879); Léon to Gambetta, [early 1880], no. 389 (cf. *Revue des Deux Mondes* 38, 1880).

59 Léon to Gambetta, 18 Dec. 1881, no. 478 (cf. *Revue des Deux Mondes* 48, 1881). Cf. Léon to Gambetta, 9 Mar. 1879, no. 295; 30 Nov. 1881, no. 472;

Gambetta to Léon, 17 Dec. 1880, 80.61/67: 'I am sending you the *Revue des Deux Mondes* to help you sleep'.

60   Léon to Gambetta, 6 July 1876, no. 191. Cf. *Histoire générale de la presse française*, 3: 61–4, 137–9.

61   Léon to Gambetta, [undated], no. 62; 30 Sept. 1873, no. 87; Gambetta to Léon, 14 May 1875, 75.28/47 (*Le Premier Paris*); 9 June 1880, 80.28/67 (*Le Soleil*); 31 Oct. 1881, 81.18/36 (*Le Danube* and *Le Messager de Vienne*). Cf. Léon to Gambetta, 2 Nov. 1881, no. 458: 'The two Austrian papers were without interest'.

62   Léon to Gambetta, 17, 19 Sept. 1872, nos. 26, 27. Cf. *Histoire générale de la presse française*, 3: 220–2; Michael Palmer, '*Le Petit Journal*', in *New Oxford Companion to Literature in French*, 617.

63   Léon to Gambetta [undated], nos. 16, 35, 36; 20 Aug. 1879, no. 360.

64   Léon to Gambetta, 29 May 1876, no. 176. Cf. *Histoire générale de la presse française*, 3: 224.

65   Léon to Gambetta, 9 Dec. 1873, no. 118. Cf. 30 Sept. 1873, no. 87.

66   Léon to Gambetta, 29 Mar. 1879, no. 304 (*L'Association Catholique*); 15 Sept. 1872, no. 24 (*La Gazette de France*); Léon to Gambetta, 23 Nov. 1873, no. 112 (*Le Gaulois*). Cf. 12 Nov. 1873, no. 105. Léon also mentions *Le Constitutionnel* (30 June 1876, no. 189), *L'Estafette* (6 July 1876, no. 191), *Le Pays* (22 June 1879, no. 339).

67   Léon to Gambetta, 17, 19 Sept. 1872, nos. 26, 27 (*Le Petit Journal*); 12 Nov. 1873, no. 105 (*Le Gaulois*).

68   Léon to Gambetta, 18 Oct. 1876, no. 234. Cf. 4 Aug. 1876, no. 210; 8 Oct. 1876, no. 230; 8 Aug. 1879, no. 357. Cf. *Histoire générale de la presse française*, 3: 194–7. For an account of the purchase of the *hôtel*, see Chapter 3, above.

69   Miriam Levin, *Republican Art and Ideology in Late Nineteenth-Century France* (Ann Arbor, MI: UMI Research Press, 1986); Anthony Langdon, 'Barbizon School', in *The Oxford Companion to Western Art*, ed. Hugh Brigstocke (Oxford: Oxford University Press, 2001), 47. Cf. Susan Foley, '"A Great and Noble Painting": Léon Gambetta and the Visual Arts in the French Third Republic', in *French History and Civilization: Papers from the George Rudé Seminar* 4 (2011), ed. Briony Nelson and Robert Aldrich, available at www. h-france.net/rude/rudeindex.html, 106–17.

70   Alphonse Daudet, *Souvenirs d'un homme de lettres* (Paris: C. Marpon et E. Flammarion, 1888), 146–7.

71   Léon [Gambetta to an unknown woman], [1865?], in Reinach, *La Vie politique de Léon Gambetta*, 229–31. See 'Silvestre, Théophile', in *Dictionnaire critique des historiens de l'art actifs en France de la Révolution à la Première Guerre mondiale*, ed. Philippe Sénéchal and Claire Barbillon, 2009, at www.inha. fr/spip.php?article2544, pdf (6 pp) downloaded 19 Mar. 2011.

72   The terms were interchangeable at this time, though Zola's work later gave 'realism' more 'scientific' connotations. Cf. John Houre, 'Naturalism', and 'Realism', in *Oxford Companion to Western Art*, 510, 619.

73   Gambetta to Léon, 14 July 1874, 74.24/55. Cf. Bury 2: 165.

74   Gambetta to Juliette Adam, 7 Oct. 1874, H&P no. 217. Cf. Paulus Potter (1625–1754), 'The Bull', *c.*1647; Royal Picture Gallery, The Hague. www.mauritshuis.nl/index/, accessed 9 Mar. 2011.

75   Gambetta to Léon, 2–5 October 1874, H&P no. 214 and editors' note.

76 Ibid. Cf. 'Silvestre, Théophile', *Dictionnaire critique des historiens de l'art*, 3. On the Academy, see Patricia Mainardi, *The End of the Salon: Art and the State in the Early Third Republic* (Cambridge: Cambridge University Press, 1993).

77 See Steven Adams, *The Barbizon School and the Origins of Impressionism* (London: Phaidon Press, 1994); Jean Bouret, *The Barbizon School and Nineteenth-Century French Landscape Painting* (London: Thames and Hudson [1973]); Houre, 'Realism', *Oxford Companion to Western Art*, 619.

78 According to Halévy and Pillias, John W. Wilson purchased 'The Angelus' for his Brussels gallery in 1874 (H&P no. 214, editors' note). However, the provenance outlined by the Musée d'Orsay, where the painting is now held, contradicts that claim, asserting that the painting was in the Van Praët collection in Brussels from 1860 but entered the Paul Tesse collection in 1864 and the Emile Gavet collection in Paris in 1865; nor does the Musée d'Orsay list an exhibition in Brussels in 1874. There can be no doubt, however, that this was the painting Gambetta saw.

79 Jules Claretie cites Antonin Proust (art critic and later Gambetta's Minister for the Arts) on this point. See 'Léon Gambetta, amateur d'art', *Gazette des Beaux-Arts* 27 (1883): 123–6. Cf. Daudet, *Souvenirs*, 146.

80 Gambetta to Léon, 2–5 Oct. 1874, H&P no. 214; Léon Gambetta, 'Discours prononcés le 19 février 1871 à l'Assemblée Nationale . . . et le 26 juin 1871 . . . à Bordeaux', *Discours* 2: 1–35 (21–2).

81 Gambetta to Léon, 2–5 Oct. 1874, H&P no. 214. See Levin, *Republican Art and Ideology*, esp. Chapters 2 and 4.

82 Gambetta to Jules Breton, 2 May 1880, H&P no. 439.

83 The unnamed work may have been the portrait of Lady Helen Dashwood and her son, painted in 1784 and reproduced as an engraving by Samuel William Reynolds in 1833, in the National Portrait Gallery, London.

84 Gambetta to Léon [2–5 Oct. 1874], H&P no. 214.

85 Gambetta to Léon, 30 Apr. 1876, 76.23/50. Cf. Gambetta to Léon, 10 June 1876, 76.29/50: 'Make your arrangements so that we can go to the Salon on Tuesday morning'. Cf. Mainardi, *The End of the Salon*, 39–48, 63–4; Levin, *Republican Art and Ideology*, 116–17.

86 Léon to Gambetta, 2 June 1879, no. 329. Cf. *Paris Salon de 1879*, no. 165: Jules Bastien-Lepage, 'Portrait de Sarah Bernhardt,' in *Catalogues of the Paris Salon 1673–1881*, 60 vols (New York: Garland Publishing, 1977).

87 *Paris Salon de 1879*, no. 2530: Émile Renouf, 'Dernier radoub, mon pauvre ami [Last refit, my poor friend]', in *Catalogues of the Paris Salon*; Arthur Baignères, 'Le Salon de 1879', *Gazette des Beaux-Arts*, 2e période, 19 (1879): 42.

88 www.culture.gouv.fr/documentation/arcade/pres.htm. The painting is in the art gallery at Issoudun (Indre). Cf. Michael Adcock, 'Pictorial Politics and "Social Art": Representations of the Working Classes in French Art, 1848–89,' Ph.D. Thesis, University of Melbourne, 2000, 307–8, 319, 331.

89 Léon to Gambetta, 'Wednesday', no. 22; 'Wednesday', no. 46.

90 See Christian Lassalle, Patrick Favardin, and Odile A. Schmitz, *Hommage à Léon Gambetta* (Paris: Musée de Luxembourg, 1982), 152–6.

91 Philip Nord, *The Republican Moment: Struggles for Democracy in Nineteenth-Century France* (Cambridge, MA; London: Harvard University Press, 1995),

140; 170; Philip Nord, *Impressionists and Politics: Art and Democracy in the Nineteenth Century* (New York: Routledge, 2000), 65–6.

92   Gambetta to Léon, 6 Mar. 1882, 82.20/73; Nord, *The Republican Moment*, 164–5, 169; *Impressionists and Politics*, 65–6; Anne-Marie Martin-Fugier, *Les Salons de la Troisième République: Art, littérature, politique* (Paris: Perrin, 2003), 181–2.

93   Tanagra figurines originated in the Greek town of that name in the late fourth century BCE. They became popular in the 1860s and 1870s, and were admired particularly for their realism.

94   See 'L'Alsace: Elle Attend' at '1789–1939: L'Histoire par Image', www.histoire-image.org/index.php; Lasalle, Favardin, and Schmitz, *Hommage à Léon Gambetta*, no. 137, where the title is given as 'L'Alsacienne: Elle Attend'.

95   Lasalle, Favardin, and Schmitz, *Hommage à Léon Gambetta*, nos. 387; 378; 'Scellés après le décès de M. Léon Gambetta'; Bury 2: 333; Nord, *Impressionists and Politics*, 44.

96   Nord, *The Republican Moment*, 165.

97   Levin, *Republican Art and Ideology*, 20–1, 126, 161, 186, 231, n. 47; Nord, *Impressionists and politics*, 50, 63–4.

7   'This religion satisfies my soul'

1   Gambetta to Léon, 16 Jan. 1878, 78.3/35.

2   Blaise Pascal (1623–62), *Les Provinciales*, letters defending a Jansenist condemned for heresy in 1656.

3   'Discours sur les menées ultramontaines, prononcé le 4 mai 1877 à la Chambre des Députés', *Discours* 6: 284–362 (354).

4   See Chapter 1, above.

5   Ralph Gibson, *A Social History of French Catholicism, 1789–1914* (London; New York: Routledge, 1989), 165–7.

6   P.-B. Gheusi, *Gambetta par Gambetta: Lettres et souvenirs de famille* (Paris: Société d'Éditions littéraires et artistiques, 1909), 8–30.

7   Gambetta to Léon, 10 Feb. 1877, 77.3/70; 29 Feb. 1878, 78.10/35.

8   Gambetta to Léon, 9 July 1879, 79.68/111. Cf. Léon to Gambetta, 7 June 1879, no. 333.

9   Gambetta to Léon, 10 Nov. 1880, 80.54/67. Cf. Gambetta to Léon [env. dated 15 Aug. 1872], 72.8/18: 'I persist in believing that it is not a matter of indifference for us that we have the same name, the same patron saint.'

10   Gambetta to Léon, 20 [env. dated 31] Mar. 1879, 79.36/111; Léon to Gambetta, 30 Mar. 1879, no. 305. Was the lost 'ribbon of the order with its medal' perhaps a Miraculous Medal on a blue ribbon, worn by Children of Mary?

11   Gambetta to Léon, 27 Jan. 1877, 77.2/70; 9 Nov. 1881, H&P no. 496.

12   Gambetta to Léon, 30 [env. dated] Aug. 1876, 76.39/50; 14 Nov. 1881, 81.23/36; 22 Apr. 1875, H&P no. 242.

13   Gambetta to Léon, 29 July 1876, H&P no. 283.

14   Gambetta to Léon, 7 Jan. 1874, 74.3/55; 12 Feb. 1879, 79.18/111; Léon to Gambetta, [undated], no. 12.

15   Gambetta to Léon, 29 July 1882, 82.50/73; 2 July 1876, H&P no. 279; 23 Apr. 1878, H&P no. 375.

16 Gambetta to Léon, 8 Mar. 1882, 82.21/73.
17 Gambetta to Léon, 29 July 1876, H&P no. 283; 10 May 1877, 77.20/70; 9 Dec. 1881, H&P no. 509.
18 Gambetta to Léon, [env. dated 15 Aug. 1872], 72.8/18.
19 Léon to Gambetta, 30 Apr. 1893, no. 103; 5 Nov. 1873, no. 166.
20 Léon to Gambetta, 28 Apr. 1876, no. 165. Cf. Gambetta to Léon, 28 Apr. 1876, 76.22/50.
21 Léon to Gambetta, 16 Nov. 1873, no. 107. Mt Tabor is not named in the gospels but Christian tradition identifies it as the site of the Transfiguration.
22 Léon to Gambetta, [undated], no. 13.
23 Léon to Gambetta, 8 Mar. 1876, no. 153.
24 Quoted in Terence R. Wright, 'The letter and the spirit: Deconstructing Renan's Life of Jesus and the assumptions of modernity', Religion and Literature 26, 2 (1994): 55–71 (62, 65). Cf. Michael Kelly, 'Renan, Ernest', and 'Vie de Jésus', in The New Oxford Companion to Literature in French, ed. Peter France (Oxford: Clarendon Press, 1997), 682–3; 836; Charles Sowerwine, France since 1870: Culture, Society and the Making of the Republic, 2nd edn (Basingstoke: Palgrave Macmillan, 2009), 42.
25 'The Syllabus of Errors condemned by Pius IX', Papal Encyclicals Online, available at www.papalencyclicals.net/Pius09/p9syll.htm, accessed 29 Sept. 2010.
26 Jacques Gadille, La Pensée et l'action des évêques français au début de la Troisième République 1870–1883, 2 vols (Paris: Hachette, 1967), 1: 89, 94, 113, 134–6.
27 T. Tackett, 'Ultramontanism', BELIEVE religious information service, available at soft.com/believe/txc/ultramon.htmUltramontanism, accessed 10 Oct. 2010.
28 Gadille, La Pensée et l'action 1: 71.
29 Ralph Gibson, 'Why Republicans and Catholics Couldn't Stand Each Other in the Nineteenth Century', in Religion, Society and Politics in France Since 1789, ed. Frank Tallett and Nicholas Atkin (London; Rio Grande: The Hambledon Press, 1991), 115.
30 Gadille, La Pensée et l'action 2: 254, 267.
31 'Discours prononcé au banquet commemoratif de la défense de Saint-Quentin, le 16 novembre 1871', Discours 2: 160–89 (175–6); Gadille, La Pensée et l'action 2: 263.
32 Adrien Dansette, Religious History of Modern France, 1: From the French Revolution to the Third Republic (New York: Herder and Herder, 1961), 17–23; Gibson, Social History of French Catholicism, 236–46.
33 Grévy, La République, 141; Claude Langlois, 'Indicateurs du XIXe siècle: Pratique pascale et délais de baptême', in Histoire de la France religieuse, 3: Du roi très chrétien à la laïcité républicaine, ed. Philippe Joutard (Paris: Seuil, 1991), 235–46.
34 Léon to Gambetta, [undated], no. 264; Gambetta to Léon, 10 June 1879, 79.56/111.
35 Émile Poulat, 'Déchristianization du prolétariat ou dépérissement de la religion?' Le Mouvement social 57 (1966): 47–59; Sanford Elwitt, The Making of the Third Republic: Class and Politics in France, 1868–1884 (Baton Rouge: Louisiana State University Press, 1975), 141 ff; Sowerwine, France since 1870, 27.

36　Jules Michelet, *Le prêtre, la femme et la famille*, nouvelle éd. (Paris: Calmann-Lévy, 1890), 2.
37　*Histoire religieuse de la France 1800–1880*, ed. Gérard Cholvy and Yves-Marie Hilaire (Paris: Éditions Privat, 2000), 179–84; Gibson, *Social History of French Catholicism*, 184–6, 244.
38　'Discours prononcés les 9, 10, et 11 octobre 1878 à Grenoble', *Discours* 8: 253–84 (269–70).
39　Bury 3: 395.
40　'Discours sur les menées ultramontaines,' *Discours* 6: 354. Bury (2: 70) cites evidence that Gambetta was mistaken and that Peyrat had not actually said these words.
41　Gadille, *La Pensée et l'Action* 2: 91. As Jérôme Grévy has established, Gambetta was initiated in Marseille in 1869 for electoral reasons, but the Lodge was largely inactive and disappeared shortly afterwards. There is no record of his joining a Lodge in Paris (*La République*, 143–4) and no trace in the correspondence.
42　Gadille, *La Pensée et l'action* 2: 92–3.
43　'Discours prononcés les 17 et 18 septembre 1878 à Valence et à Romans', *Discours* 8: 216–52 (esp. 242–8).
44　Gambetta to Léon, 2 July 1876, H&P no. 279. Cf. Bury 2: 317.
45　Cf. Joseph Reinach, *La Vie politique de Léon Gambetta, suivie d'autres essais sur Gambetta* (Paris: Félix Alcan, 1918), 201–5: Reinach reproduces Gambetta's notes on Littrés summary of Comte's philosophy.
46　Quoted in Bury 2: 249.
47　'Discours prononcés à Albertville le 25 septembre 1872', *Discours* 3: 65–88 (72, 86).
48　'Discours prononcés les 17 et 18 septembre 1878 à Valence et à Romans', *Discours* 8: 244.
49　Gambetta to Léon, 3 Feb. 1882, 82.10/73; 28 Feb. 1882, H&P no. 528. Cf. 6 June 1882, 82.38/73. Renan's daughter claimed that 'relations were quite frequent – and very friendly' between her father and Gambetta (H&P no. 528, editors' note [a]).
50　*L'Écclésiaste: Traduit de l'Hébreu; Étude sur l'âge et le caractère du livre* [1882], in *Œuvres complètes de Ernest Renan*, ed. Henriette Psichari, 10 vols (Paris: Calmann Lévy, 1947–61), 7: 531–91 (541, 545).
51　Sylvie Aprile, 'Bourgeoise et républicaine, deux termes inconciliables?' in *Femmes dans la Cité 1815–1871*, ed. Alain Corbin, Jacqueline Lalouette and Michèle Riot-Sarcey, (Paris: Créaphis, [1997]), 211–23.
52　*Abrégé de la mythologie à l'usage des pensionnats dirigés par les religieuses des sacrés-cœurs de Jésus et de Marie, dites de Louvencourt* (Amiens: Duval et Herment, 1847), 7.
53　Quoted by James F. McMillan, 'Religion and Gender in Modern France: Some Reflexions', in *Religion, Society and Politics in France since 1789*, 55–66 (55).
54　*Ibid.*, 59–61.
55　Pillias, 86.
56　*La République Française*, 15 Aug. 1872, 1–2; Gambetta to Léon, 15 Aug. 1872, 72.8/18.
57　Gambetta to Léon, 4 July 1879, 79.65/111; 4 Aug. 1879, 79.77/111.

58 Mariette Portet, *Sèvres en Île-de-France* (Condet-sur-Noireau: Imp. C. Corlet, 1963), 187–8.
59 Léon to Gambetta, 1, 17 Mar. 1879, nos. 292, 298; Gambetta to Léon, 16 Mar. 1879, 79.31/111.
60 Léon to Gambetta, 10 July 1879, no. 346.
61 Léon to Gambetta, 19 July 1879, no. 348.
62 'Triduum des morts, prêché en église Saint-Augustin [Paris], par M. l'Abbé Codant . . . , 4, 5 et 6 novembre 1878', in *Octave des Morts: Instructions et sermons sur les vérités catholiques relatives au purgatoire et aux défunts, comprenant un triduum de M. l'Abbé Codant . . . une octave de M. l'Abbé Drouin . . . et quelques autres instructions sur le même sujet* (Paris: Martin et Audier, 1879), 9–26 (11).
63 Léon to Gambetta, 'Saturday' [1872], no. 2.
64 Gambetta to Léon, 20 May 1876, 76.27/50. Whether the 'Jeremiah' was Codant is unclear but Gambetta referred to him as a 'curé' (Gambetta to Agénor Bardoux, 25 July 1878, H&P no. 384) as did Léon (Léon to Gambetta, 19 July 1879, no. 348).
65 Gambetta to Léon, 30 Jan. 1878, 78.5/35.
66 Gadille, *La Pensée et l'Action* 2: 119.
67 'Discours prononcé au banquet commémoratif de la défense de Saint-Quentin, le 16 novembre 1871', *Discours* 2: 179–80.
68 'Discours sur les menées ultramontaines,' *Discours* 6: 350–1.
69 Bury 2: 397.
70 Gambetta to Léon, 24 Apr. 1877, 77.13/70; 3 May 1877, 77.17/70.
71 'Discours sur les menées ultramontaines', *Discours* 6: 333, 334, 337, 361.
72 Gadille, *La Pensée et l'action* 2: 65; Jacques Chastenet, *Gambetta* (Paris: Fayard, 1968), 263. On the crisis of 16 May, see Chapter 4, above.
73 Gambetta to Léon, 20 May 1877, 77.26/70.
74 Gadille, *La Pensée et l'action* 2: 41, 45–77.
75 Gambetta to Léon, 20 May 1877, 77.26/70; 15 Oct. 1877, 77.50/70.
76 Gambetta to Léon, 16 Jan. 1878, 78.3/35.
77 Gambetta to Léon, 20 Feb. 1878, H&P no. 357.
78 On the Concordat and the Organic Articles that governed Church–State relations until 1905, see Dansette, *Religious History* 1: 117–37; Claude Langlois, 'Politique et religion', in *Histoire de la France religieuse* 3: 108–16.
79 Gadille, *La Pensée et l'Action* 2: 40–1, 132.
80 Gambetta to Léon, 27! [sic] Mar. 1878, 78.12/35. The exclamation mark alluded to their anniversary (27 April); they often celebrated dates ending in 7.
81 Gambetta to Léon, 27! [sic] Mar. 1878, 78.12/35; 20 May 1878, 78.15/35; 2 June 1878, 78.20/35; 23 Apr. 1878, H&P no. 375; Gambetta to Agénor Bardoux, 7, 22 May 1878, H&P nos. 380, 381. Cf. Gadille, *La Pensée et l'Action* 2: 41–2.
82 Gadille, *La Pensée et l'Action* 1: 184.
83 Léon to Gambetta, 29 Nov. 1876, no. 246.
84 Gambetta to Bardoux, 25 July 1878, H&P no. 384. Cf. Gambetta to Léon, 7 Nov. 1878, 78.31/35.
85 Gambetta to Léon, 20, 24, 30 July 1879, 79.71/111, 79.73/111, 79.76/111; Léon to Gambetta, 31 July 1879, no. 353.
86 Gambetta to Léon, 27! [sic], 28 July 1879, 79.74/111, 79.75/111.

87   Jean-Marie Mayeur, *Léon Gambetta: La patrie et la République* (Paris: Fayard, 2008), 311–12. See Chapter 9, below.
88   Dansette, *Religious History of Modern France* 2: 40–53.
89   In 1905, when the Separation of Church and State was decreed and unauthorized religious orders disbanded, the Dominican convent at Sèvres closed and the sisters moved to Belgium (Portet, *Sèvres en Île-de-France*, 178).
90   Léon to Gambetta, 22 Dec. 1881, no. 479.
91   Gambetta to Léon, 29 Oct. 1880, 5.30 a.m., 80.53/67.
92   Gambetta to Léon, 31 Dec. 1882 [*sic,* for 1881], 82.74/73.
93   Gérard Cholvy, *Christianisme et société en France au XIXe siècle, 1790–1914,* 2nd edn (Paris: Seuil, 2001), 32.

8   'What glory, to have created a new France'

1   Léon to Gambetta, 6 Jan. 1879, no. 274.
2   In June 1876, 120 of 363 republican Deputies signed up to Gambetta's Republican Union. See Grévy, *La République*, 226–31. On the republican majority, see Bury 2: 435.
3   Gambetta to Léon, 1 Feb. 1878, 78.6/35. Rouher hailed from the Auvergne region of France. Cf. 'Discours sur l'élection de l'arrondissement de Loudéac (Côtes-du-Nord), prononcé le 1er février 1878 à la Chambre des Députés', *Discours* 8: 58–98 (esp. 83, 95).
4   On Gambetta's foreign policy and international links, see Bury 2: 328–55.
5   E.g., Gambetta to Juliette Adam, 15 Nov. 1874, H&P no. 221; 5 Oct. 1875, H&P no. 251; 27 Jan. 1877, H&P no. 300.
6   Gambetta to Léon, 1, 16 Jan. 1878, 78.1/35, 78.3/35; 20 Feb. 1878, H&P no. 357.
7   Gambetta to Léon, 20 Feb. 1878, H&P no. 357; Bismarck quoted in Jean-Marie Mayeur, *Léon Gambetta: La patrie et la République* (Paris: Fayard, 2008), 506, n. 33.
8   Gambetta to Léon, 21, 23 Feb. 1878, H&P nos. 358, 359. Léon's letter has disappeared.
9   Gambetta to Léon, 19 Aug. 1875, 75.31/47.
10 Gambetta to Léon, 30 Apr. [env. dated 1 Apr.] 1876, 76.17/50; 19 Apr. 1876, 76.19/50; Léon to Gambetta, 5, 16 June 1876, nos. 178, 184.
11 Gambetta to Juliette Adam, 27 Jan. 1877, H&P no. 300.
12 Pillias, 93–103. His argument was based on research in Germany as well as in France.
13 Gambetta to Léon, 1 Mar. 1878, 78.11/35.
14 Gambetta to Léon, 2, 6, 11 Mar. 1878, H&P nos. 361, 362, 364.
15 Bury 3: 48–9; Mayeur, *Léon Gambetta*, 300–2.
16 Gambetta to Léon, 23 Feb. 1878, H&P no. 359.
17 Gambetta to Léon, 23 Apr. 1878, H&P no. 375; Gambetta to Comte Henckel de Donnersmarck, 22, 24 Apr. 1878, H&P nos. 374, 376. Cf. Pillias, 108–12; Bury 3: 49–50.
18 Léon to Gambetta, 23 Mar. 1879, no. 302.
19 This is the main purpose of Juliette Adam's polemical memoir, *Après l'abandon de la revanche*, 7th edn (Paris: Lemerre, 1910).

20 Bury 3: 56–9. Bury's analysis is based on German diplomatic correspondence and the memoirs of Henri de Blowitz, Paris correspondent for *The Times*. Cf. Mayeur, *Léon Gambetta*, 299–300.

21 Gambetta to Léon, 20 [env. dated 31] Mar. 1879, 79.36/111.

22 Léon to Gambetta, 24 Mar. 1877, no. 258.

23 Adam, *Après l'abandon de la revanche*, 55–65; Bury 2: 425, n. 2.

24 Gambetta to Léon, 23 Dec. 1877, 77.68/70.

25 Goncourt Journals, 19 Jan. 1877, quoted in Anne Martin-Fugier, *Les Salons de la Troisième République: Art, littérature, politique* (Paris: Perrin, 2003), 55.

26 Carlo Bronne, *La Marquise Arconati: Dernière Châtelaine de Gaasbeek* (Brussels: Tervuren, 1970), 60–9; Martin-Fugier, *Les Salons de la Troisième République*, 69–70, 235–6.

27 Cf. Michael Burns, *Dreyfus: A Family Affair, 1789–1945* (New York: Harper Collins, 1991), 317; Martin-Fugier, *Les Salons de la Troisième République*, 55. On Arconati-Visconti's protests, see Ruth Harris, 'Two *Salonnières* during the Dreyfus Affair: The Marquise Arconati-Visconti and Gyp', in *Confronting Modernity in Fin-De-Siècle France: Bodies, Minds and Gender*, ed. Christopher Forth and Elinor Accampo (Basingstoke: Palgrave Macmillan, 2009), 240.

28 Gambetta to Arconati-Visconti, 13, 21, 28 Sept. 1877, H&P nos. 336, 338, 341; [undated], nos. 572, 573.

29 Gambetta to Arconati-Visconti, 18 July 1879, H&P no. 418; 15 Feb., 15 Mar. 1880, nos. 432, 433; 19 Feb., 17 May 1881, nos. 465, 476; [undated], nos. 577, 578, 579.

30 Gambetta to Arconati-Visconti, 13, 21 Sept. 1877, H&P nos. 336, 338; 17 Jan., 1 Apr. 1878, nos. 355, 370. Cf. Bronne, *La Marquise Arconati*, 91.

31 Bury 3: 89, n. 17.

32 Bury 3: 56 n. 3, 185, 308.

33 Gambetta to Juliette Adam, 18 Oct. 1878, H&P no. 389; Adam, *Après l'abandon de la revanche*, 244–5; Pillias, 291.

34 Léon to Gambetta, 18 Oct. 1879, no. 373.

35 Gambetta à Mme Arnaud de l'Ariège, 18, 22 Aug., 25 Sept., 3 Oct. 1882, AD Hauts-de-Seine, 1 J 207; Mayeur, *Léon Gambetta*, 306.

36 Letter of Mme ***, 25 Aug. 1878, quoted in Pillias, 291. Pillias saw the original but kept the writer's identity secret. There is no record of subsequent sightings of the letter.

37 Adam, *Après l'abandon de la revanche*, 98. Many historians accept the story but give no sources: Jacques Chastenet, *Gambetta* (Paris: Fayard, 1968), 286; Martin-Fugier, *Les Salons de la IIIe République*, 55; Daniel Amson, *Gambetta, ou, le rêve brisé* (Paris: Tallandier, 1994), 143, 338; Jacques Silvestre de Sacy, *Le Maréchal de MacMahon, Duc de Magenta, 1808–1893* (Paris: Éditions internationales, 1960), 346; Bury 2: 425.

38 Chastenet, *Gambetta*, 286.

39 Bury 2: 425 and n. 2; Saad Morcos, *Juliette Adam* (Beirut: Dar al-Maaref-Liban, 1962), 83; Marie-Thérèse Guichard, *Les Égéries de la République* (Paris: Éditions Payot, 1991), 45.

40 Cf. Bury 3: 43; Adam, *Après l'abandon de la revanche*, 183/185, 244–6; Morcos, *Juliette Adam*, 118–19, 398 n. 172.

41   Gambetta to Adam, 7 Nov. 1876, 17 Jan. 1877, 23 Nov. 1878, H&P nos. 291, 298, 395; Juliette Adam, *Nos amitiés politiques avant l'abandon de la revanche* (Paris: Lemerre, 1908), 310.

42   BnF, Naf 12608, 'Mémoires de Scheurer-Kestner', 1878–1882: 1878, 85.

43   Gambetta to Léon, 8 Feb. 1878, 78.8/35; 26 Apr. 1878, 78.13/35; 28 July 1878, H&P no. 385.

44   Gambetta to Léon, 11 Aug. 1878, 78.26/35; 22 May 1878, 78.16/35; Pillias, 90–1, 137–8. Cf. Veronique Magnol-Malhache, with Patrick Chamouard and Denis Lavalle, *Léon Gambetta: Un Saint pour la République?* (Paris: Caisse nationale des monuments historiques et des sites, 1996) 26, 47 n. 2; O. A. Schmitz, 'Les Jardies', in Christian Lasalle, Patrick Favardin, and Odile A. Schmitz, *Hommage à Léon Gambetta* (Paris: Musée de Luxembourg, 1982), 111.

45   'Discours prononcé le 24 mai 1878 au banquet du Cercle National', *Discours* 8: 151–61. Cf. Charles Sowerwine, *France since 1870: Culture, Society and the Making of the Republic*, 2nd edn. (Basingstoke: Palgrave Macmillan, 2009), 31–2.

46   Gambetta to Léon, 24 May 1878, 78.17/35.

47   Steven C. Hause, *Hubertine Auclert: The French Suffragette* (New Haven, CT: Yale University Press, 1987), 42–4.

48   'Discours prononcés les 17 et 18 septembre 1878 à Valence et à Romans', *Discours* 8: 217–53.

49   Gambetta to Léon, 29 Sept. 1878, 78.28/35.

50   Toby Gelfand, 'Neurologist or Psychiatrist? The public and private domains of Jean-Martin Charcot', *Journal of the History of the Behavioural Sciences* 36, 3 (2000): 215–29; Mark S. Micale, 'The Salpêtrière in the Age of Charcot: An Institutional Perspective on Medical History in the Late Nineteenth Century, *Journal of Contemporary History* 20 (1985): 703–31 (709–10).

51   Gambetta to Léon, 1 Nov. 1877, 77.52/70; 29 Sept. 1878, 78.28/35; Léon to Gambetta, 30 Oct. 1879, 375.

52   Gambetta to Léon, 1 Oct. 1878, 78.29/35; 'Discours prononcés les 9, 10 et 11 octobre 1878 à Grenoble', *Discours* 8: 253–85; Bury 3: 93–4.

53   'Discours prononcés les 17 et 18 septembre 1878 à Valence et à Romans', *Discours* 8: 223. Cf. Mayeur, *Léon Gambetta*, 282.

54   Gambetta to Léon, 7, 25 Nov. 1878, 78.31/35, 78.34/45.

55   See *Dictionnaire des Ministres de 1789 à 1989*, ed. Benoît Yvert (Paris: Perrin, 1990), 461–2.

56   See Robert A. Nye, *Masculinity and Male Codes of Honor in Modern France* (New York; Oxford: Oxford University Press, 1993); Susan Foley and Charles Sowerwine, 'Rousing, Dominating, Persuading: Léon Gambetta and the Construction of Male Democracy in France, 1868–1882', 'Oratory and Democracy' Seminar, University of Melbourne, 2009.

57   Gambetta to Léon, 20, 21 Nov. 1878, H&P nos. 393, 394.

58   Police reports cited in Bury 3: 96, n. 40.

59   'Discours prononcés les 9, 10 et 11 octobre 1878 à Grenoble', *Discours* 8: 263, 272–3. On the electoral system for the Senate, see Sowerwine, *France since 1870*, 29; Bury 3: 91–2, 100.

60   Léon to Gambetta, 5, 6 Jan. 1879, nos. 273, 274; Gambetta to Léon, 6 Jan. 1879, 79.1/111.

61   Gambetta to Léon, 11 Jan. 1879, 79.4/111.

62 *Ibid.*
63 Gambetta to Léon, 13 Jan. 1879, H&P no. 399; 14, 15, 17 Jan. 1879, 79.6/111, 79.7/111, 79.8/111; Léon to Gambetta, 13, 16 Jan. 1879, nos. 276, 277. See Bury 3: 11–12.
64 Léon to Gambetta, 18, 19 Jan. 1879, nos. 278, 279; Gambetta to Léon, 19 Jan. 1879, 79.9/111.
65 Gambetta to Léon, 19 Jan. 1879, 79.9/111; Léon to Gambetta, 20 Jan. 1879, no. 280.
66 Gambetta to Léon, 20 Jan. 1879, 79.10/111; Grévy, *La République*, 238.
67 Gambetta to Léon, 20 Jan. 1879, 79.10/111; Bury 3: 108–11.
68 Léon to Gambetta, 21 Jan. 1879, no. 281.
69 Léon to Gambetta, 29 Jan. 1879, no. 284. The telegram has not survived.
70 Gambetta to Léon, 30 Jan. 1879, 79.13/111; Léon to Gambetta, 31 Jan. 1879, no. 285. Grévy was President of the Chamber before being elected President of the Republic.
71 Gambetta to Léon, 31 Jan. 1879, 79.14/111.
72 Both cited in Bury 3: 120–1.
73 Léon to Gambetta, 3 Feb. 1879, no. 287.
74 Pierre Barral, *Léon Gambetta: Tribun et stratège de la République, 1838–1882* (Toulouse: Privat, 2008), 198.
75 Grévy emphasizes Gambetta's choice (*La République*, 266); Barral emphasizes Grévy's persuasion (*Léon Gambetta*, 199); Mayeur (*Léon Gambetta*, 284) and Bury (3: 120–2) are both sceptical that this was the outcome Gambetta desired.
76 Gambetta to Léon, 9 Feb. 1879, 79.17/111.

9 'Triumphant, and full of regrets'

1 Gambetta to Léon, 8 Mar. 1879, 79.28/111.
2 The title 'Prime Minister' only came into use during the Fifth Republic. During the Third Republic the equivalent position was 'President of the Council of Ministers'.
3 Gambetta to Léon, 7 Feb. 1879, 79.16/111. Cf. Bury 3: 125–6.
4 Gambetta to Léon, 13, 14 Feb. 1879, 79.19/111, 79.20/111. Gambetta quotes or paraphrases Léon's missing letters.
5 Gambetta to Léon, 14, 16 Feb. 1879, 79.20/111, 79.21/111; Léon to Gambetta, 17 Feb. 1879, no. 288.
6 Gambetta to Léon, 12, 25 Feb. 1879, 79.18/111, 79.24/111.
7 Léon to Gambetta, 19, 20 Feb. 1879, nos. 289, 290; Gambetta to Léon, 20 Feb. 1879, 79.23/111.
8 'Discours prononcé le 16 février 1879 en réponse à une députation du XXe arrondissement au Palais Bourbon', *Discours* 9: 6–11.
9 Gambetta to Léon, 22 Mar. 1879, 79.33/111; Léon to Gambetta, 23 Mar. 1879, no. 302.
10 Gambetta to Léon, 14 [env. dated 10] June 1879, 79.56/111.
11 Léon to Gambetta, 10, 15 June 1879, nos. 334, 335; Gambetta to Léon, 15 June 1879, 79.57/111.
12 Léon to Gambetta, 8 July 1879, no. 345.

13   'Fête de la Présidence de la Chambre des Députés', *La République Française*, 16 July 1879.
14   APP, B/a 922: 1878–1880: [report by agent] 'Howe', 9 July 1879.
15   Gambetta to Léon, 6 July 1879, 79.66/111.
16   Gambetta to Léon, 9 July 1879, 79.68/111.
17   Gambetta to Léon, 20, 21 June 1879, 79.60/111, 79.61/111; Léon to Gambetta, 21 June 1879, no. 338. Cf. Bury 3: 136–8.
18   Gambetta to Léon, 16, 17 June 1879, 79.58/111, 79.59/111.
19   Léon to Gambetta, 1, 9 Jan. 1879, nos. 272, 275; Gambetta to Léon, 9 Jan. 1879, 79.3/111.
20   Léon to Gambetta, 20 Mar. 1879, no. 300; Gambetta to Léon, 20, 22 Mar. 1879, 79.32/111, 79.33/111.
21   Léon to Gambetta, 23 Mar. 1879, no. 302; Gambetta to Léon, 23 Mar. 1879, 79.34/111.
22   Gambetta to Léon, 11 Apr. 1879, 79.40/111.
23   Gambetta to Léon, 29 May 1879, 79.51/111; 1 June 1879, 79.53/111; Léon to Gambetta, 1 June 1879, no. 326.
24   Gambetta to Léon, 20, 21 July 1879, 79.71/111, 79.72/111; 12 Aug. 1879, 79.80/111; Léon to Gambetta, 31 July 1879, no. 353.
25   Gambetta to Léon, 30 July 1879, 79.76/111; 4 Aug. 1879, 79.77/111; ASP, 2 EP 1, Dr 5, sdr d: 'Alphonse Léon'; Pillias, 151.
26   Gambetta to Léon, 1, 8 Mar. 1879, 79.26/111, 79.28/111.
27   Léon to Gambetta, 9, 20 Mar. 1879, nos. 295, 300.
28   Léon to Gambetta, 20 Apr. 1879, no. 314; 29 May 1879, no. 326.
29   Léon to Gambetta, 20 Apr. 1879, no. 314; Gambetta to Léon, 20 Apr. 1879, 79.44/111.
30   Gambetta to Léon, 4 Aug. 1879, 79.77/111.
31   Gambetta to Léon, 22 Feb. 1879, H&P no. 405. There is no evidence to support the editors' view (n. [a]) that the 'wound' was caused by Gambetta's refusal to marry Léon.
32   Léon to Gambetta, 2 Apr. 1879, no. 306; Gambetta to Léon, 3 Apr. 1879, 79.38/111. Cf. J.-J. Rousseau, *La nouvelle Héloïse*, ed. Daniel Mornet, 4 vols (Paris: Hachette, 1925), letter 30.
33   Gambetta to Léon, 12 Aug. 1879, 79.80/111. Cf. 19 Feb. 1879, 79.22/111; 16 Mar. 1879, 79.31/111; 30 July 1879, 79.76/111.
34   Gambetta to Léon, 15, 20, 21 Aug. 1879, 79.81/111, 79.82/111, 79.83/111.
35   Léon to Gambetta, 12 Aug. 1879, no. 358.
36   Gambetta to Léon, 14 Oct. 1879, 79.89/111. Cf. 11 Oct. 1879, 79.88/111.
37   Léon to Gambetta, 16 Oct. 1879, no. 373.
38   Léon to Gambetta, 27 Oct. 1879, no. 374.
39   Gambetta to Léon, 12, 27 Dec. 1879, 79.101/111, 79.105/111; Pillias, 151.
40   Léon to Gambetta, 23 Dec. 1879, no. 383; Gambetta to Léon, 19 Jan. 1880, 80.2/67.
41   Gambetta to Léon, 10 Nov. 1879, H&P no. 299; 13 Nov. 1879, 79.94/111.
42   Gambetta to Léon, 1 Mar. 1879, 79.26/111; Léon to Gambetta, 2 Mar. 1879, no. 293.
43   Léon to Gambetta, 21 Apr. 1879, no. 315; Gambetta to Léon, 20, 21 Apr. 1879, 79.44/111, 79.45/111; 29 June 1879, 79.63/111; 4 July 1879,

79.65/111; Léon to Gambetta, 28 June 1879, no. 341. Waddington was born in England and his wife was American.
44 Gambetta to Léon, 5 Sept. 1879, 79.85/111; Léon to Gambetta, 6 Sept. 1879, no. 364.
45 Gambetta to Léon, 29 Nov. 1879, 79.98/111; 5, 9 Dec. 1879, 79.99/111, 79.100/111; Léon to Gambetta, 6, 11 Dec. 1879, nos. 376, 378.
46 Gambetta to Léon, 16, 23 Dec. 1879, 79.102/111, 79.106/111; Léon to Gambetta, 18 Dec. 1879, no. 381. Cf. Bury 3: 148.
47 Léon to Gambetta, 23, 24 Dec. 1879, nos. 383, 384: Gambetta to Léon, 26, 27 Dec. 1879, 79.104/111, 79.105/111.
48 Léon to Gambetta, 27 Dec. 1879, no. 385.
49 Léon to Gambetta, 24 Jan. 1880, no. 387; Gambetta to Léon, 27 Jan. 1880, H&P no. 431.
50 Gambetta to Léon, 20 Mar. 1880, 80.20/59; 4 June 1880, 80.26/67; 23 Oct. 1880, 80.50/67.
51 E.g., Gambetta to Léon, 15 Feb. 1880, 80.13/67; 13 Mar. 1880, 80.18/67; 14 May, 26 June 1880, 80.35/67.
52 Gambetta to Léon, 13 Mar. 1880, 80.18/67. Cf. 8 June 1880, 80.27/67; 4 Dec. 1880, 80.59/67.
53 Louis Andrieux, *Souvenirs d'un Préfet de Police*, 2 vols (Paris: J. Rouff, 1885), 1: 263–73. No trace of the original notes exists at the Archives de la Préfecture de Police, but there was almost certainly a secret dossier on Gambetta, which Andrieux may have taken with him on retiring (*Souvenirs*, 27–31).
54 Pillias, 287–8, doc. no. 17. The coachman's memoir is barely literate; we have adjusted the grammar in our translation.
55 Andrieux, *Souvenirs d'un Préfet de Police*, 1: 267, 1 July 1880.
56 Gambetta to Léon, 22 Jan. 1880, 80.5/67.
57 Gambetta to Léon, 26 Jan. 1880, 80.7/67; 14 May 1880, 80.24/67. See Chapter 6, above.
58 Bury 3: 150–2, 158–65.
59 Gambetta to Léon, [undated], 81.34/36. This letter is catalogued under 1881, but its contents put the date at 21 June 1880. Cf. Bury 3: 164–7.
60 Gambetta to Léon, 25 June 1880, 80.34/67; 3, 9 July 1880, 80.36/67, 80.37/67.
61 Bury 3: 162, 176–83.
62 Bury 3: 183, 229; Grévy, *La République*, 273.
63 Gambetta to Léon, 10 Nov. 1880, 80.54/67. Cambyses II ruled the Persian Empire in the sixth century BCE. That 'Cambyses' was Grévy is evident in Gambetta to Léon, 29 July 1882, 82.51/73. The nickname may reflect Herodotus' claim that Cambyses was mad. Cf. 'Cambyses II', *Encyclopœdia Britannica*.
64 Léon to Gambetta, 26, 28 Jan. 1881, nos. 424, 426. Cf. *Histoire générale de la presse française*, ed. Claude Bellanger *et al.*, 5 vols (Paris: Presses Universitaires de France, 1969–1976), 3: *De 1871 à 1940* (1972), 7–22.
65 Léon to Gambetta, 11, 13 Jan. 1881, nos. 418. 419.
66 Pierre Barral, *Léon Gambetta: Tribun et stratège de la République, 1838–1882* (Toulouse: Privat, 2008), 209.
67 Gambetta to Léon, 17 Mar. 1881, H&P no. 468. Cf. Bury 3: 231–3.
68 Gambetta to Léon, 19 Mar. 1881, 81.8/36; Léon to Gambetta, 31 May 1881, no. 444.

69 Gambetta to Léon, 3 Aug. 1881, H&P no. 483; Léon to Gambetta, 11 Nov. 1881, no. 464.
70 Gambetta to Léon, 22 Aug. 1881, 81.15/36; Léon to Gambetta, 22 Aug. 1881, no. 454. Cf. Chastenet 1: 378–81; Barral, *Léon Gambetta*, 217–20.
71 Gambetta to Léon, 1 Jan. 1881, 81.1/36.
72 *Ibid.*
73 *Ibid.*
74 Pillias, 152–3.
75 Gambetta to Léon, 13 Feb. 1881, H&P no. 464.
76 Gambetta to Léon, 4, 11, 24 Feb. 1881, 81.3/36, 81.4/36, 81.6/36; 19 Apr., 1881, 81.10/36; 22 Aug. 1881, 81.15/36; Léon to Gambetta, 11 Feb. 1881, no. 433.
77 Gambetta to Léon, 11, 15 Feb. 1881, 81.4/36, 81.5/36; Léon to Gambetta, 17 Feb. 1881, no. 435.
78 Léon to Gambetta, 10 Feb. 1881 (two letters), nos. 431, 432; Gambetta to Léon, 4 Mar. 1881, 81.7/36.
79 Léon to Gambetta, 12 Feb. 1881, no. 434.
80 Léon to Gambetta, 5 Mar. 1881, no. 440; 8 June 1881, no. 445; 30 Nov. 1881, no. 472.
81 Gambetta to Léon, 25 Oct. 1881, 81.16/36.
82 Chastenet 1: 383–92.
83 Gambetta to Léon, 8 Nov. 1881, 81.19/36 (emphasis original).
84 Léon to Gambetta, 9 Nov. 1881, no. 463.
85 Gambetta to Léon, 9 Nov. 1881, 81.20/36.
86 *Ibid.*

10 'Poor France, I had other dreams'

1 Gambetta to Léon, 28 May 1882, 82.36/73.
2 Jules Husson Champfleury, *Les Bourgeois de Molinchart* (1855), was a well-known novel sending up the provincial bourgeoisie.
3 The 1870 battle in which the Prussians defeated the French.
4 Gambetta links two well-known phrases from Claude Perrault's *Bluebeard*.
5 Chastenet 1: 394.
6 Gambetta to Léon, 12 Nov. 1881, 81.21/36.
7 Léon to Gambetta [undated, late 1881], no. 404. Cf. Grévy, *La République*, 276; Pierre Antonmattei, *Léon Gambetta: Héraut de la République* (Paris: Michalon, 1999), 372–6; Chastenet 1: 394.
8 Léon to Gambetta, 12 Nov. 1881, no. 466.
9 Gambetta to Léon, 14 Nov. 1881, 81.23/36.
10 Grévy, *La République*, 276–7. Cf. *Dictionnaire des Ministres de 1789 à 1989*, ed. Benoît Yvert (Paris: Perrin, 1990).
11 Gambetta to Léon, 30 Apr. 1876, 76.23/50; Pierre Barral, *Léon Gambetta: Tribun et stratège de la République, 1838–1882* (Toulouse: Privat, 2008), 238; Jean-Marie Mayeur, *Léon Gambetta: La patrie et la République* (Paris: Fayard, 2008), 375–7.
12 Gambetta to Léon, 14 Nov. 1881, 81.23/36.
13 Gambetta to Léon, 16 Nov. 1881, 81.24/36; Léon to Gambetta, 16 Nov. 1881, no. 468.

14 Léon to Gambetta, 21 Nov. 1881, no. 469.
15 Gambetta to Léon, 24 Nov. 1881, 81.26/36; 29 Nov. 1881, H&P no. 505. Cf. Grévy, *La République*, 227–9.
16 Léon to Gambetta, 10 Dec. 1881, no. 475; Gambetta to Léon, 11 Dec. 1881, H&P no. 510.
17 Léon to Gambetta, 14 Dec. 1881, no. 476.
18 Léon to Gambetta, 14 Dec. 1881, no. 476.
19 Grévy, *La République*, 275.
20 Gambetta to Léon, 12 Jan. 1882, H&P no. 516; 19 Jan. 1882, 82.5/73; Léon to Gambetta, 12, 14 Jan. 1882, nos. 482, 483. Cf. Chastenet 3: 404–5; Bury 3: 307–15.
21 Gambetta to Léon, 19, 21 Jan. 1882, 82.5/73, 82.6/73; Léon to Gambetta, 21 Jan. 1882, no. 486.
22 Gambetta to Léon, 19, 23 Jan. 1882, 82.5/73, 82.7/73.
23 'Discours sur le projet de révision constitutionnelle prononcé le 26 janvier 1882 à la Chambre des Députés', *Discours* 10: 213–56 (227–9).
24 Cf. Grévy, *La République*, 280; Barral, *Léon Gambetta*, 243–4; Chastenet 1: 404–6.
25 Gambetta to Léon, 19, 21, 23 Jan. 1882, 82.5/73, 82.6/73, 82.7/73.
26 Gambetta to Léon, 27! [*sic*] Jan. 1882, 82.8/73; Léon to Gambetta, 27 J[an. 18]82, no. 487.
27 Gambetta to Léon, 30 Jan. 1882, 82.9/73. Cf. Bury 3: 316.
28 Gambetta to Léon, 4 Feb. 1882, 82.11/73.
29 Gambetta to Léon, 8 Feb. 1882, 82.14/73.
30 Gambetta to Léon, 4, 6, 7 Feb. 1882, 82.11/73, 82.12/73, 82.13/73.
31 Gambetta to Léon, 8, 10, 18 Feb. 1882, 82.14/73, 82.15/73, 82.16/73; 9 Feb. 1882, H&P no. 524.
32 Gambetta to Joseph Gambetta, 19 Feb. 1882, H&P no. 527.
33 Léon to Gambetta, 2 Mar. 1882, no. 490; Gambetta to Léon, 8 Mar. 1882, 82.21/73.
34 *Le Siècle*, 9 Nov. 1881; Mayeur, *Léon Gambetta*, 520, n.18.
35 ASP, 2 EP 2, Dr 3 sdr b: Mme Marcellin Pellet to Pillias; cf. Pillias, 160; Jean-Michel Gaillard, *Jules Ferry* (Paris: Fayard, 1989), 352.
36 Pillias, 152–3.
37 Gambetta to Léon, 10 Feb. 1882, 82.15/73; 30 Mar. 1882, 82.24/73 (emphasis original); ASP, 2 EP 1, Dr 5, sdr d: 'Alphonse Léon'.
38 Léon to Gambetta, 25 Feb. 1882, no. 488; 4 Mar. 1882, no. 491; Gambetta to Léon, 11 Mar. 1882, 82.23/73.
39 Gambetta to Léon, 9 Mar. 1882, 82.22/73.
40 Gambetta to Léon, 5 Apr. 1882, 82.26/73.
41 Gambetta to Léon, 11 May 1882, 82.29/73. Cf. 9 Mar. 1882, 82.22/73; 8 May 1882, 82.28/73.
42 Gambetta to Léon, 24, 27 May 1882, 82.34/73, 82.35/73; 6 Apr. 1882, H&P no. 534
43 Gambetta to Léon, 10 Feb. 1882, 82.15/73. Léon's letter has disappeared.
44 Gambetta to Léon, 23 Feb. 1882, 82.18/73; 21 Apr. 1882, 82.27/73.
45 Gambetta to Léon, 31 Mar. 1882, 82.25/73. Cf. 8 May 1882, 82.28/73.
46 'Séance du 1ᵉʳ mai, Commission relative au recrutement et à l'avancement dans l'armée, Notes de M. Francis Charmes', in Joseph Reinach, *La Vie*

politique de Léon Gambetta, suivie d'autres essais sur Gambetta (Paris: Félix Alcan, 1918), 293.

47 Gambetta to Léon, 27 May 1882, 82.35/73; 1, 15, 23 June 1882, 82.37/73, 82.40/73, 82.41/73; 7 July 1882, 82.43/73. Cf. Bury 3: 330–3.

48 Gambetta to Léon, 15 June 1882, 82.40/73; 7 July 1882, 82.43/73; 6 July 1882, H&P no. 544. Cf. Pillias, 159, n.1; Bury 3: 344.

49 'Discours sur les évènements d'Égypte, prononcé le 18 juillet 1882, à la Chambre des Députés', *Discours* 11: 93–105 (101, 104). Cf. Bury 3: 334.

50 Gambetta to Joseph Gambetta, 11 July 1882, H&P no. 546; Gambetta to Léon, 12, 13 July 1882, 82.44/73, 82.45/73.

51 Léon to Gambetta, [undated], no. 405. This letter was catalogued with others from 1880, but its content dates it to 1882.

52 Gambetta to Léon, 13, 15 July 1882, 82.46/73, 82.47/73; 'this Friday, 1 am', 82.1/73 (the only Friday compatible with the contents of this letter is 14 July).

53 Gambetta to Léon, 22 July 1882, H&P no. 552; Pillias, 159.

54 Gambetta to Léon, 22 July 1882, 82.48/73.

55 Gambetta to Léon, 27 July 1882, 82.49/73.

56 Gambetta to Léon, 31 July 1882, 82.52/73; 3, 4 Aug. 1882, 82.54/73, 82.55.73.

57 Gambetta to Léon, 1, 4, 6 Aug. 1882, 82.53/73, 82.55.73, 82.57/73.

58 Gambetta to Léon, 6 Aug. 1882, 82.57/73.

59 Gambetta to Léon, 6, 8 Aug. 1882, 82.57/73, 82.59/73.

60 Gambetta to Léon, 27, 29 July 1882, 82.49/73, 82.50/73.

61 Gambetta to Léon, 29 July 1882, 82.51/73; 1 Aug. 1882, 82.53/73.

62 Gambetta to Léon, 31 July 1882, 82.52/73; 1 Aug. 1882, 82.53/73.

63 Gambetta to Léon, 3, 4, 5, 6 Aug. 1882, 82.54/73, 82.55/73, 82.56/73, 82.57/73.

64 Gambetta to Léon, 7 Aug. 1882, 82.58/73.

65 Gambetta to Léon, 31 July 1882, 82.52/73; 6, 7 Aug. 1882, 82.57/73, 82.58/73.

66 APP, B/a 924: Dossier Gambetta (1882–1883): report, 3 July 1882; Gambetta to Léon, 10 Aug. 1882, 82.60/73.

67 Gambetta to Joseph Gambetta, 30 Oct. 1882, H&P no. 567.

68 'Séance du 22 novembre', in Reinach, *La Vie politique de Léon Gambetta*, 300; Bury 3: 42–4.

69 Gambetta to Léon, 10 Aug. 1882, 82.60/73.

70 Gambetta to Léon, 3, 11 Aug. 1882, 82.54/73, 82.61/73.

71 Gambetta to Léon, 16, 17, 19 Aug. 1882, 82.62/73, 82.63/73, 82.64/73.

72 Gambetta to Léon, 21 Aug. 1882, H&P no. 561.

73 Gambetta to Léon, 8, 11 Sept. 1882, 82.66/73, 82.67/73.

74 Léon to Gambetta, 9 Sept. 1882, no. 493; Gambetta to Léon, 14 Sept. 1882, 82.69/73.

75 Gambetta to Léon, 21 Sept. 1882, H&P no. 564 and n. (a); Joseph Reinach, 'L'Amie de Gambetta', *Le Figaro*, 18 Nov. 1882, 1–2. Cf. Pillias, 160–1.

76 Gambetta to Léon, 21 Sept. 1882, H&P no. 564; 25 Sept. 1882, 82.70/73; Léon to Gambetta, '17 or 19' [probably 27], 29 Sept. 1882, nos. 494, 495.

77 Ignotus, 'Post-Scriptum', *Le Figaro*, 3 Jan. 1883, 1.

78 Gambetta to Léon, 25 Sept. 1882, 82.70/73; Gambetta to Auguste de Serres, 6 Oct. 1882, H&P no. 566. Cf. Adolphe Robert and Gaston Cougny,

Dictionnaire des parlementaires français, 5 vols (Paris: Bourloton, 1890), 2: 227; noms.rues.st.etienne.free.fr/rues/c.html, accessed 8 Jan. 2011.

79 Gambetta to Léon, telegrams: [undated] Oct. 1882 (82E); 31 Oct. 1882 (82 F); 31 Oct. 1882, 4pm (82 G), 18 Nov. 1882 (82 L); Gambetta to Auguste de Serres, 6 Oct. 1882, H&P no. 566, n. (a).

80 Gambetta to Joseph Gambetta, 30 Oct. 1882, H&P no. 567; Paul Strauss, Les Fondateurs de la République (Paris: La Renaissance du Livre, 1934), 93; Reinach, 'L'Amie de Gambetta'; 'Chez M. Joseph Reinach: Les heures tristes des Jardies', Le Petit Parisien, 18 Nov. 1906; Daniel Halévy and Émile Pillias, 'Lettres inédites de Gambetta', Revue de Paris, 45ᵉ année, 3 (1 Feb. 1938): 512–31 (531).

81 Gambetta to Léon, 19 Nov. 1882, H&P no. 569. Cf. Pillias, 163–4.

82 'Observation', in 'Blessure et mort de M. Gambetta', Gazette hebdomadaire de médecine et de chirurgie 3, 19 Jan. 1883: 33–46; reproduced in Discours 11: 195–228, and in Odilon Lannelongue, Leçons de clinique chirurgicale (Paris: Masson, 1905), 286–316. These detailed clinical notes were drafted by Lannelongue and, along with notes on the autopsy drafted by Cornil, were published under the signatures of the seven attending doctors. The following account is taken from this source unless otherwise specified.

83 Pillias, 177–8.

84 Professors Charcot, Verneuil, Trélat, Brouardel, Cornil; Doctors Siredey et Lannelongue. On Charcot, see Chapter 8, above. Cf. Gambetta to Charcot, 10 Jan. 1882, H&P no. 519; Gambetta to Juliette Adam, 5 June 1877, H&P no. 315; Anne Martin-Fugier, Les Salons de la Troisième République: Art, littérature, politique (Paris: Perrin, 2003), 28, 207, 284–5.

85 'L'incident de Ville-d'Avray', Le Gaulois, 29 Nov. 1882, 1; 'La Vérité sur l'incident de Ville-d'Avray', Le Gaulois, 30 Nov. 1882, 1–2; 'La Blessure de M. Gambetta', L'Intransigeant, 1, 2 Dec. 1882, 1. Cf. D. Damamme, 'Corps de la République: Blessure de M. Gambetta', Genèses: sciences sociales et histoire (1991): 160–71, n. 5.

86 Pillias, 165–7, 176–7; 288–9, doc. 17. He interviewed a number of those involved.

87 Roblin, in Pillias, 289; ASP, 2 EP 2, Dr 3: 'Léonie Léon': 'questionnaire envoyé à Marcellin Pellet le 2 XII 1933'; Pillias, 184. Walther's name is incorrectly spelt 'Walter' in 'Blessure et mort', and in Lannelongue, Leçons, 65, 290. Cf. H. Marrès, 'La Mort de Gambetta' [1883?]. An engraving of the painting hangs in Gambetta's bedroom at les Jardies.

88 Fieuzal to Joseph Léris, 8 Dec. 1882, in Pillias, 182; 'Blessure et mort': 'Renseignements complémentaires' and n. 1.

89 Lannelongue, Leçons, 300, n. 1; 'Blessure et mort', 'Renseignements complémentaires' and n. 1.

90 Lannelongue, Leçons, 285, 300, 317; Reginald Heber Fitz, 'Perforating inflammation of the vermiform appendix with special reference to its early diagnosis and treatment', American Journal of Medical Science 92 (1886): 321–46; P. Kouindjy, Appendectomie: Difficultés de l'Opération et Accidents Consécutifs (Paris: Carré et Naud, 1898), 12.

91 Joseph Reinach, 'La Maladie et la mort de Gambetta', Revue politique et littéraire, 6 Jan. 1883, 4–6 (5) (also in La République française, 7 Jan. 1883, and in Discours 11: 233); Lannelongue, Leçons, 285, 300 (Fig. 21), 317.

92   Étienne to Ranc, 31 Dec. 1882, in Arthur Ranc, *Souvenirs: Correspondence 1831–1908* (Paris: Edouard Cornély et Cie, 1913), 332–3; Pillias, 184.
93   Pillias, 184–5. Strauss, *Les Fondateurs*, 91–4. Roblin claimed to have returned to the bedroom just after Gambetta died (Pillias, 289–90).
94   Reinach, *La Vie politique de Léon Gambetta*, 120; Reinach, 'La Maladie et la mort de Gambetta', *Discours* 11: 234; Roblin, in Pillias, 289; Pillias, 184–5.
95   BnF, naf 12701: Léon to Mme Marcellin Pellet, 27 Aug. 1883, 7 Aug. 1884.
96   First quoted by Strauss (*Les Fondateurs*, 80), this comment has been repeated by other historians: P. B. Gheusi, *La Vie et la mort singulières de Gambetta* (Paris: A. Michel, 1932), 237 ff.; Antonmattei, *Léon Gambetta*, 526; Barral, *Léon Gambetta*, 254–5.
97   Kouindjy, *Appendectomie*, 12–13; Lannelongue, *Leçons*, 285, 323–5.
98   APP, B/a 924: dossier Gambetta (1882–1883), police reports: 30 Nov., 21, 27, 30 Dec. 1882; Pillias, 165–80; 'Blessure et mort de M. Gambetta'.
99   Strauss, *Les Fondateurs*, 93–4; Pillias, 185.

11   'People are weeping for the patriot, the orator'

1   Gambetta to Léon, 30 Sept. 1882, 82.72/73.
2   Véronique Magnol-Malhache, with Patrick Chamouard and Denis Lavalle, *Léon Gambetta: Un Saint pour la République?* (Paris: Caisse nationale des monuments historiques et des sites, 1996).
3   'Gambetta', *Le Temps*, 1 Jan. 1883, 1; 'City and Suburban News', *New York Times*, 6 Jan. 1883; 'The Death of Gambetta', *New York Times*, 3 Jan. 1883, 1.
4   AN F7 15.9582: Gambetta: le 1er janvier 1883, Intérieur; APP, B/a 924: Police municipale, 16e Arron., M. Féger, Paris, le 1er janvier 1883.
5   'Blessure et mort de M. Gambetta', 33–46, reproduced in *Discours* 11: 225ff; P. B. Gheusi, *La Vie et la mort singulières de Gambetta* (Paris: A. Michel, 1932), 300, 305; Odilon Lannelongue, *Leçons de clinique chirurgicale* (Paris: Masson, 1905), 318, 323; Magnol-Malhache, *et al.*, *Léon Gambetta*, 43–6, 70–6; Léon to Mme Marcellin Pellet, 17 Nov 1886, in Pillias, 215. Cf. P.B. Gheusi, 'Le nouveau tombeau de Gambetta', *L'Illustration*, 10 avril 1909: 239–42.
6   Avner Ben-Amos, 'Monuments and memory in French Nationalism', *History and Memory* 5, 2 (1993): 50–81 (60–1); Mona Ozouf, 'The Panthéon: The École Normale of the Dead', in *Realms of Memory: Rethinking the French Past*, ed. Pierre Nora, trans. Arthur Goldhammer, 3 vols (New York: Columbia University Press, 1996), 3: 325–40; Lorraine Ward, 'The Cult of Relics: Pasteur Material at the Science Museum', *Medical History* 38 (1994): 52–72; Magnol-Malhache, *et al.*, *Léon Gambetta*, 46; Carl Sagan, *Broca's Brain: Reflections on the Romance of Science* (New York: Random House, 1979), 6.
7   *La République française*, 3, 4 Jan. 1883.
8   *Discours* 11: 236–9; Pillias, 187; ASP, 2EP 6, Dr 2, sdr a: 'Lettres à sa famille': Joseph Gambetta to Victor Hugo, 12 Jan. 1883 (copy); Magnol-Malhache, *et al.*, *Léon Gambetta*, 54–7.
9   'The Death of Gambetta: France Preparing to Bury her Greatest Statesman', *New York Times*, 6 Jan. 1883; *La République française*, 7, 8 Jan. 1883; *Discours* 11: 282–92; APP B/a 924: 'Mort et Funérailles de Gambetta', Jan. 1883. For

the complete funeral, see *Le Figaro*, 6–7 Jan. 1883; *La République française*, 1–7 Jan. 1883.

10   APP B/a 924: 'Mort et Funérailles de Gambetta', Jan. 1883; *La République française*, 7 Jan. 1883; James R. Lehning, 'Gossiping about Gambetta: Contested Memories in the Early Third Republic', *French Historical Studies* 18, 1 (1981): 237-54, (esp. 240–1).

11   Magnol-Malhache, *et al., Léon Gambetta*, 63–5; *La République française*, 12–14 Jan. 1883.

12   Joseph Reinach, 'La Maladie et la Mort de M. Gambetta', *Discours* 11: 234–5.

13   ASP, 2 EP 6, Dr 2, sdr b: 'Collection Gheusi: lettres ayant appartenu au Ruiz de Léonie Léon': Léon to Ruiz, 9 Jan. 1883.

14   See Chapter 10, above.

15   Pillias, 186; BnF, Naf 12708, 'Mémoires de Scheurer-Kestner, 1877–1882', 85; 'Chez M. Joseph Reinach. Les Heures tristes des Jardies', *Le Petit Parisien*, 18 Nov. 1906.

16   ASP, 2 EP 6, Dr 2, sdr b: Léon to Ruiz, 21 Feb., 30 Mar. 1883; *ibid.*, 'Liste des souscripteurs pour rente L.L.'; Pillias, 190, 250.

17   Gambetta had explained the system to his father: Gambetta to Joseph Gambetta, 5 Sept. 1878, H&P no. 387. Cf. Bury 3: 11, n. 17.

18   ASP, 2 EP 2, Dr 1, sdr e: [information from Léon's notary]; Léon to Mme Pellet, 18 May [1883], in BnF, Naf 12701: Lettres de Mme Léonie Léon à Mme Marcellin Pellet, 1875–1887; Naf 12702: 1888–1904. All references to the Léon–Pellet correspondence refer to this collection; cf. Pillias, 190–1.

19   Gambetta to Léon, 30 Sept. 1882, 82.72/73; Léon to Mme Pellet, 1 Apr., 24 Oct. 1883; 27 Aug. 1885.

20   Léon to Mme Pellet, 25, 28 Mar., 4 Aug. 1883.

21   Léon to Mme Pellet, 19 July 1883; [24?] July [1884?].

22   Léon to Mme Pellet, 4 Mar., 20 June 1887; 10 May 1889.

23   L. Delpech to E. Spuller, *La Presse*, 7 Jan. 1883, 2; cf. Magnol-Malhache, *et al., Léon Gambetta*, 105.

24   H&P no. 542 n. a; Magnol-Malhache, *et al., Léon Gambetta*, 105–7. On the history of the house and the land, see Odile Sassi, 'Léon Gambetta: Destin et mémoire (1838–1938)', Thèse de doctorat d'histoire, Université Paris IV-Sorbonne, 1998, sous la direction du Pr J.-M. Mayeur, 2 vols. (cf. 1: 355–8, 365–7).

25   ASP, 2 EP 6, Dr 2, sdr b: Léon to Ruiz, 17, 21 Nov. 1883.

26   Magnol-Malhache, *et al., Léon Gambetta*, 105–7.

27   Sassi, 'Léon Gambetta', 1: 373–92; APP, B/a 924: dossier Gambetta: 6 Jan. 1884; *La République française*, 2 Jan. 1884. Cf. 'Discours de Eugène Étienne, Ministre de la Guerre, Président de la Société Gambetta, à la cérémonie des Jardies, le 14 janvier 1906', in *Gambetta et ses Amis*, ed. Émile Labarthe (Paris: Les Éditions des Presses Modernes, 1938), 324; for Spuller's use, see correspondence quoted by Sassi, 'Léon Gambetta', 1: 385.

28   APP B/a 924, dossier Gambetta: C[ommissionnai]re Sèvres à Préfet de Police, Paris, 7 Jan. 1900.

29   'Image d'Épinal N° 1316', fig. 7, in Magnol-Malhache, *et al., Léon Gambetta*, xiv.

30   'The Statue of Gambetta', *New York Times*, 11 Apr. 1884; Sassi, 'Léon Gambetta', 1: 422–38.

31 June Hargrove, *The Statues of Paris: An Open-Air Pantheon* (New York; Paris: Vendome Press, 1989), 162.
32 For images, see Hargrove, *The Statues of Paris*, 108–9, 256, 316.
33 Magnol-Malhache, *et al.*, *Léon Gambetta*, 112; Sassi, 'Léon Gambetta', 1: 441–59; Georges Poisson, 'La première pyramide érigée dans la cour du Louvre: La pyramide de Gambetta', *Historia* 520 (1990): 70–6; 'The Gambetta Monument', *New York Times*, 3 July 1887; Hargrove, *The Statues of Paris*, 162.
34 'Discours de M. E. Spuller à l'inauguration du monument de Gambetta, Place du Carrousel à Paris, le 13 juillet 1888', in Labarthe, *Gambetta et ses amis*, 243, 249.
35 *Ibid.*, 252–3.
36 Sassi, 'Léon Gambetta', 1: 464; Magnol-Malhache, *et al.*, *Léon Gambetta*, 111–12.
37 'Discours de M. E. Spuller', in Labarthe, *Gambetta et ses amis*, 253–4.
38 Léon to Mme Pellet, 17 Nov. 1886; 4 Mar. 1887; cf. 20 May 1883; BnF, Naf 13608: Léonie Léon: Lettres à Joseph Reinach, undated [1885?], ff.18–19.
39 Léon to Mme Pellet, 7 Aug. 1884.
40 Léon to Mme Pellet, 8, 24 Oct. 1885; Sept. 1891.
41 Léon to Mme Pellet, 12, 20 Oct. 1885.
42 Léon to Mme Pellet, 12 Jan. 1886. Cf. Chastenet 1: 444–71.
43 Chastenet 1: 472–517; Charles Sowerwine, *France since 1870: Culture, Society and the Making of the Republic*, 2nd edn (Basingstoke: Palgrave Macmillan, 2009), 57–9.
44 Léon to Mme Pellet, 17 Nov. 1886; 5 Jan. 1887.
45 Léon to Mme Pellet, 4 Feb., 20 June 1887.
46 Chastenet 1: 496–500.
47 BnF, Naf 13608: Léon to Reinach, 31 Oct. 1887, ff. 67–8.
48 Léon to Mme Pellet, 4 Apr. 1888; 10 May 1889.
49 BnF, Naf 13608: Léon to Reinach, 18 Jan. [1885?], ff. 16–17 (emphasis original); cf. 27 May [1887], ff. 59–60.
50 Léon to Mme Pellet, Jan. 1888; Oct. 1896.
51 Léon to Mme Pellet, 15 May [Mar.?] 1891.
52 Léon to Mme Pellet, 9 July 1891; Pillias, 235.
53 Léon to Mme Pellet, 5 Sept. 1889.
54 Léon to Mme Pellet, Aug., 17 Nov. 1886.
55 Pillias, 230–1; ASP, 2 EP 3, dr 2, Dr. Baratoux to P.-B. Gheusi, 29 Mar. 1933 (copy).
56 Léon to Mme Pellet, July, 14 Oct. 1891.
57 Pillias, 232–3; Léon to Mme Pellet, 14 June 1891.
58 Léon to Mme Pellet, 3 July, 20 Aug. 1892.
59 Léon to Mme Pellet, 18 Mar., 12 Apr., [undated], 1893.
60 Léon to Mme Pellet, 2 Feb., 15 Aug. 1893.
61 Léon to Mme Pellet, 22 Oct. 1893; 28 Apr. 1894.
62 Léon to Mme Pellet, Feb. 1896.
63 www.st-thom.com/didon.html; *Catholic Encyclopedia* at www.newadvent. org/cathen/04782a.htm, accessed 4 Mar. 2011.
64 Pillias, 262–3.
65 Pillias, 261.
66 Léon to Mme Pellet, 5 Nov. 1894.

67 Sowerwine, *France Since 1870*, 64–9.

68 Chastenet 2: 54–8, 290–1.

69 Pillias, 260–3; *La Croix*, 30 Apr. 1939, 1–2 (obituary for Janvier).

70 ASP, 4 EP 2, Dr 5 sdr b: 'Père Janvier'. The religious orders were gradually allowed to return after World War I.

71 Léon to Mme Pellet, Mar. 1894. Cf. undated [1893].

72 ASP, 4 EP 2, Dr 5 sdr b: 'Père Janvier'.

73 Magnol-Malhache, *et al.*, *Léon Gambetta*, 107–8; Sassi, 'Léon Gambetta', 1: 397–403, 409–11; Labarthe, *Gambetta et ses amis*, 307–9; 'Discours de Joseph Reinach prononcé à la cérémonie des Jardies, le 14 janvier 1906', *ibid.*, 331.

74 'Discours de Paul Doumer à l'inauguration du monument de Gambetta, à Bordeaux, le 25 avril 1905', in Labarthe, *Gambetta et ses amis*, 262.

75 'M. Saint-Saëns à Bordeaux', *La Revue musicale*, 1er mai 1905 (5e année, no. 9): 266–7. Saint-Saëns had written the work for morale-boosting concerts during the siege of 1870, but only the *Marche héroïque* (opus 34) was then performed. Cf. Sabina Ratner, *Camille Saint-Saëns 1835–1921: a Thematic Catalogue of his Complete Works, 1: The Instrumental Works* (Oxford: Oxford University Press, 2002), 278–82; Sassi, 'Léon Gambetta', 1: 471–81; Magnol-Malhache, *et al.*, *Léon Gambetta*, 112–15; Labarthe, *Gambetta et ses amis*, 311.

76 Sassi, 'Léon Gambetta', 1: 484–5; Labarthe, *Gambetta et ses amis*, 311.

77 Magnol-Malhache, *et al.*, *Léon Gambetta*, 81–2.

78 Sassi, 'Léon Gambetta', 1: 412–16; *Le Temps*, 29 Mar. 1920, 1–3.

79 Magnol-Malhache, *Léon Gambetta*, 79–81.

80 *Annales du Sénat et de la Chambre des députés, Documents parlementaires, 2e partie, Chambre des députés, Débats*, Session 31 July 1920, 2943; Magnol-Malhache, *et al.*, *Léon Gambetta*, 81–2; Sassi, 'Léon Gambetta', 1: 505.

81 Magnol-Malhache, *et al.*, *Léon Gambetta*, 83–5.

82 *Ibid.*, 86–8; Sassi, 'Léon Gambetta', 1: 507–8.

83 Magnol-Malhache, *et al.*, *Léon Gambetta*, 89–94; Sassi, 'Léon Gambetta', 1: 508–9.

84 Magnol-Malhache, *et al.*, *Léon Gambetta*, 94.

85 Sowerwine, *France since 1870*, 111–13.

86 Sassi, 'Léon Gambetta,' 1: 521–9; Labarthe, *Gambetta et ses amis*, 347–420; Émile Pillias, *Gambetta: Exposition organisée à l'occasion du centenaire de sa naissance* (Paris: Bibliothèque nationale, 1938).

87 Léon Daudet, *Le Drame des Jardies (1877–1882): roman contemporain* (Paris: Fayard, 1924). On Adam, see *Journal de l'Abbé Mugnier (1879–1939)*, texte établi par Marcel Billot (Paris: Mercure de France, 1985), 1 June 1924 and 439.

88 Pierre Dominique, 'Le drame des Jardies: 27 novembre 1882,' in Gilbert Guilleminault, *La Jeunesse de Marianne: Le roman vrai de la Troisième République* (Paris: Le Livre de poche, 1966), 192–219.

89 Jacques Chastenet, préface, André Beauguitte, *Le Tiroir secret* (Paris: Presse-Diffusion [1968]). Chastenet did point out that Beauguitte's 'suppositions' were unsupported by any evidence, but he nevertheless lent the book the prestige of his name.

90 ASP, 2 EP 2 Dr 3 sdr a: note by Pillias 'Lundi 28 août 1933' and photo; Letter, Pascal-Hervé Daniel, Chef du Service des Cimetières, Mairie de Paris, to the authors, 3 May 2010.

91 Jack Lang, Préface to Christian Lasalle, Patrick Favardin, and Odile A. Schmitz, *Hommage à Léon Gambetta* (Paris: Musée du Luxembourg, 1982).

92 Hargrove, *The Statues of Paris*, 315–16; Poisson, 'La Pyramide de Gambetta,' 75; Hargrove, 'Les Statues de Paris' in *Les Lieux de mémoire*, ed. Pierre Nora, 2: 1855–6 (1865).

93 Daniel Amson, *Gambetta, ou Le rêve brisé* (Paris: Tallandier, 1994); Pierre Antonmattei, *Léon Gambetta: Héraut de la République* (Paris: Michalon, 1999); Pierre Barral, *Léon Gambetta: Tribun et stratège de la République, 1838–1882* (Toulouse: Privat, 2008); Jean-Marie Mayeur, *Léon Gambetta: La Patrie et la République* (Paris: Fayard, 2008).

94 Maurice Agulhon, 'Gambetta La Défense Nationale,' in Lassalle, Favardin and Schmitz, *Hommage à Léon Gambetta*, 45.

Epilogue: 'The letters remain'

1 BnF, Naf 13608, ff. 16–17: Léon to Joseph Reinach 18 January [1885?].

2 *Ibid.*

3 Pillias, 268.

4 BnF, Naf 12702: Léon to Mme Pellet, 15 May, late July, 24 Nov. 1891; 12 Apr., 1893; BnF, Naf 13608: Léon to J. Reinach, 18 Jan. [1885?], ff. 16–17; BnF, Naf 12701: Léon to Mme Pellet, 31 Jan. 1886.

5 One copy remains in the papers of Joseph Reinach: BnF, Naf 13609. Pillias claims to have seen a second copy in the possession of the son of one of the five recipients. He also claims that Reinach lent his copy to a friend, who made a further copy. Cf. Pillias, 268–9.

6 *Revue de Paris*, 1 Dec. 1906: 419–68; 15 Dec. 1906: 673–96; 1 Jan. 1907: 57–74. These are the letters re-published in H&P.

7 Gambetta to Léon, 19 Jan. 1879, 79.9/111 (*Revue de Paris*, 1 Jan. 1907, 63); 19 Jan. 1882, 82.5/73 (*Revue de Paris*, 1 Jan. 1906, 463–4).

8 Gambetta to Léon, 27 Jan. 1882, 82.8/73 (*Revue de Paris*, 1 Jan. 1907, 73–4); 2 May 1878, 78.14/35 (*Revue de Paris*, 1 Jan. 1907, 58–9); 8 Oct. 1880, 80.45/67 (*Revue de Paris*, 1 Jan. 1907, 69–70). Cf. Pillias, 267.

9 ASP, 4EP 2, Dr 5 b, 'Père Janvier': notes by Pillias of an interview with Janvier, undated: ff. 3, 7; [copy of a letter from] Janvier to Pillias, 20 Dec. 1933, in Pillias, 265.

10 ASP, 2 EP 2, Dr 1, sdr e: 'Le Notaire de Léonie Léon,' incl. letter of C. Tollu to G. Pallain, 11 Dec. 1906. Cf. Pillias, 265–6.

11 Pillias, *Léonie Léon*, 267–8. Three women, who remained in the sitting room while the men burned the letters in the basement, later confirmed details of the event to Pillias.

12 Jacques Suffel, 'Gambetta et Léonie Léon (correspondance inédite)', *Bulletin du bibliophile* 4 (1987): 459.

13 *Ibid.*, 459–60. Suffel was unable to ascertain who had removed the letters for 1872 and 1874. A further typescript of Gambetta's letters was completed in 1999 by Mme Jeanine Dodu, assistant administrator of the BAN.

14 Léon to Mme Pellet, Jan. 1888, in Pillias, 221.

15 ASP, 2 Ep 2, Dr 1, sdr e; Pillias, 270–2 (where Janvier is quoted as saying 'one doesn't sell mud'). Pillias' account is based on the personal papers of Georges Pallain, and on his interview with Father Janvier in the 1930s.

16 Suffel, 'Gambetta et Léonie Léon,' 460.

17 In the initial correspondence with the dealer, the number of letters was given as 496, but this is wrong; the figure of 495 appears consistently from 1940 and that is the number now extant. The Chief Librarian, M. de Soulès, had further copies of the letters made after the war. See BAN, UB 535: Léonie Léon: 'Origine et authentification de la Copie dactylographié des Lettres de Léonie Léon et Léon Gambetta'; E. Fabius to E. Herriot, 26 Mar. 1938 (two letters); E. Fabius to the 'Conservateur en Chef' of the Library of the Chamber of Deputies, 29 Mar. 1938.

18 BAN, UB 535: Léonie Léon: 'Papiers provenant de la succession de LÉONIE LÉON et offerts à la Bibliothèque de la CHAMBRE DES DÉPUTÉS', cotes 1–65 (a list of the enclosed documents, which included her birth certificate, information on her finances, and correspondence with other republicans).

19 They also took a green folder containing two brief reports on the international situation by Abel Ferry, dated 29 and 30 July 1914, addressed to René Viviani, President of the Chamber. The Ferry name was still well known thanks to Jules Ferry, and may have aroused the Germans' interest.

20 BAN, UB 535: 'Vol et enquêtes': Pierre de Soulès, Chief Librarian, BAN, to Jacques Desmarest [? partly illeg.], 26 Nov. 1949, copy. This letter contains lengthy extracts from the bailiff's report, and is attached to a letter from the Director of the Service des Réparations-Restitutions, to the Director of the Banque de France [Desmarest], 9 May 1951. Cf. Sophie Coeuré, *La Mémoire spoliée: Les archives des Français butin de guerre nazi puis soviétique* (Paris: Payot, 2007), esp. 37–8.

21 Suffel, 'Gambetta et Léonie Léon,' 461.

22 BAN, UB 535: 'Vol et enquêtes: Special Enquiry Bureau, Hamburg, Objet: Recherches au profit des Autorités Françaises', 19 June 1950, and typescript of a declaration by Gottfried Schewek, 20 May 1950 (French translations); Coeuré, *La Mémoire spoliée*, 37–8.

23 BAN, UB 535: Letter from Adrien Dansette, 20 Feb 1947; reply, 7 Mar. 1947; 'NOTE concernant la disparition d'un dossier de lettres addressées par Léonie Léon à Léon Gambetta en dépôt succursale de la Banque de France à Libourne,' 4 Mar. 1947; [handwritten note by the Chief Librarian, M. Gravel, on the envelope that held the typed copies]: 'Copy of the 495 letters of Léonie Léon to Gambetta, the originals of which were taken by the Germans at Libourne in 1941. These copies were brought back today, 28 Mar. 1947, by President Hippolyte Ducos.'

24 *Ibid.*

25 Gambetta to Léon, 22 Sept. 1876, 76.41/50; BnF, Naf 12701, Léon to Mme Pellet, 19 July [1884?]; Léon to Gambetta, 25 Dec. 1873, no. 125.

26 Léon to Gambetta [undated], no. 2; cf. Chapter 2, above.

Index